W9-BUE-557

nation is a long-awaited gift of a book. It will take the reader on a journey into many kitchens, of course—including those of Gilbert's past—but also iconic works of literature and art that reveal the complexities of how ingestion has been depicted and regarded. A rich, powerful, important delight of a book to both mull over for its splendid insights but also to use for years to come as a guidebook into the most important writing about food both now and in the past."
—Louise DeSalvo

"This wonderful book is both a collection of sparkling writing and an enchanting scholarly journey, with Sandra Gilbert as a Virgilian guide. It shows us how food can be, and has been, transformed through history into memory, myth, language, and image as different artists explore the subject in different forms. This is a tour of our daily lives with a radiant light cast on our most essential item."
—Eavan Boland

More Advance Praise for *The Culinary Imagination* by Sandra M. Gilbert

"It is hard to imagine how Sandra Gilbert could have produced so broad an overview of contemporary food writing and thought, not only literary analysis but also history, memoir ("foodoir!"), and bibliography. Anyone wanting an introduction to the meaning of food culture should start here."

—Marion Nestle, professor of nutrition, food studies, and public health at New York University, and author of *Eat, Drink, Vote: An Illustrated Guide to Food Politics*

"*The Culinary Imagination*, a rollicking exploration of nourishment's latent messages, moves with the forcefulness and energy of a fast-sailing ship on epic seas. Sandra M. Gilbert brings her legendary powers of discernment and analytical gusto to the urgent subject of food, and the results—lushly entertaining, salty with anecdote and wisdom—have lyrical savor and a tenderly autobiographical richness."
—Wayne Koestenbaum

"*The Culinary Imagination* is the book Sandra Gilbert has had simmering for years. A rich and tasty dish of cultural history, gastronomical ethnology, literary criticism, and memoir, it's flavored with Gilbert's characteristic blend of erudition and humor, warmth and wisdom. I learned something from every delicious page."
—Elaine Showalter

"What a gift of pleasure the wonderful Sandra Gilbert has given us. Food, glorious food turns out to be an ample subject, with seemingly endless stores of wisdom. Along with the joy of reading about food (as pleasant for some as cooking and eating), in contemplating how we have thought about, dreamt of and imagined food for centuries, *The Culinary Imagination* serves us a delight of the mind as well."
—Susan Griffin

"For anyone like me, who believes that life is too short to have one bad meal or that thinking about and learning about food is the quickest way to understand the self, the family, and the culture, Sandra M. Gilbert's *The Culinary Imagi-*

The CULINARY IMAGINATION

ALSO BY SANDRA M. GILBERT

Prose

Rereading Women

On Burning Ground

Death's Door

Wrongful Death

Masterpiece Theater (with Susan Gubar)

No Man's Land (3 volumes; with Susan Gubar)

The Madwoman in the Attic (with Susan Gubar)

Acts of Attention: The Poems of D. H. Lawrence

Poetry

Aftermath

Belongings

The Italian Collection

Kissing the Bread

Ghost Volcano

Blood Pressure

Emily's Bread

The Summer Kitchen

In the Fourth World

As Editor

The Norton Anthology of Literature by Women
(with Susan Gubar)

Feminist Literary Theory and Criticism: A Norton Reader
(with Susan Gubar)

Inventions of Farewell: A Book of Elegies

The House Is Made of Poetry: On Ruth Stone
(with Wendy Barker)

MotherSongs (with Susan Gubar and Diana O'Hehir)

Shakespeare's Sisters (with Susan Gubar)

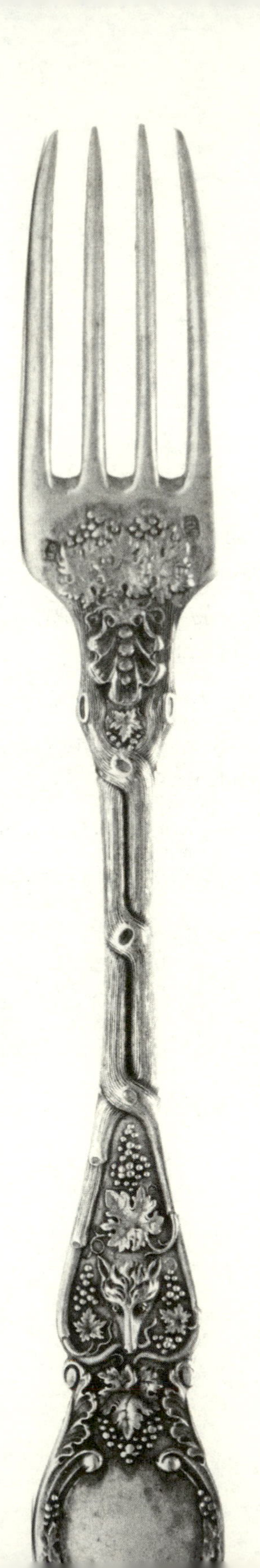

The CULINARY IMAGINATION

FROM MYTH TO MODERNITY

Sandra M. Gilbert

W. W. NORTON & COMPANY *New York • London*

Printed in the United States of America
First Edition

For information about special discounts for bulk purchases, please contact W. W. Norton Special Sales at specialsales@wwnorton.com or 800-233-4830

Manufacturing by RR Donnelley, Harrisonburg
Book design by Dana Sloan
Production manager: Devon Zahn

Library of Congress Cataloging-in-Publication Data

Gilbert, Sandra M.
The culinary imagination : from myth to modernity / Sandra M. Gilbert.
pages cm
Includes bibliographical references and index.
ISBN 978-0-393-06765-1 (hardcover)
1. Gastronomy. 2. Food—Social aspects. I. Title.
TX631.G524 2014
641.01'3—dc23

2014008788

W. W. Norton & Company, Inc., 500 Fifth Avenue, New York, NY 10110
www.wwnorton.com

W. W. Norton & Company Ltd., Castle House, 75/76 Wells Street, London W1T 3QT

1 2 3 4 5 6 7 8 9 0

For my grandchildren,

Val, Aaron, Stefan and Sophia—

with a toast to the future!

I have discovered that there is romance in food when romance has disappeared from everywhere else. And as long as my digestion holds out I will follow romance.

—ERNEST HEMINGWAY, "GASTRONOMIC ADVENTURES"

I think it is true that one gains a certain hold on haddock and sausage by writing them down.

—VIRGINIA WOOLF, *DIARY*

The galaxy is in the shape of an eating mouth.

—WILLIAM DICKEY, "KILLING TO EAT"

Contents

Foreword

Romance in Food!

In "The Wild Gastronomic Adventures of a Gourmet," a piece he published in the *Toronto Star Weekly* in 1923, the young Ernest Hemingway boasted of his dining prowess. Not only had he cheerfully consumed poison ivy in his boyhood, he bragged, but as an adult "I have eaten Chinese sea slugs, muskrat, porcupine, beaver tail, birds' nests, octopus and horse meat," along with "mule meat, bear meat, moose meat" and such other exotic items as hundred-year-old eggs and snails. And he would continue to follow his yearnings! For, he concluded, "there is romance in food when romance has disappeared from everywhere else."

I've used that last statement as an epigraph for this book because its straightforward passion may help us understand why and how we read, write, work and play with food in the gastronomically obsessed twenty-first century, especially in industrially developed countries. Throughout this volume, as I explore many modes of food writing—what we might call the *eating* words of novelists and memoirists, poets and polemicists—along with representations of food in cooking shows and movies, paintings and art installations, I've tried to contextualize our culinary imaginings with investigations of the cultural history that has shaped them, giving ever-increasing urgency to our search for romance, and sometimes even redemption, in kitchens of the mind.

My organization of the materials I cover reflects my effort to balance discussions of texts and investigations of contexts. The first section of the book, "Digging In: Tastes of Past and Present," focuses both on the philosophical meanings of the food chain to which all mortal beings belong and on the social and political dynamics that, from myth to modernity, inform our eating habits. "The galaxy is in the shape of an eating mouth," wrote the late poet William Dickey in another of my epigraphs for this book, and he was summarizing what might be considered the metaphysic of food. We eat but can be eaten! We love our dinners but don't want to become dishes on the cosmic menu. We delight in the powers that transform the raw into the cooked, yet we also fear our vulnerability at the table. We long for the delicacies that the chef broils and bakes, stews and simmers, but dread the dangers of unknown edibles. We savor festive meals, yet resolve to renounce gluttony. As I show in these first four chapters, poets from Homer to Shakespeare, Keats and Rossetti, along with storytellers from Rabelais to Alcott, Joyce and Woolf have mused on the powers of the cook and the powers of food while examining moralities of renunciation and celebration.

Despite the long history of literary fascination with food, however, I'll argue in the next section of this book—"Today's Table Talk: Recipes of the Modern"—that by the early twentieth century changing times had led to transformed aesthetic tables. Poets and novelists increasingly meditated on the dailiness of the kitchen, and memoirists began to organize autobiographical writings through culinary memories. "One gains a certain hold on haddock and sausage by writing them down," declared Virginia Woolf in one of the last entries in her famous diary. *Thinking* food had become a way of thinking about life, even while literary enterprises had become ways of thinking *about* food. The self that the great M. F. K. Fisher defined as "the gastronomical me" became a central figure in the culinary memoirs that have come to be called "foodoirs," and the cook emerged from the kitchen to perform in TV studios and to star in movies featuring what the starved orphans of *Oliver!* called "food, glorious food!" "Let's eat" is now a category in my local video store, and restaurant critics too are celebrities along with the chefs whose productions they evaluate. The genre known as "the recipe novel" has countless aficionados, and it's paralleled by the menu poem and the gastronomic Gothic.

But of course the issues raised by food and hunger have always been as political as they are poetical. Vegetarianism and the more austere veganism have roots in the writings of theorists from Pythagoras to Shelley, and current proponents include such literary figures as Jonathan Safran Foer and J. M. Coetzee. Diets and dietary diatribes have long preoccupied readers, writers, and eaters, while, as I show in the last section of this book, "Food Chained: Food Fights, Fears, Frauds—and Fantasies," eating disorders (anorexia, bulimia) and food-related diseases are equally important to the contemporary culinary imagination. Yet even while many commentators portray the twenty-first century gastronomic culture produced by industrial capitalism in dystopian terms (*Fast Food Nation; Food, Inc.)* their works are balanced by what I'm defining as the "postmodern pastorals" outlined in the writings of, say, Wendell Berry and Michael Pollan.

As I reflect on the topics I've listed here, I realize I've been thinking about this material for a long time, not just because of a personal fascination with kitchen mysteries but also from the perspective of a cultural historian. Some thirty years ago I noticed that throughout the twentieth century poetry had increasingly savored not just exotic edibles but our daily bread. "Add food and stir," the injunction I explore in the first chapter of this volume, seemed to me to have flavored much contemporary verse, even while it had deep historical origins. Together with my good friend the poet–novelist Diana O'Hehir, I assembled a delicious collection of poems, tentatively called "Eating Words," in which we represented tasty works by Williams and Stevens, Lawrence and Hughes and Plath and countless others. We shopped the prospectus around for a while before understanding that its moment hadn't yet come. But in the meantime, as both a poet and a feminist critic, I myself was over and over again drawn to the glamour of the hearth, and to the domesticity that we in women's studies were striving to reimagine as a source not of female enslavement but of feminist empowerment.

Needless to say, both as activists and theorists we feminists had always struggled to address the patriarchal politics and poetics that have so long chained women to sink and stove. Yet the lives and words of the foremothers whom the French sociologist Luce Giard so resonantly calls "the kitchen women nation" were newly fascinating to many of us. At least three of my own collections of verse had titles enlivened, or so I hoped, by culinary allusions to this ancestral "nation." *The Summer Kitchen* celebrated the second, basement kitchen to which my Sicilian aunts withdrew in hot weather, and sought to mythologize the mysteries that bewitched and bewildered me in that subterranean place. *Emily's Bread* drew on my fascination with the two Emilys—Brontë and Dickinson—who were both bakers in their families. *Kissing the Bread* brooded on my Sicilian mother's strange habit of kissing a loaf of bread before throwing it away and became a metaphor for the poignant farewells to the quotidian that inflect all our lives.

Even while I was completing *Death's Door: Modern Dying and the Ways We Grieve,* the project in cultural studies that preceded this book, I knew I wanted, finally, to turn to an examination of the central place that food had lately come to occupy in all the arts. When I went to Cornell in the spring of 2007 as the first M. H. Abrams Distinguished Professor in the English department on that campus, I talked about my ideas with the teacher who has throughout my career done the most to shape my thinking, Mike Abrams himself, and benefited from his wise advice to begin my analysis of culinary modernity by investigating the history of food writing. After that, I was helped on my journey into gastronomic culture by numerous other colleagues, friends and institutions. Here I must thank three organizations in particular for their encouragement of my work. During a month's residency at the American Academy in Rome, I researched the foods of Rome and learned on the spot about the Rome Sustainable Food Project, designed by Alice Waters and implemented by former Chez Panisse chef Mona Talbott. During a three-month residency at the Camargo Foundation in Cassis, I benefited from the hospitality of Connie Higginson and Leon Selig, and shared my ideas with other fellows—especially Barbara Weissberger, Michele Longino and Jo and Douglas Kibbee—whose works were inspiring to me. Throughout six weeks at the Bogliasco Foundation just outside Genoa, I profited from the support of Alessandra Natale, the friendship of Suzanne Branciforte and Massimo Bacigalupi, and countless dinner table conversations with other residents.

My work on this project, however, began in Paris, where I lived for part of every year with my late partner, the mathematician David Gale, who was never so immersed in his own theorems that he couldn't read and comment on my writings. As I'll explain later in the book, it was he who guided me through the local *marchés*, he who introduced me to the wonderful restaurants and bistros he had come to love throughout many francophilic years, he who accompanied me on most of my researches, helping me find the romance in food and the food in romance. Without him this book wouldn't exist. And without him I would never have come to know the lively community of Parisians—French and American—whose friendship and encouragement have energized me for so long. Here I must especially thank Penny Allen, Marta and Maria and the late Rebecca Balinska, Michel Balinsky, Margo Berdashevsky, Jonathan Birt and Graham Ingham, Shehira Davezac, Jerry Fleming, Monique Florenzano, Guiguitte and the late Joseph Frank, Linda Gardiner, Marilyn Hacker, the late Anne and Russell Harris, Ken Johnston and his late wife Ilinca Zafiropol Johnston, Annie Mouton, Roger and Ginette Roy, and Joan Schenkar for Parisian meals and mentorship, comfort and companionship over the years. I'm particularly grateful to Diane Johnson and John Murray for the thirty-year friendship that perhaps more than any other helped me settle in Paris, and to David Downie and Alison Harris for introductions to the professional world of food, not just in Paris but in Rome, Liguria and California; and I'm equally grateful to Jean and Marie-Françoise Maurin for generously opening their homes in Paris and Normandy to me.

I have also been lucky enough to have a circle of supportive friends and colleagues on this side of the Atlantic as well as a loving family endlessly tolerant of a researcher's foibles. Among the friends who have in one way or another supported and encouraged my writing, I must thank Leah Asofsky, Ben Bagdikian and Marlene Griffith, Wendy Barker, Jacqui Brogan, Martin and Virginia Davis, Shelley Errington and Leo Goodman, Joan Finton and Shelly Baumrind, Martin Friedman and Elena Servi Burgess, Danny and Hilary Goldstine, Dorothy and Melvin Lemberger, Herbie and Claire Lindenberger, and Alan Soldofsky, along with all the members of my poetry group (Dan Bellm, Chana Bloch, Jeanne Foster, Diana O'Hehir, Peter Dale Scott, Phyllis Stowell and Alan Williamson, as well as, intermittently, Anne Winters) and a host of others for ideas and dinners. And I offer special gratitude to Joanne Feit Diehl and Dorothy Gilbert for always being there at the other end of the telephone or in my kitchen.

I've also been especially privileged to form new friendships with others in the field of food studies, notably Katharina Vester, of American University, and my

Berkeley food group: Susan Griffin, Alice McLean, and L. John Harris. A key culinary colleague has been Roger Porter, of Reed College: as coeditor of *Eating Words*, the anthology of food writing that we are currently preparing for W. W. Norton, Roger has been crucial in helping me engage with culinary philosophy while drawing my attention to texts that I've found compellingly important to my work on this volume too. In addition, I should note that Susan Gubar, my longtime collaborator on numerous other projects, has as always helped me think through all my ideas and offered nourishing feedback, to use yet another food-related metaphor. Starting with the incomparable Augustus Rose and up to and through Seulghee Lee, a series of assistants have provided course after course of information, and to my amazing current assistant, Jeff Blevins, I'll be eternally grateful for work above and beyond the requirements of his job. Once again, too, I'm deeply thankful for the warmth, encouragement, and abiding good sense of my agent, Ellen Levine, and my editor, Jill Bialosky, along with the support of their assistants, Alexa Stark and Rebecca Schultz, respectively, and the incisive interventions of my copyeditor, Allegra Huston.

My partner, Albert Magid, has lovingly provided care and concern as I completed this book, and from his family, Bonnie and Rachel and especially Daniel and Robinn Magid, I've learned the laws of kashrut and the pleasures of the seder. My late husband, Elliot Gilbert, presided over our stove for many years and made my writing possible, and my old friend, the late Bob Griffin, nurtured me in a time of great loss. I like to think that both would have relished the subject matter of this new work. My son, Roger Gilbert, a professor at Cornell, joined with Mike Abrams in advising me on the structure of my project, and along with my daughters and daughters-in-law, Kathy Gilbert-O'Neil and Susanna Gilbert, Gina Campbell and Robin Gilbert-O'Neil, he cooked, consoled and encouraged throughout the years in which I devoted myself to the culinary imagination. Susanna, in particular, has researched images and evaluated titles, while Kathy has seen to it that I can even pay my taxes in the midst of literary chaos. But it is to my grandchildren—Val Gilbert, Aaron and Stefan Gilbert-O'Neil, and Sophia Gilbert—that I dedicate this book. They have lightened my life in dark times and enlivened my kitchen with their joy in the scrumptiousness of our daily bread.

PART I

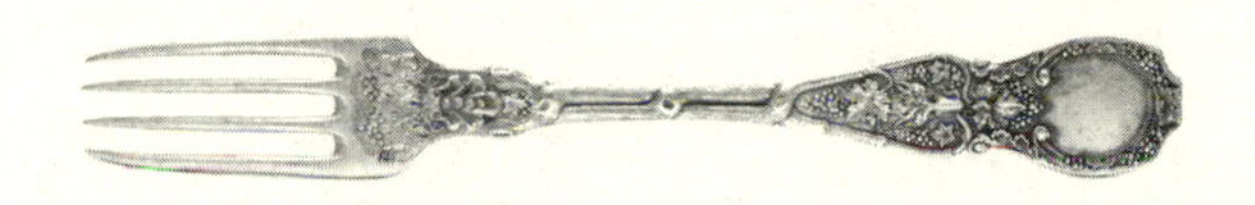

Digging In

Tastes of Past and Present

Chapter 1

Add Food and Stir: Life in the Virtual Kitchen

This year we will succeed in breaking through the envelope of the atmosphere and reach the planets. I invite you all to a banquet next New Year's Eve on the moon, where we will finally taste food of a flavor unknown to our palates and unimaginable drinks!

—FILIPPO MARINETTI, *THE FUTURIST COOKBOOK*

. . . if eating can be no more

or less meaningless
than not eating, given

that dying is as pointless
as living, existentially

speaking, of course,
why not
dig in?

—JOE-ANNE MCLAUGHLIN, "EXISTENTIALLY SPEAKING"

Writing incessantly about food is like writing porn. How many adjectives can there be before you repeat yourself?

—ANTHONY BOURDAIN, *THE NASTY BITS*

Eating Words

Food, foodies, food blogs, foodoirs, food wars, food flicks, food nets, food porn, food art, food for thought: food on the mind, everywhere. I spent an hour researching gastronomy in my local bookstore recently, and a startling number of titles had the words "food," "eat," "cook," "kitchen," or "recipe" in them: *Kitchen Wisdom. Cooked. Never Eat Your Heart Out. Women, Food and God. Kitchen Confidential. Eat Pray Love. Food Rules. Cooking for Mr. Latte. My Kitchen Wars. The Art of Eating. In the Night Kitchen.* And on and on. Some recent, some older—many selling like, well, hotcakes.

In a few of these books, cooking and eating weren't even all that central, except perhaps as lures for the hungry reader. But I was drawn to most because I almost always want to buy them. I don't count as a true foodie, like some super sophisticated diners, nor as a passionate culinary expert at the stove. Yet I share in our culture's persistent need to engage in gastronomic ruminations, devour cookbooks (some 24,000 are published annually), subscribe to culinary journals, nibble at restaurant reviews, collect DVDs of such films as *Babette's Feast, Like Water for Chocolate,* and *Ratatouille*, and gaze with fascination at Nigella Lawson or Rachael Ray or Emeril Lagasse while exercycling.[1]

Reviewing a history of Alice Waters and Chez Panisse, a writer for *Booklist* observed that the book will even interest readers who haven't been to Waters's famous restaurant "but do enjoy reading anything about food, and who doesn't?" The question is rhetorical, since just about everyone, lately, seems to want to read about one aspect or another of food. After all, my title search was limited: what if we factored in other edible words, not just "edible" itself but "stove," "cake," "spice," "appetite," and so forth? Discussing the ever more numerous novels in which recipes enrich and often leaven narratives, Adam Gopnik has speculated in the *New Yorker* that perhaps "Cooking is to our literature what sex was to the writings of the sixties and seventies, the thing worth stopping the story for to share, so to speak, with the reader."[2] But beyond what some have called "recipe novels," we now face an ever-expanding pantry full of recipe magazines, recipe poems, recipe memoirs, recipe histories, recipe travelogues, and even recipe polemics.

Beyond these recipe genres, mailboxes bulge with commercial and academic food journals, from *Saveur* to *Gastronomica*; computer monitors light up with alimentary blogs and restaurant critiques (Urban Spoon, Chowhound); bookstores are stuffed with anthologies of food writing from the Library of

America, the *New York Times*, the *New Yorker,* and others, along with volumes profiling celebrity chefs, debating the politics of food, analyzing the medical or cultural rights and wrongs of eating, and musing on both the mores of contemporary fast food chains and the morality of the contemporary food chain. Newspapers cover popular competitive eating championships, including not only the famous Nathan's hot dog eating contest but others focused on ribs, wings and grilled cheese sandwiches, the last of which once featured a sandwich on which an image of the Virgin Mary was said to have appeared. And as for other media, artists from Giuseppe Arcimboldo to Andy Warhol and Wayne Thiebaud have long focused on sometimes grotesque, sometimes luscious still lives of food, but now the pop star Lady Gaga makes headlines with costumes fashioned from flank steaks (a "meat bikini"! a "meat dress"!). In the meantime, hit movies focus on the triumphs and trials of cooking, while the Food Network and its rivals rivet viewers with stoveside counsel, culinary travel, and such pseudo-sporting competitions as *Iron Chef* and *Top Chef,* capturing larger audiences than most of the cable news channels.[3]

Why do we so massively—and often so hungrily—meditate on food, its history, its preparation, its stories, its vices and virtues? My epigraphs, drawn from three strikingly different authors, propose various explanations. Most extravagantly, Filippo Marinetti's *Futurist Cookbook* as long ago as 1932 sought to reimagine cuisine as itself an abstraction, a wholly new art form that would repudiate the bourgeois meals of tradition, and in a way his radically innovative, often bizarre meal plans foreshadowed the avant-garde "molecular gastronomy" lately made famous by Ferran Adrià. More recently and in a different philosophical mode, Joe-Anne McLaughlin defines eating as an essentially pointless existential activity that we engage in (and brood on) because "Why not?," while, with postmodern cynicism, the onetime chef Anthony Bourdain, author of the macho bestseller *Kitchen Confidential,* hints that representations of food are ultimately pornographic—as the now popular phrase "gastroporn" implies.

Musing on the fascinations of virtual food, the journalist Michael Pollan makes what appears to be a more practical, socially observant claim. The ascendancy of food TV, he declares, "has, paradoxically, coincided with the rise of fast food, home-meal replacements and the decline and fall of everyday home cooking," and asks "How is it that we are so eager to watch other people browning beef cubes on screen but so much less eager to brown them ourselves?" Pollan's historical speculation is intriguing. Has cooking in our late capitalist society simply withered away, as Marx predicted the state would do under Communism? Or have our old-fashioned kitchen ways merely morphed into a different set of culinary practices? Whatever the answers (and we'll explore many in this book) our preoccupation with food on the page, the wall, and the screen is both undeniable and unprecedented.[4]

"Tell me what you eat, and I shall tell you what you are": so goes a famous aphorism set down by Jean Anthelme Brillat-Savarin, the high priest of "transcendental gastronomy" whose groundbreaking *Physiology of Taste* was first published in 1825. Putting the matter somewhat differently, the rebellious modernist Henry Miller declared that "If the bread is bad the whole life is bad," while the contemporary food writer Bill Buford has offered a comparable culinary generalization: "You are what you eat and you eat what you are."[5] Given our turn to gastronomic fantasies, however, my investigations of the culinary imagination will supplement these maxims with an additional proposition: *Tell me what you read and write about what you eat, and I shall tell you* more *about what you are. Tell me how you envision food in stories and poems, memoirs and biographies, films and pictures and fantasies, and we shall begin to understand how you* think *about your life*. You might, after all, be munching popcorn and sipping Diet Coke while watching Meryl Streep perform as Julia Child in *Julie and Julia*; you might be nibbling on takeout sushi while riffling through the latest issue of *Saveur*. And what you eat will of course tell me something about you—but what you watch and read about eating will tell me at least as much. For, figuratively speaking, the daily bread you brood on reflects the daily life you live as accurately as the daily sandwich you pick up at the local deli.

To be sure, we'll see that representations of the lore and lure of food go back to antiquity, even to prehistory. Food taboos and other culinary practices are inscribed in the sacred texts of most cultures, while almost all religions feature holy feasts and fasts. From the six portentous pomegranate seeds Persephone nibbles in the myth that underlies the Eleusinian Mysteries and the voluptuous apple with which Eve (and Satan) transgressively tempt Adam, to the Last Supper at which Judas betrays Jesus, eating is often at the center of deadly occasions in Western song and story, even while, as the Jewish seder celebrations and the ritual Christian Communion of bread and wine suggest, religious thinking often strives to convert sin and pain into mystical pleasure.

Writings about more quotidian eating also have a long history in our culture. In the *Gorgias*, Plato inveighed against cookery as analogous to sophistry. Ancient Roman poets invited friends to dinner in verse. Medieval monks dreamed of the land of Cockayne, where houses were made of cakes and roasted fowls fell from the sky demanding to be eaten. Eighteenth-century parodists mused on the arts of cookery. Some Romantic poets protested the "blood sugar" derived from the toils of Jamaican slaves, while others fantasized magical foods. Victorian cooks produced rhyming recipes. And of course novelists built whole plots around teas and dinners, feasts and fasts.

"Sir Belly," declared Rabelais, "is the true master of all the arts," and therefore devoted much of *Gargantua and Pantagruel* to the excesses of appetite. In *A Christmas Carol*, Dickens poignantly feted the worthy Cratchit family with a communal meal of roast goose and, just as wistfully (but more ambitiously), Proust resurrected the whole world of his *temps perdu* from a morsel of a madeleine. In 1949, in her savory *Alphabet for Gourmets*, M. F. K. Fisher rejoiced in "Literature . . . and the banquets it can serve forth," and she herself served forth, in a single tasty paragraph, some thoughts on "gastronomical novels" by writers from Bennett to Bemelmans, and by "Huysmans and Saltus and Petronius and all those boys" and by "Virginia Woolf who wrote perhaps better than anyone in the Western world about the feeling of being a little drunk, or of being a hostess." "Food and cooking are not low subjects," declared the Episcopalian priest and culinary theorist Robert Farrar Capon in 1967. They "are among the richest subjects in the world."[6] Not surprisingly, then, quite a few critical works have been produced by scholars and historians studying representations of food and eating throughout a literary history crammed with dining that is by turns dangerously delicious and richly restorative.[7]

In the pages that follow, however, I'll argue that even while the products of our hungry culture are rooted in centuries of culinary writing and painting, our recipe novels and poems, our food polemics and cooking programs represent a gastronomical feeding frenzy that's both unprecedented and deeply significant. Why do we aestheticize recipes in verse and prose, narrate our personal and family histories by sharing tales of ancestral eating, venerate celebrity chefs, admire images of soup cans and layer cakes, and even predict cultural disaster through analyses of eating (or overeating) practices? Do our on-the-page, onscreen and online visions of food accompany a mass social return to dream kitchens of the mind because, as Pollan believes, we've so distanced ourselves from "real" food that we compensate by savoring virtual food? Or does our preoccupation with the rites of quotidian eating rather than the rituals of sacred food reveal some telling truths about our preference for the sensual things of this world rather than the *panis angelicus*—the angelic bread—of the spiritual realm?

Add food and *stir.* That phrase evolved out of an imperative from a verse-writing class that someone once reported to me: "when in doubt, add food." I suppose the teacher meant to say (and rightly) that adding food adds credence, adds dailiness, adds "real life." But the phrase "add food and stir" goes deeper, acknowledging that when we focus on food we focus not just on the literal schedule of meals we all consume but also on the stirrings of memory and desire and joy and, yes, even grief that those meals evoke in us. We stir readers when we add food because we remind them of their places at the complicated buffet of self, family, culture. Our recipes are histories of who we are, transmitting the tastes of the past through precept and example, even as they suggest how we can sometimes revise our lives by adjusting the menu. Yet the notion that by adding scrupulous details about the preparation of food we'll necessarily stir an audience or a readership is surely a new one! In earlier centuries, fruit—the golden apples of the Hesperides, Eve's apple, Persephone's pomegranate seeds, Homer's lotus berries—didn't usually come with recipes for pie and pudding. Milton gave no recipes for the "dulcet creams" Eve offered Raphael; Dickens didn't tell his fans how to roast the goose that stirred all the Cratchits to insist that "there never was such a goose," nor did Proust include a word or two about the ingredients of Marcel's famous madeleine. (And in any case, if such literary foods had been accompanied by culinary instructions, those would have been transmitted to mostly out-of-sight cooks and slaves.) Why have our kitchen fantasies changed so radically?

Burgers and Mâche

No one citizen of our hungry society is representative. *Fast Food Nation*, *Food, Inc.* and *Super Size Me* address the real eating habits of one constituency; *The United States of Arugula, Food Rules* and *The Julie/Julia Project* reflect the dream (and maybe the real) menus of another subculture. But gastronomic cultures mix things up, too, stirring ingredients around in the melting pot of the quotidian. How many arugula eaters have never bitten into a Big Mac? Where the old British pub staple bangers and mash might be said to have embodied a coherent set of culinary assumptions, contemporary diners in many corners of society are more likely to subsist on burgers and mâche—that is, on a diet combining commonly popular dishes with newly fashionable ingredients. And witty chefs may well have revised the burgers into innovative masterpieces while the tender mâche, also known as lamb's ear lettuce and hard to find in the States in the past, is now widely available in trendy supermarkets like Trader Joe's, Whole Foods, and Wegmans. For foie gras burgers, see Dean and DeLuca online: four for $55. As for bangers and mash, refined, cosmopolitan versions of these sizzle on bang-up menus in with-it restaurants. For an over-the-top Lucullan redaction, see Robert Irvine's recipe at FoodNetwork.com, featuring grapeseed oil, Guinness stout and elaborate "tobacco onions."[8]

Nonetheless, the obesity epidemic to which so much print has been devoted is clearly and sadly a consequence of burgers with processed cheeses, supersized colas, fat-saturated French fries—all the usual suspects. Foie gras and grapeseed oil don't make most people fat because most people don't have much access to such ingredients. Those who eat the products of our fast food nation get fat from, well, saturated fat, and high-fructose corn syrup, and salt and maybe nitrates and nitrites. They get fat, all too often, because it's cheaper to buy cheeseburgers than apples; in one famous film episode a family of migrant workers had to feed their kids drive-through meals because apples, at a dollar each, were out of reach.[9]

But burger—minus foie gras—marketing hits the middle classes, and even the so-called chattering classes too. I remember a group of graduate students sitting at a seminar table during a lunch break and comparing McDonald's branches around the world: India is interesting, said one, because the hamburgers are really lamburgers; Paris Big Macs are tastier than New York ones, volunteered another; Russian St. Petersburgers are pretty bad, opined another. And then there is the "ghostly" and elusive McRib, the widely fetishized ultimate faux food: a ground pork patty with "ribs" made of a "french toast-like substance." It has been an object of adoration on some 300 Facebook pages and appeared on *The Simpsons* and on one of David Letterman's top 10 lists—and was a postmodern object of admiration for some members of my class. Everybody in the room was munching on something healthy, perhaps even a vegan salad from our campus's dining commons, but everybody had lots of greasy meat and oily pizza creds.[10]

As I set the table for my mulling of these paradoxes, I'll begin by confessing that I too—like most of my friends, relatives and students—have a complex culinary history and divided gastronomic loyalties. I'm old enough to have experienced what I'll call the Tale of American Culinary Transformation, which some recent commentators argue divided us into a pre-Julia and a post-Julia nation. But as a first-generation American (my parents and grandparents came here from Sicily, from Liguria-via-Nice, and from Russia-via-Paris) I escaped what are generally considered traditional American eating habits. Maybe for that reason I'm more representative than I tend to think. Anyway, before I can explain how I read about eating, I'll begin to disclose a little of my own rather complicated eating history.

Tales of American Culinary Transformation

The time: 1955.

The place: the dining room of Balch II, a women's dormitory at Cornell University.

Ten of us are at one of the big round tables where the arts of "Gracious Living" are inculcated in us during sit-down meals served to the dorm's more fortunate inhabitants by scholarship girls who earn part of their keep working as waitresses. I'm looking with perplexity at bowls of tuna and noodles in a cream sauce, topped with crushed potato chips, that have been set before us.

"Oh, my mom makes this," says one girl enthusiastically. "She pours Campbell's cream of mushroom soup over the tuna and the noodles and then puts on the potato chips and bakes it." "My mom does that too," another chimes in. "And she makes great string beans. She adds a can of Campbell's cream of celery soup to a can of string beans and she bakes it and puts some crushed French fried onion rings on top. It's soooooo good."

Yet another girl explains something that *her* mother does with cream of chicken soup. And I'm astonished at all these discoveries. At eighteen, I've never heard of such culinary doings! So I ask more questions of more diners and resolve to learn how to prepare these dishes myself. Next time I go to my boyfriend's basement apartment in Collegetown, by God, I'll do a *real* tuna-noodle bake with cream of mushroom soup and maybe some canned mushrooms and maybe a topping of, oh, who knows what!

The time: 1985.

The place: the dining room of Terrace, an eating club at Princeton University.

I'm now a grownup English professor at Princeton, and seated at a small table with one of my students—let's call her Jennifer—and a few of her friends, who have invited me to dine with them. "Do be sure," says Jennifer, "to try the leg of lamb with Dijon mustard crust. It's one of our chef's specialties."

Later, I'll learn from another Princeton student that Terrace, with its dedicated chef, had been recruiting members by simply publishing menus like the one below in *The Princetonian,* the campus daily:[11]

Thursday:
Thai Marinated Chicken OR
Deep Fried Sea Bass in spicy sweet sauce

Broccoli Rabe with Ginger Butter

Rice

xxx Adult Chocolate Fortune Cookies

And Iced Coconut Cream

Thus did college dining change in three decades. And this change reflected, didn't it, an extraordinary metamorphosis of American culinary practices in the same period. One of the figures central to that transformation was the Knopf editor Judith Jones, who told the tale not too long ago in her cosy, gossipy *The Tenth Muse: My Life in Food,* which recounts her sponsorship of a series of bestsellers, beginning with *Mastering the Art of French Cooking* and moving on to books by such other luminaries as James Beard, Claudia Roden, Marcella Hazan, and Madhur Jaffrey. That story of wholesale change in tastes at table has also been examined in a range of other books, including several biographies of Julia Child along with the famous "French chef" 's own memoir, a joint "biography" of Alice Waters and her renowned Chez Panisse, and, of course, the more general culinary history titled *The United States of Arugula.* Most of these works in one way or another adhere to the master narrative that I'm calling the Tale of American Culinary Transformation—or TACT, for short.

Here is the history of contemporary American food according to TACT.

Once upon a time Americans ate Jell-O, apple pie, canned vegetables, plain old roasts, and "casseroles" made with cream of mushroom soup like those to which I was introduced as an undergraduate. Then an eager but gastronomically innocent young person of WASP or WASPish descent—Mary Frances Kennedy (Fisher), James Beard, Craig Claiborne, Julia McWilliams (Child), Judith Bailey (Jones) and yes, Alice Waters—accidentally or on purpose traveled to France. There s/he confronted, out of nowhere, a whole New World of food in the Old World: *charcuteries* or *fromagers* where postwar Parisians stood patiently in long queues, often, writes Jones, "in old carpet slippers with maybe a toe sticking through" because "no matter how hard the times, they had to have a good noonday meal."[12] And, too, there were *boulangeries* where one bought crunchy baguettes instead of cottony Wonder bread, *vergers* where the vegetables were dewily fresh, *boucheries* where one might purchase *cervelles* (brains) as well as chops and chickens, *patisseries* vending *tartes Tatin* instead of apple pie.

The WASP young person was stunned. At home in the *États-Unis,* she had never (well, hardly ever) encountered such delicacies. As Judith Jones confides, she had been raised to believe that "garlic represented everything alien and vulgar. It smelled bad, and people who handled it or ate it smelled bad." Indeed, adds Jones, "one wasn't supposed to talk about food at the table (it was considered crude, like talking about sex)," and even "spaghetti was always cut into ladylike pieces." In France the scales of American ignorance fell from the young person's eyes, the layer of American asbestos was lifted from her/his tongue. S/he became an acolyte of *la cuisine française,* with all that such devotion implied: the liberal use of garlic and herbs, the construction of sophisticated roux, the freedom to cook with real wine (instead of the dreadful liquid that used to be called "cooking wine"), and so forth.[13]

Then the transformed young person returned to the United States, determined to preach the gospel of *la bonne table* far and wide. Judith Jones championed Julia Child. Julia Child took to the airways. Craig Claiborne ruled the culinary roost at the *New York Times.* Alice Waters invented Chez Panisse. Chez Panisse invented dozens of other restaurants around the country, all devoted to the *nouvelle* purity of "California cuisine." The Food Network was born—and invented Rachael Ray. Anthony Bourdain invented himself. And so on until we reach today's culinary paradise(s) of farmers' markets, Whole Foods and Williams–Sonoma.

It's a heartwarming story, especially for wannabe foodies like me and my friends. There's only one problem: it isn't entirely true. Yes, Julia's teachings did change our lives in the kitchen just as Craig's reviews got us hooked on new restaurants, and—eventually—the top and bottom chefs of the Food Network expanded our notions of what you could whisk in a mixing bowl. But what about those of us, excluded from TACT (and mostly from Jones's memoir), who did *not* grow up eating tuna-noodle casseroles—or, for that matter, Jell-O and Wonder bread? What about those of us whose households didn't refuse garlic but were perfumed with it? What about those of us whose spaghetti wasn't "cut into ladylike pieces," and who came from homes where food was discussed as openly as politics?

Obviously the TACT narrative doesn't apply to some of us because we weren't WASPS—although some (with cosmopolitan parents) might even have been WASPS and nonetheless lived garlicky lives. But probably the TACTless population constituted by the children of immigrant families like my own most dramatically represents the gaps in our current story of American gastronomic metamorphosis. Sitting at that table in a Cornell dining hall, I was bemused by the tuna casserole because in my Sicilian–Italian–French–Russian family, where there was no elderly relative who spoke English without an accent, I'd never encountered such food. To be sure, my Sicilian-born mother, who came to the States when she was seven, longed to escape the Italianità of her large, noisy family; she was the youngest of nine, and fled from an Italian ghetto in Brooklyn to the (then) pseudo-WASP gentility of Queens right after I was born. But her notion of American food consisted mainly of lamb chops, baked potatoes, and chocolate pudding. Resolutely intellectual, she never read "ladies magazines," didn't "lunch" (except on the run, at the public school where she taught fifth grade), and certainly never heard of using Campbell's soups in such exotic ways. Nor, therefore, had I.

What I had heard of—and had eaten in happy quantities on many festive occasions—was food that the protagonists of TACT only discovered on pilgrimages to Europe: *hors d'oeuvres variés* (including *caviar d'aubergines* and mushrooms *à la grecque*) produced by my Niçois grandfather; a stuffing of Ligurian origin (made with spinach, mushrooms, sausage, parmesan cheese and, yes, lots of garlic!) with which he and my grandmother dressed our Thanksgiving turkeys; *arancini* (glowing rice balls with mushrooms or chicken livers tucked into their centers) produced by my Sicilian aunts; and *paska* (a cheese pudding) served with *koulich* (a coffee cake) that my Russian grandmother regularly procured for Russian Easter from a shop on Madison Avenue.

"The Northeast, where I grew up, had long suffered from a puritan disdain of the enjoyment of food," asserts Jones sweepingly.[14] But I don't know what Northeast she's discussing. In my family, we emphatically didn't eat Jell-O. Nor did the families of most of my friends. Rather, we ate lots of different dishes, and loved discussing them. One of my best girlfriends was Colombian, another Peruvian, and several of my earliest boyfriends were Spanish or Latin American too: one introduced me to paella, which we regularly sampled at the Sevilla in the Village. Another boy was Armenian: he took me to Middle Eastern restaurants in Manhattan where we reveled in voluptuous stuffed grape leaves, and afterward we'd go to Port Said, a place on the West Side where (though we were under age) we drank ouzo and eyed the in-house belly dancers with fascination. Other boyfriends were mostly Jewish. The first one at Cornell, for whom I made that casserole of tuna and noodles (we didn't like it), received regular care packages of Hebrew National salami from his parents in Brooklyn, and introduced me to *matzoh brei.* A later one at Cornell, whom I eventually married, brought me home to dinners in his parents' Bronx apartment that were carefully prepared by their African American cook, Mattie. Sometimes Mattie offered down-home fried chicken, but more often she concocted the Yiddish specialties she'd been taught by my mother-in-law-to-be: chopped liver, savory or sweet kugels, braised brisket.

On our first date, in 1956, the boyfriend who became my husband took me to Larré's, a popular French restaurant on West Fifty-Sixth Street that closed only a few years ago. There we feasted on *hors d'oeuvres variés* not unlike my grandpa's—and there I unwittingly ordered *escargots à la bourgogne*—snails in garlic sauce—somehow thinking, in my first-date nervousness, that they were coquilles Saint-Jacques; and thus I learned to love a French delicacy about which I might otherwise have been squeamish.

Nor were the restaurants of which I've written here lone harbingers of things to come in America. Although Jones traces the proliferation of ethnic restaurants to the late sixties, when I was growing up in New York, not that many years after she was raised there, the city was full of little bistros like Larré's, even in benighted Queens, and there were Italian restaurants everywhere, including the venerable Grotta Azzurra, founded in 1908, where celebrities from Enrico Caruso to Frank Sinatra feasted. Even more venerable was Luchow's, where my family and I ate sauerbraten, wiener schnitzel, and headcheese vinaigrette, and almost as venerable was the Russian Tea Room, where we all dined on chicken Kiev and beef Stroganoff. In their magisterial

On the Town in New York, Michael and Ariane Batterberry, founder editors of *Food and Wine* magazine, outline the geography of cuisines available throughout the city between 1914 and 1940, from Chinatown eateries to Jewish delis, from little French bistros to Italian cafés and German beer halls, noting that although the small French restaurant had

> captured New York's doting attention more than any other, [further] waves of foreign invaders staked out conquered territories in all parts of Manhattan. Turkey and Armenia commandeered the east side area from Twenty-sixth to Thirty-fourth Street . . . The Greeks held Ninth Avenue. Little Spain occupied Cherry Street . . . An Egyptian Garden bloomed on Washington Street, a Swedish Ratskeller entrenched itself on East Fifty-Second, and the steamed fish with rice at the Miyako Japanese restaurant on Fifty-eighth soon became as famous as the curries of the Ceylon India Inn.[15]

I have to admit that I remember dining at some of those restaurants, all of which were still in delicious bloom while I was growing up in the city. But of course it may be objected that I am bearing witness to the culinary delights of a very special youth—among immigrants, in immigrant-rich metropolitan New York. Yet what of cities like Chicago and New Orleans? San Francisco and Santa Fe? Richmond and Savannah? It doesn't seem likely that they were all populated by Jell-O-eaters. Polish sausages, dirty rice, gumbo, *cioppino*, chile, tamales, Southern fried chicken, greens with potlikker—these now (or do I mean still) fashionable foods didn't appear out of nowhere! The food historian Donna Gabaccia points out that many of our American "shifting, blended, multiethnic eating habits" have a complex history that goes back to the food ways of colonists and the foods introduced by indigenous peoples along with increasingly diverse masses of immigrants.[16]

What, then, is the real story behind TACT? As I reflect on it, I think it's a tale of consciousness expansion, education and institutionalization. To begin with, the consciousnesses expanded were clearly those of such WASPs as Julia

McWilliams Child and Judith Bailey Jones; in France, they learned about foods of whose existence they'd been barely aware in America even though many of their compatriots—from Alice B. Toklas and Gertrude Stein to Ernest Hemingway and M. F. K. Fisher—had already dined on such delicacies. In their pedagogical journeys, all followed the footsteps of many British travelers, whose culinary pilgrimages were extolled in the eighteenth century by the poet William King: in his "Art of Cookery," this poet demanded "Muse, sing the man that did to Paris go, / That he might taste their Soups, and Mushrooms know." Then, in an effort to analyze the nature of these new soups and other dishes, Child, Jones, and their contemporaries began what did in fact become a transformative process: they wrote in detail, or edited books about, what they had learned to eat. As educators, they were extraordinarily influential at a time when many Americans were ready to change in countless ways—in particular, when the conservatism of the fifties began to wane and the consciousness-expanding sixties "blew" what we might call the national mind.[17]

Still, given Jones's version of TACT, what did it mean for me and other children of immigrant families when Julia Child and her cohort began to preach the gospel of *la bonne table*? To begin with, I'd say that, as we'll see, the growing celebrity of Julia, Marcella, and their colleagues ultimately meant we could now affirm the excellences of our ethnicities. If we'd tried to escape toward Americanness—as my mother had yearned for lamb chops and I'd, if only briefly, sought tuna casseroles—we no longer needed to do so. We were no longer anxious, as some had been, about culinary Italianità—or Jewishness, or Hispanicity. And better still, what we'd known intuitively and experientially was now returned to us in the lucidly organized prose of accomplished gastronomic writers.

To be sure, we'd always had cookbooks of our own. In 1958 I began my married life with the *Talisman Italian Cookbook* (1950) and a range of other volumes, including (among non-Italian collections) Dione Lucas's *Cordon Bleu Cookbook* (1947), of which my husband was a particular fan, and Edward Harris Heth's marvelous compendium of seasonal recipes, *The Wonderful World of Cooking* (1956), a work that emphatically proved the strengths of a non-mushroom-soup-based American cuisine. Jones and others tend to dismiss books of this era, defining the period as (in Jones's words) a "wilderness" in which such compendia "boasted of the number of recipes they had crammed between the covers [because who] cared about the quality of the instruction"? But though I'm offended by this judgment of writings I love, I have to concede that when the heroines and heroes of TACT came to power, their productions had a far greater reach than their precursors'. Now everybody wanted to eat the way we immigrant families had always eaten![18] And we too learned to love and honor our ancestral kitchens in new ways. In her seventies, my mother (who died at the age of ninety-seven) began to reimagine some of the Italian recipes she'd renounced in her earlier efforts to become "American": *scalora in brodo,* marinara sauce, Sicilian sausages roasted with lemons. The culinary revolution of the sixties had reminded my mom that, after all, those dishes were American too.

Firing Up the Stove in the Sixties

Speaking of consciousness expansions: the countercultural sixties were after all *the* revolutionary era of the twentieth century, matched only by the flaming twenties. Even in the secluded safety of the States, the years of the Second World War had offered American citizens relatively impoverished menus. The food rationing whose rigors M. F. K. Fisher addressed in *How to Cook a Wolf* (1942) was probably more widely challenging to cooks than the straitened circumstances of the depressed thirties. But in Europe and Asia meals were far more meager for civilians and soldiers alike, while for internees in concentration and prison camps the menus of desolation were really, for some years, unspeakable. No wonder, then, that a vast sigh of gastronomic relief arose in the postwar years. Paradoxically, the prettified fifties—the "tranquillized" fifties, as Robert Lowell called that decade—laid the groundwork for all kinds of change. Suddenly there was a booming economy, an ever-growing college population, and what Betty Friedan so famously described as a "feminine mystique" for women to chafe against. And as the food historian Laura Shapiro has meticulously demonstrated, new hungers were simmering in the kitchen, fostered by a number of food writers: Poppy Cannon (who at one point collaborated with Alice B. Toklas), Samuel Chamberlain (a.k.a. "Clementine" of *Gourmet*), and of course James Beard and Dione Lucas as well as the influential British writer Elizabeth David and even "Betty Crocker." The culinary atmosphere established by these figures is usually ignored by proponents of TACT, but their gradually evolving menus, including some that had actually been encouraged by corporate-sponsored events like the Pillsbury Bake-Off (where no cake mixes were allowed!), helped lay the groundwork for *nouvelle* cooks from Julia Child to Julie Powell.[19]

New appetites were inspired, too, by new travel patterns. Functioning both as postwar "peacekeepers" and Cold War warriors, hosts of American soldiers were stationed around the world, especially in Germany. My husband and I lived "off base," outside Nuremberg, in 1958, where, in the local *gästhausen,* we and countless others posted nearby were introduced to the pleasures of *rahm schnitzel* (veal cutlet with cream sauce) and *zigeuner schnitzel* ("gypsy" cutlet, with peppers and tomatoes), carp and *kartoffelsalat.* My husband's platoon was the usual almost comically various group made famous by movies and later *M*A*S*H*—a telephone lineman from Mississippi, a mechanic from Rochester, an art historian from Rhode Island, a fire-breathing sergeant from Brooklyn, several Mormons from Utah, etc.—in other words, "guys," as in all platoons, from everywhere, many with wives and a few with kids. Almost all of us traveled around Europe, nibbling cheeses that were really strange to some and regularly scarfing not just schnitzels but scallopine and linguine.

By the sixties, increasing numbers of civilian travelers cruised and jetted across the Atlantic and even the Pacific, while the American combat vets and ex-GIs who had seen "Paree" and other gastronomic hot spots no longer wanted to stay down on the farm, or in the suburbs. The cosmopolitan epiphanies that had fed the imaginations of well-to-do WASP travelers like M. F. K. Fisher, Julia Child and Judith Jones were no longer the prerogative of the upper classes. Fed on—and fed up with—the tuna casseroles of childhood, college kids journeyed to Europe on exchange programs—and even if they didn't travel they learned about formerly exotic foods from pals who'd been abroad or from newly founded cafés in college towns and big cities. Hippies and other denizens of the counterculture, especially the Diggers, made food reform a centerpiece in their plans for the greening of America. Alice Waters and her friends constituted a sort of *nouvelle cuisine* commune in Berkeley, as did Ruth Reichl and a group of like-minded diners. Julia Child spoke to the masses on TV and Craig Claiborne pontificated in the pages of the *New York Times*. Yes, restaurant culture had proliferated in the nineteenth century (and before that there had long been inns, taverns, chop-houses and cookshops where prepared food could be bought) and there had long been restaurant reviewers, pamphlet-wielding vegetarians, and connoisseurs of fine wine and foie gras. But now what Betty Fussell has sardonically called the "kitchen wars"—or at least, the kitchen upheavals—had begun in city, suburb, and exurb.[20]

Nor did women's rebellion against the "feminine mystique" repress the new spirit of culinary innovation. Although Michael Pollan has said that Friedan's book "taught millions of American women to regard housework, cooking included, as drudgery, indeed as a form of oppression," he also concedes that "second-wave feminists were often ambivalent on the gender politics of cooking" and that even the great Simone de Beauvoir believed cooking, if sometimes oppressive, "could also be a form of 'revelation and creation.'" Still he concludes that Beauvoir's comment was "a bit of wisdom that some American feminists thoughtlessly trampled in their rush to get women out of the kitchen."[21] This blanket assertion, along with other more sweeping claims about the role of feminism in the rise of fast food and the decline of the traditional family meal, has stirred up a stew of protest among food studies scholars and feminist gastronomes, most of whom point out that the development of so-called convenience foods significantly predated the second wave of feminism and even the "feminine mystique" of the fifties. Notes one writer on the food studies listserv, "Didn't McDonald's come about in the 1940s? Burger King and KFC in the 1950s? Merriam-Webster added the term 'fast food' to their dictionaries in 1951. Fast food has nothing to do with women wanting out of the kitchen; it has to do with capitalism." Another adds that "Ray Kroc took the McDonald brothers southern California drive-in into the franchise world in 1955; Harlan 'Colonel' Sanders originally leased his fried chicken recipe and the equipment to fry it directly to restaurants on a handshake agreement of a nickel for each piece of chicken they sold, taking Kentucky Fried Chicken into the realm of stand-alone stores in the late 1950s."[22]

Indeed, my own experience in the trenches of second-wave feminism, like that of many of my contemporaries, was very different from what Pollan assumes. True, women who felt themselves to have been brainwashed by the fifties' ideologies of Betty Crocker and Betty Furness sided with the rebellious Betty Friedan in repudiating a culture that fetishized cake mixes, fancy washing machines, and shiny refrigerators (even while most made use of every convenience). Yet one of the tenets of our feminism was not a flight from the kitchen but a revaluation of the kitchen and everything it symbolized, in particular the nurturing arts and culinary secrets that had long been a source of women's power. The word "kitchen" became magical for me and others as we sought to recover what we considered the real roots of gastronomy in the hearth, the kettle, and the cauldron over which our ancestresses had presided. We didn't want to be relegated to the kitchen; we had learned to hate tuna casserole and (as Hillary Clinton would later put it) "staying home and baking cookies." What we admired was the intelligence and expertise that Julia Child incarnated: a new, smart way of reviving ancient savors.

Of course, as women increasingly entered the workforce, they encountered the stresses Pollan and others have described. And yes, such stresses meant that, on the one hand, more men collaborated at the stove, and, on the other hand, more families took out "takeout." For the revolutionaries of the sixties and seventies, though, corporate food—TV dinners, Big Macs—weren't major answers. At the least, takeout was pizza (then a relatively new phenomenon) or Chinese or reasonably high-quality deli. But we learned, too, to make fast meals—pasta with pesto, for instance, or frittatas, or fajitas—all from newly accessible recipes facilitated by a newly fascinating gastronomic culture. Besides, let's face it, convenience food is in fact convenient. Male or female, if you get home at six or seven after a day in the office, the lab, or the classroom, you won't start a *gigot d'agneau*, a *boeuf bourguignon*, or even a lasagna from scratch, not if you have kids to feed and not in what Julia Child rightly called "the servantless American kitchen." You'll need help from somewhere, no matter how gastronomically virtuous you are! Maybe a canned chicken broth instead of a homemade stock? Maybe a takeout rotisserie chicken?

But even if we feminists didn't cook, we often wrote about food, dreamed about it, fictionalized and versified it, pioneering the modes that have now been popularized by the Food Network, by foodoirs and by food bloggers. As befitted women torn among the various Bettys (Crocker, Furness, and Friedan), our musings were sometimes ambivalent. The young Sylvia Plath confided to her journal that she hoped to be "spare[d] from cooking three meals a day . . . from the relentless cage of routine and rote." In *The Bell Jar*, her protagonist, Esther Greenwood, is poisoned by crab salad–stuffed avocados at a luncheon hosted by the magazine *Ladies' Day*. Yet, as Lynda Bundtzen has shown in a fine essay in *Gastronomica*, this author was a passionate cook, as were quite a few other writers of her generation. In "Making the Jam without You," the poet Maxine Kumin bestowed a fantasy of foraging and simmering on a traveling daughter, wishing that she'd be accompanied by a mysterious figure who would bring her buckets of fat, "plum-size" blackberries "crooked on his angel arms" so that she could bear them "to a square/white unreconstructed kitchen/not unlike this one" and fill her own jelly glasses "with the bright royal fur." And before she popularized the zipless fuck in her bestselling *Fear of Flying*, Erica Jong made her debut as a poet with a volume of delicious verses titled *Fruits and Vegetables*.[23]

As we'll see, women have a long relationship not just to "the relentless cage of routine and rote" associated with the drudgery of three meals a day and tuna casseroles but also to the virtual or fantasy food we have come to associate with "transcendental gastronomy." In nineteenth-century America, Emily Dickinson reimagined her kitchen as "Domingo," in the Spice Islands, even while she protested against Victorian constraints. And in the mid-twentieth century a group of women imprisoned at the Terezin (Theresienstadt) concentration camp produced one of the most moving of all virtual cookbooks. As many neared death from starvation, they obsessed about food, the way almost all inmates did, and spent their time cooking in the mind—"platonically," as one of them put it. Unlike other prisoners, however, they confided their thoughts to paper, and the chief author, Wilhelmina Pächter, bequeathed the manuscript to a survivor friend. Years later, it was published, its sometimes skewed or fragmented directions attesting both to the ravages of internment and the powers of the culinary imagination.

Here is one of the more triumphant recipes:

Cold Stuffed Eggs Pächter

Hard boil 10 eggs, cut them in half. Remove yolks and press them through a sieve. Add 5 decagrams butter, 2 anchovies pressed through a sieve, a little mustard, 3–4 drops Maggi [liquid seasoning], ⅛ liter whipped heavy cream, parsley, lemon juice. Now put eggs on a platter. Pour [liquid] aspic over. Before [pouring on the aspic] let fantasy run free and the eggs are garnished with ham, [smoked] salmon, caviar, capers. One can put the eggs into paper cuffs and serve them with hot sliced rolls.[24]

Let fantasy run free! A legacy from the darkest kitchen of the twentieth century to our online, onscreen world of virtual kitchens, foodoirs and food blogs? But the women of Terezin were wasting away on concentration camp fare, whereas we in the contemporary West are sated, even glutted, with more than we need. In a reversal of historical culinary hierarchies, the rich are thin, the poor are fat, and neither class is driven by relentless hunger to fantasize. Yet visions of sugarplums (and even more outré delicacies) dance in most people's heads, on countless pages, and millions of TV screens. Have we fled the responsibilities of the real kitchen, as Pollan defines them, broken the barriers of imagination and entered Marinetti's futuristic dreamland? Do our voyeuristic culinary reveries border on porn, as Bourdain hints? Or do we just brood on eating because life is pointless anyway, so—as McLaughlin slyly wonders—"why not / dig in" however we can?

Come, let's enter and explore the contemporary cathedral of gastronomy, its history, its arts and sciences, its warring sects, its prophets and profiteers!

Chapter 2

Black Cake: Life (and Death) on the Food Chain

The part of the soul which desires meats and drinks and the other things of which it has need by reason of the bodily nature, they placed between the midriff and the boundary of the navel, contriving in all this region a sort of manger for the food of the body; and there they bound it down like a wild animal which was chained up with man, and must be nourished if man was to exist.

—PLATO, *TIMAEUS*

We can smell only what is in the process of wasting away, and we can taste only by destroying.

—G. W. F. HEGEL, *LECTURES ON FINE ART*

Cooking is one of those arts which most requires to be done by persons of a religious nature.

—ALFRED NORTH WHITEHEAD, *DIALOGUES*

The Mystery of Food
Increased till I abjured it
And dine without Like God—

—EMILY DICKINSON, 1311

What We Eat—and What We Are

"Tell me what you eat and I shall tell you what you are." I've already expanded Brillat-Savarin's famously magisterial, even arrogant, claim to say, "Tell me what you read and write about what you eat and I shall tell you what you are." But for the moment let's analyze the statement as the transcendental gastronome himself formulated it, and read it from various perspectives: anthropologically, psychologically, metaphysically. That Brillat-Savarin himself ate certain kinds of foods—foie gras, let's say, and (as he enthusiastically recorded) "the curate's tuna omelet"—would tell us his cultural identity even if we didn't know his name and language: he was obviously a Frenchman. That he liked eating in certain ways, at certain times, and with particular friends, might convey his personality: he was convivial, a *professeur* and *amateur* of gastronomy who enjoyed the company of other gourmands. That he ate at all—that he *had* to eat and had to eat food that had once been alive—is of course tautological, yet crucial. Like all of us, Brillat-Savarin ate what he *was himself*: as a mortal being, he ate other mortal things, he ate mortality. Thus what he ate was what he was. He ate *because* he was, and he *was* because he ate. He resided, like the rest of us, on the food chain.

In *The Devil's Dictionary,* the American writer Ambrose Bierce, who knew and enjoyed Brillat-Savarin's writings, succinctly and sardonically evoked the food chain in a definition of the word "edible," which means, asserted Bierce, "Good to eat, and wholesome to digest, as a worm to a toad, a toad to a snake, a snake to a pig, a pig to a man, and a man to a worm."[1] Food, as Plato has Socrates observe with distaste in one of my epigraphs, is about materiality, about the "wild animal" that, from his perspective, was "chained up" with the immaterial soul. Centuries later Hegel elaborated, noting in another of my epigraphs that the substances we smell and taste are in the process of dissolution, as we ourselves are. Indeed, he observed, "smell, taste, and touch have to do with matter as such and its immediately sensible qualities—smell with material volatility in air, taste with the material liquefaction of objects, touch with warmth, cold, smoothness, etc. For this reason these senses cannot have to do with artistic objects." In this philosopher's view, then, as in Plato's, the very concept of "culinary art" would be an oxymoron.

Medieval theologians agreed, counting gluttony among the seven deadly sins, and moralizing poets and painters from Dante to, later, Bosch and

Bruegel consigned overly enthusiastic diners to miserable afterlives: Dante's gluttons wallow, starving, on heaps of garbage, while Bosch's and Bruegel's sinners are themselves stewed, sautéd and roasted even as they yearn for inaccessible delicacies. Chaucer's hypocritically ferocious Pardoner summarizes such views of the perils posed by the "wild animal" of the belly, beginning with an allusion to St. Paul:

> *"For they are foes of Christ and of the Cross,*
> *Whose end is death, whose belly is their god."*
> *O gut! O belly! O you stinking cod,*
> *Filled full of dung, with all corruption found!*
> *At either end of you foul is the sound.*
> *With how great cost and labour do they find*
> *Your food! These cooks, they pound and strain and grind;*
> *Substance to accident they turn with fire,*
> *All to fulfill your gluttonous desire! . . .*
> *But truly, he that such delights entice*
> *Is dead while yet he wallows in this vice.*[2]

If you turn your mind to it, you may discern rather a lot of gloom and doom surrounding food. For Buddhist monks, as for the Pardoner and the Christian theologians whose views he parodies, the body is merely a sack of guts with openings at each end, the prey of desire and prone to decay. The mouth is violent and ruthless in consumption; the anus a helpless victim of excremental workings. And Cartesian dualism affirmed such notions in later Western centuries: from a dualistic point of view, I both *am* a body and *have* a body. The me that *has* a body ought to transcend my fleshly heaviness, my place on the food chain; the me that *is* a body is destined to be something's dinner. Yet the conundrum of my condition, a version of the enduring mind–body problem, is biologically inescapable: what wants to liberate itself from the belly's animality ultimately depends on the labors of that organ, as Aesop wittily observed in his fable of the "belly and its members," here put into a sonnet by the poet Judith Goldhaber:

A popular revolt against the belly
was cooked up by the foot, the brain, the hands,
the eyes, the nervous system, and the glands.
"What do you think this is? An all-night deli?
To keep you well supplied with bread and jelly
we must bow ceaselessly to your demands!
We've voted that it's time to take a stand
against your bossy ways! So take your smelly
job and stuff it!" And they went on strike!
Quite soon the hands grew weak, the eyes grew dim;
too late, they all repented of their whim.
The Members of the body, rather like
those of the state, must live in brotherhood
and work together for the common good.[3]

Kafka's great story "A Hunger Artist" might be an extended riff on Aesop's observation: the protagonist, seeking to exhibit his skill at fasting to a public that was once enthusiastic but has grown indifferent, dies alone, his wasted flesh hidden under rotten straw in a circus cage. He is quickly replaced by a wild young panther, who "enjoys the taste of food" and whose "noble body, equipped with everything necessary, almost to the point of bursting, even appeared to carry . . . around with it" a freedom "located somewhere or other in its teeth, and its joy in living came with . . . strong passion from its throat." One with his body, Kafka's panther appears to live in his bite, his swallow, while the hunger artist, in eschewing teeth—and throat and belly—has devolved into a heap of dried grass, ironically enough evoking the biblical line that "all flesh is as the grass."[4]

Given a choice between soul and belly, must we become beasts, succumbing without consciousness to the drive for food? Or have our increasingly intellectualized gastronomical interests emerged out of a revisionary theology that unites spirit with matter in a devotion to the quotidian pleasures of our daily bread (and beef and wine and gourmet vegetables)? In our increasingly secular Western societies we're torn on these issues, even though medieval injunctions against gluttony now seem passé. On the one hand, whether we dream of prime ribs or McRibs, fries or frittatas, tofu or tapas, we are immersed in a foodie culture. On the other hand, we're surrounded by dietary sermonizing not unlike the Pardoner's, as Francine Prose has incisively noted: vegans urge efforts to escape the food chain, or at least the part of it that involves animals; nutritionists preach regimens of low fats or low carbohydrates or raw foods or high proteins; glamour magazines celebrate slenderness, equating anorectic bodies with wealth ("You can never be too thin or too rich"). And finally, on, as it were, the third hand, for those who embrace some form of "transcendental gastronomy," food becomes both physical and metaphysical, both sensual and emotional. In the words of the Provençal novelist Jean Giono, "There are things which by flavor or color make you taste joy . . . and others which make you taste grief. Three parts of joy, one of mourning—that is the taste of life." As Brillat-Savarin argued, directly contradicting Plato and Hegel, eating can be spiritually significant as well as materially pleasurable in its complex melding of presence and absence.[5]

Indeed, Bierce's definition of the word "eat" incorporates an important allusion to the French master:

> EAT, v.i.: To perform successively (and successfully) the functions of mastication, humectation, and deglutition.
>
> "I was in the drawing-room, enjoying my dinner," said Brillat-Savarin, beginning an anecdote. "What!" interrupted Rochebriant; "eating dinner in a drawing-room?" "I must beg you to observe, monsieur," explained the great gastronome, "that I did not say I was eating my dinner, but enjoying it. I had dined an hour before."[6]

The pleasure of eating, according to this story, transcends the merely physical acts of "mastication, humectation, and deglutition." Indeed, the virtual pleasures of contemporary food blogs, foodoirs and food shows are implicit in Brillat-Savarin's remark. One may already have dined but still recall the pleasures of gastronomy while watching Mark Bittman sup in Spain or reading

M. F. K. Fisher's tales of Provence. Not only the creation of culinary delicacies but the appreciation of the idea of such delicacies gives joy to the diner, whose imaginings of meals past, present and possible, like Proust's memory of his childhood madeleines, bestow on food an insubstantial, perhaps even aesthetic cast. From this perspective, we eat, yes, because we are mortal and must eat—just as we must ourselves sooner or later be eaten. Yet not only are we sustained by what we eat, we are consoled, comforted, and even, sometimes, transfigured by it, since gastronomic experience is ultimately more mental than it is physical.

Historically, the language of love, the language of food and the language of survival often blend, as if melded in a magic bowl. Declares the Shulamite woman in the Song of Songs, as she savors the thought of her lover:

> As the apple tree among the trees of the wood, so is my beloved among the sons. I sat down under his shadow with great delight, and his fruit was sweet to my taste. He brought me to the banqueting house, and his banner over me was love. Stay me with flagons, comfort me with apples: for I am sick of love.[7]

The fear of pain, argued Brillat-Savarin, "makes man throw himself . . . toward the opposite extreme, and give himself up completely to the small number of pleasures which Nature has permitted him." And among these, the "pleasures of the table" are crucial, for although such pleasures "do not presuppose ravishment nor ecstasy nor bliss . . . they gain in duration what they lose in intensity, and are above all distinguished by their own merit of making all the others more intense for us or at least of consoling us for their loss."[8]

Stay me with flagons, comfort me with apples. Indeed, averred the great gastronome, if the "pleasure of eating is one we share with animals," the "pleasures of the table are known only to the human race" for they involve careful preparation and communal delight, so that even if we are theologically austere, "we still enjoy ourselves at marriages, baptisms, and even funerals."[9] Thus neither the purely physical panther nor the fanatically ascetic hunger artist can share in the distinctively human communal rituals of mealtime. Despite Plato's definition of the belly as a wild animal, what makes our daily bread the staff of life on which we lean is more than the brute nourishment we gain when we devour it. The idea of bread accompanies the physical fact of the bread itself. The starving women of Terezin ate "Platonically," recall, as they scribbled their cookbook. For it isn't just flagons and apples that stay and comfort us; it's the knowledge that there *are* flagons and apples, along with the idea of the nurture such good things of this world represent. Whether we are sick with love, sick with fear or sick with grief from the loss of love, such knowledge is comforting.

Cooking—and Coping

In my own case, certainly, our daily bread has figuratively as well as literally become a staff of life, its wordings and workings an essential source of literary affirmation as well as literal nourishment. In February 1991 my husband of thirty-four years, Elliot Gilbert, died of a medical accident, and for the next fifteen years I mourned him, elegized him, analyzed and reported the catastrophe that killed him, then meditated more broadly on mourning in contemporary culture. And my years of stewing in grief while studying it issued in a number of books—a memoir, a collection of my own elegies, an anthology of elegies by others, and finally a massive investigation of modern dying and the ways we grieve. And yet much of this time—for a long while without really noticing what I was doing—I was cooking and collecting culinary writings. Confronting the anxiety, dread and despair that inevitably accompany grief, I became, if not a gastronome, an increasingly interested reader and writer of and about gastronomy.

My loss had forced me to contemplate the food chain so darkly described by Bierce in his definition of edible ("Good to eat . . . as a pig to a man, and a man to a worm"). But family and friends had comforted me with apples, too, and I gradually learned to comfort myself with, at the very least, ideas about apples. As a wife and mother of three, I'd always been at least in part responsible for family meals. But gradually, in the course of a long and loving marriage, my husband had grown increasingly central in the kitchen. Indeed, by the time his sudden death swept him out of our household, I was mostly sous-chef, pot-washer, and dishwasher-loader. Nor did I in general object to those roles. I liked cooking and (in my view) had taught Elliot many of his culinary skills, but he was tenacious about what he wanted to eat as well as how he wanted to cook it, and it was easy, and very comfortable, to let him feed us all on deviled eggs, petrale sole poached with mushrooms, *boeuf bourguignon*, lamb croquettes with avgolemono sauce, veal marengo, roast turkey with Genovese spinach stuffing, salmon mousse, roast beef with Yorkshire pudding, crème caramel, German chocolate cake, and on and on.

I intervened at the stove only rarely. Now and then I produced specialties I'd learned in my family's various immigrant kitchens—for instance, I made the spaghetti sauce my Sicilian mother and her sister had taught me along with the meat loaf stuffed with hard-boiled eggs they'd introduced me to; and for picnics I did a macedoine of vegetables I'd learned from my Russian grandmother as well as the marinated artichokes and mushrooms she and my Niçois grandfather had regularly included in their *hors d'oeuvres variés.* Once in a while, too, I experimented with curries or with stir-fries, neither of which much interested Elliot. But my cooking was increasingly desultory and intermittent.

And when he died? For a while I was largely fed (to the extent that I could swallow food) by other, equally devoted male chefs: my close friend the late Bob Griffin, my son Roger, and even, at the beginning of my relationship with him, my late partner, David Gale, who became a major inspiration for this book. I think for at least a year Bob brought over casseroles and soups—from the Southern rice and bean dish known as Hoppin' John to the Tuscan soup called *ribollito*—or orchestrated offerings by others, and Roger came with his wife and four-year-old son to live with me for four months in the spring of 1991, during which he produced delicate cannelloni, superb curries and splendid barbecues. In fact, one of the first things I wrote during those early years of bereavement that was neither an elegy nor some other kind of grief work was a gastronomic tribute to the men whose cooking had sustained me for so long, from my Niçois grandfather to my father, my husband, Bob and Roger.[10]

Then, in the spring of 1993, when I first met David, he fêted me with roast lamb and zabaglione, his major accomplishments at the stove. (He also attempted a cheese soufflé at one point, although, like the absent-minded mathematician he now and then could be, he made it with sugar instead of salt!) But when it became clear that our relationship was no passing fancy, he invited me to join him on a trip to Paris, where he had a place in the Marais. And since his culinary repertoire was limited, I would perforce become the household cook—in France.

Thus, there I was, in the fall of 1993, presiding over a tiny Paris kitchen, in a small apartment to which I had shipped so many books on death and dying, grieving and mourning, elegy and apocalypse, that the shelves could barely hold them. Embarking on a decade in which I'd pore over weighty theoretical tomes by such writers as Kristeva (on abjection), Derrida (on loss), and Barthes (on grief and photography) along with cultural studies of numerous death-drenched topics (from the institution of hospice to the horrors of the Holocaust), I had to learn to navigate the local outdoor market, to *faire les courses* (do the shopping) on the nearby rue St. Antoine, to store food in a half-size refrigerator, and most important, to cook for myself and a man who preferred peeling the garlic and loading the dishwasher to stirring the sauce or ladling the gravy. I was no longer a sous-chef; David had taken over that job. Now I really was the chef, or anyway an amateur *cuisinière*—in other words, some kind of a *cook*—and as I plunged into the quotidian rituals of the market and the kitchen I found myself reviving and renewing a culinary imagination I'd forgotten while also educating myself in the ways of a gastronomic culture that was simultaneously new and, thanks to my Niçois grandfather, oddly familiar.

Oh the joys of the marché Richard Lenoir, not far from the rue de Sévigné, the street where David and I settled down for our first three months of what would become fifteen years on and off together in Paris. The two of us soon began trundling through this three-block-long, biweekly outdoor market with our little *chariot* (the wheelie in which most Parisians transport food from shop to home) every Sunday morning, and like most other buyers we developed a stylized route among the narrow, intricate alleys that ran between the clusters of stalls. Our itinerary would start with the nearest fishmonger at the outermost edge of the market, whose elaborate ring of icy shelves—laden with glistening *truites de mer*, ivory fillets of sole, rosy strips of salmon, langoustines tensely curved in their grayish carapaces—was always dense with customers, loud with the shouts of sellers *and* buyers. But never buy at the first stand you see, or so I was told. First inspect as much of the *marché* as you can struggle through. Which means on to the next fishmonger, and thence from one *verger*—or vegetable stall—to another, one *fromager* to another, one *traiteur* or *charcutier* to the next one, until you've chosen the queue you want to join: the one next to the stall that has what look like the most succulent chanterelles, the ripest tomatoes, the most tempting *saucissons,* the creamiest brie de Meaux, the most silvery trout.

Then you pounce and point and buy and load your little cart with the weighty gifts of earth and sea—a kilo of this, 200 grams of that, a loaf here, a bouquet there—and you wheel them back to your kitchen, to cheer and nourish yourself for the next few days. And all the time, all around you, everyone else at the *marché* is doing the same thing, some noisily, some suavely, some anxiously, while the vendors hawk their wares and (now and then) a group of singers and an accordionist, positioning themselves at the center of the whole seething mass, add to the general good-humored cacophony.

On a fine October Sunday, when the herb stall is still fragrant with basil and rosemary but the wild mushroom stand is already heaped high with golden *girolles*, thick-legged *pieds de mouton* and slim black *trompettes de la mort*—the strangely slippery forest-dwellers whose name means "trumpets of the dead"—the *marché* isn't just lively; it often seems, in its bustle of bargains and riches, to signify life itself. No wonder I found it so restorative to journey through its web of plenty after a week of investigating the permutations of loss, fear and grief. Even (or perhaps especially) among autumn's tokens of mortality, the eating end of the food chain, as opposed to the being eaten one, is figuratively as well as literally comforting. At the same time, when I first came upon those *trompettes de la mort*, a tangle of black at the heart of the *marché*, I was curiously unnerved. Grief theorist that I was, and memoirist of mourning, I thought them almost as eerie as their name. Did they really arise from the breasts of the dead like miniature foreshadowings of the Day of Judgment? If I bought 300 grams, as I did on the spot, would I be stir-frying messages from the other world? Were these magic-seeming mushrooms supernatural funereal objects meant to be consumed as reminders of mortality or as farewells to the luscious materiality of life itself? Musing on weirdly symbolic fungi while meditating on grief, I was turned to thoughts about the end-time of eating, especially the ceremonial significance accorded to those last meals that mark a finale to the appetite most central to life itself—the desire for food. Jesus's Last Supper had sacred meanings and liturgical consequences, but in our culture quotidian farewells to food have their own curious importance.

In the United States, for instance, doomed prisoners are often offered ritual "last meals." Quite a few websites are devoted to the final menus chosen by Americans on death row. A recent roundup of choices, according to one source: "Karla Faye Tucker requested a fruit plate but didn't eat it. John Wayne Gacy asked for shrimp, fried chicken, French fries, and a pound of strawberries. Timothy McVeigh ate two pints of mint chocolate chip ice cream. In 1992, Arkansas convict Ricky Ray Rector, who had brain damage from shooting himself in the head after killing a police officer, ate a final meal of steak, fried chicken, and cherry Kool-Aid, but famously said he wanted to save his pecan pie for later."[11] And for some of those who die as a result of physical illness rather than legal edict—specifically for those who are conscious enough to want to say goodbye to gastronomy—last meals are also resonant.

Perhaps the most notorious such supper in contemporary times is the one to which the late French president François Mitterrand invited thirty guests, all of whom joined him in dining on oysters, foie gras, roasted capon, and—*les pièces de resistance*—ortolans, the tiny songbirds illegal to eat in France. Drowned in Armagnac, then roasted for six to eight minutes in high heat, each ortolan is eaten whole: the diner, his own head covered with a large white cloth, bites off and discards the bird's head, then crunches on the rest of the creature. Some devotees "claim they can taste [its] entire life as they chew in the darkness: the wheat of Morocco, the salt air of the Mediterranean, the lavender of Provence." Is the taste of the ortolan, then, the taste of the past, of mortality? And why the covering of the diner's head? Jean-Louis Palladin, a French chef who is said to have once smuggled four hundred ortolans into a restaurant he owned in Washington's Watergate Hotel, claims that "It is for concentrating on the fat going down the throat. It is really like you are praying, see? Like when you take the [Communion wafer] into your mouth from the priest's hand in church and you think about God. Now that is what eating *l'ortolan* is really most like."[12]

The quotidian and the sacred: the quotidian *as* the sacred! In our era, these distinctions are increasingly blurred, but whatever our religious leanings, it's perhaps inevitable that, when we're feeling funereal, the trumpets of the dead, like those slender dark *trompettes de la mort* I found so alluring at the marché Richard Lenoir in Paris, rise from shadow and call us to the table. The world over, many cultures prescribe special ways to feed the hungry dead along with particular kinds of feasts and fasts to assuage the sorrows of those who mourn. The culinary imagination, in its dream of transcendental gastronomy, often yearns to dissolve the boundaries between soul and body, dead and living.

The Funeral Baked Meats

The day after I consigned the final typescript of *Death's Door: Modern Dying and the Ways We Grieve* to my sterling research assistant Augustus Rose so that he could mail it to my editor, he came into my study with a charming congratulatory gift, a little book called *Death Warmed Over* that's a discussion—with recipes—of "Funeral Food, Rituals, and Customs from Around the World." And of course, mourners do need to warm themselves over (and over again) with food that says yes, you're still alive, your body's fires still need stoking. When Hamlet laments to his friend Horatio that "the funeral baked meats / Did coldly furnish forth the marriage tables" at the unseemly and untimely wedding of his mother to her brother-in-law, the funeral meal to which he refers evokes what is surely an almost universal custom. Whatever the cuisine, people must nourish themselves after bidding ceremonial farewells to the dead. Sometimes (as when mourners partake of the Eucharist at a requiem Mass) the food they consume is sacred, but more often it's secular—although, even while addressing ordinary bodily needs, the secular has a kind of ritual function on such an occasion. The Victorian novelist Elizabeth Gaskell observes in *Cranford* that "Many a one has been comforted in their sorrow by seeing a good dish come upon the table." And in one of his most brilliant stories, Raymond Carver depicted the surprising, if brief, consolation that a bereaved couple find in a bakery, whose proprietor urges them to "eat one of my hot rolls" because "Eating is a small, good thing in a time like this"—a resonant phrase that becomes the title of the tale. As Brillat-Savarin noted, one can appreciate the pleasures of the table at funerals as at other ceremonial occasions. But even while mourners seek to comfort themselves with apples or apple pie, they usually gather and share food to honor the dead while healing the rift in communal life left by the departure of the one they loved.[13]

If, as anthropologists have noted, the universal "ritualized commemoration of the dead" has been so central to comparative ethnography that the discovery of graves is generally considered proof that a humanoid strain became human, social scientists and evolutionary biologists have also found that sustained food sharing distinguishes humans from animals. Yes, from ants and bees to wolves and bats, many creatures divide the spoils of foraging or hunting; but "the patterning and complexity of food sharing among humans is truly unique." We share within and among families, between generations, between tribes and cultures, and, in various ways, across time. In his ambitious *Catching Fire: How Cooking Made Us Human*, the biological anthropologist Richard Wrangham argues that both the availability of food made easily digestible by cooking and the communal activity of shaping that cuisine were not just important but crucial links in human evolution.[14]

In many societies, the bereaved feel an urgent need to share food with the dead as well as with one another, sometimes to placate the ancestors, sometimes to renew bonds of love and sympathy. Souls that have left their bodies require nourishment, it's often thought, to strengthen them for journeys to other realms or for survival in the afterlife. Ravenous, sometimes furious with loss, they hunger for nurture. In the *Odyssey*, "the ghosts / of the shambling, shiftless dead" thirst for the blood of a ram and a heifer that the protagonist and his men have sacrificed; disembodied, they can only speak to Odysseus when the fluid of life infuses them with power; thus the mythical prophet Tiresias, from whom the wandering hero wants counsel, commands him to "Stand back . . . / so I can drink the blood and tell you all the truth." Nor were

Homeric Greeks alone in such visions of the needy dead. In other parts of the ancient world, Egyptians and Etruscans provided feasts for the dead inside the tomb. Describing one of many depictions of ritual dining in the "painted tombs of Tarquinia," D. H. Lawrence notes that it is a representation of "the death-banquet"—the funeral feast of the living—"and at the same time [a picture of] the dead man banqueting in the underworld," for in the view of the Etruscans (as of the Egyptians), while "the living feasted out of doors, at the tomb of the dead, the dead himself feasted in like manner . . . away in the underworld."[15]

Even now, in the early days after a death Chinese mourners "set food, flowers, and candy beside the fresh grave" while some Jamaicans "place several johnnycakes—the original term was *journey cakes*—in the casket with the deceased" to ensure that the soul has nourishment for its voyage outward. In a twist on this theme, the Badaga sect of northern India requires that relatives "dip a coin in butter and place it in the mouth of the dying person" because he'll need the money to buy food and drink en route to the afterlife, while "the butter will provide him with strength for the trip." And speaking of butter, Zoroastrians believe that once the bones of the dead have been exposed on Towers of Silence and picked clean by vultures, their souls will travel across the Bridge of Judgment either to a place of endless light where they'll be perpetually nourished by "the butter of early spring" or to a horrendous underworld where they'll have to sustain themselves on rotten food.[16]

In a few cultures, departed souls return periodically to be entertained by the earthly families they left behind. A Chinese "Summons of the Dead" from the second century BC offers luscious lures to a departed child, whose parent urges him to return and dine on "Ribs of the fatted ox cooked tender and succulent;/Sour and bitter blended in the soup of Wu," accompanied by "Jadelike wine, honey flavored."[17] And the Indian memoirist Shoba Narayan reports that in her Kerala family there was an "annual *shraadham*, a daylong ceremony when the entire clan gathered to pay obeisance to our ancestors" with "an elaborate, five-course feast that would feed twelve Brahmin priests, two cows, our entire family, and all the crows in the neighborhood"—birds who were "supposed to carry the souls of our forefathers, so the more crows we fed, the better it was for our lineage."[18] Perhaps most famously, Mexicans assign great importance to el día de los Muertos, the Day of the Dead, when altars known as *ofrendas*—cloth-covered tables "bearing fruits, dainties, beverages, and votive lamps"—appear all over the country to invite the dead "to descend upon the earth and enjoy the celebration in the company of friends and relatives." On that day the living feast too, dining in homes and cemeteries on special delicacies, including *pan de muerto*, often made into "life-size skull-shaped cakes with the name of the deceased written in frosting on the forehead."[19]

Similar ritual delicacies appear in Italian bakeries—for example, *fave dolci*, sweet pastry "beans," sometimes known as *ossa dei morti*, "bones of the dead." Like the customs that mark Mexico's Day of the Dead, the habit of eating such sweets is thought to have a pagan origin; the great gastronome Pellegrino Artusi opined that *fave dolci* represent "beans from the garden" whose significance "is rooted in antiquity, as the fava bean was offered to the Fates, to Pluto, and to Persephone, and was used in superstitious rituals." These legumes, he added, "specially the black variety, were used as funerary offerings because the ancients believed the beans contained souls of the dead and were shaped like the doors of hell."[20]

If certain holiday pastries function as sometimes comforting, sometimes scary chains of sugar that bring the living and the dead together, the rituals of the wake and the funeral banquet are more likely to mark the inexorable separation of the bereaved from those who love them. The pleasures of the table from which the dead are excluded emphasize their absence even while offering signs of life to those who mourn. The ancient custom of "sin-eating"—practiced well into the nineteenth century in parts of England, Wales and even Appalachia—may be one of the most curious culinary expressions of the gulf between life and death. The designated sin-eater, a kind of scapegoat who was usually shunned and impoverished in his community, would consent, for a small price, to drink a cup of beer or wine and eat a dry biscuit in the presence of the newly dead body, reciting a set formula of transferred guilt. At a resonant moment in her novel *Precious Bane* (1928), Mary Webb describes the procedure:

> Now it was still the custom at that time, in our part of the country, to give a fee to some poor man after a death, and then he would take bread and wine handed to him across the coffin, and eat and drink, saying—
>
> *I give easement and rest now to thee, dear man, that ye walk not over the fields nor down the by-ways. And for thy peace I pawn my own soul.*
>
> And with a calm and grievous look he would go to his own place. Mostly, my Grandad used to say, Sin Eaters were such as had been Wise Men or layers of spirits, and had fallen on evil days. Or they were poor folk that had come, through some dark deed, out of the kindly life of men, and with whom none would trade, whose only food might oftentimes be the bread and wine that had crossed the coffin.[21]

If the sin-eater is a Christ-like figure who takes the evil deeds of others upon himself through the ingestion of bread and wine, the grievous loss of the dead is more often marked by ceremonial feasting. Sometimes, to be sure, a fast precedes a feast. Among both Indian Hindus and Sri Lankan Buddhists, death is considered unclean, so cooking is forbidden in the home of the deceased, and although friends can bring food to the bereaved, mourners often fast for at least a day. Devout Jews, too, mark a death with a meager meal—a hard-boiled egg (symbolizing regeneration) and salt (standing for incorruptibility)—before beginning the ritual of sitting shiva, seven days during which the bereaved and their guests often indulge in what one observer describes as an "orgy of eating." The foods, provided by visitors to the bereaved household, range from chips and dips, lox and pickled herring, to cakes, cookies and sodas. Just a few days ago as I stood by a table laden with such delicacies, someone urged me to partake, observing that "It's a mitzvah to eat in a house of mourning." Perhaps sharing the food is a way of sharing the grief?

Of course, the best-known "funeral baked meats" may be those consumed at an Irish wake. Supplemented by what's called a wake cake—oddly reminiscent of the biscuit devoured by the sin-eater—such foods accompany great quantities of fiery drink. And as Lisa Rogak points out, both a New Orleans jazz funeral and a Cajun funeral give you "the impression that you've arrived at a party," so lavish is the food and so flowing the drink. But even the more abstemious Belgians, Dutch and English are famous for funeral cakes, on which, in some cases, the initials of the dead are inscribed. As the great Russian critic Mikhail Bakhtin pointed out, "No meal can be sad. Sadness and food are incompatible (while death and food are perfectly compatible)." Thus the funeral banquet, with its affirmation of the needs of the living, appears at the end of many folk tales, because the "end must contain the potentialities of the new beginning, just as death leads to a new birth."[22] After all, even the reviled sin-eater chews and swallows so that the dead will stay *away* in peace—"walk not over the fields, nor down the by-ways"—and leave the living in peace too.

What of us—foodies and non-foodies—in contemporary America? Across our melting pot of a land we've always consumed funeral feasts of various kinds, depending on our ethnic origins, as we marked wakes and shivas and offered food to mourners and their friends. Frequently, of course, the deeply stricken ones—the bereaved themselves—have little appetite. I remember that I had trouble eating in the days after my husband died, and I had the same difficulty seventeen years later, when David suddenly suffered cardiac arrest. On both occasions, it was as if I literally couldn't swallow the pain of what had happened—and I later learned that "anorexia and other gastrointestinal disturbances," "feelings of emptiness and heaviness," and "feeling that something is stuck in your throat" are among a range of physical symptoms "not unusual in grief." For years, therefore, such custodians of etiquette as Amy Vanderbilt and Emily Post advised those who would comfort the grieving to offer soft foods—gentle custards, delicate broths, coddled eggs—or simply tea and toast.[23]

Still, the community that gathers following a funeral and a burial has to share a ritual meal, here as elsewhere. Thus, in the heart of the country, according to many sources, services for the dead are often followed by the consumption of what Rogak, citing Garrison Keillor's wry phrase, calls a "hot dish"—that is, a kind of easy casserole—offered to guests after the ceremony or delivered later to the grieving family at home. Some recipes for this dish can be hilarious. Here's one that's almost a parody of the tuna and mushroom soup casseroles I learned to eat as an undergraduate. From the Minneapolis–St. Paul *City Pages*, it's meant for large—and perhaps not too picky—groups:

American Legion Funeral Hot Dish

5 lbs. ground beef
1 large onion, chopped
1 16-oz. bag frozen sliced carrots
1 16-oz. bag frozen cauliflower florets
1 16-oz. bag frozen chopped broccoli
1 50-oz. can of cream of mushroom soup
1 50-oz. can cream of chicken soup
1 bunch celery, chopped
¼ c. soy sauce
1 t. white pepper
3 12-oz. bags chow mein noodles

Fry hamburger and chopped onion in a large cast-iron pan, breaking it up into small pieces with a potato masher. Place in a large roaster. Mix frozen vegetables, soups, chopped celery, soy sauce, and pepper in a bowl. Pour into roaster and blend with meat. Fold in two bags of chow mein noodles, cover, and bake at 325 degrees for 75 minutes. Remove from oven. Sprinkle remaining bag of chow mein noodles on top. Put cover back on and bake another 15 minutes. Serves 50.

Although the indifference with which this recipe calls for smashing together a strange range of ingredients suggests that the ensuing casserole is merely designed to address what M. F. K. Fisher called "a glum urge" for a lot of filling food, the dish is evidently still popular in the Midwest. At the same time, as the reporter who transcribed the recipe observes, "Here in the Twin

Cities, the trend in funeral food is moving away from the hot dish, toward apricot-coriander meatballs and crème brûlée." And she quotes the comments of a local caterer:

> It's no longer about Jell-O and casserole and five different kinds of cake. . . . Today, people expect casual, upscale fare at funerals. We offer a chicken pasta salad with grapes and mandarin oranges and hot pork tenderloin on croissants with honey mustard. Our garlic-pecan stuffed mushrooms are very popular. And our desserts are all homemade: strawberry-layered whipped cream cake, pies, éclairs, tiramisu.[24]

Okay, it's easy to laugh. Like so-called designer funerals with posh caskets and hip music ("a little AC/DC, ZZ Top, maybe 'Butterfly Kisses' or 'Wind Beneath My Wings' . . . songs of today, not a hundred years ago"), gourmet funeral food comes off as weirdly dissonant, considering the occasion for which it's prepared. Yet that the traditional (and boring) "hot dish" has been replaced by more elaborate and exotic fare, from garlic-pecan stuffed mushrooms to tiramisu, suggests how crucial earthly sustenance is to mourners even while revealing how radically contemporary attitudes toward such sustenance have changed. To return to the theology of food: is it possible that the gourmet service has become *the* farewell service for our time? In a post-existentialist age, when the sacred has lost much of its sacramental ritual meaning, perhaps rites of passage have become gastronomic rather than religious events.[25] Was François Mitterrand's real last communion with roasted ortolans rather than with the Eucharist of old? And are our communions sacred or secular?

The Pulse of the Kitchen

Consider the materials and mysteries of the kitchen. The materials: the leaves, beans, fruits, flesh, blood, waiting for metamorphosis. The mysteries: the procedures of metamorphosis. Whether it's a stone hut in Crete or a beautifully tiled workspace in California, the kitchen's heart is some kind of hearth; its heartbeat the cooking fires that seethe and simmer, bake and stew, grill and transform. The pulse of the kitchen is the pulse of human life, which triumphs over death by turning nature into nurture, and, often, the raw into the cooked.

The magic of the flames that accomplish such metamorphoses has been known for at least half a million years. Archaeologists have found the remains of hearths in northern Chinese caves, where so-called Peking Man left a litter of charred animal bones. As James Boswell put it two and a half centuries ago, "My definition of man is, 'a Cooking Animal'. The beasts have memory, judgment and all the faculties and passions of our mind, in a certain degree; but no beast is a cook. . . . Man alone can dress a good dish; and every man whatever is more or less a cook, in seasoning what he himself eats." More whimsically, the Romantic essayist Charles Lamb speculated, in his "Dissertation Upon Roast Pig," that "the art of roasting" accidentally emerged in ancient China when a certain swineherd's cottage, housing a litter of fine piglets, burned to the ground, and the man's son discovered just how unexpectedly delicious grilled pork could be. For a while, Lamb ironically opines, the swineherd, his son, and their fellow citizens took to setting their homes on fire in order to savor the pleasures of cooked meat, until at last "a sage arose" who observed "that the flesh of swine, or indeed of any other animal, might be cooked (burnt, as they called it) without the necessity of consuming a whole house to dress it. Then first began the rude form of a gridiron" while "Roasting by the string, or spit, came in a century or two later, I forget in whose dynasty." By "such slow degrees," concludes the writer, "do the most useful, and seemingly the most obvious arts, make their way among mankind."[26]

Implicit in Lamb's tale is, of course, a fantastic recipe: take three little pigs, lock them into a wooden cottage and burn it down. Voilà, roast pork! But his mini history of cooking then offers an innovator—a sage!—who modifies the recipe by replacing the cottage with an oven inside the cottage, which will eventually become an oven inside the kitchen inside the cottage. And if that kitchen pulses with mysteriously transformative powers, the powers guiding those powers are most often summarized in the cultural documents we call recipes.

The word "recipe," as it happens, connotes a gift, the term itself having descended from the Latin *recipere*, meaning "to take, receive," and the Latin word, in its turn, deriving from the Indo-European *kap*—"to grasp"—which yields, among other English words besides "recipe," "receive, recover, recuperate, [all equally] from Latin *capere*, to take, seize, catch."[27] Recipes, then, are culinary procedures that we've inherited from history, ancestral gifts meant to guide us through the mysteries of the kitchen. In daily life, as well as in times of mourning, they are prescriptions for the cultural recovery or recuperation of the goodness that is all too fleeting in nature.

According to M. F. K. Fisher, around 2800 BC a "wise emperor in China . . . compiled a great cookbook, the *Hon-Zo*" and "In forty-seven centuries we have not learned much more about food than it can tell." Whether or not this is the case, it's certainly true that few Western recipes survive from the deep past. In or around AD 228, Athenaeus of Naucratis—an Egyptian-born gastronome and philosopher—mused on wines and waters, fruits and meats, in his weighty *Banquet of the Learned,* inserting a recipe here and there along with advice that the cook's "mind must comprehend all facts and circumstances." Fisher notes that when "the cover was lifted from" his signature "dish of bird brains, eggs, wine, and spices, pounded with very fragrant roses and cooked in oil," the "sweet excessive perfume" of the concoction "made all the guests drop their eyelids with pleasure." But the collection of Roman recipes known as *Apicius,* thought to have been compiled in the late fourth or early fifth century, is one of the earliest Western works primarily devoted to cooking instructions.[28]

To the modern reader the ancient delicacies described in these gatherings are frequently mysterious, if tantalizing. What, for instance, can we make of "Delian sweets," special cakes Athenaeus said were sacrificed "to Iris, goddess of the dawn" and described as "wheat dough, boiled, with honey and the so-called *kokkora* (which are a dried fig and three walnuts)"? Athenaeus's description is notably enigmatic (*one* fig? *three* walnuts?—serves how many?). But *Apicius* hardly clarifies the problem in offering instructions for a comparable pastry:

> Take durum wheat flour and cook it in hot water so that it forms a very hard paste, then spread it on a plate. When cold cut it up in lozenges, and fry in best oil. Lift out, pour honey over, sprinkle with pepper and serve.

In their invaluable *Classical Cookbook,* Andrew Dalby and Sally Grainger remark that this "gives something remarkably like choux paste," but I personally am not sophisticated enough to imagine the quantities of water, flour, and so forth that would yield anything recognizable from the words above.[29]

That we need to understand the specifics of any recipe is obviously essential. When we read such a text, we're communing with someone who's far away yet with us in the kitchen. Her (or his) voice may come from centuries ago and from a culture whose assumptions about the world we barely understand—but if so, it's all the more thrilling when that voice tells us, in terms we *do* understand, how to contrive a meal with eternal staples: eggs, sugar, oil, butter, wheat or corn or rice—and perpetual variables: fruit, meat, vegetables. And as recipes convey these instructions, they also hint at ways of managing in the world, surviving winter, living through loss. Although the recipe for Delian sweets meant to slake the appetite of Iris is cryptic, its author clearly intends us to combine grain, honey, figs, and nuts—fruits of the earth—so judiciously that the goddess will remember her duty to brighten the sky and empower wheat, flowers, fruits and nuts to keep on rising from the soil.

An Elizabethan recipe that tells us how "To make fine Cakes" celebrates the pleasures of culture's ability to organize ingredients so as (at least temporarily) to preserve pleasure for its own sake:

> Take fine flowre and good Damaske water you must have no other liquor but that, then take sweet butter, two or three yolkes of egges and a good quantity of Suger, and a fewe cloues, and mace, as your Cookes mouth shall serue him, and a lyttle saffron, and a little Gods good about a sponfull if you put in too much they shall arise, cutte them in squares lyke vnto trenchers, and pricke them

> well, and let your ouen be well swept and lay them vppon papers and so set them into the ouen. Do not burne them if they be three or foure dayes olde they bee the better.[30]

Not insignificantly, modern scholars translate "Gods good" as hartshorn, a medieval compound of powdered horn that functioned, like yeast, as a leavening agent: the key ingredient facilitating the magical metamorphosis of slithery batter or sticky dough into risen bread or puffy cake. Gods good, the phrase implies, is an alchemical power that comes to us through the goodness of the God who gave us reason and culture.

Arguably, all recipes constitute such instructions for recuperation, transformation, preservation. Even the bizarre if boring funeral hot dish I transcribed above implies an urge to strengthen and comfort diners with a representative melange of plant and animal foods (albeit frozen vegetables and ground beef), soothing broths (cream soups), and presumably lively flavors (soy sauce, chow mein noodles). And perhaps such an emphasis on representing and recovering the diversity of earthly foods can be traced back to ancient and medieval stews like this *monokythron*, meaning "one-pot meal," that Andrew Dalby has translated from the medieval Byzantine *Prodromic Poems:*

> If you like I'll tell you all about this *monokythron*. Four hearts of cabbage, crisp and snowy white; a salted neck of swordfish; a middle cut of carp; about twenty *glaukos* [sic]; a slice of salt sturgeon; fourteen eggs and some Cretan cheese and four *apotyra* [sic] and a bit of Vlach cheese and a pint of olive oil, a handful of pepper, twelve little heads of garlic and fifteen chub mackerels, and a splash of sweet wine over the top, and roll up your sleeves and get to work—just watch the mouthfuls go.

Here are quantity and diversity enough for even—to risk a pun—the most byzantine of ancient or modern funerals![31]

In this context, my all-time favorite recipe—and the one I imagine as having the most restorative potential—is the set of instructions for making a

Black Cake that Emily Dickinson included in a letter to a friend. Although this greatest of American woman writers was surrounded by born-again Christians and immersed in a culture whose Victorian mystique of domesticity was at least as powerful as what Friedan called the feminine mystique of the 1950s, she herself was theologically skeptical and socially defiant. Pressed as a young girl to accept Christian evangelism, she refused—and as an adult she insisted that "Eden is that old-fashioned House / We dwell in every day," preferring quotidian pleasures to sacramental promises. Nor did she celebrate the ladylike ways to which she had been born and raised; she consistently decried the "dimity convictions" of the "soft-cherubic—gentlewomen" whose company she refused to join.

Yet Dickinson did compose poems in the kitchen as well as in the bedroom that was her sanctuary, and she was an accomplished baker who won prizes for bread-baking and judged culinary contests. Although her comment on the "Mystery of Food" that I have included in my epigraphs here suggests that she could imagine dining without earthly sustenance—like God, or Kafka's hunger artist—her equation of food with mystery implies reverence and even an equation of the quotidian culinary imagination with sacred rites, or mysteries. The Black Cake whose recipe I give—drawn from a letter she wrote to a friend—was one of her specialties, and with her knack for identifying the everyday and the magical, her claim that this "swarthy cake [was] baked only in Domingo" implies that she took communion in the legendary spice isle that was really her own kitchen, just as Eden was her own old-fashioned house. Indicating the almost mythic size of the dish she plans, the poet admonishes her correspondent to "take a milk pail" and then follow the instructions below (note that she can conceive of using several cake pans as alternative vessels):

2 pounds Flour—
2 Sugar—
2 Butter—
19 Eggs—
5 pounds Raisins—

1½ Currants—
1½ Citron—
½ pint Brandy—
½—Molasses—
2 Nutmegs—
5 teaspoons Cloves—Mace—Cinnamon—
2 teaspoons Soda—

Beat Butter and Sugar together—
Add Eggs without beating—and beat the mixture again—
Bake 2 ½ or three hours, in Cake pans, or 5 to 6 hours in Milk-pan,
if full—[32]

I don't know whether this lyrical food—crammed with raisins and currants and citron, rich with brandy, molasses, cloves, mace, cinnamon, nutmeg—was ever offered at a funeral banquet, although Dickinson's recipe yields enough delicious morsels to serve most of the citizens of mid-nineteenth-century Amherst. But I do know, because I've made it myself, that even if you halve the quantities because you don't own a "Milk-pan," this Black Cake will last nearly forever, more deliciously consoling every day. And if you too commune with it, it will remind those who mourn and indeed all who are mortal—especially those cooks who are, as Whitehead puts it, "of a religious nature"—that the mysteries of food, tenuous though they are, can restore, redeem, and at least temporarily preserve a few of the fleeting things of this world.

Chapter 3

All That Is Toothsome? Sacred Food, Deadly Dining

Man, king of all nature by divine right, and for whose benefit the earth has been covered and peopled, must perforce be armed with an organ which can put him in contact with all that is toothsome among his subjects.

—JEAN ANTHELME BRILLAT-SAVARIN, *THE PHYSIOLOGY OF TASTE*

And the fear of you and the dread of you shall be upon every beast of the earth, and upon every fowl of the air . . . Every moving thing that liveth shall be meat for you; even as the green herb have I given you all things.

—GENESIS, 9:2

The Powers of the Cook

"The serious cook,"declared Julia Child, "really must face up to the task personally." Specifically, using "a sharp knife or lobster shears, [she must] cut straight down ½ inch into the back of the lobster . . . thus severing the spinal cord and killing the lobster instantly." Which is to say, "the serious cook" must confront her place in the food chain and learn not just to eviscerate a chicken but actually to kill a living being. For to be serious, implied the great culinary instructor, is to understand that life lives on death, and that, more specifically, the kitchen is the locus classicus where the dead—whether animal or vegetable—are reshaped and transformed into substances that can sustain the lives of others.[1]

Wrote Alice B. Toklas in her legendary cookbook/memoir:

> Food is far too pleasant to combine with horror. All the same, facts, even distasteful facts, must be accepted and we shall see how, before any story of cooking begins, crime is inevitable. That is why cooking is not an entirely agreeable pastime. There is too much that must happen in advance of the actual cooking.

The chapter in which this passage appears is entitled "Murder in the Kitchen" and features an episode in which Toklas—the designated chef de cuisine for the Stein–Toklas household—dispatches a "lively carp" by stabbing it (the way Julia Child was later to counsel impaling a lobster) until, "horror of horrors" the fish is "murdered in the first, second and third degree" and the writer finds herself guiltily smoking a cigarette while waiting "for the police to come and take me into custody."[2]

As the contemporary poet Ruth Stone has more recently put it, the kitchen is "the cutting room" where each of us goes "like an addict / To eat of death" or anyway to reconstruct death so that others can eat it. Thus the cook may at times become, herself, an assassin of lobsters for lobster Newburg, or a murderer of carp for "carp stuffed with chestnuts." "Man not only dines; he also kills and sacrifices," mused Father Capon in *The Supper of the Lamb*, his meditative cookbook. "Blood is not pretty," but no effort "to say what cooking is about . . . can afford to let it slide by out of mind." Even if the cook doesn't do the requisite killing herself, she profits from the deeds of other murderers—the slaughterers who end the pulsing lives of cows, pigs, sheep and chickens so that their flesh can find its way to her oven; the farmers who tear carrots, potatoes and onions from snug beds for her soup pot; the gardeners who pluck pears and peaches from sunny branches for her fruit bowl. For as another recent poet, William Dickey, has written, "The galaxy is the shape of an eating mouth. . . . We must eat to live, and we must kill to eat. / The serious cook will always face this problem." And the great Brillat-Savarin, otherwise a man of considerable sensitivity, declared that a "true gourmand is as insensible to suffering as is a conqueror." Indeed, the author of *Transcendental Gastronomy* offered as chilling a description of eating as any we have:

> As soon as an edible body has been put into the mouth, it is seized upon, gases, moisture, and all, without possibility of retreat.
>
> Lips stop whatever might try to escape; the teeth bite and break it; saliva drenches it; the tongue mashes and churns it; a breath-like sucking pushes it toward the gullet; the the tongue lifts up to make it slide and slip; the sense of smell appreciates it as it passes the nasal channel, and it is pulled down into the stomach to be submitted to sundry baser transformations.[3]

But if the activities of the diner are terrifyingly destructive, the powers of the cook are yet more dangerous because they facilitate the destruction that allows the kitchen to thrive and keep others alive.

Because they do keep others alive, however, the powers of the cook are also beneficial and preservative: cooking, mused John Ruskin in the mid-nineteenth century, "means the knowledge of Medea, and of Circe, and of Helen, and of Rebekah, and of the Queen of Sheba. It means the knowledge of all herbs, and fruits, and balms, and spices, and all that is healing and sweet in fields and groves, and savory in meats."[4] Though problematic (Medea, Circe), the cook's talents are essential to life, so much so that they can be imagined as primordially creative. In Western tradition, after all, God is in a sense the first cook. He takes a lump of clay, pats and pokes it into shape until it's a sort of strange cake, then breathes on it with a hot breath from the furnace that is his Being—and lo, it's a man. Then he takes a rib of the man, breathes another transformative breath on that raw bit of flesh and bone—and lo, it's a woman.

In at least one version of the Eden in which he places the newly made couple, the woman begins preparing food right away, harvesting "fruits, and balms, and spices": Milton's Eve, eventually the temptress of *Paradise Lost*, gathers and crushes "the Grape" for drink, and "From many a berrie, and from sweet kernels prest / She tempers dulcet creams." When the archangel Raphael comes to dine, he joins her and her mate in eating heartily of these "viands," with "keen dispatch / Of real hunger, and concoctive heate."[5] And once she has ripped an apple from a branch and thereby torn herself and her man from the stasis of Eden, where nothing ever happens and all is always good to eat, she is destined to become an even more remarkable cook, at least figuratively speaking, for before she brings forth new bodies in pain and suffering, they rise like magic loaves inside the oven of her womb—and lo, they're babies. More, after they've been expelled from that paradise into the outside world, she transforms her own flesh and blood into warm milk for them, to grow them from tiny mewling helpless things into walking talking children.

Yet when they're weaned of Eve's milk, those children are still doomed, as the Bible tells us, to brood on food—and even, indeed, to murder one another (along with the beasts of the earth) for the sake of food. Arguably the first vegetarian, "Cain brought of the fruit of the ground as an offering unto the Lord, / And Abel, he also brought of the firstlings of his flock and of the fat thereof. / And the Lord had respect unto Abel and to his offering / but unto Cain and to his offering he had not respect." Jehovah, the God of the Old Testament, was a carnivore—as we also know from the many meat offerings he demands from the Israelites—yet as such he turned the vegan Cain into a murderer. Thus if the primordial creation of man was a deific recipe, and the original sin a fruit theft, the first homicide was a food fight.[6] For indeed, as Lord Byron put it, "all human history attests / That happiness for man—the hungry sinner!— / Since Eve ate apples, much depends on dinner."[7]

But beyond such originatory events, the Judeo-Christian Bible is, of course, stuffed with food. God the cook gave the Jews recipes of a kind, consisting of meticulous dietary laws (for instance, "Thou shall not seethe a kid in his mother's milk") whose significance is to this day analyzed and debated. And the Old Testament tells us that as they wandered through the desert he gifted them with manna—a "bread" that was "like coriander seed, white; and the taste of it was like wafers made with honey"—which may well have been, it's speculated, "a mosslike lichen, *Lecanora esculenta*, that clings to cliffs in the Middle East": high "winds will sometimes scatter this stuff through the desert until it falls like rain on Bedouin settlements; [and it] has a naturally sweet flavor."[8]

The desert wanderings of the Jews, moreover, are commemorated with special Passover foods, transcribed, as it were, from the texts of prophets and rabbis who became, in this connection, sacred cooks and menu planners: unleavened bread (*matzohs*) to symbolize the haste with which the people left Egypt, before the dough in their ovens could begin to rise; bitter herbs (*maror*) to represent the bitterness of slavery; a mixture of apples, nuts, wine, and cinnamon (*charoses*), reminiscent of the mortar that the Israelites used in constructing buildings for their Egyptian masters; a roasted egg (*beitzah*) that symbolizes life and rebirth, like the egg that's consumed after a Jewish funeral; a vegetable (*karpas*), preferably parsley or celery, that stands for renewal, served with a bowl of salted water symbolizing tears; a piece of roasted lamb shankbone (*zeroah*), that functions as a sacrificial offering; and finally four glasses of wine, imbibed during the seder meal, to recall the fourfold promise of redemption, with a special glass left for Elijah the prophet.

Perhaps it was such a Jewish seder that became the Christian Last Supper—Western culture's most powerfully resonant meal. Combining the redemptive overtones of the traditional Passover feast with Mithraic and neo-Platonic allusions, the story of this event has the man called Jesus brilliantly manipulating *ur* foods—bread and wine—to construct a riveting ritual that seems to be based on, but revises, the seder. Thus, where the seder evokes history, with each food symbolizing one of the pains of the past, the new Christian communion invokes a sacramental future, with each food promising a transformation and redemption to come. "This is my body, and this is my blood": as the controversial Galilean proffered these foods to his disciples, he appeared to be transforming himself into a sacrificial animal, whose dedication to the well-being of his disciples would be manifested in his willingness to die so that others could eat him.[9]

Like the God whom he claimed as Father, and who had created All, Jesus presented himself as in effect a magical cook, or proposed to be such a chef de cuisine by infusing his very being into the flatbread of Passover, the ritual wine of the seder. And though sophisticated contemporary Catholics warn that in what's called the doctrine of transubstantiation the phrase "this is my body" could mean "this represents" my body rather than "this actually is" my body, almost any child brought up in the Roman Catholic Church can testify that the very nature of Communion—the skinny wafer melting in the mouth, the willed refusal to bite it—means, in particular to the youngest members of the congregation, that "I have God in my mouth, I don't want to hurt him, I can't bite or chew him!"

In the Middle Ages even grownup theologians puzzled over this problem, wondering, as the historian Caroline Bynum puts it, how Christ could "be present in physical elements so distressingly fluid or breakable? Would not the pious draw the risible conclusion . . . that little bits of Jesus fell off if crumbs were spilled or that one hurt God by chewing the host? [In reaction,] theologians such as Aquinas affirmed that Christ's entire body was present in every particle. Thus his body was not physically broken in the fraction of the host." But by the time the Reformation had inspired widespread hostility to the Roman Catholic Church, the Puritan poet John Milton performed a heated *reductio ad absurdum* on the concept of material transubstantiation, declaring that such a notion turns "the Lord's Supper into a cannibal feast," and adding that if we literally eat Christ's "flesh," "to speak candidly, after being digested in the stomach, it will be at length exuded."[10]

In early Christian thinking, however, not only the Savior's flesh but his blood had a mythic vitality of its own. As a divine bodily fluid–become–wine, it was obviously sacred because it signified the godly life that drained out of Jesus as he hung on the Cross, the life he sacrificed for the redemption of humanity. But it was also resonant because Arthurian tradition associated the sacred blood with the magical powers of the Holy Grail, the bowl or cup consecrated by Jesus at the Last Supper and sometimes said to have been used by the devout Joseph of Arimathea to catch the Savior's blood.[11] Enchanted cornucopias of food and drink were of course persistent tropes in European fairy tales, but the Grail was a theological version of such a vessel, brimming over with heavenly nourishment. And that glimmering wine was matched by what a famous hymn calls "*panis angelicus*": the "bread of the angels," constituted—so it was believed—out of the literal as well as the symbolic flesh of Christ, handed down, as it were, from heaven, so that even the "poor, the servant, the lowly" might "eat God" along with his priestly hierophants. For, declared the fourteenth-century Dominican mystic John Tauler, "There is no kind of matter which is so close to a man and becomes so much a part of him as the food and drink he puts into his mouth; and so God has found this wonderful way of uniting Himself with us as closely as possible and becoming part of us."[12]

As Bynum observes, countless other early mystics waxed ecstatic at the prospect of such holy feasts. "Oh God," exclaimed one monk, "to love you is to eat you. You refresh those who love you so that they hunger more, for are you not simultaneously food and hunger?" And others, notes the historian, had equally impassioned appetites. In the later Middle Ages, she explains, the Eucharist offered itself to the senses of the faithful "with astonishing familiarity": it "dissolved on the tongue into honeycomb or bloody flesh, and announced its presence, when profaned or secreted away, by leaving a trail of blood. Christ appeared again and again on the paten and in the chalice as a baby, a glorious youth, or a bleeding and dying man."[13]

Christianity wasn't the only ancient religion in which the god transformed himself into a sacramental food. Sometimes thought to have helped shape Catholic liturgy, the Roman worship of the savior called Mithras originated in the Persian theology of Zoroastrianism, and obsessively centered on a "tauronoctony," a kind of early bullfight, in which the hero/god or his priestly representative slays a sacred bull, whose blood the congregation may have drunk, or in which they supposedly bathed. After literal bull-killing was replaced by a sculpture or mural representing the tauronoctony, the religious practice of this cult was sheltered in an underground "mithraeum" and focused on a ritual common meal of bread and wine, not unlike the meal that constitutes the Mass. And it was thought that such a culinary communion—like the Communion in the Mass—would unite the worshipper with his deity, whose sacred foods could bestow eternal life.

In the Americas, maize—the dietary staple on which most early cultures here depended—was considered in and of itself a sacred substance whose powers originated in a god's self-sacrifice. Writes the food historian

Margaret Visser, "Corn, for the Indians . . . was a tragic and sacred plant": the farmer who cultivates it "feels sorrow and guilt because he must cut it down in order to live, and he feels joy and gratitude because the plant accepts death and agrees in time to return—if due respect is paid to custom and science—to feed its murderers again." A "central myth of the Indians," she adds, tells of a culture hero who is forced to wrestle with a "spirit guide"—a godly young man "dressed in yellow and green, with a headdress of green feathers"—until he kills him and consigns his body to the earth, from which "the tips of the warrior's plumed headdress" reappear and grow "into a plant as tall as a man." The food into which this maize god transforms himself may not be sacramental in the Christian or Mithraic sense, but it is nonetheless sacred, and divinely alive. "Corn must never be wasted, for this was sacrilege," notes Visser, adding, "Mexican Indians still say that scattered corn which has not been picked up will complain to God about it. Corn was afraid of being cooked, so a woman must breathe on the corn before throwing it into the pot, to comfort it and accustom it to heat."[14]

The myths and practices of classical Greece also yield visions of sacred foods, divine cooks and food fights between humans and deities. According to the first-century writer Apollodorus, the Titan Prometheus "molded men from water and clay," kneading them into life much as Jehovah transformed Adam from earth to flesh. But the rebellious Titan was even more renowned for his theft of fire, as documented by the ancient author Hesiod. In a nasty gastronomic plot, Prometheus tricked the ruler of the gods into choosing an inferior sacrificial offering: instead of accepting real meat hidden inside the unprepossessing stomach of an ox, the greedy Olympian chose inedible bones wrapped in savory-looking "glistening fat." Zeus fought back, said Hesiod, by hiding fire from men, thereby denying them its crucial culinary properties. But the cunning Prometheus deceived the god yet again, absconding with fire hidden "in a hollow fennel-stalk, so that Zeus who delights in thunder did not see it." Zeus's revenge was ferocious: he created woman, in the form of the duplicitous Pandora, to let loose evil on the world, and he chained Prometheus to a rock where the Titan's liver was daily devoured by an eagle, continually regenerating itself only to be consumed again. Thus, like culture heroes who are credited in societies around the world with the discovery of cooking fire, the hero and cook who made civilized cuisine possible for mortals became himself a kind of eternally suffering foodstuff.[15]

If the tale of Prometheus constituted one Greek culinary myth of origin, the powerfully influential Eleusinian Mysteries revolved around several other, perhaps even more primal narratives. The major story underlying this ritual, which was at the center of a festival annually celebrated in ancient Greece, begins when Hades, king of the underworld, kidnaps and rapes Persephone, daughter of the earth goddess Demeter. The grieving mother searches the world for her daughter, and in her sorrow neglects fields and crops, causing a terrible famine. Finally, Zeus intervenes to demand that the god of the dead restore Persephone to her mother so that earth can bloom again. But just before returning the girl to the upper world, says the *Homeric Hymn to Demeter*, Hades "stealthily" feeds her "the honey-sweet berry of the pomegranate"—and because she has consumed this otherworldly food she is forced to spend four months in his underground realm, the months that correspond to the season of fruitlessness. All the more reason, though, why Demeter rejoices, and the fields renew their fertility, when the beloved daughter is annually reborn.[16]

In at least one offshoot of this narrative, Demeter's travels bring her to Eleusis, the land of Triptolemus, a heroic figure sometimes said to have been the son of Gaia and Okeanos (earth and ocean)—that is to say, a "primordial man." There, in gratitude for his family's hospitality, she teaches him the secrets of agriculture that are so central to the tale of regeneration that is also the story of Persephone.[17] And the mysteries of agriculture are also, of course, central to the celebration of the Eleusinian Mysteries, which featured rites of initiation, the display of sacred objects, and—most important—a day of ceremonial fasting followed by the consumption of a drink called *kykeon*, described in the *Homeric Hymn to Demeter* as a mixture of "barley and water with / delicate pennyroyal."[18]

Recently some scholars have speculated that this drink's powers weren't merely mythic and mystic; they may have been psychedelic. Although the theory has met with considerable skepticism, several researchers have argued for the centrality of a "hallucinogenic drug in one of the ancient world's most venerable rituals, the initiation ceremony at Eleusis," noting that such "drugs, when administered in a strictly religious context, are now called 'entheogens' " —literally meaning "that which causes God (or divine inspiration) to be within an individual"—and citing the emergence of what came to be called magic mushrooms in Mesoamerican shamanism. The *kykeon,* these scholars claim, may have been "parasitized by the fungus ergot, which contains the psychoactive alkaloids lysergic acid amide (LSA), a precursor to LSD," or the beverage may have been hallucinogenic because the Greeks actually had access to "a variety of Psilocybe mushrooms, and various other entheogenic plants, such as *Amanita muscaria* mushrooms."[19]

The controversy over the *kykeon* should remind us that what some cultures consider godly foods may seem, to others, scandalous, diabolical, or even poisonous. And of course, if the Judeo-Christian God is an originatory cook, his persistent opponent, Satan, has comparable—although more malevolent—culinary skills. It's Satan, after all, who lures Eve into eating an apple that may have been the most dangerously delicious fruit course ever offered. And it's Satan whose devils boil the wicked in oil even while priests and ministers roast his acolytes at the stake. The powers of the cook are always potentially evil because they're always potentially destructive. The apple that the serpent offers may look golden and delicious—and yet . . . Similarly, the potion a seductive lady—Circe, for instance—serves you may taste marvelous, and yet . . . Or what if someone tempts you with a sweet—derived, say, from a kind of lotus—and it just puts you to sleep?

Even a kindly maternal cook may turn into a witch, such as the one who wants to bake children into cookies in "Hansel and Gretel," or an ogress, who wants to stew them alive. Consider the horrendous tale of vicious King Tereus, his wife Procne, and her sister Philomela. Lasciviously desiring the lovely Philomela, Tereus—supposedly accompanying her on a visit to his queen—locked her in a remote cabin in the woods, raped her, and cut out her tongue so that she could never proclaim his offense to the world. But the resourceful young woman wove "a clever fabric, working words / In red on a white ground to tell the tale / Of wickedness" and sent it as a message to

Procne, who rushed to her rescue. Then, plotting revenge, Tereus's enraged wife looked at her little son Itys "with ruthless eyes," and "planned / In silent rage a deed of tragedy" that she and Philomela carried out forthwith. "Alive, / And breathing still, they carved and jointed [the boy], / And cooked the parts," then summoned Tereus to a dinner where he "swallow[ed] down / Flesh of his flesh" until the women announced their "deed of doom." Erring husbands, beware of luscious ragouts: the more savory the meat you eat, the more succulent the fleshly sins for which it may be a punishment![20]

And needless to say, children should stay away from cooks, kitchens—and sometimes parents or other relatives. In the Greek myth of Thyestes, a tale from which the woes of the house of Atreus evolve, the rivalrous twin sons of Pelops, king of Olympia, engage in a battle for power, and at one point, Atreus slays Thyestes' children and cooks them, though he saves their hands and feet in order to taunt their father with them after the unwitting man has consumed the broth, stew, pie, whatever. Seneca the Younger wrote a Roman play based on this story, a work that may have been performed during gladiatorial combats. And in the sixteenth century Seneca's drama very likely influenced Shakespeare's early, astonishingly bloody *Titus Andronicus*, a tragedy whose plot alludes in several ways to the story of Philomela as well as to the feast of Thyestes, although it demonstrates that guilty mothers, too, may suffer culinary torment as a penalty for their misbehavior. At the very end of this gory play, when the adulterous queen Tamora asks to see her sons, the vengeful Titus declares that

> There they are both, baked in that pie;
> Whereof their mother daintily hath fed,
> Eating the flesh that she herself hath bred.[21]

But perhaps a pattern for all these tales of what the culinary philosopher Carolyn Korsmeyer calls "Terrible Eating" may be derived from myths of the primordial gods themselves, whose originatory father, Saturn, fearing a prediction that he would be overthrown by one of his children, routinely gobbled up his offspring. The horror of such hunger has psychoanalytic meanings in

Francisco Goya, *Saturn Devouring His Son* (1821–23).
Museo Nacional del Prado, Madrid, Spain.

fantasies of the "devouring mother," or murderous and castrating father, that have been explored by theorists from Sigmund Freud and Carl Jung to Melanie Klein and Jacques Lacan. But stories and images based on these anxieties are cross-culturally common. In Western society, one of the most devastating representations was produced in the early nineteenth century by Francisco Goya. Known as *Saturn Devouring His Son*, this is a portrait of a nakedly savage, wild-eyed Saturn gnawing with mindless ferocity on a small headless body. According to some sources, the work was influenced by Rubens's more "refined" 1636 painting of the same subject—although in Rubens's work the deity looks cunning rather than ravenous, while the child is a screaming baby, an image more suggestive of intentional cruelty than "refinement."[22] But the history of Goya's picture is odder than that of Rubens. Bizarrely, this portrait of divine cannibalism—one of the group known as Black Goyas—was

Peter Paul Rubens, *Saturn Devouring His Son* (1636).
Museo Nacional del Prado, Madrid, Spain.

painted directly on the wall of the artist's dining room and only later transferred to canvas.[23]

Such cannibal behavior—called anthropophagy or "man-eating" by the Greeks—has probably been practiced in a few cultures, alarmingly so from a Western perspective. "Somewhere at the back of our minds," remarks Margaret Visser, "carefully walled off from ordinary consideration . . . lies the idea of cannibalism—that human beings might become food, and eaters of each other," since, as the "serious cook" knows, violence "is necessary if any organism is to ingest another." Visser argues that table manners have evolved to further "the determination of each person present to be a diner, not a dish," for one of the "chief roles of etiquette [is] to keep the lid on the violence which the meal being eaten presupposes." Yet, as she shows, even cannibalistic societies, most notably perhaps Aztec civilization, have always "surrounded the eating of human flesh with carefully prescribed ritual"—and the absence of such ritual might make the taboo-breaking meals of Tereus, Thyestes, Tamora and Saturn horrifying even to a cannibal king.[24]

In fact, in his classic essay "On Cannibals," Michel de Montaigne compared the behavior of so-called savages with that of his civilized contemporaries, declaring that in his view "there is more barbarity" in European modes of torture—"tearing a body limb from limb by racks and torments, that is yet in perfect sense" than in roasting and eating an enemy "after he is dead." The Stoics, he added, perhaps with an intent to shock, believed "that there was no hurt in making use of our dead carcasses, in what way soever for our necessity, and in feeding upon them too; as our own ancestors, who being besieged by Caesar in the city of Alexia, resolved to sustain the famine of the siege with the bodies of their old men, women, and other persons who were incapable of bearing arms." Such behavior was after all, he proclaimed, preferable to "treachery, disloyalty, tyranny, and cruelty, which are our familiar vices."[25]

That Montaigne, writing in the 1500s, knew a good deal about Aztec civilization becomes quite clear in his essay "Of Coaches," in which, noting that "Our world has lately discovered another . . . as large, well peopled, and fruitful, as this whereon we live," he marvels at the "astonishing magnificence of the cities of Cusco and Mexico." Yet the cannibals Montaigne celebrated appear rather more like noble savages than did the citizens of Cusco and Mexico as they were depicted by the conquistadors. The Aztecs, Visser notes, were historically the largest and most sophisticated man-eating culture, although anthropologists continue to dispute the nature and motive—not to mention the historical reality—of their cannibalism. Was it simply a legend, was it a ritual act of communion with the gods, or did it arise from nutritional deficiencies?[26] When the Spaniards entered the Aztecs' domain in the sixteenth century, some estimated that as many as 250,000 prisoners of war had been consumed by the society's elite, but most historians consider this number much exaggerated. In any case, the killing and cooking of the Aztecs' hapless victims, no matter their number, was reportedly as scrupulously ceremonial as any Elizabethan feast—or any European torture. According to what may be merely a myth constructed by the invaders, the victims' hearts—described as "precious eagle-cactus fruit"—were torn from their breasts while they were still living and sacrificed "to the sun, Xipilli, Quauhtleuanitl," and then, as soon as they were dead, their bodies were carefully flayed and butchered, with a thigh of each supposedly consigned to the emperor Moctezuma. Finally, we're told, their flesh "was cooked with peppers and tomatoes, and served up upon bowls of maize, the universal sacred staple of the Aztecs."[27]

Along a similar culinary line, Patrick Leigh Fermor has noted of more recently observed cannibals that their "victims were prepared while still alive, by cutting slits down the back and sides into which pimentos and other herbs were stuffed." Cannibal rituals were, according to this account, inflected by gastronomical sophistication. Leigh Fermor quotes a seventeenth-century French Dominican monk who "observed that the Caribs had most decided notions of the relative merits of their enemies. As one would expect, the French were delicious, by far the best. . . . The English came next [but the] Dutch were dull and stodgy, and the Spaniards so stringy, they were hardly a meal at all, even boiled." Adds Leigh Fermor dryly, "All this sounds sadly like gluttony."[28] Thus, if the Mesoamerican culture of the Aztecs was really cannibalistic, it was very likely the only "imperialist state . . . fully to institutionalize cannibalism," but its practices, Visser claims, "included many attitudes that are found only in part in much smaller cannibal groups."[29]

Such behavior has been intermittently recorded and its authenticity debated by ethnographers, but perhaps more importantly for us as Western readers, it has been *dramatized* in major literary texts whose focus (unlike that of the tales of Tereus and others) is on brute eating rather than on blind revenge. The dauntless hero of the *Odyssey*, for instance, encounters quite a few anthropophagic types as he struggles to reach his home in Ithaca. Polyphemus, the horrendous Cyclops, "stuff[s] his enormous gut / with human flesh, washing it down with raw milk," and his table manners are particularly disgusting. After ripping the mariner's crewmen "limb from limb to fix his meal / he bolted them down like a mountain-lion, left no scrap, / devoured entrails, flesh and bones, marrow and all!" Later in the epic, the "tremendous Laestrygonians . . . not like men, like Giants," skewer Odysseus's "crews like fish / and whisk them home to make their grisly meal." And even later in this narrative that Henry Fielding rather darkly called "the eatingest epic," such behavior is manifested by monstrous mythic creatures who don't even take human form, Scylla and Charybdis. The latter gulps and vomits, gulps and vomits, while the former stretches out six heads to "seize as many men" and gobble them "raw— / screaming out, / flinging their arms toward" their helpless captain.[30]

But one writer's horror story is another's black comedy. In 1728, many centuries after Homer scandalized audiences with tales of savage diners radically different from "men like us, who live on bread," the great satirist Jonathan Swift offered his sardonic "Modest Proposal for Preventing the Children of Poor People in Ireland From Being a Burden to Their Parents or Country, and for Making Them Beneficial to the Public." Since it was so hard to feed these impoverished babies, the public had better feed on them—for, declares Swift's speaker blandly (with a slight dig in the ribs of Americans), "I have been assured by a very knowing American of my acquaintance in London, that a young healthy child well nursed is at a year old a most delicious, nourishing, and wholesome food, whether stewed, roasted, baked, or boiled."[31]

Less than a century later, Lord Byron produced his equally sardonic ottava rima "epic" of *Don Juan*, where at one point the hero, along with his tutor Pedrillo, is shipwrecked and set afloat in a raft with a crew of starving sailors, who grow increasingly ravenous, since, as Byron dryly observes, "man is a carnivorous production, / And must have meals, at least one meal a day." Thus, according to a time-honored "custom of the sea," the men draw lots and the "luckless Pedrillo" is chosen to be dinner, meekly requesting to be bled to death—and dying, "as born, a Catholic in faith." For, notes Byron ironically, "first a little crucifix he kiss'd, / And then held out his jugular and wrist."[32] A similar but not very amusing scene forms a key part of a central episode in Edgar Allan Poe's unnerving "Narrative of Arthur Gordon Pym." Here, the eponymous protagonist, adrift on a pitiless sea with a few other survivors of a mutiny, finds himself indulging in a "fearful repast," of which he notes, "Such things may be imagined, but words have no power to impress the mind with the exquisite horror of their reality," then goes on to describe how "having in some measure appeased the raging thirst which consumed us by the blood of the victim . . . we devoured the rest of the body, piecemeal."[33]

Thirty years after Poe's grisly scene appeared, Mark Twain satirized such representations of the so-called custom of the sea in a hilarious vision of a hypothetical "custom of the land." "Cannibalism in the Cars" is a tale of polite parliamentarians resorting to cannibalism when snowbound in a railroad car en route to Chicago. Twain has the narrator of the episode, who turns out to be a madman, describe his deadly dining with parodic relish:

> We . . . sat down with hearts full of gratitude to the finest supper that had blessed our vision for seven torturing days. . . . I liked Harris. He might have been better done, perhaps, but I am free to say that no man ever agreed with me better than Harris, or afforded me so large a degree of satisfaction. Messick was very well, though rather high-flavored, but for genuine nutritiousness and delicacy of fibre, give me Harris.

In real life, of course, considerably less comic scenes have been enacted following numerous shipwrecks, air crashes and other disasters. The ghastly doings of the Donner Party, stranded in the snows of the California sierra, come to mind, as does the Andean air crash in 1972 that became the subject of *Alive*, both a book and a movie.[34]

No doubt writers from Swift to Byron, Poe, Twain and other more recent authors have brooded in their various ways on such doings because these true stories horrify and haunt us. Commenting that press coverage of Jeffrey Dahmer's cannibalism was "obsessive" although the man was really being tried for murder, the critic Claude Rawson notes that "We shrink from the subject [of cannibalism] but cannot leave it alone." Indeed. Detailed reports about Dahmer included a report that when "police searched [his] kitchen, they found nothing but the refrigerated flesh of his victims . . . no condiments; no fruit, vegetables, cereals or dessert." And yet in the face of such fascinated horror (or perhaps because of it), the great Mexican painter Diego Rivera declared in his autobiography that he had as a young art student come to think of human flesh as the healthiest meat and subsisted on it for several months. He noted that "During the time of our experiment, I discovered that I liked to eat the legs and breasts of women, for as in other animals, these parts are delicacies. I also savored young women's breaded ribs. Best of all, however, I relished women's brains in vinaigrette."[35]

In fact, insisted Rivera—who may or may not have cooked up a tall tale here—although he never returned to this culinary practice, he came to believe that "when man evolves a civilization higher than the mechanized but still primitive one he has now, the eating of human flesh will be sanctioned. For then man will have thrown off all of his superstitions and irrational taboos." In the meantime, however, revulsion persists. Think, after all, of the fictive cannibal psychiatrist Hannibal Lecter, whose portrayal won an Oscar for Anthony Hopkins and who keeps reappearing in book after book, film after film. Think of the murderers who capture headlines in tabloids by cooking victims en brochette.[36] Perhaps our fascination with all this tells us that you have to be wary not just of "serious cooks" but of the powers of hunger if you want to be a diner, not a dish.

And it may help to be virtuous too. In Dante's *Inferno*, the pilgrim's vision of the wretched Count Ugolino, whom hunger drove to eat his own sons when he was imprisoned in a Florentine tower, is followed, in the very deeps of hell, by the sight of a triple-headed Satan gnawing on three sinners, all three defined as traitors by the author and each "kept / As by a flax rake." The shade of Brutus silently writhes in the grip of "the black mouth" and he's joined in his torment by his fellow conspirator, "sinewy Cassius." But the "soul . . . who suffers most / Is Judas Iscariot; head locked inside / He flails his legs" as he struggles within the maw of Satan, that chef of evil, sliding eternally down the diabolical gullet, destined never even to reach the oblivion of the devil's dark gut.[37]

The Powers of Food

The bizarre permutations of human and inhuman appetite, along with the daunting powers of the cook to create and destroy, suggest that it's always wise to watch what you eat while ensuring that you yourself aren't eaten. Or so myth and literature make clear. Whether contrived by culture or evolved in nature, many foods have uncanny, often unnerving properties. Sometimes, indeed, the powers of food are double-edged. For instance, the entheogens that might have initiated the acolytes of Eleusis into untold ecstasies can also have dire consequences. It's lately been speculated that the Salem witch trials began when a group of young girls were poisoned by ergot that had grown on rye in the Massachusetts Bay Colony. The symptoms that seemed to document their victimization by witchcraft are all, evidently, consistent with ergotic poisoning: the "girls were often stricken with violent fits that were attributed to torture by apparitions [but the] spectral evidence of the trials appears to be the hallucinogenic symptoms and perceptual disturbance accompanying ergotism [and the] convulsions appear to be epileptiform [while] accusations of choking suggest the involvement of the involuntary muscular fibers that is typical of ergot poisoning," and so forth. Perhaps, then, if the Almighty has decreed that the "fear" and the "dread" of humans—and especially of human cooks—"shall be upon every beast of the earth," we humans have long had, for our part, every reason to dread even the most familiar-looking contents of the larder while also regarding unknown foodstuffs with justifiable anxiety.[38]

Closing your mouth against temptation, whether through holy fasting or through sheer anticipatory disgust, might seem the safest strategy for survival, spiritual or physical. Declared the celebrated medieval theologian and poet Alan of Lille, "If Adam had fasted in paradise . . . he would not have been exiled into damnation. If Esau had fasted . . . he would not have lost his birthright. If Noah had fasted . . . he would not have lost his modesty. Therefore, through fasting the body is purged that it may receive the Eucharist sacramentally, and the spirit that it may receive it spiritually."[39] More practically, some of the dead might rue delicious dinners as feasts that cost them their fleshly lives.

Poisons—both those that occur naturally and those that are deliberately deployed—have of course a long history. Ergotic poisoning of the kind from which the supposed victims of Salem witchcraft may have suffered has also been blamed for "the outbreaks of 'dancing mania' and other aberrations which affected whole villages in the Middle Ages," according to the food historian Alan Davidson. In fact, the last major outbreak in Europe was relatively recent, occurring in France in 1951: four people died and 200 were affected.[40] Among other substances that rightly inspire dread, the toxin that causes botulism "has been described as the most poisonous substance known; 1 gram could kill between 100,000 and 10 million people." But it doesn't have the long and mythic history associated with such substances as deadly nightshade, hemlock, arsenic, and death cap (amanita) mushrooms. These are the foods that can deceive innocents wandering in pleasant forests—children who naively swallow poisonous berries, foragers who unwittingly pick the poisonous toadstool. In Mary Wilkins Freeman's "Old Woman Magoun," pretty little Lily is one of those unfortunates and dies after consuming the sweet berries of the deadly nightshade. And according to some sources, the Buddha himself was accidentally killed by a peasant who offered him a deathcap mushroom, thinking it a delicacy.[41]

These are the foods that legendary cooks and poisoners manipulate. The Greek sorceress Medea was a mistress of the arts of toxicity, for, said Apollonius Rhodus, "the goddess Hecate taught [her] to handle magic herbs with exceeding skill," and her favored instrument was wolfsbane (aconitum), also known as monkshood and chariot of Venus, infused at one point into a cup of wine with which she attempted to murder the Greek hero Theseus. But, as Ruskin noted, she could also deploy her botanical knowledge on behalf of those she loved. In the *Argonautica*, she makes Jason invulnerable by giving him "the charm of Prometheus," a plant that "shot up" when "the ravening eagle on the rugged flanks of Caucasus let drip to the earth the blood-like ichor" of tortured Prometheus. And Medea's culinary witchery may have been hereditary, since, besides being a priestess of Hecate, she was a niece of that consummate gastronomic seductress Circe, who so famously stirred "wicked drugs" into a delicious potion of "cheese, barley / and pale honey mulled in Pramnian wine," thereby transforming Odysseus's hungry sailors "bristling into swine—with grunts, / snouts—even their bodies, yes, and only the men's minds stayed steadfast as before."[42]

Of course, the fermentation that transforms grapes into wine, grains into beer, honey into mead, potatoes into vodka, is a primordial example of thrilling, potentially perilous metamorphosis. Circe's special cocktail may have literally turned men into pigs, but most alcoholic drinks have the potential to bring out the beastly in those who overindulge. On the one hand strengthening and even sacred, on the other hand dangerously intoxicating and debilitating, wines and liquors are substances—unlike, say, entheogens—that are subject to quotidian abuse. If Christ's blood offers salvation in a wine chalice, Dionysus—the mysterious god of the vine and of drunkenness—brings both solace and frenzy, joy and rage, when he unleashes the power in the cup. For centuries alcoholic beverages were used as anesthetics and restoratives. Yet consider the fate of Pentheus, the righteous voyeur of Euripides' *Bacchae*: his own mother tore him limb from limb when he spied on the ferocious celebrations of the Maenads. Consider, more generally, the madness represented by the Roman rites of the Bacchanalia. And consider, even to this day, the dangers of drink as outlined by protesters from the pious members of the Women's Christian Temperance Union (WCTU), led by Carrie Nation, known as the Kansas Smasher (for the two-foot hatchet she wielded in her effort to "physically destroy every saloon in the country"), to, more poignantly, the angry grievers of MADD. Volumes can be, and have been, written about the ambiguities of this history.[43]

But Medea, Circe and Dionysus are only a few legendary wielders of magic whose foods might (or might not) be dangerous. Many who devise problematic meals have unequivocally bad intentions. In European fairy tales, perhaps the most prominent villainess is the wicked queen in "Snow White," who retreats to "a very secret, lonely room" where she makes a poisoned apple with which she plunges the story's heroine into a trance. Historically, real-life poisoners included the city of Athens, whose official instrument of execution was hemlock, as we know from Plato's powerful account of the death of Socrates: the cup of hemlock was actually called the state poison. And for centuries kings have insisted on the services of tasters—human as well as animal—to ensure that their roasts and casseroles didn't kill them.

Some were no doubt justified in worrying since they themselves were so adept at annihilating their enemies with deadly potions. La Cantarella, much used by the murderous Borgias, was a mixture of arsenic and phosphorus whose secret "had been divulged to [them] by a Spanish monk, who also knew the antidote for it, as well as an antidote for arsenic" so that the famous family was itself "well armed" against sinister plots. Nonetheless, whether accidentally or on purpose, Rodrigo Borgia, who became Pope Alexander VI, himself died of poison.[44] And of course Shakespeare played with poisons: in *Romeo and Juliet*, where the heroine swallows a potion that seems to kill her; in *Hamlet*, where both Hamlet senior and his erring widow die of poison, the latter by mistakenly drinking from a cup that was intended for someone else, as the Borgia pope may have done; and perhaps most famously in *Macbeth*, where the three witches mutter fabulous incantations as they cook up their notorious brew of "Eye of newt and toe of frog, / Wool of bat and tongue of dog, / Adder's fork and blindworm's sting," et cetera. Diversely repellent—even poisonous—in and of themselves, the ingredients that these ill-intentioned cooks toss into their communal pot blend and bubble to create a potion that can cause double or triple trouble, as each lends extra power to every other.

To be sure, foods that cause illness and death aren't the only edibles to be avoided. In almost any culture there are kinds of food—usually meat and seafood—that are taboo for religious reasons. Jews and Muslims don't eat pork; Jews don't eat shellfish; Hindus don't eat beef—and these kinds of flesh are forbidden because theological texts proclaim them unclean, polluting. For similar (though not theologically argued) reasons, many peoples don't eat domesticated "pet" animals—cats, dogs, canaries, parrots—and most of us in the West don't eat insects, worms or snakes. (Few, for instance, consume "wool of bat and tongue of dog.") We in the West define these creatures as improper foodstuffs because, on the one hand, it would be quasi-cannibalistic to braise Fido the pup or Felix the cat in a stew; and on the other hand, it would be nauseating to gobble up bugs and worms that we consider in themselves disgusting—although (a caveat here) such "bizarre foods" as rotten fish, grilled rat, and beetles in various forms have been spectacularly consumed by Andrew Zimmern on the Travel Channel and now and then by hapless contestants on *Fear Factor*.[45]

There are also fruits and vegetables that have historically unnerved potential diners, just as braised cat and grilled rat horrify most of us today. When Columbus brought the humble tomato back to Europe from the New World, Europeans found it profoundly sinister, likening it to the apple Eve fed Adam

(Hungarians called it *Paradice appfel*, the apple of Paradise) or defining it as an aphrodisiac (the French called it *pomme d'amour*, love apple). As recently as the twentieth century, the French scientist Henri Leclerc considered tomatoes, like mandrakes, an "evil fruit . . . treacherous and deceitful."[46] For quite some time, the eggplant—which happens to be a member of the same botanical family as the tomato, the mandrake, and the deadly nightshade—suffered the same fate: it's said that its modern Italian name, *melanzana*, derives from the Latin *mala insana*, meaning "apple of madness." Arab doctors supposedly warned their patients that consuming this vegetable would cause not only madness but also cancer, freckles and hoarseness, among other evils.[47]

An even more voluptuous, apparently sacred—and controversial—comestible was chocolate. Venerated by the Aztecs, who served it as a kind of liqueur to their nobility and as a ritual potion to those marked for sacrifice, it was also thought (like the tomato) to be an aphrodisiac. When the European conquerors of the New World took it up, it retained a reputation for inciting "both violence and lust." According to one source, some Catholic ladies in colonial Mexico liked to sip it during Mass, a practice the local clergy condemned as blasphemous; chocolate, fulminated one bishop, was "a damned agent from the witch's brew." Back in the Old World, it was fashionable among the French and Italian aristocracy, and became so associated with lasciviousness and even erotic cruelty that the theorist Roland Barthes coined the phrase "Sadean chocolate" to define the substance "as an aphrodisiac that symbolized power: the luxurious sacred beverage stolen from Indians who were massacred, both bitter and sweet."[48]

In Charles Dickens's *A Tale of Two Cities*, a link between chocolate and tyranny is incarnated in the person of "Monseigneur, one of the great lords in power at the Court," who "was by some few sullen minds supposed to be rather rapidly swallowing France" but cannot take his morning chocolate "without the aid of four strong men," all "ablaze with gorgeous decoration." After such a strengthening *petit déjeuner*, this depraved nobleman issues forth to meet his admirers, who greet him, appropriately, with "submission . . . cringing and fawning . . . servility [and] abject humiliation."[49] As for coffee, chocolate's breakfast-time rival, by the seventeenth century it had become, as

Fernandez-Armesto wittily puts it, "the counter-opiate of the Rococo West, the potential home-breaker satirized in Bach's Coffee Cantata." And indeed, a partly sardonic, partly serious women's petition against the substance in 1674 complained that "the Excessive Use of that Newfangled, Abominable, Heathenish Liquor called COFFEE [. . .] has [. . .] Eunucht our Husbands, and Crippled our more kind Gallants, that they are become as Impotent, as Age."[50]

Even more exotic and literally mind-blowing foods than tomatoes, eggplants and chocolate might be pleasurably but dangerously enervating. In book 9 of the *Odyssey*, before they encounter the cannibalistic Cyclops and the seductive Circe, some hapless members of Odysseus's crew meet up with the fabled lotus-eaters, and, after tasting "the one-sweet fruit," languish in a primordial hippie paradise, stoned on flowers—maybe opium poppies, maybe (according to the food historian Alan Davidson) a wine concocted from jujubes. They were to reappear in Tennyson's Victorian redaction as weary wanderers who self-destructively secede from the world of work. Having "grazed" on lotus, they now long only for "rest or death, dark death or dreamful ease."[51] As writers from Homer to Tennyson revealed, not all problematic potions are poisonous. Some (like Circe's mysterious brew) turn men into swine; some (like the mystical lotus) turn them into hopeless dreamers. And there may even be enigmatic foods whose effects are more equivocal.

In Lewis Carroll's classic *Alice in Wonderland*, the young heroine is confounded, when she reaches the bottom of the rabbit hole, first by a little bottle whose "beautifully printed" label commands, "DRINK ME," and then by a "very small cake, on which the words 'EAT ME' [are] beautifully marked in currants." After ascertaining that the bottle is "not marked 'poison' " (in which case, thinks the wise child, "it is almost certain to disagree with you sooner or later"), Alice tastes the potion in the bottle, and, "finding it very nice," with a "mixed flavour of cherry-tart, custard, pine-apple, roast turkey, toffy, and hot buttered toast"—all favorite nursery foods—she finishes it off, whereupon she immediately begins to shrink "like a telescope" until, in a panic at the rapidity with which she is disappearing, she finds and eats the little cake. Then, exclaiming "Curiouser and curiouser," she finds herself "opening out like the largest telescope that ever was!"[52]

Later, encountering another bottle, the adventurous Alice drinks it more readily, observing "I know something interesting is sure to happen . . . whenever I eat or drink anything." And indeed, in a series of extraordinary episodes she expands and contracts like an accordion until eventually she meets a hookah-smoking caterpillar who initiates her into the properties of a remarkably prophetic magic mushroom: "One side will make you grow taller, and the other side will make you grow shorter." Her surreal growth-and-shrinking spurts may reflect Carroll's own knowledge of consciousness-altering substances, but at the same time they reveal an uncanny understanding of the experiences children have in a world where, even as they inexplicably gain in size, they're still helplessly small. That these episodes are triggered by enchanted foods is on the surface just plain common sense, but at the same time the weird cakes and drinks that present themselves to this little girl also dramatize food fantasies most children have—along with perfectly reasonable anxieties most develop at one point or another about ingesting unknown dishes.[53]

Grownups, of course, imagine more wide-ranging food narratives than children. If some potions are in one way or another deadly, others—love potions—supposedly drive people mad with desire. Aphrodisiacs may be rare in nature, but culture has fantasized for centuries that certain sorceresses can cook them up. Whether versified by medieval romancers or dramatized in the nineteenth century by Richard Wagner, the story of Tristan and Isolde turns on a love potion administered to the unhappy pair that plunges them into the passionate affair leading to their famous Liebestod. Similarly, in Keats's ballad "La Belle Dame Sans Merci," a knight-at-arms is discovered on a cold hillside, "alone and palely loitering," because he met "a lady in the meads, / Full beautiful—a faery's child," who found him "roots of relish sweet, / And honey wild, and manna dew" that plunged him into a hopeless fever-dream of love. A happier aphrodisiac appears in Keats's "Eve of St. Agnes," where Porphyro, the poem's hero, woos his beloved Madeline with a festive bedside spread of "candied apple, quince, and plum, and gourd, / With jellies soother than the creamy curd," among other delicacies. Soon and sexily, after wakening her with "an ancient ditty, long since mute, / In Provence call'd, 'La belle dame sans mercy,'" he "melt[s]" into her dream, "as the rose / Blendeth its odour with the violet,— / Solution sweet." Yet even here, although the lovers achieve a consummation that eludes the lovelorn knight of "La Belle Dame," their fate is uncertain: "they are gone: ay, ages long ago" into a wintry storm, where their destiny must be unknown.[54]

Other providers of problematic foods, sometimes even the beloved whom one has trusted, may be yet more dangerous than Keats's seducers. The old ballad "Lord Randall," one of a group of folk lyrics that deeply influenced Keats and his circle, tells in poignant dialogue the devastating tale of a young man who confides to his mother that his true love has poisoned him with "eels boiled in broo'" (broth) so that he is "sick at the heart, and . . . fain would lie down"—to die. Laura, one of the two virginal protagonists of Christina Rossetti's monitory Victorian poem "Goblin Market," nearly pays as terrible a price as Keats's knight for swallowing the lures of sinister otherworldly creatures. Though her wiser sister Lizzie warns her not to listen to "the fruit call" of the goblins, Laura hungers for their luscious "Apples and quinces . . . plump unpecked cherries . . . Bloom-down-cheeked peaches"—and after all, who wouldn't be drawn to this cornucopia of forbidden fruit? But once the unfortunate Laura has eaten the fruit, her gastronomic virginity is lost; fallen, like a new Eve, into a state of sin where the goblin merchants no longer seek her out, in a fever of "passionate yearning," she "gnashe[s] her teeth for balked desire." In the end, she can only be redeemed when her more virtuous sister visits the goblins and, with mouth closed against their wares, allows them to rub her all over with juicy fruit, in a kind of culinary rape scene. When she goes back home and gives herself to Laura to be licked and sucked ("Never mind my bruises, / Hug me, kiss me, suck my juices"), the sweet pulps function as an antidote for the poisoned girl, who now finds that the "juice was wormwood to her tongue, / She loathed the feast"—and yet, in an access of bitterness, it cures her.[55]

What Dickinson called the "Mystery of Food" is perpetually perplexing. Dionysus's wine cup can delight or destroy. The mushroom that may have poisoned the Buddha may also have induced in him a hallucinogenic ecstasy, or so one interpreter of his tale has claimed. And in the view of the late, somewhat eccentric ethnobotanist Terence McKenna, the same magic mushrooms, or some very like them—psilocybins—may have facilitated the evolution of great apes into human beings. Contemporary scientists find little merit in McKenna's "stoned ape" theory of human evolution, but that one can interpret certain foods in radically different ways gives words about eating a resonance that should interest the serious reader as well as the serious cook. If some dishes can plunge you into love or lethargy, others, like magic mushrooms, can inspire amazing visions and visionary songs. Samuel Taylor Coleridge's Romantic masterpiece, the ostensibly fragmentary poem "Kubla Khan," was such a production. The work, said the poet—himself, as an opium addict, a kind of lotus-eater—was "composed, in a sort of Revery brought on by two grains of Opium taken to check a dysentery." But besides its origin in a consciousness-altering potion, this richly enigmatic fantasy celebrates such transformative foods, concluding with an almost apocalyptic revelation of the way the relationship between the poet and his muse might be empowered by sacred "honey-dew" and "the milk of Paradise." In fact, the speaker reimagines himself as a kind of shaman, with the special access to supernatural knowledge bestowed on shamans and sorcerers around the world by strange things to eat and drink.[56]

Coleridge wasn't the only Romantic writer to use mind-altering substances. Thomas De Quincey, famously the author of *Confessions of an English Opium-Eater* and an impassioned disciple of both Wordsworth and Coleridge, attested at length to "the pleasures of opium." Wrote De Quincey, while wine "disorders the mental faculties," opium "introduces amongst them the most exquisite order, legislation, and harmony." Yet in his *Confessions* he confronted not only the terrors of addiction but what he called the "pains of opium": melancholy, torpor, intellectual incoherence, terrible dreams, distressing withdrawal symptoms. Like the "roots of relish sweet, / And honey wild, and manna dew" with which La Belle Dame feeds her hapless knight-at-arms, the opium that is at first so delicious may leave those who partake of its delights on the "cold hill-side" of reality, "alone and palely loitering."

In France, not long after *Confessions* appeared, Charles Baudelaire wrote in *The Artificial Paradises* (of which the first half was titled "Poem of Hashish" and the second was a translation of De Quincey's book) that the substance magically induces "a superior sharpness in each of the senses" while, as De Quincey had, he warned of its pernicious effects.[57] Along with such other luminaries as Théophile Gautier, Gérard de Nerval, and Alexandre Dumas père, he was a member of the esoteric Club des Hachichins (Hashish Club), founded in the 1840s by the psychiatrist Jacques-Joseph Moreau, who wanted to study the effects of the drug on mental functioning in order to analyze the causes of insanity. Like the English Romantics, these French counterparts were enthralled by the visionary imaginings hashish bestowed—even while they feared its dangers. Gautier's popular Gothic tale "The Hashish Club" summarizes a number of the hallucinatory effects experienced by those who sit down to a surreal dinner after nibbling the substance that a scientist based on Dr. Moreau doles out in the form of a spoonful of "green jam" not unlike something Alice might have imbibed in Wonderland. Among the first of the bizarre phenomena the speaker recounts is a change in the nature of the meal itself, namely "a complete transformation in taste": the "water I drank seemed the most exquisite wine, the meat, once in my mouth, became strawberries, the strawberries, meat. I could not have distinguished a fish from a cutlet."[58]

Recent literary historians have argued that the Romantic aesthetic itself—with its emphasis not only on the visionary imagination but also on what Wordsworth called "wise passiveness" and on what the critic M. H. Abrams has defined as "natural supernaturalism"—was fostered by the ingestion of substances like opium and hashish, both of which are classed as entheogens like the *kykeon* used in Eleusis and the psilocybin mushrooms ritually eaten by shamans. Such Romantic experimentation was to exert a powerful influence on a range of later writers, from Walter Benjamin to William Burroughs. Benjamin's "protocols" for investigating hashish were inspired by a reading of Baudelaire's *Artificial Paradises* but extended into a rather fuller testing of the drug than the earlier writer had attempted. In the course of at least ten or eleven carefully controlled experiments with hashish, the great critic evolved a concept of "profane illumination" that seemed to him "intimately related" to his "philosophical observations." Among the insights he recorded as part of a drug-induced "toe dance of reason" was a feeling of "understanding Poe much better now" because the "entrance gates to a world of grotesques seem to open up," along with a curious sense that "food belongs to another world" because he is "prevented from eating by a dividing wall of glass."[59]

Written between 1927 and 1934, the "protocols" that constitute much of Benjamin's *On Hashish* were only recently translated into English and published in the United States, but a more notorious set of instructions for achieving mental metamorphosis was widely circulated in the 1960s. The recipe for "Haschich Fudge (which anyone could whip up on a rainy day)" that Alice B. Toklas included in the popular cookbook that she published in 1954 was supplied by her friend Brion Gysen.[60] He added a somewhat tongue-in-cheek comment that sent a whole generation of hippies in search of the appropriate spices, mixed fruits and nuts, "canibis sativa" [sic], and ovens, but made Toklas's volume famous. (She herself claimed to have inserted the recipe at the last minute, without reading it.) Explained Gysen, a filmmaker and sometime collaborator of William Burroughs:

> This is the food of paradise—of Baudelaire's Artificial Paradises: it might provide an entertaining refreshment for a Ladies' Bridge Club or a chapter meeting of the DAR . . . Euphoria and brilliant storms of laughter; ecstatic reveries and extensions of one's personality on several simultaneous planes are to be complacently expected. Almost anything Saint Theresa did, you can do better if you can bear to be ravished by "*un évanouissement reveillé*."

"Two pieces" of the fudge, he added dryly, "are quite sufficient."[61]

But words themselves can also be envisioned as enchanted edibles. Christ himself, the prophet who gave himself up to be eaten by his worshippers, was defined as the "Word made flesh." And in one of her most intriguingly enigmatic lyrics, Emily Dickinson extended the meaning of that phrase, with its emphasis on the Word of God, to imply that *all* words may be divine flesh, to be partaken of in the impassioned banquets of art. "A Word made Flesh," she wrote, "is seldom / And tremblingly partook," yet "each one of us has probably tasted the very [mystical] food debated." For this aesthetically voracious poet, the communion of language meant that one might feast with furtive reverence on the pleasures of vocabulary, eating words with delight.[62]

Dickinson's poem reminds us yet again of the ambiguities with which the powers of food have been represented through the centuries. But to go back to yet another biblical image of ambiguous dining, we might note that even Eve's apple—that sinister fruit packed with the seeds of evil—led to what's been called the *felix culpa*, the fortunate fall, as one of the loveliest medieval lyrics makes clear:

Ne hadde the appil take ben,
The appil taken ben,
Ne hadde never our lady
A ben hevene quene.[63]

In other words, if Eve hadn't eaten the apple, Mary wouldn't have given birth to Jesus, and thus, according to this reasoning, the first deadly and sinful meal led inevitably to a sacred supper of redemptive bread and wine. Who knows what the cosmic cupboard may yet have in store—not to mention the cryptic power that cooked up the food chain?

Chapter 4

Master Belly and Our Daily Bread: A Brief History of the Literary Kitchen

> . . . there's no way to hide the belly's hungers—
> what a curse, what mischief it brews in all our lives!
> Just for hunger we rig and ride our long benched ships
> on the barren salt sea, speeding death to enemies.
>
> —HOMER, *ODYSSEY*, BOOK XII

> Master Belly is the true master of all the arts. . . . The name of his command is: do as I say, and at once, or die. . . . The whole world is busy serving him, everyone working. And in return he brings all sorts of good things to the world, inventing all the arts, every engine known, all trades and crafts, all machines and subtleties.
>
> —RABELAIS, *GARGANTUA AND PANTAGRUEL*

Transcendental Gastronomy?

An unforgettable literary moment: Marcel, the speaker of Proust's *Remembrance of Things Past,* is cold and "dispirited after a dreary day." His mother offers him what may be the world's most famous bedtime snack: a madeleine, with its distinctive scallop-shell shape. Writes Proust:

> I raised to my lips a spoonful of the tea in which I had soaked a morsel of the cake. No sooner had the warm liquid, and the crumbs with it, touched my palate than a shudder ran through my whole body, and I stopped . . . An exquisite pleasure had invaded

> my senses . . . I had ceased now to feel mediocre, accidental, mortal. Whence could it have come to me, this all-powerful joy? I was conscious that it was connected with the taste of tea and cake, but that it infinitely transcended those savours, could not, indeed, be of the same nature as theirs. Whence did it come? What did it signify?

Like the holy bread and wine out of which Christian liturgy is constituted, this transcendent pick-me-up consists of something baked (a transformation of flour and other ingredients into a breadlike substance) and something brewed (a metamorphosis of leaves, rather than grapes, into a beverage). However, unlike the ceremonial food that is sought by worshippers with religious reverence and bestowed by priests with due solemnity at the center of the Mass, the restorative that Marcel's mother administers evokes a secular Sunday service centered on "the little piece of madeleine which on Sunday mornings at Combray . . . my aunt Léonie used to give me, dipping it first in her own cup of real or lime-flower tea."

Proffered casually to a child, Proust's madeleine has a humble pathos. Not even a whole—merely a segment, nearly a crumb—it's been dipped in someone else's tea, and its origins are doubly domestic: first Aunt Léonie administers this homely eucharist, then the grown-up narrator's mother offers it to him. No hieratic churchly establishment sponsors it: it is in and of the home—women's bedrooms and kitchens. Yet out of—indeed, because of—its quotidian domesticity, a world of the past resurrects itself, just as the Savior is supposedly resurrected by and within the wafer of the Mass. More, besides reviving the times past that made the speaker who he is, the tea and cake bring into being the words of the book, the very *being* of the book, in which he will incarnate his memory of those times. For as soon as he recognizes the taste of the madeleine "soaked in" his aunt's lime-blossom tea, a whole world magically appears, in a passage crucial to modernist understandings of both consciousness and creativity:

> . . . the old grey house upon the street, where her room was, rose up like the scenery of a theatre to attach itself to the little pavilion,

> opening on to the garden, which had been built out behind it for my parents . . . and with the house the town, from morning to night and in all weathers. . . . And just as the Japanese amuse themselves by filling a porcelain bowl with water and steeping in it little crumbs of paper which until then are without character or form, but, the moment they become wet, stretch themselves and bend, take on colour and distinctive shape . . . so in that moment . . . the whole of Combray . . . sprang into being . . . from my cup of tea.[1]

Thus, though the effect of Proust's madeleine is in some sense sacramental, it isn't theological. Rather, the little meal offers a transcendence of the quotidian that is paradoxically *derived* from the quotidian in all its humdrum imminence. Like Walter Benjamin's definition of his hashish experiences, Proust's biscuit—with its scallop shape emblematic of holy pilgrimage—yields a "profane illumination" that will guide him on his journey toward the (re)creation of the past.[2]

Despite Plato's scorn for the "wild animal" that is the belly and the "sophistry" he associates with cookery, and despite Hegel's contempt for the transience of taste and smell, everybody's daily bread can arguably offer comparable illuminations. The word "taste" itself, after all, is linguistically ambiguous, signifying both the gastronomic ("that cake tastes good") and the aesthetic ("that tablecloth is in good taste"). Certainly, countless novelists and poets in European culture have explored and dramatized the significance of quotidian food. And, in Asian society, apparently "ordinary" activities—for instance, the tea ceremony as outlined by the Zen priest Takuan—ritualize the quotidian. Participants are to enter "a small room in a bamboo grove or under trees" and will be greeted by the tea utensils "arranged in order." Suggested Takuan:

> . . . let this all be carried out in accordance with the idea that in this room we can enjoy the streams and rocks as we do the rivers and mountains in Nature, and appreciate the various moods and sentiments suggested by . . . the transformation of seasons. . . . As

> visitors are greeted here with due reverence, we listen quietly to the boiling water in the kettle, which sounds like a breeze passing through the pine needles, and become oblivious of all worldly woes and worries.[3]

"A breeze passing through the pine needles"! The boiling kettle literally symbolizes both transience and transformation—water to steam, leaves to tea, season to season. Such a contemplative practice reminds us again that the phrase "meditations on transcendental gastronomy" ultimately refers not only (as Brillat-Savarin suggests) to the spiritual pleasures of the table but to both the apparent insubstantiality of taste *and* the way in which the sensations associated with eating (not only taste but also smell, touch, sight) bestow on food the strange ability to transcend its own materiality.[4]

Inevitably, our dependence on our daily bread does link us to our animality, for we are like beasts in our obedience to the imperatives of "Master Belly." The great Russian critic Mikhail Bakhtin begins an important discussion of eating and "the grotesque body" in Rabelais's *Gargantua and Pantagruel* with a passage that could apply as easily to a dog as to a man:

> Eating and drinking are one of the most significant manifestations of the grotesque body. The distinctive character of this body is its open unfinished nature, its interaction with the world. These traits are most fully . . . revealed in the act of eating; the body here transcends its own limits; it swallows, devours, rends the world apart, is enriched and grows at the world's expense.

But the point that Bakhtin derives from this preliminary description is telling:

> The encounter of man with the world, which takes place inside the open, biting, rending, chewing mouth, *is one of the most ancient, and most important objects of human thought and imagery.* Here man tastes the world, introduces it into his body, makes it part of himself. *Man's awakening consciousness could not but concentrate on*

> *this moment, could not help borrowing from it a number of substantial images determining its interrelation with the world.* [emphasis added][5]

Odd as it may seem to compare the voracious Pantagruel with the fastidious Marcel, both fictional characters meet, as it were, the "meat" of the world "inside the open, biting, rending, chewing mouth"—and thereby determine, in a distinctively human manner, some sort of connection with that which surrounds them.

If a dog could speak, it might say—in a revision of the Cartesian *cogito ergo sum* ("I think therefore I am")—"I eat therefore I am; I am therefore I eat." But a man or woman can say, "I eat and *contemplate* what I eat, therefore I am." Or, as the anthropologist Claude Lévi-Strauss observed, appropriate food must be "not only good to eat, but also good to think."[6] Thus, rather than being a wild beast chained up in the body, the human belly is a master, from Rabelais's perspective as from Aesop's, for its material consumption empowers the mind's intellectual consumption of experience. "Animals feed themselves," goes one of the aphorisms that Brillat-Savarin considered "a lasting foundation for the science of gastronomy"; "men eat; but only wiser men know the art of eating."[7]

More specifically, though, how does human eating differ from animal eating in its encounter with the world? To begin with, and to turn again to Lévi-Strauss—this time to his famous model of the distinction between culture and nature—most humans cook their food while animals eat food that's raw (unless humans cook it for them). As we've seen, fire-bringers like Prometheus are invariably culture heroes, for they instruct their societies in the arts of transformation and preservation that are crucial to civilization. In addition, as we've also seen, human eating is usually communal: we are the only species that shares food in regular, stylized ways. Finally, human food transcends mere eating in its engagement with history and memory. Proust's representation of such a confrontation with history is essentially modern in its interiority, its privacy, but—transculturally and transhistorically—carefully formulated ways of eating and preparing food link long chains of generations.

And in many societies, offerings of food to the dead also reinforce connections with the human past.[8]

Because our consumption of our daily bread is, in Bakhtin's words, "one of the most ancient, and most important objects of human thought and imagery," it is a topos for art of all kinds. Food, wrote the French thinker Roland Barthes, is not only "a collection of products" but also "a system of communication, a body of images, a protocol of usages, situations and behavior." In fact, he added, "One could say that an entire 'world' (social environment) is present in and signified by food." In a similar vein, the anthropologist Mary Douglas pointed out that "Eating, like talking, is patterned activity, and the daily menu may be made to yield an analogy with linguistic form." Which is to say that menus and other culinary protocols often dramatize and symbolize complex social and cultural realities.[9]

Just as food's significance and the powers of the cook have long been elaborated in tales and poems, the *dailiness* of such edibles as Marcel's madeleine has been a subject of aesthetic representation, literary analysis and philosophical discussion. It is of this quotidian gastronomy that Brillat-Savarin, Proust, Rabelais and Bakhtin speak—of the gastronomy that is "transcendental" not in mystifying or sanctifying food but in reflecting self-consciously on the physical, emotional and social experiences of obtaining and preparing food, tasting it, swallowing it, feasting on it or rejecting it. "Transcendental gastronomy" has been represented by literary artists from Homer and Horace to all the major European and American novelists, the great modernists and the contemporary poets and novelists whom I will discuss later in this book. In particular, until the last century or so, such writings on "Master Belly" and "his" need for daily bread have focused on food for three apparently quite different reasons: first, to moralize on right and wrong attitudes toward eating; second, to analyze the manners and mores of eating—that is, the customs surrounding food in various kinds and levels of society; and third, to celebrate the community represented by culinary modes. But the three motives for gastronomic writing are interlinked, too, since moralizings on food inevitably reflect the diverse mores of the table, and celebrations of food frequently reinforce or repudiate the morals and manners of dining.

The Morality of Renunciation

One of the most notable meals in nineteenth-century American literature isn't eaten by those for whom it's been cooked. Early on Christmas morning, as the four young heroines of Louisa May Alcott's *Little Women* are gathered at the table, "eager for breakfast," their adored Marmee bursts into the room with a greeting—and a sermon.

> Merry Christmas, little daughters! . . . But I want to say one word before we sit down. Not far away from here lies a poor woman with a little newborn baby. Six children are huddled into one bed to keep from freezing, for they have no fire. There is nothing to eat over there, and the oldest boy came to tell me they were suffering hunger and cold. My girls, will you give them your breakfasts as a Christmas present?

And indeed, although the girls are "unusually hungry, having waited nearly an hour" for their mother to return from holiday errands, they happily agree to her request, so we soon see them officiating at the impoverished family's table, feeding the six immigrant children "like so many hungry birds, laughing, talking and trying to understand the funny broken English." Perhaps because what is good to eat must be good to *think*, the experience of watching the deprived children eat what was to have been the March family's Christmas morning meal becomes a spiritual festivity for Meg, Jo, Beth, and Amy.[10]

"That was a very happy breakfast, though they didn't get any of it," comments Alcott, adding that when the sisters "went away, leaving comfort behind . . . there were not in all the city four merrier people than the hungry little girls who gave away their breakfasts and contented themselves with bread and milk on Christmas morning." Here food—cream, muffins, "buckwheats"—is powerful to the story's protagonists precisely because they haven't consumed it. Instead, the renunciation practiced by the "little women" gives special meaning to the *idea* of food as a sign of a "transcendental gastronomy" rooted in hunger and service. To be sure, the children are almost immediately compensated for their morality with a communal meal of bread and milk not unlike the meal of madeleine and tea that Proust's Marcel consumes, and also, therefore, not unlike the simple bread and wine of the Christian service. But perhaps even more important, they are ultimately rewarded at a secular banquet whose magical appearance sets the plot of Alcott's novel in motion, just as Proust's madeleine—very differently—triggered the author's remembrances of things past: Old Mr. Laurence, the eccentric recluse next door, sends over "ice cream, actually two dishes of it, pink and white, and cake and fruit and distracting French bonbons" because, explains the all-wise Marmee, he heard from "one of his servants about your breakfast party" and wanted the children to "have a little feast at night to make up for the bread-and-milk breakfast." And the very next day the girls meet his grandson Laurie, the hero—if there is one—of their story.

In traditional theological texts the renunciation of food isn't usually rewarded with such profane pleasures as ice cream, bonbons and boyfriends. The medieval nuns, monks and saints whose habits of fasting Caroline Bynum has so brilliantly studied became, as in one of Emily Dickinson's poems, "inebriate[s] of air," not gastronomic delicacies. If they were rewarded with any physical foodstuff, it was the *panis angelicus* of the Eucharist, the "celestial bread" that "hell cannot digest." But the discipline that Marmee imposes on her daughters isn't the rule of the convents and monasteries—a rule essentially founded on Gregory of Nyssa's assertion in the fourth century that taste is "the mother of all vice."[11] Rather, her devotion to humility and service is rooted in the Protestant—originally Puritan—ethic of the New England in which Alcott herself was raised. In addition, it has connections with the Transcendentalist philosophy practiced by Henry David Thoreau, Ralph Waldo Emerson, and Louisa May Alcott's unworldly father, Bronson Alcott.

Thoreau famously spent several hermit-like years on the shore of Walden Pond, where his diet was virtuously frugal. In *Walden*, he notes that his "expense of food for eight months" was a mere $8.74, adding that he also consumed "potatoes, a little green corn, and some peas, which I had raised" along with some of the beans he grew in his two-and-a-half acre bean field. The purchases he lists include:

Rice . . . . $ 1.73 ½
Molasses . . . . 1.73 Cheapest form of the saccharine.
Rye meal . . . . 1.04 ¾
Indian meal . . . . 0.99 ¾ Cheaper than rye.
Pork . . . . 0.22 . . .
Flour. . . . . 0.88 Costs more than Indian meal, both money and trouble.
Sugar 0.80
Lard 0.65
Apples 0.25
Dried apple 0.22
Sweet potatoes 0.10
One pumpkin 0.06
One watermelon 0.02
Salt . . . . 0.03[12]

Bronson Alcott's version of this austere culinary morality was even more radical, and his daughter certainly understood it even while she significantly modified it—and explained why in a scathing account of bitter experience.[13]

"Transcendental Wild Oats" dramatizes Louisa's view of the Alcott family's trials at Fruitlands, a utopian community that Bronson helped found in the early 1840s. Residents of this idealistic enclave forswore most of the pleasures of the table. Wrote the reformer Charles Lane, another of its founders, "Neither coffee, tea, molasses, nor rice tempts us beyond the bounds of indigenous production," and he added that "No animal substances neither flesh, butter, cheese, eggs, nor milk pollute our tables, nor corrupt our bodies." In fact, notes one historian, "nothing from animals (including wool, honey, wax, or manure) nor even animal labor were used by the community. The founders felt men should not take anything from animals, for they should be as free as humans. Bronson Alcott's idealism was so strong, in fact, that he would not permit canker-worms to be disturbed, and forbade the planting of such vegetables and roots as grow downward instead of upward into the air."[14]

Unfortunately, this utopian experiment proved to most of the participants that the renunciation of worldly goods and desires along with the traditional techniques of agriculture would be unrewarded on this earth, for the vegan paradise that Fruitlands was supposed to become proved fruitless. Without fertilizer and with no animals to help plant and harvest, the table over which the woman who was the original of Marmee had to preside was meager indeed, as Alcott sardonically observed:

> Unleavened bread, porridge, and water for breakfast; bread, vegetables, and water for dinner; bread, fruit, and water for supper was the bill of fare ordained by the elders. No teapot profaned that sacred stove, no gory steak cried aloud for vengeance from her chaste gridiron; and only a brave woman's taste, time, and temper were sacrificed on that domestic altar.

Given such a history, it isn't surprising that in her role as author of *Little Women* Alcott bestows an ice cream party on her young heroines even while she celebrates the holiday goodwill that shapes their willingness *not* to eat breakfast.[15]

But that the food the four sisters eat or don't eat is by and large simple (buckwheats, muffins, cream, bread and milk, ice cream), with the exception of those French bonbons, reflects not only a Puritan ethic but an early American gastronomic ideology that defined itself very self-consciously against what the colonists considered the excesses of Old World cuisine. Of course, the settlers' culinary virtue was partly born of geographical necessity. Some of the more realistic novelists writing in the first decades of the nineteenth century garnished stories of Puritan hardship with accounts of strange—and tough or sparse—New World foods. The narrator of Lydia Maria Child's *Hobomok* described a breakfast "only of roasted pumpkin, a plentiful supply of clams, and coarse cakes made of pounded maize," and the protagonist of Catharine Sedgwick's *Hope Leslie* remembers a time when "the best in the colony were reduced to living upon muscles [sic], acorns, and ground nuts." But by and large, as the critic Mark McWilliams has noted, American colonists made the best of gastronomic hardship by evolving a "myth of republican simplicity" that celebrates "the simple, wholesome food" of their new land—"baked beans, cornbread in all its forms, roast game and pork, and the New England boiled dinner."

Corn, in particular—perhaps the most widely available local ingredient—was lauded as "a good wholesome and simple dish" in comparison to "the monstrous and hellish compositions of modern cookery" consumed in England and on the continent.[16] In 1793 Joel Barlow's popular poem "The Hasty-Pudding" lauded this "delicious grain" in what became a quintessential American culinary manifesto:

> *To mix the food by vicious rules of art,*
> *To kill the stomach and sink the heart . . .*
> *From this the kitchen Muse first framed her book,*
> *Commanding sweats to stream from every cook;*
> *Children no more their antic gambols tried,*
> *And friends to physic wonder'd why they died.*
> *Not so the Yankee—his abundant feast,*
> *With simples furnished, and with plainness drest,*
> *A numerous offspring gathers round the board,*
> *And cheers alike the servant and the lord;*
> *Whose well-bought hunger prompts the joyous taste,*
> *And health attends them from the short repast.*

"A simplicity in diet, whether it be considered with reference to the happiness of individuals or the prosperity of a nation, is of more consequence than we are apt to imagine," declared Barlow in a preface to his mock epic. And indeed, according to the vision of the virtues of corn meal (or "Indian") pudding that the poem offers, the luxury-loving "kitchen Muse" of the Old World prepares dishes that don't just metaphorically "kill the stomach," they actually kill little children, who cease "their antic gambols" and sink into the grave after consuming viciously artful dinners! No wonder Marmee feeds her girls a plain diet of muffins and buckwheat pancakes, bread and milk. Health, as well as morality, "attends [the] short repast."[17]

To be sure, despite colonial American attacks on the excesses of the "kitchen Muse" who ruled Old World cuisine, there is a long European tradition of gastronomic moralizing that, in its way, equals American admonitions about simplicity. In *The Republic*, for instance, Plato sermonizes against "Syracusan dinners, and the refinements of Sicilian cookery" as well as "Athenian confectionery," noting that "such feeding" is like "melody and song composed" in a style that engenders "license" as well as disease. Thus, just as "simplicity in music" is "the parent of temperance in the soul," so simplicity in cuisine fosters health. When "intemperance and disease multiply in a State, halls of justice and medicine are always being opened; and the arts of the doctor and the lawyer give themselves airs." In fact, as the philosopher Elizabeth Telfer has remarked, "the doctrine of false pleasures [Plato] expounds in *The Republic*" is "a particularly striking attempt to show that the pleasures of food are not worth having" because they merely relieve from the discomfort of hunger rather than functioning as positive delights in themselves. If the belly is a wild animal, its savagery can perhaps be tamed by abstemiousness. In this view of matters gastronomic, Plato was probably influenced by Pythagoras, who was noted for repudiating animal food and who had himself been influenced, according to some scholars, by vegetarian Brahmin sages. Later, the Neoplatonist philosopher Porphyry also advocated a "fleshless diet."[18]

Among the great Roman writers, the poet Horace eloquently advocated moderation in all things. Worldly and witty, he never denied the primacy of material life as Plato did, but celebrated the virtues of simplicity much as the American colonists later would. Although in one of his satires Horace recorded with bemused interest a friend's "disquisition on gastronomy," in another he noted flatly that "A hungry stomach rarely despises common food," expressing contempt for the "man who is pale and bloated from gluttony" and explaining that if

> you've a deep-rooted inclination, when a peacock is served,
> to caress your palate with it rather than a chicken[,] Your judgement
> is impaired by what doesn't count: the bird is hard to come by,

it costs a packet, and its spreading tail is a colorful sight—
as if that mattered a damn! Do you actually eat those feathers
which you find so gorgeous?

Even when Horace extended an urbanely versified dinner invitation to a friend—working in a genre that was popular with other Roman poets—he modestly proposed that "If you can . . . face smallish helpings of vegetarian food, / I shall look forward . . . to seeing you here at sunset."[19]

Roman banqueting habits were, of course, notoriously marked by intemperance and extravagance, with some very wealthy diners even indulging in a form of bulimia: commented the poet-playwright Seneca, "They vomit so that they may eat and eat so that they may vomit." The longest extant portion of Petronius's *Satyricon* is devoted to an episode that's become known as "Trimalchio's Feast," in which a vulgarly rich Roman (who some think was modeled on the dissipated emperor Nero) hosts a bizarrely immoderate dinner, featuring such delicacies as "a wild boar of the largest possible size . . . wearing a freedman's cap on its head" and a calf "brought in on a two-hundred pound plate: it was boiled whole and wearing a helmet." Descending into chaos, the "absolutely sickening" meal sardonically proves the virtues of moderation. With almost the same verve, Horace depicts a comparably grotesque collation hosted by a "rich parvenu," at which an awning collapses on the dinner table but the host and guests recover from the accident to confront a banquet that includes "a huge dish with a crane / a male, ready-carved, liberally sprinkled with salt and meal" and "the liver of a white female goose fattened on figs" as well as other "tasty things" that no one really wants to swallow.[20]

The classical tradition of gastronomic moralizing persisted throughout the Middle Ages and the Renaissance into the eighteenth century and beyond, although specific arguments changed as society evolved in different ways. Where the medieval St. Gregory of Nyssa had declared that taste is "the mother of all Vice," the English Augustans and Romantics, along with the American Transcendentalists, joined Horace in praising the benefits of "natural" eating. In his magisterial "Essay on Man," Alexander Pope advised his readers that they should "from the creatures thy instructions take / Learn from the birds what food the thickets yield; / Learn from the beasts the physic of the field," while Nathaniel Hawthorne, recording a meal of fish he'd caught himself, accompanied by beans, corn and cucumbers from the family garden, exuberantly noted that "this day's food comes directly and entirely from beneficent Nature" and Thoreau, echoing Pope, declared that "Our diet, like that of the birds, must answer to the season."[21]

Similarly, just as Petronius and Horace satirized culinary excess, later poets scornfully critiqued the disease and degradation they associated with culinary immoderation. As we've seen, Dante consigned gluttons to the third circle of his *Inferno*, where they wallow in soil that "gives off a putrid odor" and are guarded by "Three-headed Cerberus, monstrous and cruel," who—like a horrific canine incarnation of uncontrolled hunger—ceaselessly barks at them from his "triple throat":

> *His eyes are red, his beard*
> *Grease-black, he has the belly of a meat-feeder*
>
> *And talons on his hands: he claws the horde*
> *Of spirits, he flays and quarters them in the rain.*
> *The wretches, howling like dogs where they are mired*
>
> *And pelted, squirm about again and again.*[22]

Some centuries later, Jonathan Swift's "Modest Proposal" to roast and eat year-old Irish babies indignantly parodied the moral indifference of the voracious organ Rabelais called "Master Belly," whose cravings, he implied, prompted the English imperialists to swallow the land that belonged to the starving people of Ireland.

By the late eighteenth century, as Tristram Stuart has shown in *The Bloodless Revolution,* his magisterial history of vegetarianism, poets and polemicists were railing as passionately as Porphyry against the eating of meat: Bronson Alcott's experiment at Fruitlands arguably had its origin in their theories.

Many were acolytes of doctrines formulated by the notorious British physician George Cheyne, who had been a "drunken fatso" before converting to "a diet of milk with *Seeds, Bread, mealy Roots,* and *Fruit*" while averring that "I cannot find any great difference between feeding on human flesh and feeding on animal flesh, except custom and practice." The novelist–publisher Samuel Richardson followed Cheyne's "Regimen" and renounced "Wine, Flesh, and Fish." In France, Jean-Jacques Rousseau, the *philosophe* who helped devise the dream of the "noble savage," propounded vegetarianism in *Julie, ou La Nouvelle Heloïse* and *Émile, ou de l'Éducation*, declaring in the latter work that the "indifference of children towards meat is one proof that the taste for meat is unnatural."[23]

A political as well as aesthetic radical, Percy Shelley advanced the same ideas in verse and prose. In "A Vindication of Natural Diet" (1813) he argued that "There is no disease, bodily or mental, which adoption of vegetable diet and pure water has not infallibly mitigated, wherever the experiment has been fairly tried" and noted with revulsion that "It is only by softening and disguising dead flesh by culinary preparation, that it is rendered susceptible of mastication or digestion; and that the sight of its bloody juices and raw horror, does not excite intolerable loathing and disgust." Mary Wollstonecraft Shelley, his wife and the author of the bestselling fantasy *Frankenstein, or, The Modern Prometheus,* agreed, creating an innately benevolent monster who explains that "My food is not that of man; I do not destroy the lamb and the kid to glut my appetite; acorns and berries afford me sufficient nourishment." Clearly both Percy and Mary Shelley saw their vegetarian remarks as not only medical and ethical but political statements about the distinctions between those arrogant (and wealthy) enough to eat luxurious meat meals and those who subsist, humbly and gratefully, on "acorns and berries."[24]

In a comparably political vein, the American ex-slave Frederick Douglass detailed in one of his autobiographies the gulf between the diets of slaves and masters on the Maryland plantation where he grew up. The slaves, he explained, lived on "ash cake"—a coarse flat bread baked in the hearth, which, "with its ashes and bran, would disgust and choke a northern man"—while their owners indulged in Lucullan feasts:

> The table groans under the heavy and blood-bought luxuries gathered with pains-taking care, at home and abroad. Fields, forests, rivers and seas, are made tributary here. Immense wealth, and its lavish expenditure, fill the great house with all that can please the eye or tempt the taste. Here, appetite, not food, is the great *desideratum*.

And yet, added Douglass, the "poor slave, on his hard, pine plank . . . sleeps more soundly than the feverish voluptuary who reclines upon his feather bed and downy pillow." For "to the indolent lounger," food "is poison, not sustenance. Lurking beneath all their dishes, are invisible spirits of evil, ready to feed the self-deluded gourmandizers with," among other ills, "dyspepsia, rheumatism, lumbago and gout."[25]

Though writers in all genres persistently brooded on gastronomic morals, it was often in prose narratives that such issues were most fully dramatized. Flaubert's *Madame Bovary*, for instance, tells the painful story of Emma Bovary, a romance-reading young provincial woman whose dissatisfaction with the bourgeois narrowness of her life leads her into several ill-fated adulterous affairs. Quite early, the book documents this protagonist's desirousness through her disgust with the simple fare her husband loves and her yearning for delicacies like those she first encounters on a visit to a local chateau. Whereas Charles eats plain "boiled beef and onions" along with pieces of cheese, an apple, and water, then goes to bed and snores, Emma finds the "iced champagne" at the chateau so enticing that she "shiver[s] all over," feeling it "cold in her mouth." Here too she sees exotic fruits for the first time—pomegranates and pineapples—while even the sugar seems "whiter and finer than elsewhere."[26] Later in the novel, when Emma's rich lover, the libertine Rodolphe, decides to leave her, he hides a farewell note beneath a gift basket of apricots from his estate—and ironically, just when her innocent husband is urging one on her at dinner, she catches sight of her lover's carriage leaving town and falls down in a faint. Her husband explains to his friend, the local pharmacist, that "she had been taken ill suddenly while she was eating some apricots" and the chemist comments that perhaps "the apricots had brought on the syncope." And indeed, as a stand-in for the world of deceptive luxury in which she has been ensnared, the roué's apricots have sickened Emma.

In the end, however, it is the ingestion of a different substance—the arsenic she seizes from the same pharmacist's storeroom—that sickens her unto death. Tellingly, she experiences her demise on her tongue, in her mouth and gullet. As she lies dying—in one of the most explicitly horrifying death scenes in the nineteenth-century novel—she notes, to begin with, "the frightful taste of ink" and keeps "constantly opening her mouth as if something very heavy were weighing upon her tongue"—figuratively speaking, the ink and paper of the romantic fantasies she has so gullibly devoured. Then begin hours of spasmodic vomiting, literally a consequence of arsenic poisoning, but again figuratively a reaction to all the illicit delicacies this eager adulteress has swallowed. A famous physician is sent for but pronounces that nothing can be done. And as Emma fades on her deathbed, in another moment of gastronomic irony the pharmacist begs the celebrated doctor to do him "the signal honour of accepting some breakfast" and sends "quickly to the 'Lion d'Or' for some pigeons; to the butcher's for all the cutlets that were to be had; to Tuvache for cream; and to Lestiboudois for eggs." As for the unfortunate Madame Bovary, even in death she continues to regurgitate the poisonous food of romance: as she is being dressed for the grave in her wedding gown and bridal wreath, someone has to raise her head for a moment, "and a rush of black liquid issue[s], as if she were vomiting, from her mouth."

Where Flaubert powerfully delineated the terrible consequences of Emma's hungers for socially forbidden foods, three of his contemporaries just as scathingly dramatized the immorality of a culture that smugly allows the poor to hunger for any food at all. In Victor Hugo's *Les Miserables,* the convict Jean Valjean has been imprisoned for stealing a loaf of bread to feed his family—an event that triggers the whole plot of the novel—while in Charles Dickens's *Oliver Twist* the nine-year-old orphaned hero is rebuked when, "desperate with hunger, and reckless with misery," he tremblingly asks a "fat healthy" master of his workhouse for more gruel:

> The master aimed a blow at Oliver's head with the ladle; pinioned him in his arms; and shrieked aloud for the beadle . . .
>
> "Mr. Limbkins, I beg your pardon, sir! Oliver Twist has asked for more!" . . .
>
> "For more!" said Mr. Limbkins. "Compose yourself, Bumble, and answer me distinctly. Do I understand that he asked for more, after he had eaten the supper allotted by the dietary?"
>
> "He did, sir," replied Bumble.
>
> "That boy will be hung," said the gentleman in the white waistcoat. "I know that boy will be hung."[27]

This classically Dickensian scene is almost comic in the contrasts between the little that the child requests to supplement the dangerously meager "supper allotted by the dietary" and the stout solemnity of the well-fed "gentleman" who predicts his doom. But, like Jean Valjean's theft of bread, Oliver's poignant plea for food has far-reaching consequences, shaping the plot of the novel that follows, in which the child only gets the sustenance he needs when he becomes a member of a gang of thieves. Almost as bizarre—and similarly poignant—are the scenes in Charlotte Brontë's *Jane Eyre* where the orphaned heroine finds herself freezing and starving at the charity institution allegorically named Lowood. Quite early in her stay there, the hypocrisy of the school's administrator, the horrific Mr. Brocklehurst, is dramatized when he complains to the kindly principal, Miss Temple, "that a lunch, consisting of bread and cheese, has twice been served out to the girls during the past fortnight. How is this? I looked over the regulations, and I find no such meal as lunch mentioned. Who introduced this innovation? and by what authority?" When Miss Temple responds that she ordered the meal because "the breakfast was so ill prepared that the pupils could not possibly eat it; and I dared not allow them to remain fasting till dinner-time," he responds with a gastronomic homily:

> "Madam . . . You are aware that my plan in bringing up these girls is, not to accustom them to habits of luxury and indulgence. . . . Should any little accidental disappointment of the appetite occur,

> such as the spoiling of a meal, [the incident] ought to be improved to the spiritual edification of the pupils [by reminding them] that man shall not live by bread alone. . . . Oh, madam, when you put bread and cheese, instead of burnt porridge, into these children's mouths, you may indeed feed their vile bodies, but you little think how you starve their immortal souls!"[28]

If the overfed guardians who plan such an inadequate "dietary" for Oliver and his mates represent a system of profound economic injustice fattening and battening on the poor, Brocklehurst—whom Jane initially describes as a "black pillar" with a "grim face at the top . . . like a carved mask"—is not only an agent of such injustice but also a pillar of righteous patriarchal culture that would starve orphan girls in the name of the law and the Lord. Both children, however, are granted furtive moments of culinary celebration in the midst of starvation. Oliver's is more problematic, for he's decently fed only when he encounters the Artful Dodger, who will later lead him into a life of crime but at first gives him a "long and hearty meal" of beer and "ready-dressed ham and a half-quartern loaf." Jane, by comparison, has a more spiritual experience, with more elegant food. She joins her saintly friend Helen Burns in Miss Temple's private parlor, where they feast on "generous slices" of a seed cake that they experience as "nectar and ambrosia," though, remarks Jane, "not the least delight of the entertainment was the smile of gratification with which our hostess regarded us, as we satisfied our famished appetites on the delicate fare she liberally supplied."

The morals here are clear. The food that the Dodger offers out of cynical self-interest is at the least ambiguous; though Oliver requires it, it has at first quite dire consequences for him. But the food that Miss Temple produces out of pure kindness embodies a maternal ethic grounded in a Christian charity utterly foreign to the sanctimonious Brocklehurst—or, for that matter, to Dickens's fat gentlemen. Thus, while Oliver has to learn to refuse the meals prepared by Fagin and his gang, Jane will be nourished through all her trials by Miss Temple's allegorically resonant "seed cake." Arguably, indeed, the celebratory moment that she and the dying Helen enjoy in their beloved teacher's warm room will sustain them through dark tribulations to come—Helen's death, Jane's grief, and Jane's onward pilgrimage to adulthood. Such celebrations are akin not only to the ice cream supper that Alcott's four little women revel in but also to what is perhaps an even better known feast: the holiday dinner that Dickens's Scrooge provides in *A Christmas Carol* when, redeemed and renewed, he sends the impoverished Cratchits a turkey that's "twice the size" of their hungry, crippled child, Tiny Tim, and in his generosity seconds the little boy's Christlike prayer, "God bless us, every one."[29]

The Morality of Celebration

Dickens described Christmas, with its feasts and gifts, as a "charitable, pleasant time: the only time I know of in the long calendar of the year, when men and women seem by one consent to open their shut-up hearts freely, and to think of other people below them as if they really were fellow-passengers to the grave, and not another race of creatures bound on other journeys." But the Christmas holiday is arguably a time of charity—*caritas*—in an even larger sense, for its seasonal placement, as many scholars agree, suggests its origins in the Roman feast of Saturnalia, a holiday whose festive generosity and liberation from quotidian laws make it a paradigm of what Bakhtin has called the carnivalesque. Celebrated annually around the time of the winter solstice, Saturnalia was a festival where customary hierarchies were revised or dissolved. In this period, notes one historian, "the roles of master and slave were reversed in the household. Either the master and his family dined with the slaves [or] the slaves ate extravagantly." And every night, after meals, there were wild, merry, and drunken games over which any one in the group—including slaves—could be chosen by lot to act as Saturnalian "king," with the power to order others to "commit any absurdity."[30]

Writes Bakhtin, the Saturnalia was "perceived as a true and full, though temporary, return of Saturn's golden age upon earth" and its tradition "remained unbroken and alive in the medieval carnival, which expressed this universal renewal and was vividly felt as an escape from the usual official way of life." Great tables laden with food were invariably part of this return of a "golden age" where both want and renunciation were unknown. Whether on the Roman equivalents of ice cream and seed cake, on turkeys twice the size of little boys, or hams and sausages and suckling pigs crowned—as in *Satyricon*—with a "freedman's cap" or decked with holly and ivy, the celebrants of Saturnalia, like our celebrants of Christmas and New Year, banqueted freely, even excessively, as they reenacted what Bakhtin describes as an entrance into "the utopian realm of community, freedom, equality, and abundance." The pieties enunciated by the Bumbles and Brocklehursts who rule the official institutions of workhouse and orphanage were shattered; even the sincere austerities of Alcott and Thoreau were vigorously repudiated. The motto of such a festivity is perhaps best expressed by Sir Toby Belch, Feste the clown, and Sir Andrew Aguecheek in *Twelfth Night* (a play whose title refers to the feast of the Epiphany that is the twelfth day of the traditionally extended Christmas holidays). Scoffing at the prim steward Malvolio, the two carousing knights, accompanied by the fool, stagger about the stage taunting the man's puritanism: "Dost thou think, because thou art virtuous, there shall be no cakes and ale?" sneers Sir Toby. "Yes, by Saint Anne," echoes Feste, "and ginger shall be hot i' the mouth too!"[31]

Sir Toby's dream realm—and the kind of space inhabited by Rabelais's gigantic eaters—is akin to the medieval fantasy kingdom known as the land of Cockayne. Here the whole world is a kind of utopian kitchen in which food and wine—and sexual pleasure too!—offer themselves endlessly to luxuriating consumers. Even the buildings are edible, and roasted birds (geese, "with plenty of garlic," and delectable larks) jump into wide open mouths:

> *There are private rooms and large halls;*
> *The walls are all of pies, of meat, of fish, and rich food,*
> *The most pleasing that a person can eat.*
> *All the shingles are cakes made of flour,*
> *On the church, the cloister, and the hall.*
> *The pegs are fat sausages.*

And all this "Rich food fit for princes and kings" is available to hungry peasants, starved travelers, and supposedly abstemious monks: Master Belly rules indeed![32]

Not everyone was ready to celebrate that rule. In the moralizing tradition to which fictional and real figures (Malvolio to Bronson Alcott) belong, satirists inveighed against the unearned satiety that was its hallmark. A painting by Pieter Bruegel the Elder, titled *Het Luilekkerland*, meaning "the lazy-luscious-land," depicts slothful gluttons lying limply beneath a table bent under the weight of half-eaten goodies, next to a river of milk and under a cloud of pudding from which one unfortunate is struggling to extricate himself. And in the New World Benjamin Franklin, an advocate of colonial austerity, warned "Those Who Would Remove to America" that "America is the land of labour, and by No means what the English call Lubberland, and the French Pays de Cocagne, where the streets are said to be paved with half-peck loaves, the houses tiled with pancakes, and where the fowls fly about ready roasted, crying *Come eat me!*" Nonetheless, the fantasy of endless easy food is hard to eradicate: it is inherent in biblical visions of the land of milk and honey and it persists in American dreams of the Big Rock Candy Mountain; it speaks to and for children (as we'll see in a later chapter) in tales about gingerbread houses and giant peaches, about chocolate factories and "the Good Ship Lollipop"; and of course it literally manifests itself in all-you-can-eat buffets and in saturnalian New Year's Eve parties.[33]

In exploring the writings of Rabelais, Bakhtin examines legends about "the utopian land of gluttony and idleness (for instance, the *fabliau* of the *pays de Cocagne*)." But his powerful theories of the carnivalesque are deeply rooted in his analysis of Rabelais's *Gargantua and Pantagruel,* a spicy fantasy about ravenously hungry giants and their friends whose actions and meditations frequently turn to the sort of irreverent banqueting in which Shakespeare's appropriately named Sir Toby Belch indulges. From Gargantua's birth in the midst of a feast at which Gargamelle, his mother, has eaten "sixteen barrels, two casks, and six pots besides" of tripe to his son Pantagruel's encounter with the worshippers of Master Belly, Rabelais's work focuses on fabulous lists and quantities of foods, dishes, kitchens, cooks and cauldrons to celebrate the culinary arts of the quotidian rather than the sacred meals of the Church. That swallowing and imbibing are thematic is dramatized, too, when Gargamelle's gastronomic feat ends with a treatment causing "every sphincter in her body" to lock up so that her child is born from her ear shouting "Drink! Drink!" instead of "Wa! Wa!" That such carnal consumption is irreligious, even blasphemous, is hinted at by this birth scene's parodic reversal of the Virgin Mary's supposed impregnation with the Word of the Holy Ghost through her ear, an image depicted in numerous Renaissance paintings of the Annunciation.

Beyond these moments, Rabelais's plot turns throughout on bizarre culinary events. Book 1 features a war between the Bakers of Lerné and the Bakers of Gargantua's Country, which ends in a "fine feast of flatcakes and grapes," while book 4, a picaresque narrative in which the hero and his friends undertake a journey in search of the Oracle of the Divine Bottle, relates the extraordinary history of the battle between "the furious Sausages" who inhabit "Wildmen's Island, the Ancestral Home of the Fat Sausages" and an army of cooks sailing against them in the good ships *Monk's Drinking Mug, Toasting Glass*, and *Market Basket.* In between, the infant Pantagruel gobbles half a cow from whose udders he's nursing and snacks on "a great bear" his father keeps as a pet, "crunching him up like a chicken, and making a fine hot mouthful of him," while his friend, the monk Brother John, describes his dream of heaven as "God's fine kitchen" and explains that "monks like being in kitchens" just as much as poets do. Finally, book 4 climaxes with an enormous catalog of the foods the gluttonous Belly Worshippers sacrifice to "Their Belly-Potent God," and book 5 ends with a ceremonial visit to the Oracle of the Sacred Bottle.[34]

The menu dear to the Belly Worshippers occupies many pages and includes such savory items as:

shoulder of mutton in garlic
meat pies in hot sauce
pork chops with onions
roast capons in gravy
chickens
ducks
goats
fawns and bucks
rabbits and hares
partridges and chicks

beef royale, sliced
breast of veal
boiled chicken and fat capons with blancmanges

And "on Fish and Fasting Days":

caviar
pressed caviar
fresh butter
thick pea soup
spinach
sweet white herring

And on and on for several more pages. By contrast, Pantagruel's final encounter with the parodically Divine Bottle ends when "the sacred Bottle gave forth a sound like that made by bees bred in the flesh of a young bull, sacrificed and dressed [for cooking] . . . or like the roar of a crossbow . . . or like a strong summer rain. . . . And then a single word sounded: " '*Trink!*' " The pilgrims inevitably and rightly interpret this single utterance as meaning "that it is drinking, not laughter which makes men human" and specifically understand that it is an imperative to drink wine, for "in drinking wine you find yourself divine." Thus, with a celebration of principled intemperance following an immoderate listing of the pleasures of the table, the mock *Odyssey* of Pantagruel concludes.

In his Christian sentimentality as well as in his realistic depictions of Victorian courtrooms, prisons and workhouses, Dickens is to be sure profoundly different from Rabelais. Yet his comment that Christmas is a time "when men and women seem by one consent to open their shut-up hearts freely, and to think of other people below them as if they really were fellow-passengers to the grave" implicitly proposes the same utopian time-out-of-time feasting that the sixteenth-century French writer praises. As a journey toward the grave, quotidian reality requires the relief of the timeless holiday banquet, whose culinary rituals preserve in themselves a celebration of life for its own joys, a delight in how time-bound flesh is redeemed by timeless fleshly delights. Thus though the Christmas celebrations Dickens imagines may not be instances of

Rabelaisian carnival like those Bakhtin defines, they are in their own ways instances of festive liberation and liberality. Like Alcott's ice cream party, the Christmas dinner that Scrooge attends at his nephew's house, as well as the Cratchits' meal over which the author envisions Tiny Tim presiding, represent moments of reconciliation through communal dining—through, that is, a sharing of food that sacramentalizes the ordinary. Bakhtin notes that "even within bourgeois culture the festive element did not die" because the "feast is a primary, indestructible ingredient of human civilization." Thus the "private" feast "still preserves the ancient spirit; on feast days the doors of the home are open to guests, as they were originally open to 'all the world,' " and, like the banquet of Rabelais's fantasy, the later, "bourgeois" banquet marks "a temporary transfer to the utopian world."[35]

Nor is the private party that Bakhtin calls the bourgeois feast necessarily linked to specific holidays, although, like the Bakhtinian feast, it occupies a kind of regenerative time-out-of-time. Such resonant banquets appear in—among numerous later works—Kate Chopin's *The Awakening,* James Joyce's "The Dead," and Virginia Woolf's *To the Lighthouse.* In the first of these, the protagonist's gradual awakening to a larger reality than her life as a properly dutiful wife and mother is marked, at key points, by ceremonial meals. A kind of revisionary Emma Bovary—Willa Cather dismissively called her "a creole Bovary"—Chopin's Edna Pontellier achieves selfhood through romance although she ultimately chooses to cast aside the trappings of erotic desire. But one of her first literal and figurative awakenings takes place on the Louisiana island of Chenière Caminada, where she has gone to attend Mass with her almost-lover Robert Lebrun after a midnight swim the night before. When she's overcome with drowsiness during the service, the attentive Robert brings her to the nearby cottage of Madame Antoine, where she naps in "a strange, quaint bed" like the heroine of a fairy tale, then awakens to discover that a ritual meal of bread and wine has been left for her:

> She was very hungry. No one was there. But there was a cloth spread upon the table that stood against the wall, and a cover was laid for one, with a crusty brown loaf and a bottle of wine beside the plate. Edna bit a piece from the brown loaf, tearing it with her

> strong, white teeth. Then she went softly out of doors, and plucking an orange from the low-hanging bough of a tree, threw it at Robert, who did not know she was awake and up.

Here a secular collation of bread and wine—accompanied by the plucking of what may be allegorically forbidden fruit—literally replaces the eucharistic feast of the Mass, and then is followed by another meal in which, in a revision of gender arrangements that parallels the revision of theological tradition, Robert prepares and serves Edna a broiled fowl.

Toward the end of the book, once she has decided to leave her husband's house for a small space of her own, Edna arranges for herself a more public banquet. On this occasion, notes the narrator,

> There was something extremely gorgeous about the appearance of the table . . . There were wax candles in massive brass candelabra, burning softly under yellow silk shades; full, fragrant roses . . . abounded. There were silver and gold . . . and crystal which glittered like the gems which the women wore.
>
> The ordinary stiff dining chairs had been discarded for the occasion and replaced by the most commodious and luxurious which could be collected throughout the house.

And here, "Before each guest stood a tiny glass that looked and sparkled like a garnet gem"—a special cocktail that Edna's father has "composed." As for Edna herself, we are told that "There was something in her attitude, in her whole appearance when she leaned her head against the high-backed chair and spread her arms, which suggested the regal woman, the one who rules, who looks on, who stands alone."[36] In fact, in its worldliness this banquet constitutes a kind of mock Last Supper, marking Edna's definitive transformation from her old bourgeois self to a new "solitary soul" who can no longer live within the structures she has heretofore inhabited. The feast over which she now presides is as bitter as it is sweet, marking her turn away from the communities of her past in search of a new communion—a consummation she is to find only in a final swim toward death.[37]

In Joyce's "The Dead," as in Woolf's *To the Lighthouse,* similarly worldly—and poignant—feasts are celebrated. "The Dead" is set at an annual Christmas dance hosted by the spinster aunts of the protagonist, Gabriel Conroy—but Gabriel does the honors at the table, carving the meats and toasting the assembled company. Joyce describes the heavily laden banquet board in meticulous culinary detail, as if touring a geography of gastronomy:

> A fat brown goose lay at one end of the table and at the other end . . . lay a great ham . . . and beside this was a round of spiced beef. Between these rival ends ran parallel lines of side-dishes . . . In the centre of the table there stood, as sentries to a fruit-stand . . . two squat old-fashioned decanters of cut glass, one containing port and the other dark sherry. On the closed square piano a pudding in a huge yellow dish lay in waiting and behind it were three squads of bottles of stout and ale and minerals, drawn up according to the colours of their uniforms.[38]

It's notable that underlying this holiday plenitude there's an extended military metaphor: the ham and beef are "rival ends"; the fruit stand is flanked by "sentries"; the other drinks are lined up in "squads" and known by "the colours of their uniforms." The feast here, as in Bakhtin's account of Rabelais, seeks to triumph over death and yet—unlike most Rabelaisian feasts or, for that matter, Dickens's Christmas party—it struggles to hold off death.

Perhaps a key element of the modernist banquet inheres precisely in the explicit failure of Chopin's and Joyce's festivities to defeat death either through fantasies of regeneration or through a vision of eternal renewal. Though Edna Pontellier is depicted as "the regal woman," she is also (perhaps for this reason) "the one who stands alone"—and in the course of her dinner, enthroned among her guests, she experiences the sense of "hopelessness which so often assailed her, which came upon her like . . . a chill breath . . . from some vast cavern wherein discords wailed." Similarly, although Gabriel Conroy gallantly toasts his hostesses and leaves their party in a fever of desire for his wife, his passion is chilled when he discovers that a song sung by another guest has brought back—like a ghost at the feast—her memory of Michael

Furey, the long-buried lover of her youth. Paradoxically, rather than cheering and comforting him, the Christmas dinner has reminded Gabriel that "one by one," he, his aunts, and their other guests "were all becoming shades," so that he feels his soul approaching "that region where dwell the vast hosts of the dead [and his] own identity . . . fading out into a grey impalpable world."

A comparable melancholy marks the dinner that is a climactic moment in *To the Lighthouse.* Almost as famous as Proust's madeleine in the history of the modernist novel is the great casserole of *boeuf en daube* that the beautiful, mythically maternal Mrs. Ramsay ladles out for the guests in her summer home. Collected around the table, the company are knit together, like Edna's friends, in a candlelit circle where they enact their various roles in an almost stylized fashion—the host is irritable because one guest has asked for more soup, the hostess's children are mocking her passion for clean dairies, the rebellious Lily Briscoe is dreaming of her painting—but all ultimately partake of the ceremonial meal put before them, which, Mrs. Ramsay privately decides, should honor the just-announced engagement of two young friends at the dinner party:

> The cook had spent three days over that dish. . . . And she peered into [it], with its shiny walls and its confusion of savory brown and yellow meats and its bay leaves and its wine, and thought, This will celebrate the occasion—a curious sense rising in her, at once freakish and tender, of celebrating a festival.[39]

Triumphing as she doles out this delicious concoction based on "a French recipe of [her] grandmother's," Mrs. Ramsay muses that such moments of festive unity "partook, she felt, carefully helping Mr. Bankes to a specially tender piece, of eternity." And from a Bakhtinian perspective, the group has in a sense eaten a tender piece of eternity as they briefly enter a utopian space in which they are "all conscious of making a party together in a hollow, on an island; [where they have] their common cause against that fluidity out there." Yet as she rises from the table Mrs. Ramsay is suddenly overwhelmed by the same intuition of mortality that engulfs both Gabriel Conroy and Edna Pontellier. Hearing the voices of her husband and his friend Augustus Carmichael chanting lines about the passage of time—"all the lives we ever lived and all the lives to be"—she realizes that the scene she is leaving "was vanishing even as she looked," that "it had become . . . already the past."

In one sense, all feasting—from the Roman to the Rabelaisian, from the Dickensian to the Woolfian—is transcultural and ahistorical. "Our feasts are the movement of the needle which sews together the parts of our reed roofs, making of them a single roof, one single world," explained a New Caledonian native to the renowned anthropologist Marcel Mauss.[40] And we in the industrialized West are also knitted together by the traditions of public and private feasting we continue to celebrate today—Christmases and birthdays, seders and New Years' suppers, Thanksgivings and Easters. Yet our ways of feasting are also radically transformed by time. Indeed, in almost all the banquet scenes that have appeared in fiction the ghost at the feast is arguably the specter of history that continually reshapes not only gastronomic manners and mores but the metaphysics that underly such ways of being in the world.

Needless to say, too, our menus change along with the culinary ideologies they reflect. For instance, many of us are, at least intermittently, eating even more exotic foods than those available at the festivities of the Pontelliers, the Ramsays, and the Morkans, not to mention those bestowed upon the March sisters of *Little Women* by kindly Mr. Laurence. Remember Bronson Alcott's experiment with asceticism at Fruitlands, the austerely utopian colony he helped found in 1843? Well, Fruitlands is now a museum of Transcendentalism in which contemporary foodies would find themselves quite content. The dishes in its restaurant vividly dramatize a change in our feelings about food that, as we'll see, is intricately linked to twentieth-century transformations in the kitchen and in writings about the kitchen. Here are some samples of dishes recently on offer at Fruitlands:

Tuna Salad Niçoise

A composed salad of tonnato in olive oil, red new potatoes, tomatoes, green beans, kalamata olives, and hard-cooked egg
$13.00

Quiche of the Day
Served with our signature salad . . . mesclun, strawberries, goat cheese, sugared pecans and lemon poppy-seed vinaigrette
$13.00

Cobb Salad Wrap
Flour tortilla filled with roasted chicken, avocado, apple smoked bacon, tomatoes, lettuce, gorgonzola and our homemade green goddess dressing
$13.00

Grilled Prosciutto, Provolone and Tomato Confit Panini
Spread with our basil pesto, white balsamic vinegar and chef's choice side salad
$13.00

Panko Crusted, Boursin and Spinach Stuffed Chicken Roulade
Served on a bed of field greens with Fresh Basil Vinaigrette
$14.00

Asian Salmon
Poached salmon on a bed of greens with honey ginger dressing and topped with ginger and garlic Asian vegetables
$14.00

What would Bronson Alcott think? And how did the changing culinary habits of his literary and philosophical descendants help shape this now quite ordinary menu, so radically different from those to which the Transcendentalists aspired?[41]

PART II

Today's Table Talk

Recipes of the Modern

Chapter 5

The Kitchen Muse: The Modernist Cookbook and Its Sequels

Come, Muse, migrate from Greece and Ionia;
Cross out, please, those immensely overpaid accounts,
That matter of Troy, and Achilles' wrath, and Eneas',
Odysseus' wanderings;
Placard "Removed" and "To Let" on the rocks of your
snowy Parnassus. . . .
She comes! this famous Female—as was indeed to be
expected. . . .
Smiling and pleased, with palpable intent to stay,
She 's here, install'd amid the kitchen ware!

—WALT WHITMAN, "SONG OF THE EXPOSITION"

. . . why is there a shadow in the kitchen, there is a shadow
in a kitchen because every little thing is bigger.

—GERTRUDE STEIN, *TENDER BUTTONS*

Changing Times and Tables

In a 1974 interview, the sociologist Norbert Elias, author of a groundbreaking study titled *The Civilizing Process,* commented that "If you stick your hand into the soup bowl or the meat dish, I doubt if your table companions would feel very much at ease. That said, why not? Everyone did so back when people did not feel the need to use a fork."[1] Elias traced a history of extraordinary changes in quotidian customs that no one before him had bothered to explore. First published in the late 1930s but not translated into English until the late

1960s, *The Civilizing Process* focused on transformations of table manners in order to demonstrate the ways in which people gradually began to distance themselves from their own bodies and the bodies of others. Until just a few centuries ago, noted Elias, Western diners of all classes ate with their hands, from common bowls into which each plunged a piece of bread, took a bite, and then returned the bread for more.

The fork, Elias explained, seemed like "an exotic instrument" when it first appeared in Europe at the end of the Middle Ages, and "courtiers who made use of it were mocked." In fact, Elias added, even in the seventeenth century this now ordinary utensil was a luxury item. Yet by the nineteenth century, etiquette books were declaring that it would be cannibalistic or unhygienic to eat with one's fingers—as people had, for instance, in Rabelais's time. Thus, Elias argued, between the era of Rabelais and the age of Dickens, people began "to construct an affective wall between their bodies and those of others. The fork has been one of the means of drawing distances between other people's bodies and one's own."[2]

The banquet is a recurrent festivity appearing in most cultures, but the ways in which people approach the food on the table, as well as the food itself, continually change, reflecting and shaping other social changes. The decorum that marks Mrs. Ramsay's bourgeois dinner party—as well as the dinner parties described by Chopin and Joyce—would be utterly alien to Rabelais, and to Sir Toby Belch and Sir Andrew Aguecheek. And even that decorum is itself inflected by differences in class and place. Edna and her guests, for instance, use their knives and forks in the American manner, holding the fork in the right hand with tines upward and the knife in the left hand, a manner that seemed barbaric to many Europeans. Touring America in the 1840s, Dickens remarked that people thrust these instruments "further down their throats than I ever saw the same weapons go before, except in the hands of a skilled juggler."[3] The Ramsays and Gabriel Conroy hold knives and forks European style—knife in the right hand, fork, tines down, in the left. But there are even more notable differences among these diners. Edna Pontellier and her guests drink what the author calls cocktails from tiny, sparkling glasses—a sign that Edna is moving among people who are rather "fast"—whereas Gabriel

Conroy toasts his aunts in old-fashioned (and rather anglicized) post-prandial port after discussing both Catholicism and Irish nationalism with several other guests, revealing what he eventually decides is his problematic status in his own community. As for Mrs. Ramsay, she serves—or, rather, her cook serves—her *boeuf en daube* to a table of English guests few of whom truly understand the origin of her grandmother's French recipe.

The differences in household staffing that mark these three dinner parties are also suggestive. Edna, the wife of a wealthy businessman, has a number of servants—including a nurse for her children—as well as a long-time personal retainer, Celestine. Mrs. Ramsay, the wife of a professor of philosophy, has a Swiss maid (who pines in the attic) and a cook, as well as a couple of local cleaning ladies. Gabriel's aunts, the Misses Morkan, and their singing teacher niece Mary Jane have only a single servant, "Lily, the caretaker's daughter," who is "run off her feet" at their party. But perhaps even more striking than the differences between the staffing arrangements in these three households is the distinction between these systems of household management and those that were to follow them within a few years on both sides of the Atlantic. For shortly after Chopin's death, but even when Joyce and Woolf were writing their novels, middle-class homes increasingly functioned without servants. Certainly by the 1950s few bourgeois families in England and America could boast of cooks, and most had only intermittent help in housecleaning.

The metamorphoses of such households, brought about by the dispersal of servants into a more generalized industrial population of factory workers, sales clerks, secretaries and other blue- and pink-collar laborers, was extraordinary. When Edna's husband complains bitterly that his soup is badly seasoned, she studies a cookery book in the hope of giving better instructions to her cook, and Mrs. Ramsay does of course give her cook excellent directions when she provides her with that heirloom French recipe. The Misses Morkan are closer to our own era: they have prepared at least some of the food themselves, with a bit of help from Lily. But none of these families has the kind of unmediated relationship with food and its conversion from raw to cooked that working-class families would have had, or that families of almost every class have today.

What if Mrs. Ramsay had to prepare that *boeuf en daube* herself? What if Mr. Ramsay had to help with the washing up—or even with the peeling of the many cloves of garlic a good *daube* requires? And what if Edna had to improve on her own the soup that so displeased her husband? Or suppose Gabriel, besides carving the goose, had to select it at the butcher shop, carry it home, truss it, shove it into the oven? To be sure, Chopin, Joyce and Woolf do now and then represent activity in the kitchen. In *The Awakening,* Robert Lebrun grills a fowl for Edna by himself. In *Ulysses*, Leopold Bloom prepares a morning meal of tea and toast for his perpetually recumbent wife, Molly, while planning to saute a pork kidney for his own meal: "Kidneys were in his mind as he moved about the kitchen softly, righting her breakfast things on the humpy tray. . . . Another slice of bread and butter: three, four: right. She didn't like her plate full. Right. He turned from the tray, lifted the kettle off the hob and set it sideways on the fire." And in *Mrs. Dalloway,* Woolf describes the cook, Mrs. Walker, "among the plates, saucepans, cullenders, frying-pans, chicken in aspic, ice-cream freezers, pared crusts of bread, lemons, soup tureens, and pudding basins . . . while the fire blared and roared, the electric lights glared, and still supper had to be laid."[4]

Still, the educated classes rarely labored in the kitchens whose workers they supervised. Yes, historically there have been what one critic calls "Poetical Maids and Cooks Who Wrote." The wonderfully witty eighteenth-century poet Mary Leapor, who supported herself as a cook and kitchen maid, amusingly praised the servants of "Crumble-Hall," including

> *Sophronia sage! whose learned knuckles know*
> *To form round cheese-cakes of the pliant Dough;*
> *To bruise the Curd, and thro' her Fingers squeeze*
> *Ambrosial Butter with the temper'd cheese:*
> *Sweet Tarts and Puddens, too, her skill declare;*
> *And the soft jellies, hid from baneful Air.*[5]

But Leapor died at twenty-two—and in any case such "poetical maids" were few and far between, given the difficulties of the servant class in attaining literacy. As for poetical housewives, their thoughts of daily bread only recently became literary—or philosophical.

Among those who brooded, if only briefly, on food and cooking was, as it happens, Virginia Woolf herself. In 1941, living with her husband in Sussex while the Blitz raged over Britain, she had little household help and had now and then to take charge in the kitchen. As she sank into the final depression that would lead in a few weeks to her suicide, she welcomed culinary activity. "Occupation is essential," she wrote in her diary. "And now with some pleasure I find that it's seven; & must cook dinner. Haddock & sausage meat. I think it is true that one gains a certain hold on sausage & haddock by writing them down."[6] Food, as Lévi-Straus put it, must be not only good to eat but good to think, good to write. And with these words about the *writing* of food Woolf herself joined a new cadre of novelists, poets, and essayists who were representing food in the kitchen, not just on the dinner table.

If Mrs. Ramsay and Lily Briscoe and Mrs. Dalloway found themselves, suddenly and rather surprisingly, at the stove, they would have understood that, bourgeois or even aristocratic as they were, they were joining a long line of workers—like, for instance, Mary Leapor who had labored over stoves and in pantries for centuries before them. The French sociologist Luce Giard, collaborating with the philosopher Michel de Certeau on his magisterial study of *The Practice of Everyday Life,* was at first anxious about studying culinary gestures and confessed her own initial hesitations about cooking: "I thought that I had never learned or observed anything, having . . . always preferred my room, my books . . . to the kitchen where my mother busied herself." Yet eventually, admitting her discovery of the pleasure "of manipulating raw material, of organizing, combining, modifying, and inventing," she found herself wanting to speak for and to the generations out of whose accumulated gastronomic wisdom her newly learned culinary practices had evolved.

More overtly than Woolf, Giard sought a writing equal to the culinary imagination she hoped to transcribe, and she addressed her precursors—whom she imagined as a distinctive group that she called *le peuple feminine des cuisines* ("the Kitchen Women Nation") in a moving apostrophe:

> Women bereft of writing who came before me, you who passed on to me the shape of your hands or the color of your eyes . . . you who carried me, and fed me . . . you whose beliefs and servitudes I have not preserved, I would like the slow remembrance of your gestures in the kitchen to prompt me with words that will remain faithful to you; I would like the poetry of words to translate that of gestures; I would like a writing of words and letters to correspond to your writing of recipes and tastes.[7]

The "kitchen nation" of our era isn't populated only by women, however, nor are its inhabitants bereft of writing. For when the usages and practices of the quotidian came under scrutiny by such social scientists as Norbert Elias and Roland Barthes, as well as Giard and her mentor/collaborator Certeau, they had already become the standard stuff of fiction and poetry: the same social and cultural transformations that turned the attention of these theorists to apparently humdrum "everyday life" had also affected artists and writers. Redefinitions of the sacred and the profane, the changing relations between the sexes, the gradual disappearance of the servant class and even of other class hierarchies, the rise of the restaurant, new kinds of household appliances and new kinds of households—all played a part in changing times and tables. Thus in the twentieth and twenty-first centuries Luce Giard is only one of countless writers—male as well as female—who seek to transcribe the powers and pleasures of the cook along with the joys of transcendental gastronomy. Some are modestly hedonistic, investigating humble culinary delights and conflicts; others, as we'll later see, strive to research, recount—and even institutionalize—the flavors of the exotic, the new, the alien.

Spaghetti and Beans?

The ingredients of one of the most striking meals in modernist fiction are almost shockingly commonplace: Nick Adams, the stressed-out World War I veteran who is the protagonist of Hemingway's "Big Two-Hearted River" (1925), goes on a fishing trip in the woods of Michigan where the author himself grew up, and over the first campfire he makes, treats himself to what becomes a strangely ritual dinner, though it derives from a can of pork and beans, a can of spaghetti and some ketchup.

> Nick was hungry. He did not believe he had ever been hungrier. He opened and emptied a can of pork and beans and a can of spaghetti into the frying pan.
>
> "I've got a right to eat this kind of stuff, if I'm willing to carry it," Nick said.
>
> His voice sounded strange in the darkening woods. He did not speak again. . . .
>
> Nick put the frying pan . . . over the flames. He was hungrier. The beans and spaghetti warmed . . . The little bubbles were coming faster now. Nick sat down beside the fire and lifted the frying pan off. He poured about half the contents out into the tin plate. It spread slowly on the plate. Nick knew it was too hot. He poured on some tomato ketchup . . . he was not going to spoil it all by burning his tongue. . . . His tongue was very sensitive. He was very hungry. Across the river in the swamp, in the almost dark, he saw a mist rising. He looked at the tent once more. All right. He took a full spoonful from the plate. "Chrise," Nick said, "Geezus Chrise," he said happily.

"I have discovered that there is romance in food when romance has disappeared from everywhere else," wrote Hemingway in the newspaper article that I discussed in the foreword to this volume. "And as long as my digestion holds out I will follow romance." His relentless gastronomical pursuit, as we've seen, had already led him to sample such exotic delicacies as Chinese sea slugs, muskrat, porcupine, beaver tail, birds' nests, octopus, horse meat, mule meat, bear meat, moose meat, frogs legs and "fritto misto."[8]

But romance in a couple of canned foods plus some ketchup? Perhaps because these dishes become the center of a makeshift kitchen in the wilderness, they do radiate romance. Paradoxically, the spaghetti and beans (followed by a can of apricots) are industrial food, cooked and packed in factories, rather than such traditional pastoral delicacies as fried fish, grilled meats, fresh fruits. Yet these unlikely substances, bubbling over the campfire, take on the glamour of Nick's desire ("He was very hungry"), his rebellious insistence on their propriety ("I've got a right to eat this kind of stuff, if I'm willing to carry it") and his gastronomic intensity ("His tongue was very sensitive"). Finally, as darkness falls and a mystical mist rises from the river where he plans to fish the next day, Nick's supper becomes a kind of mock communion: " 'Chrise,'" he mutters with his mouth full of ordinary joy. " 'Geezus Chrise.' " And the next morning, after a night's sleep in the wilderness, he tucks two equally humble onion sandwiches into his pocket.

"To Be Hungry Is To Be Great"—and perhaps to eat onion sandwiches. The modernist poet and physician William Carlos Williams insisted on the first point in the early 1930s in the title of what may be one of the first recipe poems, and demonstrated the second in a brief verse celebrating the "small, yellow grass-onion," an apparently trivial vegetable that grows in early spring and is a savory wild "precursor" to the concrete sidewalks of Manhattan. When it's "plucked as it comes, in bunches, / washed, split and fried in / a pan," notes the hungry doctor, it's "inclined to be / a little slimy." Yet, if "well cooked / and served hot on rye bread," he adds, it's "to beer a perfect appetizer— / and the best part / of it is they grow everywhere."[9] Always available and yet evoking primordial places, this wild onion is the opposite of both Hemingway's canned goods and the big domestic onion Nick finds in his travel pack, yet it is gastronomically as ordinary, "served hot on rye bread" with beer, a workingman's treat inside or outside the city. To be hungry for this—not just for caviar and oysters—*is* to be great; it is to be human and desirous and to partake of the wonder of what grows "everywhere." The raw materials of the kitchen nation aren't rare, and the genius of the literary cook who celebrates them in pot and skillet is fueled by hunger.

A Rape of the Icebox

In the same decade when he praised wild onions and rye bread, Williams also drafted one of the most notoriously innovative twentieth-century poems, although it's neither pornographic nor unintelligibly avant-garde. Rather, it is apparently straightforward, colloquial—and unabashedly gastronomic.

Indeed, it's so simple and conversational that numerous readers have long questioned its aesthetic status as a poem, especially because this famous verse actually presents itself as a casual note left on a kitchen table or counter:

This Is Just To Say

I have eaten
the plums
that were in
the icebox

and which
you were probably
saving
for breakfast

Forgive me
they were delicious
so sweet
and so cold

Queried by an interviewer about this piece, Williams declared that it was "really just a passing gesture," part of an event that "actually took place just as it says here." Still, he mused, perhaps its "virtue . . . is its simplicity," though he insisted on its formal symmetry ("it's metrically absolutely regular.")[10]

Further discussion yielded more about the poet's attitude toward the work. When the interviewer pointed out that "this [poem] goes against so many preconceived ideas of poems . . . because it's the kind of thing that almost anybody might say," Williams responded, "Yes, because no one believes that poetry can exist in his own life," then added that "you have to get used to the fact that in your own life, that which touches you, such as your affection for your wife," might lead to a poem, even if the occasion seems trivial. "If you address something to her, you feel a little sorry—probably the poor kid had these things saved for supper and here you come along and raid it. Why it's practically a rape of the icebox!" Note that here the wife of the house—not a cook or kitchen maid—rules and guards the kitchen, but the husband, too, can enter what might have been, for Mr. Ramsay, alien territory. Note, too, that his claim for the status of his confession (later theatrically described as nearly "a rape") is both modest and ambiguous: this is *just* (merely) and *just* (fair) and *just* (accurate) to say. Despite such ambiguity, however, his transgressive eating of forbidden fruit is depicted lightly, casually, and yet at the same time with gusto: "they were delicious / so sweet / and so cold." But, too, the plums ("in / the icebox"—an appliance the Ramsays may not have had) are common fruit, though perhaps interdicted, and the young husband who ate them has surely not brought about the fall of humanity![11]

The story of this work was charmingly continued when the poet's wife, Flossie, supposedly replied to his versified note with a note of her own, which he himself later versified, titled "Reply (Crumpled on Her Desk)," and described as "a little more complex, but quite as good." Here, patiently domestic, she told "Dear Bill" that she'd made him some sandwiches and that he'd now find blueberries in the icebox, presumably to replace the missing plums, along with "a cup of grapefruit" and "a glass of cold coffee." There's a teapot on the stove "with enough tea leaves / for you to make tea if you / prefer," she told him too, calmly explaining that he should "just light the gas— / boil the water and put in the tea." Her conclusion, besides stressing the availability of other comestibles ("Plenty of bread in the bread-box / and butter and eggs") was affectionate but openly bewildered.[12]

I didn't know just what to
make for you. Several people
called up about office hours—

See you later. Love. Floss.

Please switch off the telephone.

A little more complex indeed! Floss, whether in her own person or in her doctor-husband's imagination, gets her own back with pointed allusions to what might be his culinary incapacity ("Just light the gas— / boil the water and put in the tea"), to what suddenly seems to be his pickiness ("I didn't know just what to / make for you"), and to his forgetfulness around the house ("Please switch off the telephone").

Whether complex or simple, however, it's hard to imagine these domestic lyrics, beginning with a husbandly "rape of the icebox" and a wifely offer of quotidian culinary abundance—sandwiches, tea, coffee, blueberries, grapefruit, bread, butter—seeing print in the nineteenth century. When he was a young man, Williams often noted, his favorite poet was John Keats, whose poems brood on magic foods ("La Belle Dame Sans Merci," "The Eve of St. Agnes") or celebrate, more abstractly, the natural richness that fills "all fruit with ripeness to the core" ("To Autumn"). But a kitchen? An icebox? Scribbled or crumpled notes about plums and sandwiches? Yet if a focus on forbidden fruit suggests that Milton's *Paradise Lost* might be a distant ancestor of Williams's "This Is Just To Say," a web of associations implies that a Keatsian antecedent could be "Ode on a Grecian Urn" with its "bold lover" yearning for erotic bliss, its ceremonial vessel that is an "unravish'd bride of quietness," and the "cold pastoral" whose tale it dwells on. But in Williams's poem the well-wrought urn becomes a homely appliance sheltering a breakfast "ravish'd" by a hungry husband—and the emblems of "cold pastoral" are the plums he devoured, delighting that they were "so sweet / and so cold." How and why has the American poet transmogrified Keats?[13]

As several recent commentators have pointed out, the Romantic movement that shaped Keats was an era when culinary matters gradually became "integrated into all literary genres"—an era, in particular, where the mention of food in "a lyric context" had begun to call "into question the doctrine of good [aesthetic] taste" that defined eating as a "low" (thus grotesque or comic) activity. "La Belle Dame" and "The Eve of St. Agnes" featured magical or exotic foods that were crucial to fantastic narratives. But in his influential Preface to *Lyrical Ballads* (1803), Keats's near precursor William Wordsworth had revalued the supposedly ordinary so that it had as much glamour as the exotic. The poet, he declared, should write about "incidents and situations from common life . . . in a selection of language really used by men."

And in attending to common life, such Romantics as Percy Shelley, Charles Lamb and Thomas De Quincey were producing important culinary essays, including Lamb's speculations on the origins of cooking, Shelley's vegetarian polemics and De Quincey's memoir of "opium-eating."[14]

Ultimately, however, it was in America that a poetics based on "situations from common life" and "language really used by men" shaped an aesthetic context that influenced Williams's radical metamorphosis of Keats's pastoral. And Walt Whitman had almost everything to do with the change. The passage from his "Song of the Exposition" that I've used as an epigraph here—featuring the fabled muse of ancient Europe now "install'd amid the kitchenware"—elegized the "Embroider'd, dazzling world . . . Blazon'd with Shakespeare's purple page, / And dirged by Tennyson's sweet sad rhyme" to which Keats, too, had belonged. In Williams's view, as in that of so many other modernists, Whitman was "a key man" who "broke through the deadness of copied forms": in Ezra Pound's comparable phrase, he "broke the new wood." And while such comments suggest that Whitman's importance was primarily his contribution to a freer prosody, the place of his muse amid the clatter of kitchenware rather than in the cathedral-like hush of the embroidered study emphasizes the unprecedented newness of a culinary poetics that could focus, as the novel does, on the daily rather than the sacred meal.[15]

Meditating further on "This Is Just to Say," Williams articulated this poetics too: "everything in our lives, if it's sufficiently authentic to our lives and touches us deeply enough with a certain amount of feeling, is capable of being organized into a form which can be a poem." He demonstrated this point in countless works, especially in a few others where the very activity of eating dramatizes what "touches us deeply." In one poem, for instance, he poignantly delineates a "poor old woman" who is "munching a plum / on the street" from a paper bag, and in a bravura stanza imagines the "solace of ripe plums" from her perspective, reiterating her pleasure by reenacting every bite with a different line break:

They taste good to her
They taste good

to her. They taste
good to her

And in another poem he depicted two young girls in an empty summer cityscape, with cotton candy like "pink flames in their right hands . . . touching their avid mouths / with pink sugar on a stick— / like a carnation each holds in her hand." As the ripe plums solaced the old woman, and the stolen plums pleasured the thieving poet, so the candy comforts the girls—helps them "while the time away"—as "they mount the lonely street." "No ideas but in things," Williams famously declared in several texts, and foodstuffs are among the most concrete of things with which to demonstrate that "everything in our lives can be organized into a poem." Even candy on a stick, a fried green onion, fruit in a paper bag, a kitchen, an icebox, a bowl of plums. Or an ordinary ripe peach.

The Modernist Fruit Bowl

Who dares to eat a peach? Not the speaker of T. S. Eliot's famous monologue "The Love Song of J. Alfred Prufrock." If Williams immortalized some everyday plums by stealing them, Eliot's antihero brought a peach into the pantry of modernism by dithering about it. Aging and anxiety-stricken, Prufrock hides his whole name from the world behind an initial initial, and measures his days with "coffee spoons" and other culinary paraphernalia—"sawdust restaurants with oyster shells," tea with cake and ices and marmalade—but worries that he's puny and balding. Before his utterance rises to a climactic vision of indifferent mermaids ("I do not think that they will sing to me"), he wonders whether he should "part his hair behind" to disguise his baldness, and asks himself "Do I dare to eat a peach?" Is he nervous about the fruit because it's juicy and messy, as one critic has suggested? Or because it's fuzzy, and fuzz bothers him on female arms that are "downed with light brown hair"? Or because, besides balding, he's lost some teeth, and can't bite into a peach, even if it's decorously cut in pieces? Whatever the answer may be—and Eliot occludes it just as he occludes the man's given name, which might be anything from John to Jehosephat—the fruit in question is both quotidian and forbidden.[16]

In a belligerent gastronomic and literary manifesto, D. H. Lawrence took on this problematic delicacy in a peachy poem of his own that might well be a reply to Eliot's masterpiece of irony. "Would you like to throw a stone at me?" Lawrence begins argumentatively. Then, "Here, take all that's left of my peach." Like Prufrock, he has an invisible interlocutor, but where Prufrock's listener very likely shares the indifference of the mermaids from whom the timorous J. Alfred expects no speech, Lawrence's unnamed listener might be Prufrock himself, since he (or a Prufrockian she) is evidently as troubled by the peach's voluptuous body as Prufrock is by juice and fuzz and femininity. Indeed, the poet of "Peach" imagines that his auditor would prefer to sanitize and in effect unsex the peach. A series of questions, like a set of Renaissance *blazons* naming the physical parts of the beloved, implicitly explain why Prufrock *won't* eat a peach:

> *Why the groove?*
> *Why the lovely, bivalve roundnesses?*
> *Why the ripple down the sphere?*
> *Why the suggestion of incision?*

And then the poet replies with a sardonic thrust at both Puritanism and the Industrial Revolution:

> *Why was not my peach round and finished like a billiard ball?*
> *It would have been if man had made it.*
> *Though I've eaten it now.*
> *But it wasn't round and finished like a billiard ball.*
> *And because I say so, you would like to throw something at me.*
> *Here, you can have my peach stone.*[17]

In a triumph of gustatory pleasure over inhibition, Lawrence has gobbled his peach, just as Williams swallowed his plums. And now he offers its erotic core—"wrinkled with secrets, / and hard with the intention to keep them"—to his audience: not a "billiard ball" but a body with a seed at its heart, his fruit will crack open to admit new growth.

Although the cultural and social web of modernism that linked Williams, Eliot and Lawrence dates back to Whitman and reimagines fruit as ordinary rather than sacred, material rather than magical, it was still full of contradictions. Lawrence wrote frequently of his love–hate relationship with Whitman, who became a central figure in his *Studies in Classic American Literature.* Williams not only admired Whitman but paid homage to Lawrence throughout his career, especially in "An Elegy for D. H. Lawrence," where he praised him for his "unenglish greatness." At the same time, he considered Eliot a sort of literary villain, arguing that *The Waste Land* was a disaster for American poetry ("I felt at once that it had set me back twenty years and I'm sure it did"). As for Eliot, he once remarked that "Hawthorne, Poe and Whitman are all pathetic figures; they are none of them as great as they should have been," but he was arguably influenced by Whitman in many ways, and despite Williams's hostility, he and the New Jersey doctor were connected through their common friend, the modernist poet Ezra Pound. A scathing attack on Lawrence, however, was the centerpiece of Eliot's irascible (and anti-Semitic) tract *After Strange Gods*, a set of lectures delivered at the University of Virginia in which he asserted that Lawrence had "an incapacity for what we ordinarily call thinking."[18]

Both the aesthetic differences and the similarities among these three powerful modernist figures are vividly embodied in their depictions of fruit and eating. Williams is perhaps the most radical and immediate in his apparently scribbled confession that he's stolen some plums from an icebox set in what one can easily imagine as a real, nighttime kitchen. Lawrence's peach-eating isn't clearly situated: where are he and the (already consumed) peach when he utters his poem, and whom is he debating? But his peach is luscious with its own flesh, as he muses, in a moment of sensual memory, on how this "rolling, dropping, heavy globule" evolved "from silvery peach-bloom," from a "shallow-silvery wine-glass on a short stem." Eliot's peach is even more distanced from any context: first, it's Prufrock's peach, not a fruit belonging to someone representing the poet himself; and second, it's never eaten—and may never have existed. Further, though, it's surrounded with negative culinary images: tiny coffee spoons, uncomfortable receptions featuring tea and cakes and *ices* that don't tempt the speaker's appetite, and (en route to the embarrassment of the tea party) streets populated by "sawdust restaurants with oyster shells"—vulgar and clearly repellent to Prufrock.

Nonetheless, the three poets are alike in their choice of fruit that is neither divinely forbidden nor magically dangerous but ripe for daily consumption. Nor do they speak of the fruit in elevated language, though Lawrence is certainly celebratory. Finally, their encounters with fruit, while explained to significant others (Williams, after all, tells the story to his presumably sleeping wife), are solitary; they eat alone, rather than at festal boards, and meditate on food as an object of gastronomic interest. Further, the fruits that concern them are the raw materials of the kitchen: no stewed plums, no peach jam, and therefore no need for either coffee spoons or the alienating bourgeois forks and knives whose social function Norbert Elias studied. In fact, like a number of their contemporaries and descendants, many of whom admired the luscious still lives of fruits produced by such powerful painters as Renoir, Cézanne and Matisse, they were plucking their plums and peaches out of a common fruit bowl that had become central in a newly valued modernist genre. For depictions of kitchen tables laden with the products of the farm and orchard (called, in French, by the rather deprecating term *nature mort*—dead nature) had long been considered inferior to more elevated subjects: heroic battle scenes, portraits of the great, and most important, Madonnas, angels, crucifixions, creations, resurrections.[19]

Williams's friend the lawyer–poet Wallace Stevens would have understood this. He was an art collector and connoisseur (late in his life he lectured at the Museum of Modern Art on "The Relations Between Poetry and Painting") who imported fine comestibles from all over the world. In one poem he extolled the solitary pleasures of "citron to nibble / And coffee dribble" when "Frost is in the stubble," and in another he imagined himself as a Russian exile singing the joys of peaches "full of the colors of my village": "I did not know," his speaker declares, "that such ferocities could tear / One self from another, as these peaches do." And in a late poem titled "Someone Puts Together a Pineapple," Stevens takes the physical attributes of this tropical delicacy as an occasion for fantasy. The pineapple reminds him of a "hut" that "stands by itself beneath the palms" (i.e., green fronds grow from the top of the fruit); but he also observes that "Out of their bottle the green genii come" (so the pineapple is also a bottle out of which the green leaves emerge), and he comments that a "vine has climbed the other side of the wall" (the greenery hovers over the golden brown studded side of the fruit), and so on.[20]

Yet, Stevens tells himself in the meditation on metaphor that prefaces this fantasy, "He must say nothing of the fruit that is / Not true, nor think it, less." He is similarly "truthful" as he deploys tropes and images in the early poem "Floral Decorations for Bananas," which chastises these "insolent, linear peels . . . Blunt yellow in such a room" while suggesting (as if anticipating Williams) that "You should have had plums tonight" instead of "bananas hacked and hunched" at a "table . . . set by an ogre." "The Motive for Metaphor"—to cite the title of one of his most self-reflexive poems—both inheres in and struggles against reality, the "ABC of being." Thus Stevens—in his own life a portly gastronome ("One eats one pâté, even of salt")—once declared that the "plum survives its poems." Indeed, it "may hang / In the sunshine placidly . . . Harlequined and mazily dewed and mauved / In bloom. Yet it survives in its own form, / Beyond these changes, good, fat, guzzly fruit."[21]

There it is: the modernist fruit bowl. Good, fat, guzzly fruit—juicy or dangly, fuzzy or slick, stolen or given but always quotidian. Always sitting there on the sideboard of poetry, where it had never appeared in quite such a form before. Was it what Lawrence called the "appleyness" of Cézanne's "appley" apples, along with the other still lives of the Impressionists and post-Impressionists that gave these fruits their imaginative glow for early- and mid-twentieth-century poets? Or was it that, for poets and painters alike, the foods of the gods had merely become the simple foods of those everyday folk Giard called the kitchen people, men and women alike? Historical answers, as we've seen, multiply, but one fact is incontrovertible: the influence and ubiquitousness of that guzzly stuff changed the taste of poetry. As Erica Jong was later to put it in *Fruits and Vegetables* (1971):

> In general, modern poetry requires (underline one): a) more fruit; b) less fruit; c) more vegetables; d) less vegetables; e) all of the above; f) none of the above.[22]

Over the years, a) and c) increasingly became the most popular choices. Add apples and artichokes, plums and peaches, and stir.

A Sudden Slice Changes the Whole Plate

It was probably Gertrude Stein who first cut up the "guzzly" fruit of modernism, simmered it in the skillet of the avant-garde, defamiliarized it, and brought it to table. *Tender Buttons*, her new bible of the quotidian, examined the materials of gastronomy from all kinds of strange angles, perspectives influenced by (and influencing) the odd abstractions pioneered by her friend Picasso and his Cubist contemporaries. Writes the critic Marjorie Perloff:

> Prufrock's question "Do I dare to eat a peach?" has no place in the world of *Tender Buttons,* where indeed one dares to eat peach and where, in any case, the issue is not conformity to this or that social norm, but the nature of *peachness* itself. Potatoes and cranberries, eggs and milk, carafes and boxes—to meditate on these ordinary things is to refigure one's place in the world of objects.[23]

Yet what refigurings! Stein's punning, jingle-jangling musings start with menus but end in esoteric observations that are as much about life and language as they are about food. Indeed, from the perspective of the ordinary reader of culinary prose—the average educated but not super-sophisticated person Virginia Woolf called "the common reader"—Stein's edible objects become not-food, precursors to what has lately been called "Eat Art," as she turns meals inside out and even into linguistic Möbius strips in which the original roast beef or mutton or milk evolve into estranged variations of themselves.

The culinary philosopher Carolyn Korsmeyer has stressed that "the discontinuities between meals and art should not be gainsaid," and such discontinuity is nowhere more evident than in the "Food" section of *Tender Buttons.* Here the ordinary is isolated from the context of the quotidian so that it becomes both extraordinary and confusing, as if seen through a distorting mirror. Of "roastbeef," the first item in her culinary catalog, Stein notes that "In the inside there is sleeping, in the outside there is reddening, in the morning there is meaning, in the evening there is feeling." Yet soon enough in this same piece she argues that "There is no use there is no use at all in smell, in taste, in teeth, in toast, in anything, there is no use at all and the respect is mutual." No *use*? No practical value? No point or purpose? If so, why?[24]

That Perloff considers Stein's gastronomic universe a space "where indeed one dares to eat peach" seems questionable following this comment. Prufrock's peach, after all, was implicitly as seductive as the fruits Williams and Lawrence celebrated—too seductive, from that prissy speaker's perspective, to be eaten. But if Stein sees "no use" (in several senses) in smell, taste, etc., then what use is there in hunger, what point in gastronomical desire? Who, toothless and numb to flavor, would want to eat a peach if she couldn't relish it? Even more than the bread, fish, wine and fruit that appear in Cubist paintings, Stein's foods seem at first to evoke not food but representations of what might or might not be foodness: her breakfasts, lunches, teas and dinners appear to exist on canvases of the mind without flavor or aroma. Readers of "Big Two-Hearted River" and "This Is Just To Say" probably experience culinary longings rather often (even for the weirdness of canned beans and spaghetti), but who has ever yearned for Stein's cranberries ("Could there not be a sudden date, could there not be in the present settlement of old age pensions, could there not be by a witness, could there be"), mutton ("A letter which can wither, a learning which can suffer"), and cream ("In a plank, in a play sole, in a heated red left tree")?[25]

To be sure, as Korsmeyer observes, all food art isolates ordinary fruits and meats from the "real" ordinariness of daily life, yet most such art also alludes to, and implies, a connection with the daily. Thus it's both the familiarity and (in an aesthetic setting) the *de*familiarization of food that converts a bowl of plums into a poem, the contents of a pantry into a *bodegón* or a Warhol, a recipe into a climactic moment in a novel. Yet to defamiliarize, as all art does, is not necessarily to drain away the juices of meaning, as if squishing the ideas of eating through a philosophical sieve. This is what Stein's texts tend to do, however, as they disrupt not only our normative ideas of food but also our accepted notions of meaning. Some critics have, yes, strained to extract particles of conventional significance from these apparently abstract blocks of prose (often considered prose poems). Sarah Garland, for instance, argues that "Asparagus"—

> *Asparagus in a lean in a lean to hot.*
> *This makes it art and it is wet wet weather wet weather wet.*

—traces a "fairly literal chain of associations between the way asparagus is bundled to sell and often to serve (which getting to stand on a plate may indeed be art)" and, more tenuously, the asparagus-growing "wetter northern areas of Spain that Stein and Toklas visited in 1912." But does this interpretation intensify any yearning that readers may have for a particular vegetable course, and does it suggest any important points about the sight, smell, and taste of asparagus?[26]

And yet. As a number of critics have noted, Stein's innovations in *Tender Buttons* don't just disrupt received concepts of culinary matters and literary manners by their adoption of the avant-garde experimental techniques that characterized the arts of such male contemporaries as Picasso (the Cubist) and Joyce (the punster). They also disrupt, by domesticating, some of the strategies of the avant-garde itself. *Tender Buttons,* as Susan Gubar long ago observed, is a kind of "demonic *Mrs. Beeton's*," and as readers from William Gass to Judy Grahn and Marjorie Perloff have remarked, its very title, along with many of its texts, encodes a celebration of lesbian sexuality, and especially of Stein's relationship with Alice Toklas, whose name flowers into a number of puns throughout ("alas," "ale us," "eel us," "a little lace"). And what are the eponymous "tender buttons," after all? To begin with, the English phrase appears nonsensical, or at least oxymoronic: if buttons were literally tender, modifiable by that adjective and thus soft and easy to chew, they wouldn't hold anything in place, would they? But they might be edible, even delicious—like button mushrooms, for example! And metaphorically, if the buttons were tender—loving and kindly—perhaps they would and could hold the sensitive world together. In that case, the phrase evokes a sort of Victorian celebration of domestic caring: the good woman fastens things up with the tender buttons of her love.

There are further puns in the title, though. *Boutons tendre* is colloquial French for nipples, so tender buttons might be the nipples of sexual delight and maternal nurture, while they might also, if imagined erotically, equate to similarly tender clitoral buttons. Further, if the word "tender" is read punningly as a verb, then the title might mean "tender [her] buttons"—i.e., *give* her buttons—or even "tend her buttons"—i.e., care for her buttons. Considering most of these possible interpretations, then, this cryptic sequence becomes not just a strangely skewed and fragmented guide to domesticity but a deconstructed and reconstructed handbook of female desire. The two topoi are obviously linked, however. Beginning with odd meditations on "Objects" (a chair, a purse, an umbrella, a petticoat) and ending with a tour de force of abstraction on "Rooms," this experimental manual of domesticity centers on "Food" in a section that moves through a day's menus in what is evidently both a parody of a cookbook and an homage to the cook in charge of the kitchen—in Stein's life, Alice Toklas, who was later to become the author of a best-selling cookbook cum memoir.

If there is anything immediately rational and graspable in Stein's food musings, it is the sequence of titles that give structure to the section: Roastbeef, Mutton, Breakfast, Sugar, Cranberries, Milk, Eggs, Apple, Lunch, Rhubarb, Fish, Cake, Custard, Potatoes, Asparagus, Butter, and so forth—the topics in the prefatory outline that the writer offers sound like either the table of contents of a gastronomical tome or a shopping list, and though the motions of the mind that it elicits form deviating patterns, the list in itself might even be mouthwatering to some. And Stein did love to eat, just as Toklas loved to plan meals and to cook. Wrote Stein, "nothing more interesting than that something that you eat," and as for Toklas, her cookbook was ultimately a major sequel to the compelling *Autobiography of Alice B. Toklas* that her lover claimed to have penned on her behalf. That the two had long summered in Belley, the birthplace and home of Jean Anthelme Brillat-Savarin, doesn't seem to be a coincidence. Both remarked on the delights of the local cuisine, and their longtime country house , Bilignin, was filled with the transcendental gastronomer's furnishings and clearly pervaded by his spirit.[27]

At the end of the nineteenth century, Paul Cézanne decided to make a powerful contribution to the increasingly popular genre of the *nature mort.* "I will astonish Paris with an apple," he declared, and proceeded to paint some of modernity's most famous apples. One of those pictures was jointly owned by Gertrude and her brother Leo, until they divided their art holdings in 1914 after Alice Toklas had moved into their home at rue de Fleurus, in Paris. Leo, leaving for Italy, insisted on taking the Cézanne with him, asserting that the "Cézanne apples have a unique importance to me that nothing can replace" so that his sister should "look upon the loss of the apples as an act of God." For her part, Gertrude chose to keep the Picassos. But the loss of the apples to "an act of God" must have haunted her. Fat with the sunshine of Provence, Cézanne's astonishing apples are reminders of earthly shape in an aesthetic realm that was gradually decomposing. Gastronomically they evoke what D. H. Lawrence called the essence of "appleyness" as they capture the radiance of the fruit for which Adam and Eve sacrificed the innocence of Paradise.[28] Perhaps for this reason, Stein opens "Apple," one of her most accessible contributions to the modernist fruit bowl, with an incantatory celebration of the forbidden apples—both literal ones, perhaps, and painted ones. Then she gradually swerves into the Picasso-esque revisions of reality that she chose for herself and finally concludes with a straightforward statement of desire:

> *Apple plum, carpet steak, seed clam, colored wine, calm seen, cold cream, best shake, potato, potato and no no gold work with pet, a green seen is called bake and change sweet is bready, a little piece a little piece please.*
>
> *A little piece please. Cane again to the presupposed and ready eucalyptus tree, count out sherry and ripe plates and little corners of a kind of ham. This is use.*

Paul Cézanne, *Three Apples* (1878–79).
The Barnes Foundation, Philadelphia, PA, USA.

"Calm seen": calm scene? "Potato, potato": in French a *pomme* (apple) *de terre* (of earth) is a potato. "A little piece please": a little peace please?[29]

These tentative meanings surround a fleshy core of language that evolves into a traditional kitchen imperative to "count out sherry and ripe plates and little corners of a kind of ham. *This is use*" (italics added). "There is no use there is no use at all in smell, in taste," the writer had claimed in "Roastbeef," but here she reconciles herself to ripe plates of usefulness in a kitchen where, to quote one of the epigraphs I've used for this chapter, "every little thing is bigger" because it may bring a little piece of peace to the musing body by the hearth. Preparing to turn to a cookbook chapter on "Little-known French Dishes suitable for American and British Kitchens," Alice Toklas would write years later of recipes that are "most of them a slow evolution in a new direction, which is the way great art is created—that is, everything about is ready for it, and one person having the vision does it, discarding what he finds unnecessary in the past." Could she have been remembering the verbal delicacies imagined by her longtime "hubby," Gertrude Stein? "Even a way of cooking an egg can be arrived at in this way," Toklas added. "Then that way becomes a classical way" and "It is a pleasure for us, perhaps for the egg."[30]

Perhaps it was a pleasure for eggs and apples and plums to discover that they had been reenvisioned by Picasso, Cézanne and Stein?

Sculpted Meat

But can revisionary eggs and fruit actually be used in the real world by the experimental artists who imagine them on canvas and in strange dreams of language? The Italian Futurist Filippo Marinetti thought so, wrote a cookbook devoted to such innovation (*La Cucina Futurista*) and eventually opened a restaurant based on his avant-garde culinary ideology: La Taverna del Santopalato (The Tavern of the Holy Palate). "Ice cream on the moon," "consumato of roses and sunshine," "roast lamb in lion sauce," "little salad at daybreak": some of Marinetti's fantasy foods sound as though they were invented by a cross between Roald Dahl, William Blake and Gertrude Stein herself, so perhaps it isn't surprising that they were characterized by the British cookbook writer Elizabeth David as "preposterous new dishes."[31] At the same time, while his precepts seemed peculiar to contemporaries, a number of them prophesied culinary innovations that were eventually to be put into practice by such divergent food theorists as the diet gurus Robert Atkins and Jane Brody as well as the molecular gastronomer Ferran Adrià.

One of the foundational principles of Marinetti's cuisine, for instance, was "the abolition of pastasciutta [i.e., all forms of dried pasta], an absurd Italian gastronomic religion," which he felt was making his countrymen sluggish and flabby. And, added one of his followers, "the struggle against pasta is not enough. We need to pull down other idols . . . *to affirm that white bread*, for example, heavy and tasteless, *is a useless food* [and] should be replaced by wholegrain bread . . . *that rice is a precious food* but only as long as it is not deprived of its organic qualities by polishing; *that vegetables contain real trea-*

sures for the human organism . . . as long as these treasures are not stupidly destroyed through absurd cooking," and so on. "It is well," declared this writer, "that people should know a raw carrot finely chopped with oil and lemon, a plate of onions or olives or a combination of these things, together with a few nuts and a slice of brown bread, are a much more suitable and useful fuel for the human stove than the notorious *maccheroni al ragù* or *tagliatelle alla bolognese*."[32] Sound familiar? Contemporary advocates of whole foods and high-protein, low-starch diets would feel right at home in this polemic.

To be sure, Marinetti's Futurism was at least obliquely related to the Fascist movement that engulfed Italy even as he wrote manifestos and recipes. Fascist fitness was, in fact, one of the goals of his cookbook. Glorifying "war—the world's only hygiene—militarism, patriotism . . . and scorn for women," he insisted that "men think dream and act according to what they eat and drink," so that beginning with the repudiation of the "massive heaviness" of pasta, he would trigger a "renewal of Italian pride" associated with an unprecedented "religion of speed" and a devotion to "the aesthetics of the machine." Yet as an avant-garde artist he was clearly scornful of the bourgeoisie to whom Mussolini appealed. Thus he counseled the "abolition of traditional mixtures in favour of experimentation with new, apparently absurd mixtures" concocted through the sophisticated deployment of a "battery of scientific instruments in the kitchen: *ozoners* to give liquids and foods the perfume of ozone, *ultra-violet ray lamps* . . . *electrolyzers* to decompose juices and extracts, etc. in such a way as to obtain from a known product a new product with new properties, *colloidal mills* to pulverize flours, dried fruits, drugs, etc.; *atmospheric and vacuum stills, centrifugal autoclaves, dialyzers*." Of course, he noted, "the use of these appliances will have to be scientific, avoiding the typical error of cooking foods under steam pressure, which provokes the destruction of active substances (vitamins etc.) [and] *chemical indicators* will take into account the acidity and alkalinity of the sauces."[33] Sound familiar too? Perhaps not as familiar as the ideology of whole foods, fresh vegetables and low starches, but certainly analogous to the culinary discourses of, on the one hand, industrial food, and, on the other hand, molecular gastronomy.

Just the other day, my local paper offered a glossary of new culinary terms to go with a piece called "Molecular Magic," describing the "preposterous dishes" that have been made famous by Ferran Adrià at his world-famous (now closed) restaurant El Bulli: molecular gastronomy ("cooking that pushes the experimental boundaries of culinary chemical interactions"), sous-vide ("slowly heating vacuum-sealed food in a precise, low-temperature water oven"), the whipper ("an NO_2-powered canister . . . used to produce food froths and foams"), flash freezing (often to "freeze the exterior, while leaving the interior liquid") and meat glue (a "slang term for transglutaminase, enzymes used to bind proteins together," used not just by celebrity chefs but for "fast food McNuggets"). Some of Marinetti's signature dishes may have seemed odd to patrons of his restaurant, the Holy Palate, in the 1930s, but they probably wouldn't appear so strange to diners at El Bulli, in Roses, Spain.[34]

"Sculpted meat," for instance, "created by the Futurist painter Fillìa, a symbolic interpretation of all the varied landscapes of Italy, is composed of a large cylindrical rissole of minced veal stuffed with eleven different kinds of cooked green vegetables and roasted." As phallic as it is geographic, it stands "upright in the centre of the plate . . . crowned by a layer of honey and supported at the base by a ring of sausages resting on three golden spheres of chicken." Odd, perhaps, but probably not inedible. And similarly, the "edible food sculpture *Equator + North Pole,*" created by another Futurist, offers "an equatorial sea of poached egg yolks seasoned like oysters with pepper, salt and lemon," from the center of which "emerges a cone of firmly whipped egg white full of orange segments looking like juicy sections of the sun" and "strewn with pieces of black truffle cut in the form of black aeroplanes conquering the zenith."[35]

With their literary and historical allusions, such foods recall the elaborate confections of the great early-nineteenth-century royal French chef and patissier Marie-Antoine Carême along with the often grotesque gastronomic centerpieces described by Petronius in the "Trimalchio's Feast" section of *Satyricon*. Given these aristocratic roots, it isn't surprising that one recent culinary historian observed that "the growing interest in food as art in contemporary Western culture presupposes an audience satiated and wealthy enough to have the leisure to contemplate foodstuff as conceptual, rather than nourishing, at a time when 'knowing about food and being able to discourse about food . . . [have become] desirable social attributes' and could be considered 'gastronomic capital,' a subset of Bourdieu's 'cultural capital.'"[36] Marinetti, Carême, Stein, Stevens, Lawrence, Eliot, Williams—how much do they have in common? None, after all, are "potato eaters," like the drab peasants who hunch over Dutch platters in the darkness of an early (and great) Van Gogh pastoral.

Yet what we see in the writings of all these contributors to the modernist cookbook, from Imagists to Futurists, is always and already a new and fierce sacramentalizing of the quotidian, a change in our attitude toward our daily bread. Think, after all, of the phrase "holy palate" and its Italian equivalent: the Taverna del Santopalato alludes, in its Turin context, to the most famous relic in Turin, the Sacra Sindone or Shroud of Turin. In the Santo Palato or Holy Palate, however, the Holy Grail and sacred bread have yet again become sacralized emblems of the natural world, a realm of sculpted meat that points not to the celestial weavings of an ineffable heaven but to the artifacts of an all too peculiar earth. Some of the meals served in the aluminum-walled Taverna were sardonic jokes (a chicken with a bulletlike piece of steel embedded in its shoulder), and others were surprisingly healthful or oddly prophetic. All dramatized modernist foodways with which a range of artists would increasingly experiment: on the page, in the pantry, and in the palate. As Gertrude Stein put it in one of her many comments on food, "Well there are really quite a number of things to make different kinds of things to eat and everybody likes it all very much & then they do not like it at all & then they change their minds about it all & then they begin an entirely different way."[37]

Beginning "in an entirely different way," as modernists from Hemingway and Williams to Lawrence, Stevens, Stein and Marinetti did, radically changed the culinary imaginations of the twentieth and twenty-first centuries. If, as Ezra Pound declared, Walt Whitman "broke the new wood" of poetry, his descendants bit into its new fruits and began cooking up revisionary aesthetic recipes for transcendental gastronomers. Their ranks, as we'll see in a later chapter, include poets from all over the world—Pablo Neruda, Francis Ponge, Robert Bly, Sylvia Plath, Maxine Kumin, Nancy Willard and others—along with such artists as Wayne Thiebaud and Andy Warhol. But it was the American Beat author of *Howl* who made explicit the link between Whitman and the poetry of food. In "A Supermarket in California," one of his warmest, wittiest and most moving lyrics, Allen Ginsberg transformed Walt Whitman into his personal muse as he toured a late-night mid-century market:

> *I saw you, Walt Whitman, childless, lonely old grubber, poking among the meats in the refrigerator and eyeing the grocery boys.*
>
> *I heard you asking questions of each: Who killed the pork chops? What price bananas? Are you my Angel? . . .*
>
> *We strode down the open corridors together in our solitary fancy tasting artichokes, possessing every frozen delicacy, and never passing the cashier.*[38]

"To Be Hungry Is To Be Great." So, remember, wrote William Carlos Williams, who became a kind of patron saint for Ginsberg: both were from Paterson, New Jersey: Ginsberg sought literary advice from the New Jersey doctor; and for his part Williams cast Ginsberg as a kind of aesthetic son in his great long poem *Paterson.*

And, too, remember Hemingway's maxim: "there is romance in food when romance has disappeared from everywhere else." His sometime friend Gertrude Stein made the same point in her own inimitable way as she brooded on "American Food and American Houses": "Now what has all this to do with anything, well anything always has something to do with something and nothing is more interesting than that something that you eat."[39]

Chapter 6

Tastes of Clay: The Many Courses of the Culinary Memoir

> The Proust *madeleine* phenomenon is now as firmly established in folklore as Newton's apple or Watt's steam kettle. The man ate a tea biscuit, the taste evoked memories, he wrote a book. This is capable of expression by the formula TMB, for Taste>Memory>Book.
>
> —A. J. LIEBLING, *BETWEEN MEALS*

> One of the great charismas of food is that it's about cultures and grandmothers and death and art and self-expression and family and society—and at the same time, it's just dinner.
>
> —BILL BUFORD, *NEW YORK TIMES*

> We must eat. If, in the face of that dread fact, we can find other nourishment and tolerance and compassion for it, we'll be no less full of human dignity.
>
> —M. F. K. FISHER, *GASTRONOMICAL ME*

Feeding the Foodoir

Musing on winter foods, M. F. K. Fisher confessed late in her gastronomic career that "It seems very strange to try to remember the best meal of my whole life, especially one that I ate in the winter," but stranger still is the repast she remembers—neither the voluptuous raw (ice-cold plums) nor the exquisite cooked (a delicate madeleine), neither foreign (her own honeymoon meal) nor sophisticated (sole meunière), but furtive and transgressive. As a seven-year-old, she tells us, she belonged to a subterranean little club, in which she and several other neighborhood children mused on sacrosanct foods: their "whole project," she explains, "though we did not really put it in words, was to find out what our parents forbade us to eat, that we most craved and needed and wanted and loved"—oddly enough, for instance, such quotidian vegetables as tomatoes and celery. But bizarrely, the project culminates in a peculiar tasting of a quite ordinary tuber: a stolen raw potato, cut into "little slices."

> We all squatted on the cold dirt floor very solemnly, six or seven little girls, and nibbled and appraised, and whispered about the flavor, the texture, the wetness, the crunchiness, the grainy taste—or did it taste like clay?
>
> It was very strange, as I look back on it. It was a mirror held up to our futures, to all the solemn seminars and tastings we were preparing for.
>
> We analyzed and guessed and pondered.[1]

Analyzing, guessing, pondering: can there be any more appropriate intellectual processes for food writers, in particular for those authors of the culinary memoirs that have come to be called foodoirs?[2] Yet the object on which this famous gourmet-to-be remembers turning her keen intellectual attentions was hardly the kind of food Brillat-Savarin (or for that matter Ludwig Bemelmans, Waverly Root, or A. J. Liebling) would have savored. No sauce to deconstruct! No spices to sniff! No *croûte* to crumble in imagination! Not even a delicate drop of juice to lick! Eventually, as cook and cooking critic, the writer would turn her attention to the preparation of potatoes ("If I ever had my way, I thought, I would make such delicious things of potatoes that they would be a whole meal"), but here, in a moment emblematic of her most intense autobiographical epiphanies, the ordinary vegetable is wrenched out of its quotidian context, dragged into a basement under the kitchen and weirdly defamiliarized. Transgressive, yes, but parodically so, as if Eve's apple grew underground in the dirt of dailiness, and the Fall were a fall into knowledge of what is disturbing in the domestic: "the flavor, the texture, the wetness, the crunchiness, the grainy taste—or did it taste like clay?" Was this taste of clay indeed "a mirror held up to our futures, to all the solemn seminars and tastings we were preparing for"?[3]

I was going to write here about the memoir as a celebration of gastronomic recollection ("Feast, Memory!"as Nabokov might have put it), and yet Fisher's taste of clay gives me pause and redirects my attention. Like Williams's sweet and cold plums, stolen from a resonant icebox, powerful culinary memoirs often link eating and transgression as they dissect the most ordinary supper and the most extraordinary feast in an effort to analyze gastronomic memory. And what of the formula that, in one of my epigraphs, Liebling so trenchantly calls "Taste>Memory>Book"—or what might also be named "the *madeleine* phenomenon"? Even while Liebling's point is a perfectly reasonable one, it doesn't quite get at the ambiguities of the genre he describes, among them its linguistic difficulty. Yes, we can write about the meaning of dinner metaphorically, but how can we really recapture the flavors of the meal? The act of eating—like the sexual act and the experience of pain—would seem to take place in an eternal present. It's virtually impossible for language to describe the "physiology of taste" in the pure moment of biting, chewing, swallowing. Yes, some savor "explodes" in the mouth—sourness, saltiness, sweetness, bitterness, or the newly fashionable umami—yet what does it mean to say so? Verbal representation isn't adequate to the instant of dining just as, in Elaine Scarry's view, it can't capture physical torment. Odd but true: the pleasures of a rack of lamb are as nonverbal as the agony of the torturer's rack. Nonetheless, some of the most interesting contemporary writers persist in trying to find words for the unspeakable acts and facts of eating.[4]

If you are what you eat—and there can be little doubt about that, either historically or theoretically—must you also *write* what you eat and are? So it seems, lately, as foodoirs proliferate like cookies and cupcakes, pizzas and pastas, on bookstore shelves that used to be crammed with romance novels. Now even highbrow journalists confess to lying in bed dog-earing the pages of cookbooks (Adam Gopnik) and novelists take time off from plotting storylines to discourse on garden plots, dig into memories of dinners past or fulminate about meats and fruits that ought to be forbidden (Barbara Kingsolver, Jonathan Safran Foer). And in recent years, food porn or gastro-porn has come to be a label for the over-the-top luscious images and imaginings of meals ranging from sensual starters to sexy desserts featured in movies, magazines, videos, and even art galleries.[5]

No wonder the term "foodoir" echos "boudoir," as if kitchen and bedroom had merged in a fantasy collaboratively concocted by Julia Child, Doctor Ruth, Quentin Tarantino and maybe even the Marquis de Sade. Is food the new sex, as a few commentators have claimed, and are foodoirs versions of the old *True Confessions* that riveted some of us in high school? If so, why? What is good to eat may be good to think, as Lévi-Strauss declared, but apart from dedicated gastronomes like Grimod de la Reynière, Brillat-Savarin and Alexandre Dumas, few writers have thought it as intensively and extensively as twentieth- and twenty-first-century culinary autobiographers. There is the food memoir as coming-of-age story, even Künstlerroman—generally a portrait of the artist and sometimes a portrait of a troubled soul; the food memoir as the story of a marriage or cook's tale; the food memoir as history of origins; the food memoir as cultural record; the food memoir as polemic; and on and on: all modes of culinary writing that fit into customary literary genres, but now oddly transformed by a newly intense focus on stove and table, market and fridge. Many of the most famous food memoirs draw, of course, on all these genres. Fisher's *The Gastronomical Me*, for instance, arguably the paradigmatic twentieth-century work of this sort, is primarily a coming-of-age story, but it is also a cultural history, a culinary polemic, a first-person tale of love and death—and thus a grief memoir—and even an informal cookbook. Similarly, foodoirs ranging from Judith Moore's *Never Eat Your Heart Out* and *Fat Girl* to Betty Fussell's *My Kitchen Wars* and Ruth Reichl's *Tender at the Bone* gain intensity from a seamless melding of genres.

In many ways, these books are indeed celebratory tales of initiation into the pleasures of the table, with John Updike's definition of Fisher as a "poet of the appetites" a governing claim about almost all food writers, many of whom recount classic moments of culinary awakening, often in France. Fisher herself describes such a moment in an essay titled "The Most Important Meal I Ever Ate": "Falling in love for the first time since I was nine, being married for the first time, crossing the Atlantic for the first time . . . they all led irrevocably to 1:43 p.m., September 15, 1929, when I picked up a last delicious crust-crumb from the table, smiled dazedly at my love, peered incredulously at a great cathedral on the horizon, and recognized myself as a new-born sentient human being, ready at last to live." Betty Fussell, too, records a Gallic epiphany: outside Calais, "in the smallest of dockside cafés, I had my first bite of real butter and real bread. The wonder of those simple flavors and textures [sustained] our travels through France for the next twenty years in search of real food." And of course Julia Child recorded her life-changing encounter with sole meunière: its flesh "was delicate, with a light but distinct taste of the ocean that blended marvelously with the browned butter. I chewed slowly and swallowed. It was a morsel of perfection. . . . at 'La Couronne' I experienced fish, and a dining experience, of a higher order than any I'd ever had before. . . . It was the most exciting meal of my life." Young American wives abroad, the three women imply experiences of gastronomic defloration that would make each a lifelong sensualist, stories of a kind frequently reiterated by other memoirists.[6]

As a commentator on her own work, too, Fisher stresses love, warmth, nourishment and satisfied desire in her famous preface to *The Gastronomical Me:*

> [W]hen I write of hunger, I am really writing about love and the hunger for it, and warmth and the love of it and the hunger for it . . . and then the warmth and richness and fine reality of hunger satisfied . . . and it is all one . . . there is food in the bowl, and more often than not, because of what honesty I have, there is nourishment in the heart to feed the wilder, more insistent hungers.[7]

Yet this passage is quickly followed by the darker comment that I have used as one of my epigraphs here: "*We must eat.* If, in the face of *that dread fact,* we can find other nourishment and tolerance and compassion for it, we'll be no less full of human dignity" (emphasis added). Ultimately, for Fisher the "dread fact" of eating is the ontological fact of primal hunger and of the food chain in which we too are mortal links, dining on mortality and in the end destined to become dinner ourselves, whether for worms or flames or vultures. Yet at the same time, in the face of the existential anxiety associated with food—*will I have enough to eat? will I have* anything *to eat?* even, *must I or can I eat?*—another "fact" balances the truth of dread, the voluptuous fact of eating: *I have eaten well and fully,* meaning not only, *I have survived* but *I have survived with pleasure!* At its strongest, the food memoir does celebrate the deliciousness of survival, but sets that delight against the dread it also represents. Its flavors, then, are sweet *and* sour, salt *and* bitter. Perhaps, in fact, they please us so much because to the solemn, subterranean taste of clay—a taste not only of Fisher's raw potato but of the substance out of which we ourselves, too, are made—they add a comforting reminder of the "delicious things" that can be done with potatoes.

Still, if Fisher's underground childhood "seminar" was transgressive in its challenge to what parents and cooks didn't want little girls to eat, the culinary memoir itself is transgressive (or started out that way) in challenging what readers aren't supposed to want to read. To be sure, gravy-spotted cookbooks have for at least a century had a place in every bourgeois kitchen and ruled even longer among professional chefs, while since Grimod produced his series of *L'Almanach des gourmands* (1803–12) countless restaurant guides have studded the shelves of gourmets and weighed down the suitcases of travelers. But food on the nightstand? A food book as pillow book? As Fisher notes, it wasn't even proper to discuss the menu at the early twentieth-century American table. When she and her younger sister praised the cuisine of one of the household cooks, she confides, their righteously Victorian grandmother declared that "Their table manners are getting worse"—and this was true, the author adds, "if you believed as she and unhappy millions of Anglo-Saxons have been taught to believe, that food should be consumed without any comment of any kind but above all without sign of praise or enjoyment."[8]

The kitchen, after all—whether inhabited by servants or (in lower classes) wives and mothers—wasn't a place to discuss in polite society. Still lives of fruits and vegetables had long been admired, and genre paintings of butcher shops and bakeries go back as far as ancient Rome, while there are countless cosy novelistic limnings of peasant mamas in clean aprons. But Virginia

Woolf puts the issue best in "Mr. Bennett and Mrs. Brown," one of her most quoted essays: "in or about December, 1910, human character changed. In life [she added] one can see the change, if I may use a homely illustration, in the character of one's *cook*. The Victorian cook lived like a leviathan in the lower depths, formidable, silent, obscure, inscrutable; the Georgian cook is a creature of sunshine and fresh air; in and out of the drawing-room, now to borrow *The Daily Herald*, now to ask advice about a hat" (emphasis added). Like the bathroom or indeed the bedroom, the kitchen long represented "the lower depths" in Western society—"formidable" and somehow embarrassing. Surely it isn't coincidental that Leopold Bloom journeys from outhouse to butcher to kitchen (where he panfries pork kidneys) and that his adored but faithless wife lies in bed like "potted meat" with her "mellowy smellowy buttocks" and chamber pot. Joyce shocked moralists by bringing all these human intestinal workings—sexual, sensual and scatological—into daylight, if not "sunshine and fresh air." And of course it might be said that the revolutions of modernism facilitated the surprising innovations of the culinary memoir, though that genre might not at first seem to be as revolutionary as *A Portrait of the Artist as a Young Man, Ulysses, The Sun Also Rises* and *Women in Love.*[9]

Even Woolf, however, finds herself a bit flummoxed by her metaphor of cook and kitchen. "Do you ask for more solemn instances of the power of the human race to change?" she wonders, having introduced us to past and present cooks. Well, then, "consider the married life of the Carlyles and bewail the waste, the futility, for him and for her, of the horrible domestic tradition which made it seemly for a woman of genius to spend her time chasing beetles, scouring saucepans, instead of writing books. All human relations have shifted—those between masters and servants, husbands and wives, parents and children." Note, here, that while analyzing cultural metamorphoses the famous celebrant of Mrs. Ramsay still relegates the kitchen to—well, the kitchen. How unseemly it was, she declares, "for a woman of genius to spend her time . . . scouring saucepans, instead of writing books!" And of course, we almost at once do sympathize with Jane Carlyle.[10] But what about the cook—or even Jane Carlyle as cook? By the 1940s, as we've seen, Woolf herself had begun to acquiesce in the grounding realities of the kitchen. Exiled from London by the war and with only one domestic helper, she turned her own hand to "haddock and sausages," and, on the verge of suicidal depression, found the thought of doing so a stay against the death around and in her. The Georgian cook was in the process of metamorphosing into the modern writer who is also perforce a cook, and whose kitchen, a place of sunlight and air, is figuratively, if not literally, next door to the room of her own that is (at least sometimes) a place of sunlight and art.

And when the cook, whether female or male—and gender is germane here too—began moving from stove to study, dishpan to desk, the culinary memoir began to become a mainstream genre. Until fairly recently, as the food writer Bill Buford has commented, such writing "has been a niche thing, like writing about airplane tires or computer software or snowboards. But I think people have recognized a need for food writing that acknowledges everything food can be about."[11] A literary development that facilitated the rise of the genre was the relatively recent ascendancy of the novel itself, with its frequent focus on the quotidian and its elaboration of domestic detail: sexual feasting in *Tom Jones*, a rotting wedding cake in *Great Expectations,* strange picnics in *In Our Time* and *The Sun Also Rises, boeuf en daube* in *To the Lighthouse*—and my list could go on much, much longer. At the same time, though, as a genre the culinary memoir was framed and informed by the increasing popularity of the cookbook in the ever more servantless twentieth century, along with the concomitant growth of mass cultural modes of personal and household instruction, including how-to books, food polemics, self-help diets, and even testimonial advertising. That cultural icon *Mastering the Art of French Cooking* was intended, remember, for the *servantless* American cook. And though Fisher herself really wanted to be a novelist and indeed published a considerable body of prose fiction, she began her writing career with *Serve It Forth,* a set of autobiographical essays judiciously dotted with recipes ("like birds in a tree—if there is a comfortable branch") and studded, too, with culinary maxims ("if you are in a bad temper you should not be thinking of food at all") along with confessional polemics ("For my own meals I like simplicity above all. I like newness in what I serve [and] leisure [and] a mutual ease"). And *Serve It Forth* was followed by further culinary advice manuals (the wartime *How to Cook a Wolf*), journalistic meditations on gastronomy (*Consider the Oyster*), food histories (*An Alphabet for Gourmets*), and travel memoirs (*Two Towns in Provence*).[12]

Various as they are, however, all these works present themselves in one way or another as autobiographical and all depend on Fisher's brilliant construction of herself as a narrator of gastronomy who is a seductive and confident diner–cook and has become such a figure through a series of painful as well as pleasurable episodes. In all her writings, but especially in her masterpiece, *The Gastronomical Me,* she recounts these episodes with the gusto of a woman who considers herself as tasteful as she is beautiful even while she must disclose that she has become elegantly self-sufficient through suffering.

A Portrait of the Transcendental Gastronome as a Young Woman

"Now I am going to write a book," explained the young Mary Frances Kennedy (M. F. K.) Fisher in the preface to her early *Serve It Forth* (1937), and "It will be about eating and about what to eat and about people who eat. . . . Brillat-Savarin will haunt it, and very probably show himself in an inevitable aphorism. *The Settlement Cook Book* and Paul Reboux will peer shyly and with little recognition at their ancestors *The Harleian Manuscript* and Mrs. Glasse and Carême and Roselli. And people I know will talk a little and eat more." Despite this intelligent account of cultural roots, however, *Serve It Forth,* especially as part of the sequence later titled *The Art of Eating,* is more about Fisher herself and her coming to culinary consciousness—indeed, her aesthetic development or *Bildung*–than it is about Brillat-Savarin, *The Settlement Cook Book* or gastronomic gossip.[13]

To begin with, in a chapter about childhood tellingly titled "When a Man Is Small," Fisher assumes that the gastronomic subject is male—a little boy who "loves and hates food" with special "ferocity," and who can't understand his younger sister's calm hoarding of cookies. Suddenly, though, in the midst of this portrait of a young man Fisher segues into self-revelation: a tale of the sophistication with which, as a teenager on dates, she would order "a German pancake with hot applesauce and sweet butter" while murmuring nonchalantly "Salted butter ruins the flavor" to "my Tommy or Jimmy." That this soon-to-be acolyte of Brillat-Savarin is exceptional among women becomes even clearer a few chapters later, when she remarks that "cooking in itself is, for most women, a question less of vocation than of necessity. *They* are not called to the kitchen by the divine inner voice of [an] Escoffier" but "by the piping of *their* husbands' empty stomachs," so they "cook doggedly, desperately, more often than not with a cumulative if uninspired skill" (emphasis added).[14]

Fisher's implicit identification with the masculine continues intermittently throughout *Serve It Forth.* After, for instance, confessing that for "my own meals I like simplicity above all," she adds that "I do not agree with the Greeks and Romans that women should be reserved for the end of a meal and served with the final wines and music." The speaker of this passage might as well be a middle-aged male gastronome—Jean Anthelme Brillat-Savarin, for instance, or Alexandre Laurent Grimod de la Reynière—while "women" might as well be a species of petits fours. Yet by the time Fisher wrote *The Gastronomical Me,* she was portraying herself not only as a "predominantly female" diner but a diner who (despite any male identification) is indisputably a femme fatale. In one of her most notable disquisitions on dining alone, she revels in her own voluptuous union of culinary intelligence with sexual sophistication, even while she continues to define herself as an *exceptional* woman.[15]

I quote the passage below at length because it is one of her major self-portraits and arguably a culminating moment in this memoir. "More often than not people who see me on trains and in ships, or in restaurants, feel a kind of resentment of me since I taught myself to enjoy being alone," she declares.

> Women are puzzled, which they hate to be, and jealous of the way I am served, with such agreeable courtesy, and of what I am eating and drinking, which is almost never the sort of thing they order for themselves. And men are puzzled too, in a more personal way. I anger them as males.

> I am sorry. I do not like to do that, or puzzle the women either. But if I must be alone, I refuse to be alone as if it were something weak and distasteful, like convalescence. Men see me eating in public, and I look as if I "knew my way around"; and yet I make it plain that I know my ways around without them, and that upsets them.
>
> I know what I want, and I usually get it because I am adaptable to locales. I order meals that are more typically masculine than feminine, if feminine means whipped-cream-and-cherries. I like good wines, or good drinkin'-likka, and beers and ales. I like waiters; I think the woman who said that waiters are much nicer than people was right, and quite often waitresses are too. So they are always nice to me, which is a sure way to annoy other diners whose soup, quite often, they would like to spit in.
>
> And all these reasons, and probably a thousand others, like the way I wear my hair and what shade my lipstick is, make people look strangely at me, resentfully with a kind of hurt bafflement, when I dine alone.[16]

Self-possessed, seductive, ready to *épater les bourgeois,* the gastronome we encounter in this passage might be a modernist heroine. (Is she Brett Ashley? Is she Gudrun Brangwen?) Certainly she is in some sense both a literary character and almost a cinematic auteur—with considerable hauteur. Though she may be projecting her wish for admiration onto those around her, she claims to be sure she knows how people react to her: both sexes are puzzled or resentful, except for the waiters and waitresses who respect her connoisseurship, even while the audience that observes her (and she is clearly onstage) is transfixed by her glamour. She pities them (she is "sorry" that she baffles them) yet she unhesitatingly enacts her experience of dining for them, and at the same time for herself: she isn't just a poet of the appetites, she's a performer of the appetites. And all these qualities are hers perhaps primarily because she has taught herself to eat alone in restaurants ("slowly, voluptuously, and with independence"), one of the most problematic social acts in a world of public eating spaces not usually so masterfully conquered by women on their own.

Cultural critics have long remarked that restaurants are in some sense theatrical arenas, with meals at upscale venues a favored form of bourgeois entertainment, in which diners perform not only for their own tablemates but also for others in the room, even the servers and the maître d'. But, as many commentators have also noted, most people—quite a few men and almost all women—find eating alone in public difficult. Even solitary dining in private feels like a "stigmatized behavior because," notes one sociologist, "it defies the [communal] expectations we have of eating" and is even "thought of as an unfortunate activity of the social outcast." Adds this writer, "When I spoke with friends, family, and colleagues about this topic, the overwhelming response was one of embarrassment, as if we were discussing their masturbation rituals. And who wants to admit they're having it, food or sex, alone?" In the theatrical arena of the restaurant, the solo diner is vulnerable to a kind of voyeurism that verges on the "predatory."[17]

Clearly Fisher is intensely conscious of the problems implicit in gastronomical solitude. She declares, after all, with considerable satisfaction that she "baffles," "hurts," or "puzzles" observers of both sexes even while admitting that "I taught myself to enjoy being alone" and conceding further that "if I must be alone, I refuse to be alone as if it were something weak and distasteful, like convalescence." Yet it's plain too, from the pleasure she quite literally exhibits in "slowly, voluptuously" dining among an admiring circle of waiters and waitresses, that she imagines the arena of the restaurant as a stage for a bravura one-woman show, with the servers as walk-ons and the other diners as puzzled audience. Because she wears her hair a certain way, and her lipstick is a certain shade—because she is properly coiffed and literally as well as figuratively made up—she has herself become a spectacle, a star of the art of eating.[18]

The erotic flavor of Fisher's gastronomic mastery is illuminated by a passing anecdote she relates with considerable gusto in *Consider the Oyster,* a book her biographer says she wrote to amuse and distract her second husband, Dillwyn Parrish, when he was dying. Quoting the French poet–gourmet Jean-Louis Vaudoyer, she notes that in his *Éloge de la Gourmandise* he "speaks of a woman he once watched eat something especially delicious. She savored her enjoyment with a carefully sensuous slowness, and then she sighed, as it came to its inevitable end, 'Ah . . . what a pity that I do not have little taste-buds clear to the bottom of my stomach!'" To a curious prefiguration of the rearranged anatomy of pleasure that is the premise of *Deep Throat*, this little tale adds subtler thrills of voyeurism and exhibitionism. The food writer watches the diner while the diner, eating with careful sensuousness, watches him watching her and watches, too, her own performance.[19]

Most of Fisher's memoiristic writings, but especially *The Gastronomic Me,* are narrated by a culinary celebrity even more skilled at enacting her role than Vaudoyer's female gourmet, and they are marketed—with their glamour-girl portraits of the author—as seductive performances on paper of her voluptuously tough, even hard-boiled, persona as a transcendental gastronome: "I know what I want, and I usually get it because I am adaptable to locales. I order meals that are more typically masculine than feminine, if feminine means whipped-cream-and-cherries. I like good wines, or good drinkin'-likka, and beers and ales." That the tone here is Hemingwayesque isn't surprising, given Fisher's disclosure that she had been "more than once bolstered in [her] timid twenties" by an "early Hemingway phrase": "Never be daunted in public."[20] Her pose and poise as Hemingway heroine is certified, too, by the story of Cesar, the misogynistic but lascivious Spanish butcher, with which she concludes *Serve It Forth.* As she and her then husband Al Fisher feast on "a massive filet of beef" and "plenty of good wine,"

> Cesar put down his knife and fork.
>
> "She likes it, she likes good food!" he said wonderingly, to Al. "She cannot be a real woman!"
>
> After that things were very pleasant.[21]

Yet even while Fisher records such triumphs with keen satisfaction, we learn that they are hard-won. Most of her memoirs, but again especially *The Gastronomical Me,* are records of the pressures that shaped this charismatic speaker as she learned how to come to terms with the "dread fact" of eating. In some of her writings, to be sure, Fisher portrays herself as having had a kind of

Frank Capra childhood in the Southern California small town of Whittier—bicycling among orange groves, close to her siblings and her honorary Aunt Gwen, and beloved by parents who were "young and beautiful and intelligent."[22] But as a culinary narrative *The Gastronomical Me* is rich with tension, beginning in a kitchen that is at first presided over by a puritanical grandmother and then by a magnificent cook who turns out to be a madwoman.

"The first thing I remember tasting and then wanting to taste again," the author rather surprisingly confides, was "the grayish-pink fuzz my grandmother"—a "grim woman"—"skimmed from a spitting kettle of strawberry jam. I suppose I was about four." Weird though sugary, this primordial "fuzz" from a "spitting" pot out of a fairy tale may be nicer than raw potato—and it's followed in the next chapter by a more prepossessing peach pie Kennedy père offers his two little daughters—but still, a conventional "poet of the appetites" would be more likely to begin her memoir with peaches and cream than with blurry fuzz. Then both fuzz and pie are succeeded by the advent of Ora, a self-contained woman who cooks "in a kind of ecstasy" and whose savory foods Grandmother hates, especially because they inspire excited (and improper) commentary from the children.[23]

"I was very young," Fisher explains, "but I can remember observing . . . that meat hashed with a knife is better than meat mauled in a food-chopper; that freshly minced herbs make almost any good thing better"—and, in short, "that most of my observations were connected in some way with Ora's knife." But of course the cook's knife is always potentially a weapon, even while it is a tool that produces delicacies. Thus, one day, quite unexpectedly, "Ora cut her [elderly mother] into several neat pieces," then "ripped a tent thoroughly to ribbons," then "cut her wrists and her own throat, expertly. The police told Father there wasn't a scratch or a nick in the knife."[24]

Food and foodways prove, this early in Fisher's memoir, to involve strangeness (fuzz) and, worse still, violence. Yet in the eagerness of appetite, the writer and her sister are, at least on the surface, unfazed, if slightly depressed. "The way of dying was of only passing interest to us at our ages, but our inevitable return to ordinary sensible plain food was something to regret," confesses Fisher, adding rather mysteriously, "We were helpless then, but we both learned from mad Ora, and *now we know what to do about it, because of her*" (emphasis added)—know, presumably, how to wield a chef's knife without unleashing its dread powers, but know, too, how dreadful its powers can be. And that even when the cook eschews a knife she has the power to harm becomes clear enough in the next chapter of *The Gastronomical Me.* Here Fisher insists that the "first thing I cooked was pure poison": a pudding ("a little round white shuddering milky thing") that she decorated with blackberries, to which her mother was ferociously allergic. And the next dish she prepared was equally deadly: a plate of excessively curried "Hindu eggs" so spicy that she and her sister, "with the desperate intuition of burned animals," immediately raced to fill their scorched mouths with soothing mineral oil.[25]

Fisher's portrayal of her childhood cuisine as sometimes problematic—from the strictures of an ascetic grandmother to the deeds of a mad cook to the unpleasant experiments of a feckless schoolgirl—is central to her culinary–literary enterprise at its most successful. For whether as public performance or private experience, dining is always a source of some danger as well as carefully cultivated delight in this writer's imaginative world. And for these reasons it is often associated, as well, with both eroticism and gamesmanship. One of the most dramatic episodes in *The Gastronomical Me* marks the young Mary Frances's initiation into sexuality—and specifically lesbian desire—by counterpointing her first swallow of a raw oyster, her first experience as a "belle of the ball" at a girls' school Christmas dance (where two older girls fight to partner her), and her first confrontation with same-sex love gone wrong in the person of the school's weeping housekeeper and the fat nurse (dressed up as Santa Claus) whom the superficially straitlaced housekeeper adores. Noting, "I stood staring . . . like a paralyzed rabbit. I was terrified [of] the costumed nurse, and of Mrs. Cheever so hideously weeping and of all old women," the writer confesses in a moment of mingled erotic nostalgia and revulsion. "If I could still taste my first oyster, if my tongue still felt fresh and excited, it was perhaps too bad. Although things are different now, I hoped then, suddenly and violently, that I would never see one again."[26]

Less dramatic but equally telling is an episode in which the emerging gastronome forces herself to order from a menu properly as she travels across the country—and toward adulthood—with a sophisticated uncle: "I looked at my menu, really looked with all my brain, for the first time. 'Just a minute please,' I said, very calmly [and] stayed quite cool, like a surgeon when he begins an operation, or maybe a chess player opening a tournament." And "never since then have I let myself say, or even think 'Oh, anything,' about a meal, even if I had to eat it alone, with death in the house or in my heart." Just as "My First Oyster" is an early instance of dining as erotic theater, so this seemingly minor anecdote about the interpretation of menus is a foreshadowing of what was to become dining as performance, even gamesmanship.[27]

But as *The Gastronomical Me* moves toward its sorrowful last course, the erotic tension becomes stranger—sometimes sadomasochistic—and intensifies. Following the "Sea Change" of her first marriage and first trip to Europe, the narrator recounts culinary initiations that are often paralleled by sexual, or more generally moral, transformations of innocence into experience. In the first Dijonnais *pension* where she and her husband settle after their journey to France, they encounter the monstrous proto-Nazi Klorr—"the most rat-like human I have ever seen"—whose prediction of a "Uranic" renaissance in Germany marks him as an acolyte of the misogynistic and anti-Semitic Viennese philosopher Otto Weininger, a notorious theorist of both Aryan superiority and "the third sex." In a household already marked by hostile dynamics—a warring couple, an effeminate stepson—Klorr is passionately loved by the pale, ghost-story-teller Maritza Nankova, a Polish student whose gaze seems to Fisher to have a "kind of religious lewdness." One night, when the quiet is disrupted by mysterious soft sounds, the author finds Klorr feasting on grapes and cakes, set out on the girl's naked body as on a table. Though the German disappears, "silent and unruffled as a rat, with [a] napkin in his hand," "I knew," Fisher says, that he "had been supping there, while Maritza lay naked on the bed and moaned for him. And I knew that he had put the empty grapeskins on her unprotesting flesh without ever touching her."[28]

Theatrical as this episode is—framed by bed and bedroom like a scene in what Fisher refers to as "the second act of an old-fashioned bedroom comedy"—it draws from the narrator a commentary that she even more self-reflexively pronounces as melodramatic. Confronting Klorr in the hallway, she declares in the most "completely pompous French that has ever been spoken outside a national theater," that "Mademoiselle Nankova . . . is suffering from an extreme sexual overexcitement," enunciating her syllables as in "a quotation from Racine." Linking sex, food, cruelty, perversion and performance, the encounter recapitulates the "wild" hungers dramatized in the painful oyster-eating sequence in the girls' boarding school, even while it allows the author once again to take what she persistently calls "the measure of my powers" as both actress and observer.[29]

In a restaurant scene later in the book, the narrator herself becomes the object of a kind of odd culinary desire when, alone at an old inn in northern Burgundy, she meets a mad waitress who is "fanatical about food, like a medieval woman possessed by the devil." Obsessed with serving her solitary guest the treasures of a meal prepared by the famous Paris chef "Monsieur Paul," who owns the place, the girl produces an interminably luxurious lunch, and eventually it's clear that her gastronomic efforts are inspired not just by an almost insane devotion to the cook but also by a weird desire to seduce Fisher—who is as usual, despite her professed bewilderment, an artist of eating. As the writer sipped *marc* at the end of the meal, she confides, the waitress "watched me intently, her pale eyes bulging in the dimness and her lips pressed inward as if she too tasted the hot, aged *marc*"—and then, suddenly, " 'Permit me!' she said, and I thought she was going to kiss me. But instead she pinned a tiny bunch of snowdrops and dark bruised cyclamens against my stiff jacket . . . and then ran from the room with her head down."[30]

Throughout all these emotionally charged anecdotes of culinary and erotic desire—and a number of others set in parlors and *pensions* throughout Burgundy and Switzerland—the young Mary Frances is learning not just to perform as a poised and seductive diner but also as a masterful cook, always in control of the voluptuous, sometimes eccentric repasts she serves to friends. Her account of her decision-making in her own kitchen parallels her description of the decisiveness with which she enacts the role of gastronome in public (and sometimes private) spaces. In the first tiny flat that the couple rents in Dijon, she tells us, she was becoming convinced that it is "foolish" to serve a multi-course meal "just because the guests who are to eat it have always been used to" such dinners. "Let them try eating two or three things, I said, so plentiful and so interesting and so well cooked that they will be satisfied." And when Al objects that this way of entertaining may seem inhospitable, she adds firmly that "I still believe this, and have found that it makes cooking for people exciting and amusing for me, *and often astonishingly stimulating for them"* (emphasis added). Indeed, she insists, "My meals shake them from their routines, not only of meat–potatoes–gravy, but of thought, of behavior," although now and then she has to concede that "women past middle age" may experience a "spiritual upset" when she serves "an exotic or eccentric dish [that] would do more harm than good," so she must "bow" to their requirements."[31]

Here again, as in her self-portrait as diner, Fisher defines herself as a "transcendental gastronome"—a chef soaring above not only traditional bourgeois conceptions of the menu but also the conventional sex roles of domesticated women who cringe from culinary innovation. By the time she has parted from Al Fisher and is living at the beautiful Le Paquis in Switzerland with her beloved Chexbres (the name she gives Dillwyn Parrish throughout her memoir), she has confirmed her kitchen style. Although she recounts idyllic pastoral picnics *en famille*—for instance, fresh-picked peas from the couple's garden, "with little cold pullets cooked for us in Vevey"—she entertains as theatrically as she dines. On one occasion, she alarms guests by showing them into "what they could only guess to be a kind of stage-kitchen," where they perceive no signs or smell of an upcoming meal. Then after "Chexbres and I let them suffer" a bit, the couple, "with the smug skill of two magicians," astonish them with a simple meal of homemade stew, rolls and salad. The proprietor of a nearby luxury hotel is especially astounded, murmuring *"Ça alors! Formidable!"*; he refused "to believe that I had made the stew . . . convinced that in our pride we were hiding a famous chef somewhere in the cellars."[32]

As a couple, too, Chexbres and the narrator perform for each other, with Chexbres at one point inviting his love to join him for a spectacular Easter supper of gin and caviar and Fisher trumping his romantic move by politely drinking and dining—and then, surprisingly, retiring to her own bedroom.

But gradually, in the midst of magic meals and glamorous meadows, a foreboding darkness creeps into *The Gastronomical Me*. Klorr was the first herald of the horrors that were soon to engulf Europe, and then, at Le Paquis, the "very pretty pale limp" young woman with whom the writer's brother, David, is in love unwittingly picks up the dreadful thread. Marked by a "stony lethargy" throughout her visit, the vaguely sullen girl suddenly comes to life at the dinner table as she reminisces about the excitement of the "escape[s]" she has witnessed on the beach at San Sebastián—"refugees [from the Spanish Civil War] trying to swim past the border into France, pretending they were summer people. It was simply breath-taking! The guards always spotted them . . . and then there was always shooting."[33]

On ships and in trains, the drama of Europe's catastrophic slide into the Second World War is enacted and reenacted, as the author too dines on disaster. For while she crosses the Atlantic alone, to tell her family that she is going to divorce Al and marry Chexbres, she finds herself on a boat laden with Jews fleeing the Nazis and is filled with forebodings, not only of the death of the life she has lived abroad but also of her beloved's impending demise. By the time she returns to Switzerland, toward the end of *The Gastronomical Me*, the book itself has evolved into a grief memoir. Chexbres's death takes place offstage (as did the suicide of Dillwyn Parrish, who left their home to shoot himself) but his sufferings from Burger's disease, including the amputation of one leg, occupy center stage, as the pair elegiacally cross and recross the ocean like "two happy ghosts." The brilliant chapter titled "The Flaw" recounts the terror of a train journey from Vevey to Milan, during which Fisher and Chexbres witness the capture of an Italian political prisoner, who, they later learn, manages to escape from his jailers only by smashing a window and cutting his throat on its jagged edge: an offstage suicide that also prefigures Chexbres's self-inflicted death. Throughout the train trip the two have continued to experience themselves as ghosts, "free forever from the trouble of life, surrounded with a kind of insulation of love," but at this moment, as war and the fear of war seep through their shell, the insulation cracks: "We were not two ghosts, safe in our own immunity from the pain of living. Chexbres was a man with one leg gone, the other and the two arms soon to go. . . . And I was a woman condemned . . . watching her true love die too slowly," as there, "in the train, we knew for a few minutes that we had not escaped . . . knew no knife of glass . . . could keep the pain of war outside."[34]

Finally, the school of love, loss and loneliness in which Fisher has learned to be both an artist of eating and an artificer of meals yields the monitory tale of Juanito, the Mexican woman who sings mariachi in male disguise and is hopelessly in love with the writer's brother David. Fleeing to Mexico after Chexbres's death, Fisher encounters this forlorn being—a transvestite, a passionate drinker, and a powerful musician—whose wailing of "La Malagueña" rises wildly above the background of the beer hall where she is entertaining to enact the grief that the recently widowed author cannot bring herself to fully articulate. She recognizes Juanito–Juanita's dramatization of pain as one performer recognizes another's genius, and claims that she is thankful "we were leaving" so that the singer would be "free again, as much as anyone can be who has once known hunger and gone unfed." And with the admission that hunger can and perhaps inevitably must go unfed, Fisher implicitly returns to and revises her earlier statements of culinary (and human) self-sufficiency. As she was ultimately to admit in *An Alphabet for Gourmets*, the book that succeeded *The Gastronomical Me,* although "the slightly depraved ramifications of dining alone are plainly limitless . . . I prefer the category of Two . . . above all the company of One other, making the rarest kind of Two."[35]

Two Portraits of a Hunger Artist as a Young Woman

Although Fisher frequently insists that she is writing about hungers—the "wilder, more insistent" ones and those that go unfed—she is really, as she tacitly admits, an aesthete of eating and a performer of culinary skill, style and sophistication. Though her art is everywhere darkened by dread, it's not so much energized by the force of gastronomic desire as it is by the memories that flavor past appetites. By comparison, Judith Moore, perhaps her most distinguished descendant, is a brilliant artist of quotidian hungers—the wildest and most insatiable ones. The author of two culinary memoirs—*Never Eat Your Heart Out* (1996) and *Fat Girl* (2006)—Moore died just after the second of these books was published to wide acclaim, so hers, unlike Fisher's, was a career cut short by an untimely death. But even in her accomplished writings she was almost the opposite of Fisher.

Where Fisher, for instance, scorned women who "cook doggedly, desperately" in response to "the piping of their husbands' empty stomachs," Moore transcribes the ordinary pleasures of domesticity, canning, gardening, pie-making, and she revels, with some amusement and no little delight, in the cakes and casseroles of mid-century middle-class America. In *Never Eat Your Heart Out,* for instance, she painstakingly records the menus of the ritual potluck supper, including her own "cheesecake topped with canned cherry pie filling, to which I added red food coloring to make it brighter red," and "Mrs. Delacorte's famous sweet potato–pineapple Hawaii luau bake" and "Mrs. Hopper's Tater Tot casserole." "I didn't like the taste of much of this food," she confesses, "and it wasn't what I cooked at home," but, as she trenchantly observes, it was "public food, like 'good' clothing," and when someone died, you left it on his widow's kitchen counter, along with a note saying "Our prayers are with you in your time of bereavement."[36]

Where Fisher's extramarital romance with Chexbres mostly takes place offstage, Moore tells all—or a great deal of it—in a chapter boldly titled "Adultery" that is at the center of *Never Eat Your Heart Out.* And gastronomy is at the center of her adultery, as she announces even before introducing her readers to her lover:

> I don't think I ever better got the feel for that complicated business of insinuating cold butter into flour and thence into a high-pitched oven . . . that produces *mille-feuilles* pastry, don't think I ever stirred, sniffed, and tasted my way to a more provocative lime–ginger–garlic–soy–molasses marinade for duck than during the year I went out on my husband.

And where Fisher boasts of her pleasure in dining alone, Moore—recalling years of solitude after her affair has ended in separation—records the sorrow of dusk in the supermarket, cataloguing the solitary shoppers who line up with lonesome cans of cat food and Diet Coke: "The supermarket's pneumatic door wheezes. What does one person eat? . . . one pushes the cart down aisles, reads about chili on the Hormel can, chicken divan in the freezer case, and because to eat this food elicits more hope than can come true, one grabs bread, cheese, and pressed ham, gets a can of chicken noodle just in case."[37]

Finally, where Fisher recalls a secure childhood among the orange groves of Southern California, Moore records the traumas of growing up in an almost Dickensian hell, especially in *Fat Girl.* Here she tells of being fattened like a piglet by a hog- and chicken-raising farmer grandmother and then being confined to diet after diet by a whip-wielding slender, ambitious, singer mother. Ultimately, then, where Fisher commands and performs her appetites, Moore suffers hers: she is subjected to her own appetites and to those of others, victimized by the gastronomic yearnings of body and soul. By the time she writes *Fat Girl,* her narrative is a tale of struggle with such victimization, as if she were a female Prometheus chained to a mountain of flesh, clawed by the vultures of hunger. For this reason, perhaps, where Fisher's texts are elliptical and elegant, Moore's are headlong, ferocious and, yes, thick with feeling. "You're too fat to fuck," a man tells her as they dine on cheeseburgers in the first chapter of her case history of culinary desire.[38]

Arguably, Fisher was sui generis, the first to write what is basically an autobiography focused on food, but she had models, including not only such revered precursors as Brillat-Savarin and Grimod de la Reynière but also, in English, Elizabeth Robins Pennell, the author of a voluptuary's food guide titled *The Feasts of Autolycus, the Diary of a Greedy Woman*, along with such other memoirists and travel writers as the *New Yorker* writer A. J. Liebling (*Between Meals: An Appetite for Paris*) and his journalist counterpart Waverly Root (*The Food of France*). Her contemporaries included such popular memoirists as Betty MacDonald, whose *The Egg and I* was a bestseller in the 1940s, and Marjorie Kinnan Rawlings, whose anecdotal *Cross Creek Cookery* detailed the delights of "Coot Surprise" and "Alligator Tail Steak." Yet as a memoirist of hunger, Moore too had significant ancestors. Kafka's "A Hunger Artist" was surely not one of these, with its spectacular display of anorectic mastery, nor is Moore—as she takes pains to tell us—writing the history of an eating disorder. But though she confines herself to a personal case history, Moore's *Fat Girl* has a place among more politicized histories of starvation. In her fleshly entrapment, she is the opposite of a concentration camp prisoner, but her obsession with hunger is acutely described by Primo Levi, who recalls the horror of hunger at Auschwitz: "a need, a lack, a yearning that had accompanied us now for a year, had struck deep, permanent roots in us, lived in our cells, and conditioned our behavior." Less mortal but equally poignant memories of hunger preoccupy George Orwell in *Down and Out in Paris and London,* when he recalls how he and a friend, impoverished and desperate, "wrote dinner menus on the backs of envelopes [because we] were too hungry even to try and think of anything except food."[39]

Of course it's odd—it might even seem immoral—to compare a book about being overweight to tales of real, deadly deprivation. Yet the paradox of Moore's *Fat Girl* is that, although she is surrounded by plenty, the fat girl is starving. From her earliest autobiographical writings, she defines her Grammy, the witchlike cook of her childhood, as "brutal, powerful, and repulsive." And though this ferocious grandma "never feeds me a bad meal," her food itself evokes Hobbes's classic observation that life in the state of nature—a state in which Grammy nearly lives—is "nasty, brutish and short." Her meals

> do not hide the hard facts of the heavy thingness of things. Her cooking does not conceal being born, hard work, and bloody death; does not deny its roots; nor does it smother its origins in sauces. It smells like itself. It uses lard, thick cream, the fatback off the hog. . . . It is mixed with the hands and fried in iron skillets.
>
> Nothing goes to waste. When Grammy butchers hogs she pickles the cloven feet . . . the pointed, cartilaginous ears, and the curling bone-and-gristle tails. . . . Any pork remnants she grinds down into sausage, which she stuffs into the hog's intestines. The last renderings and bacon grease, hoarded over the months in Mason jars, she turns into a smoke-blackened iron pot of swilling lye to make soap.

Gross in its materiality, this food evokes primitive hungers—and primordial fears: "Grammy makes pork roast in the iron roaster while I think of how the witch tried to fatten up Gretel for her oven. I see if I can still measure my wrist with my thumb and finger."[40]

Grammy appears both in Moore's early "Blue Plate Blues," from which I've just quoted, and then, even more dramatically, in *Never Eat Your Heart Out*, which features a grisly memory of a "hog sticking day" and its aftermath, a nightmare of culinary violence over which she presides, attended by her sidekicks, Bushels and Buckles.

> Hog-sticking nights, while I got ready for bed, my grandmother and Bushels and Buckles, blood dried on their clothing, worked under the kitchen's dim overhead light. Bugs seethed, circling the bulb. . . . The kitchen resembled a butcher shop where a crazy drunken butcher was in charge. Disassembled hog crowded every surface. Hoofless legs and snoutless, earless heads and slabs of fatback and squares of what would be smoked into bacon were puzzled pieces. . . . The trio worked quickly, to keep the meat from going bad. . . . I don't remember what my dreams were, those nights. I had nightmares back then from which I'd wake, screaming, in the high four-poster bed, from which I always feared to fall.

After such knowledge, what hunger, one is tempted to inquire. Yet loveless, stranded with one or another wicked stepmother figure, the frightened, spiritually starved child becomes a desperate mouth, longing for fruits and pies, creams and puddings, delectable recipes for satiety, comfort, belonging. Thus she becomes both a victim of her own desire and its hideous representative.[41]

Its representative: Moore depicts her own body, over and over again, as a monstrosity. She recalls scornful young men shouting "Sooey pig, sooey pig!" and describes herself almost as she describes the hogs in her grandmother's kitchen, in an orgy of self-dismemberment. "Between what would be my waist if I had one and my pudenda hang fat rolls. The rolls form swags, drapes of loose fat that droop between my hip bones. My freckled breasts lay flat on my chest, and from under my breasts sweat runs." And its victim: as she separates her body into its grotesque components, she herself becomes a mouth, like the perpetually hungry, chewing, dangerously self-defeating mouth of the hog.

> My mouth is dangerous. My lips and my teeth and my tongue and the damp walls of my cheeks are always ready. . . . When I walk through the kitchen—when I walk through the world—my mouth is on the prowl. . . . I am scared of the big, hot hole my mouth is. My mouth always wants something and most of what my mouth wants, I can't give it.

For like the hog, the fatter she gets, the more likely she is to become meat for the slaughter, or at the least, a sacrifice to the scorn of a society in which her flesh imprisons, isolates and stigmatizes her.[42]

If Fisher, then, is a beautiful and beautifully made-up face, musing on the attractions of the way she wears her hair and what shade her lipstick is, Moore is an abject body, experiencing herself as nearly faceless though—in Sylvia Plath's phrase—"Allmouth."[43] Indeed, like Chexbres's limbs, amputated or ravaged by Burger's disease, the body threatens to disappear by the end of *The Gastronomical Me,* while it rules all except language in Moore's work, as if this writer were speaking flesh deconstructing itself into a series of horrified anti-*blazons* in a reversal of the Renaissance rhetoric whereby the lover celebrated his beloved's multiple physical attractions: eyes, hair, breasts, hips, etc.

"Life is so brief that we should not glance either too far backwards or forwards . . . therefore study how to fix our happiness in our glass and in our plate," wrote Grimod de la Reynière. And yet this notorious connoisseur, called by Sainte Beuve the "Father of the table," also meditated on the life and death implications of the stuff "in our glass and on our plate," staging some of his most elaborate dinner parties as funeral feasts.[44] Despite their radically different narratives, all these writers would agree with Betty Fussell that the kitchen is the one place in which we're all required to begin again, each day, at ground zero—reborn after the death of sleep to feed the gut, brain and soul by daily murder and redemption. And we too, their readers, are at the mercy of the same cosmic strictures, what Fisher called the "dread fact" of eating. When we walk through the world, our mouths, like Moore's, are "on the prowl." We submit to the voracity of the mouth, the sorrow of the mouth, concede our mortal knowledge that, as William Dickey put it, the galaxy is in the shape of an eating mouth. But we also rejoice in the adventures of the mouth, remember them, write about them. Our dread and our delight feed the foodoir that has become so fascinating to us in a servantless world where the quotidian sacrament of dinner so often replaces the sacred ancient feasts of bread and wine.

Chapter 7

Bitter Herbs or the Spices of Life? The Ambiguities of the Transnational Foodoir

> Dinner, "unordered," comes through the streets [of Florence] and spreads itself on our table, as hot as if we had smelt cutlets hours before.
>
> —ELIZABETH BARRETT BROWNING, *LETTERS*

> And, no, my grandparents said, they would never go back to that place, they spit on that place, they said, though not because of the wild things that were there. They spit on that place because [it] was like a parent who wouldn't feed its hungry children.
>
> —LOUISE DeSALVO, *CRAZY IN THE KITCHEN*

> It must be annoying to Italians the way we Americans romanticize them. We use their country for our fantasies and fill our kitchens with Tuscan-inspired tablecloths and earthenware. We cook "Italian" dishes that never existed east of Brooklyn.
>
> —LAURA SCHENONE, *THE LOST RAVIOLI RECIPES OF HOBOKEN: A SEARCH FOR FOOD AND FAMILY*

How I Ate and Who I Am

A few years ago I started to write a culinary memoir that I was going to call "The Spices of Life," and it was going to be full of contradictions—savory with celebration though salty, too, with some of the sorrow that often flavors memories of menus past. What I found myself writing, though, was more elegiac than I'd expected it to be, not just salty but bitter with what I think I recognize as the alienating taste of loss that accompanies cultural displacement, the mouthful of bitter herbs that immigrants swallow as they journey from the known to the unfathomable, from the table of the familiar to the walls of estrangement.

Beginning the writing again, I've put a question mark after my new title, hoping that as I remember more deeply, the bitter will turn sweet, or at least bittersweet. "You had a happy childhood, Sandra," my schoolteacher mother used to say in her most authoritative classroom voice when she read some of my poems. "So why must you be so *mor*bid?" And it's true that as a child, raised in times and places that must have been at least intermittently harsh for my elders, I rarely recognized the tastes and scents of loss. I thought the flavorings were always happy, frequently festive. But I myself was often sad, for reasons I couldn't understand, as if now and then I too had dipped into a dish of bitterness. Now I can read my sorrows as well as my joys through a vocabulary of the herbs that perfumed my early life, even when I didn't quite know what they were called.

Tarragon is the herb with which my story here begins. One Paris summer some years ago, when I opened a new little vial of dried *estragon*, its aroma flooded out and into and all around me, and just as if I were Proust, I was overcome. Tears pricked at my eyes—not, like Marcel, for a town unfolding its roads and roofs out of the past, but for just one person: my mother, Angela Maria Caruso Mortola, dead at ninety-seven in January 2001, who seemed to spring like a genie from that small bottle. She alone, or rather she and her long, lonely life in Jackson Heights, Queens: her widowhood, her isolation, her ambivalent loyalties to Sicily, the land she barely remembered, and to America, the country whose company she so much longed to keep.

It's often said that we know our ethnicity and its history through the foods we inherit from our families, the scents and savors of what was once the quotidian. And certainly we hyphenated Americans have produced so many recipes for and of nostalgia that any memoirist must now fear her ancestral kitchen can no longer yield much more than kitsch: Nonna's marinara sauce, Zia Teresa's inimitable *polpette*, or for that matter Grandma Molly's gefilte fish. Foodoir after foodoir, many of which I'll discuss here, investigates these gastronomic recollections. But my weepy memories of my mother were different, or so I then believed. My tears didn't well up as I sniffed the tarragon because I was reminded of some Sicilian specialty of hers. Rather, they came because she mostly didn't cook during her thirty years of marriage to my father—or if she did drag herself to the stove, she produced lamb chops or pork chops in a portable broiler-oven, instant mashed potatoes, canned peas or frozen green beans. When, throughout the more than thirty-five years of solitude she endured after Daddy died, she was obliged to prepare special meals for me and my family on our intermittent visits to New York, tarragon was the rather unlikely herb she chose to use as seasoning for most salads, soups and sauces—maybe because, along with oregano, it was one of the first dried herbs to appear on the shelves of supermarkets in Jackson Heights. So the distinctive, not especially Italian (but instead rather Frenchified) aroma of tarragon perfumed all her "company" dinners, though by "all" I mean just a few concoctions that she labored over: a quite nice preparation of breaded (and herbed with tarragon) chicken cutlets, a kind of veal stew with a light (tarragony) sauce, and a salad of (tarragon-flavored) marinated artichoke hearts.

Paradoxically, my kitchen-phobic mother came from a Sicilian household with quite a zesty culinary tradition, and there were many family stories centered on food—most notably, perhaps, the tale of my father's trial by sausage. The son of a Russian mother and a Niçois–Ligurian father, Alexis Joseph Mortola wasn't really used to things Sicilian when he first came a-courting my mother. So the older sister with whom she lived felt obliged to test his love. It was New Year's Eve, and she offered him a ferociously hot sausage along with the *pasta infornata* she'd prepared. All innocence and love, the skinny young man bit right in, for this was long before the days when you could buy a package of standard-issue hot Sicilian sausages in your local Safeway, and he had no reason to be suspicious. He manfully chewed as tears came to his eyes.

"Sandrina, we knew he really loved her," my aunt Frances would assure me, with each telling of this tale.

Maybe my mother was daunted by the complexity of a culinary heritage that included trials by sausage along with magnificent *pasta infornata* (the family name for what, I later discovered, was analogous to lasagna) along with miraculously orange *arancini*, the incomparable Sicilian rice balls whose recipe is, I suspect, genetically transmitted to a select few citizens of Persephone's island. Or perhaps, as a proto-liberated woman (a flapper and a free spirit, she always told me), she scorned the humdrum drudgery of the stove. Or perhaps—a corollary of this—she thought cooking would turn her into a stereotypical Italian mamma, redolent of garlic and olive oil and *basilico*. Because in our two-bedroom, gray-carpeted, genteelly furnished Jackson Heights apartment my father cooked and she mostly washed dishes or scrubbed floors—tasks that, oddly enough, seemed more *simpatico* to her than hovering over the stove.

Well, there was at least one distinctively Sicilian dish that she did now and then make for me. When my father went off by himself to a meeting, she would now and then assemble a dish she remembered fondly from her childhood: *scarola in brodo*, with spaghetti. This was a preparation my father heartily disliked—and so, for that matter, did I at that time, though now I can imagine what its merits would have been if my mother had cooked it with Sicilian abandon instead of WASPish restraint. Done right, *scarola in brodo* means sautéing lots and lots of crushed fresh garlic and maybe a little hot pepper in good, rich, fruity olive oil, then adding big handfuls of rinsed escarole, squeezed almost dry, to the garlicky oil and sauteeing some more, and finally uniting the vegetables with several quarts of broth into which, after a while, one would introduce a half pound or so of cooked spaghetti. The whole would then be served piping hot with lots of freshly grated parmesan, romano, or pecorino. And many traditional cooks would probably also dress the dish up with little meatballs, some white beans, and/or some slices of cooked Italian sausages, hot or mild. But alas, my mother's humble and conflicted version of this recipe was usually as bitter as it was watery—not enough garlic! overcooked escarole! not even a bouillon cube to simulate chicken broth!—even while it was the most elaborate effort she made in the kitchen, at least until Daddy died and, for thirty-five years, she took up tarragon.

My mother didn't really need to linger alone in Jackson Heights for all those decades. When my husband and I moved to Northern California with our three young children two years after my father succumbed to the long-term aftereffects of boyhood rheumatic fever, we urged her to join us, first in the little Sacramento Valley town of Davis, then in more sophisticated Berkeley. Installing herself with, or near, her daughter (I was an only child) would have been the old-fashioned Sicilian modus vivendi for widowhood. But to my determinedly modern mother, with her memories of free-spirited flapperhood, such a solution was utterly unacceptable. Just as she'd scorned the aromatic *Italianità* of the Sicilian ghetto in Brooklyn where she grew up, she renounced the role of aproned Nonna, nor did she want to seem to depend on me, her professorial daughter. No, she too was a professional—a retired schoolteacher, a would-be clinical psychologist, an avid reader of the *New Yorker* and the *New York Times Book Review*. No pantry theatricals for her, no perpetual second bedroom in someone else's home, and no diminished quarters around the corner from the daughterly Big House either. She would manage on her own, thank you, like any other up-to-date American.

And for a while she did. She had a few friends nearby, and—for maybe a decade—a number of relatives. But gradually the friends migrated south, to the sunny retirement homes of Florida, or west, to be near their kids, and gradually, too, the relatives who hadn't already moved in with their children began to die, until my mother, surviving into her late nineties, was left almost entirely alone for the last fifteen or twenty years of her life, except for our intermittent visits: alone and still stubbornly refusing to move. Perhaps it was then that the scent of tarragon became, for me, the perfume of her loneliness, the scent of a solitude into which only the voices of successive *Late Show* comedians brought something resembling company.

Yet paradoxically, it was in these last years of widowhood that she enthusiastically rediscovered the ethnicity she'd so roundly repudiated as a young woman fleeing the Sicilian ghetto of her girlhood. Indeed, in these years she kept a file of clippings from the restaurant reviews that ran in the *New York Times* and would take us excitedly to Italian restaurants recommended by Craig Claiborne or Mimi Sheraton, places whose proprietors treated her with exactly the deference due the nonna she now was—but had never (she thought) wanted to be. And in another of life's little ironies, she repeatedly congratulated me, my husband and our children on our attempts to replicate not just her sister's and mother's Sicilian recipes but even my paternal grandfather's Niçois–Ligurian achievements in the kitchen.

Oregano was often central to these enterprises. My father's father was an artist manqué, born in Nice, who had, he said, come to the United States from Paris toward the end of the first decade of the twentieth century to study, of all things, painting. Like Rick, Humphrey Bogart's most famous role, who claimed that he'd gone to Casablanca to take the waters, Grandpa was obviously misinformed. So he became first a waiter and then the co-owner of a restaurant on Franklin Street, in the heart of New York's market district. As I recall, his establishment was what T. S. Eliot would call a "sawdust restaurant with oyster shells," a lunch or supper place for truckers hauling vegetables to town and for buyers or sellers of produce.[1] I remember a black and white ceramic tile floor sprinkled with drifts of sawdust on which stood tables surrounded by what would no doubt now be extremely expensive because authentic early twentieth-century bentwood chairs. And in this form the restaurant prospered for more than thirty years. But chairs, tables and sawdust alike vanished into the shadows of history when Grandpa and his partner decided to modernize the restaurant in 1948, replacing the old accoutrements with shiny new linoleum tile floors, "leatherette" banquettes, and chrome-edged vinyl-topped tables, the best that mid-century America could offer, so that the place looked like a painting by Hopper.

Then there was a labor dispute: the longtime, old-fashioned waiters didn't want to join some union or other that tried to organize them, the union threw a picket line around the restaurant, the truckers wouldn't cross the line, and so the restaurant itself went the way of the bentwood chairs, the sawdust and the old black and white ceramic tiles. Grandpa and his partner declared bankruptcy. The only money left to Grandpa's family was what my grandmother had saved from her household allowance. Throughout this complex history, however—whether his restaurant succeeded, faltered or failed—Grandpa kept on cooking. If the aroma of tarragon is the perfume that evokes my mother's solitude, the scent of oregano—mingled with odors of garlic and inhaled through clouds of cigar smoke—conjures Grandpa's kitchen, both its early prosperity and its late defeat. Over the years I've written often, even obsessively, about this kitchen, from which regularly emerged enormous and intricately festive meals to mark the turnings of the seasons. Our New Year's supper featured a rather Americanized baked ham but one that was garnished with Grandma's own mellifluous version of *salade russe*, side by side with Grandpa's stuffed mushrooms, *caviar d'aubergines*, and—pièce de resistance!—lobster salad. Then there was a spring menu of roast lamb accompanied by Really French flageolets (they were canned and my aunt bought them at Bloomingdale's gourmet grocery) and completed by a cake topped with strawberries macerated in some brilliant combination of liqueurs in which Grand Marnier played a prominent part. Best of all, the cycle of the year was crowned by a Thanksgiving dinner, joyously followed in just a month by a Christmas feast centering on a roast turkey stuffed with Grandpa's inimitable spinach–mushroom–sausage stuffing.

I don't remember what my grandparents served for dessert at Thanksgiving. Pumpkin pies were certainly alien to them, so perhaps we had one of my Grandpa's splendid crèmes caramel, a golden ring of custard lapped in bittersweet burnt-sugar syrup. I know that Christmas dinner never ended with pumpkin or mince pie, though it sometimes theatrically climaxed in blue flames flickering over a plum pudding and sometimes in a luxurious Mont Blanc of pureed chestnuts happily married to whipped cream. But the stuffing with which Grandpa lavishly garnished his turkeys was the sine qua non of his cuisine, the dish for which he was and still is most famous among our extended network of family and friends. It is the dish that now tells me how deeply Ligurian he was.

My grandparents, Amédée Mortola and Alexandra (Sasha) Zelenzoff, had met and married in Paris. Like so many children of immigrant families, I haven't a clue how and where they came together, nor do I know exactly when and where they wed. Yet of course the family's Gallic connections are evident in their menus—the *salade russe* that Russians call *salade Olivier* but that we actually called "Russian salad," the *caviar d'aubergines* always described to me as eggplant caviar, the various marinades of artichokes and mushrooms and roasted peppers that you can buy from most French *traiteurs*. My grandparents' vast lazy Susan was always heaped with *hors d'oeuvres variés* that included these and other succulent starters for an overture to every feast, although the course itself was often metonymically described as "the lazy Susan." But though Grandpa was called Frenchy in the New York market district, and Grandma's domestic frugality was no doubt fostered in Paris, and the French army tried to draft my French-born father when he was eighteen, Grandpa's stuffing was definitively Ligurian in origin, as I've learned in recent years from friends who actually have a house on a little street in San Rocco, a *frazione* of the Ligurian town of Ruta. Their street is called Via Mortola—a name which persuades me that in some distant ancestral lifetime I too would have been the owner of such a house.

The Via Mortola is probably too rough and certainly too narrow for any vehicles except motorcycles to brave its bumps and cracks. It curves around a hillside on the Portofino peninsula that's thicketed with chestnut trees, dotted with olive and lemon groves, and blooming with bay, rosemary, thyme and other leaves and herbs whose names I don't know. From this road, really a path or track, you can clamber down to the little fishing village of San Fruttuoso or the small resort town of Camogli or up and around the hilly peninsula to elegant Portofino itself, where a dazzle of international yachts bobs in the harbor, admired by strolling masses of tourists nibbling at paper cups filled with the wonderfully portable sundae called a *paciugo*. But if you stay on this hillside, from here on the Via Mortola you can see the great plateful of blue that is the Mediterranean and the hilly spine of the Riviera whose Italianità once stretched all the way to Nice.

I guess the farm where Grandpa grew up was reached by another narrow road, not unlike the Via Mortola, high in the hills above Nice, perhaps set among olive and lemon groves, studded with bushes of rosemary and looking toward fields of other herbs—lavender? thyme?—evoking the greenery of Liguria because really once part of it. His famous stuffing was green with spinach—which I now realize was a stand-in for the wild herbs that Ligurian cooks pack into ravioli—and dense with sausage and salty with parmesan cheese and creamy with mushrooms and lively with garlic, onion, celery, all bound with a couple of beaten eggs and several cupfuls of good stale bread or breadcrumbs, and all seasoned with Grandpa's all-purpose Italian–American herb: oregano.

Why oregano instead of basil or rosemary? Perhaps, if tarragon was the herb my mother fastened on when she searched the shelves of the A & P in Jackson Heights, oregano was what caught Grandpa's eye. Perhaps there weren't many other herbs available in the forties and fifties. Could anybody in Queens buy basil, rosemary, thyme at a local supermarket? Surely there weren't any fresh herbs, but there must long have been dried oregano, even then widely used in pizza and pasta sauces, and it kept well. So when Grandpa dictated recipes to me and my young husband as, in the early sixties, we sat at his kitchen table bent over our graduate-student notebooks, taking down his every word, he always said: "And add a little oregano." Add it to the marinades. Add it to the sauces. Add it, most important of all, to the stuffing.

The indescribably delicious stuffing was essential to the turkey, and better, indeed, than the turkey itself, which Grandpa tended to overcook, perhaps out of some fundamental mistrust of American turkeys. Following its sojourn in the turkey, however, Grandpa's stuffing had many more uses. On the days after Christmas, Grandma rolled out noodle dough and together she and grandpa made ravioli that they crammed with leftover stuffing, thus returning their mix of greens and meat and cheese to its original Ligurian function as a filling for pasta. And then if there was more stuffing—as, if one was lucky (or provident), there may well have been—it could be used, can be used, to stuff mushrooms, or even zucchini, peppers, who knows what other vegetables, in time-honored Ligurian fashion.

To be sure, the most famous Ligurian recipe—and one often encountered in Nice as well—is the one for pesto, a summery sauce that sanctifies greenery in the marriage of basil with olive oil, pine nuts, garlic, cheese and sometimes butter. Oddly, my grandfather never produced a single pesto that I can remember, nor did any of my other relatives. I learned to make this sauce by reading cookbooks, despite the ancestry in which I take such wistful pride. And this is strange indeed, since everyone now knows that *pasta al pesto* is what one can and should eat on the Italian Riviera. My friend the food and travel writer David Downie quotes in his wonderful introduction to Liguria a passage that he calls "florid" but which nevertheless exactly summarizes the privileged place of pesto among my ancestors:

> "What is that scent of alpine herbs mixing so strangely with the sea spray on the Riviera's cliffs," asked writer Paolo Monelli. . . . "It is the odor of pesto: that condiment made of basil, Pecorino, garlic, pine nuts, crushed in the mortar and diluted with olive oil. . . . [It] is purely Ligurian; it speaks Ligurian; the mere smell of it makes your ears ring with a dialect at once sharp and soft, full of sliding sounds, of whispered syllables, of dark vowels."[2]

Yet this is a taste of Liguria I never encountered in my family. Did Grandpa favor oregano as his invariable seasoning because it wasn't quintessentially Ligurian? Or did he choose it so often because in the taste of oregano there is a darker hint of basil, as if oregano were basil grown more intense, a little more bitter, a little older? But basil must have grown on the farm in the hills above Nice just as it blooms in small, intensely fragrant and flavorful leaves in all the kitchen gardens of Liguria, waiting to be picked and merged with olive oil, garlic, pine nuts, pecorino.

Basil wasn't actually absent from my childhood, although when I was a little girl and even when I was a teenager I don't think I knew what it was, so I couldn't have understood that it had been mysteriously replaced by oregano in my Niçois–Ligurian grandfather's cooking. Yet I was often surrounded by basil, as I realized when I first began to cook with its distinctively peppery, aromatic leaves. In the tiny yard behind his three-story brownstone in Williamsburg, Brooklyn—then a stronghold of Sicilian culture—my uncle Frank, the husband of my mother's only sister, Frances, had laid out a miniature formal garden. Just behind the house there was a grape arbor, with a porch swing in its leafy shade, and above the arbor flapped Aunt Frances's clothesline, on which she could pin her wash while standing in her big, second-story kitchen. But for maybe twenty or thirty feet beyond the arbor stretched the sunny *giardino*, with a stone bird bath at its center and little plots of herbs and flowers radiating in all directions.

From these tiny beds of exuberant bloom rose many fragrances as fascinating as they were mysterious to a child who lived in a fourth-floor two-bedroom gray-carpeted apartment in a stolid brick building surrounded by prickly, boxy hedges of some dismally indeterminate plant. One late afternoon in California, when I was tearing the leaves from a bunch of basil in preparation for a pesto, I thought, as I often had, how familiar their perfume was, and wondered why I felt that I had long ago—somewhere, but where?—inhaled it. And then I remembered the hot flagstone paths in the miniature Williamsburg garden and the little beds of herbs and flowers. The aroma that rose when the sun leaned hard on them was mostly basil, or basil dominated the others, and I think that when I was very young I came to consider this distinctive perfume coextensive with summer in that garden in that part of New York City.

My uncle Frank, the garden designer, was swarthy, mustachioed, slightly bald, and very bitter. He almost always wore an unbuttoned suit vest and his sleeves were almost always rolled up, as though he was determined to Get Down to Things—or anyway, to do some work in the garden. He was an architect, born on one of the Lipari Islands off the coast of Sicily, I don't know which one, and I believe his family name was Adami. But when he arrived on Ellis Island, the immigration officer who greeted him said, "Here we call you Adams." So a genteelly WASPish Adams he became, though the name sat strangely on him, given his belligerent, even rather piratical air.

Uncle Frank chainsmoked Camels, a habit that eventually led to his death from emphysema, but in his healthy middle age, the time I remember best, he neither coughed nor wheezed, but vigorously breathed in and out great hot blossoms of smoke as he pounded on the table, elaborating his rage at America: New Deal, Old Deal, every deal was a bad deal. For he was an impassioned Communist (though I doubt that he was what used to be called a card-carrying one) who admired Stalin, loathed almost every other politician, and articulated his unswerving beliefs in English, Sicilian, and Italian. Most likely it was the Depression that drove him to such heights and depths of apoplectic, chain-smoking fury. Things had happened before I was born, I gathered, that had imposed some professional torment on him. My mother said he "had to work for the WPA," and she made this acronymic fate sound awful to me. Uncle Frank worked for the WPA and as part of his labors he made a beautiful little model of a Mayan temple, which he kept downstairs in his study. But his family—a wife, two daughters and a son—had sunk into genteel poverty during his years at the WPA, or so my mother implied when she discussed family history.

I have to admit that to this day I don't quite grasp why Uncle Frank constructed a model of a Mayan temple as part of what was defined as a "demeaning" job for the WPA. But even as a child I understood the reasons for his bitterness, his rage, his intransigent Communism. After all, he outlined his grievances in the course of each one of the countless political debates that surged around the long dinner table at which my parents and I frequently joined him, my aunt and my three cousins for festive meals featuring—yes—hot Italian sausages and platters of *arancini* or great roasting pans laden with Sicilian-style pizza or with marvelously layered *pasta infornata* and cannoli filled with sweet ricotta. My three Williamsburg cousins were significantly older than I, and I worshipped them all. Theirs was the home I wanted: a tall house, three children, a long table heavy with pans of pasta, people shouting and laughing in a language incomprehensible to me—Sicilian!—but that seemed somehow a source of the strange vitality that kept everyone making convivial noises and pounding the table, and a garden warm with that inexplicable scent I now know to have been the perfume of basil.

In his garden, stooping over his herbs and flowers, perhaps tending his basil with special care, Uncle Frank did sometimes smile. His sleeves rolled up, his vest loosened, a Camel fuming in the corner of his mouth, he was nevertheless more amiable there than he was at the dinner table. The aroma of basil must have penetrated that cloud of smoke, its sunny flavor must have left a trace on his tongue. When, years later, I went with my daughters to Sicily, we spent a day in the windswept, hilly town of Sambuca–Zabut, where my mother, her sister and her seven brothers were born a century ago. Not far from there, we visited the great ancient ruins of Agrigento—so superb one doesn't want to call them ruins since they look almost as if someone had wanted them to have the special majesty they have, set against those vine-covered hills and sun-baked fields. I wondered why Uncle Frank hadn't made a model of Agrigento for the WPA. But with his rage, his cigarettes, his frustrated architectural dreams, my uncle had been forced into strange compromises. One of the few "real" buildings he designed was my grandpa Mortola's restaurant in the New York market district. The one that failed in 1950.

Rosemary. Rosemary for remembrance, says Ophelia, and for all I know it grew alongside basil in Uncle Frank's garden. But though I studied *Hamlet* in high school, I didn't get the reference since I didn't actually know what rosemary was and how it can grow wild in fields, cultivated in hedges and gardens. There were songs we sang in the sixties, when we were young and hopeful—"parsley, sage, rosemary and thyme"—but what did those refrains mean? Until I became a serious cook such lines were nearly as opaque to me as Ophelia's ravings, even though I knew they referred to herbs, meaning (to a young New Yorker) dried leaves people used in the kitchen. But in early September 1970 my husband and I went with our three small children—two daughters and a son, like my dream family in Brooklyn, along with an au pair babysitter—to vacation for two weeks in a holiday villa in Portofino.

Our villa was really a large apartment on the hillside above the town, exactly two hundred steps up from the piazza that was even then basically a parking lot. (Perhaps all those steps up kept the rent down.) But though it was inexpensive, the apartment had cool marble floors, tall shuttered windows, a fine view over rooftops all the way to the glitter of the harbor where the sleek yachts rode at anchor, and a large terrace partly shaded by the vast leaves of a grape arbor like the one in Uncle Frank's garden. Almost every day Elliot and I took the children to the beach in the nearby town of Santa Margherita di Ligure, where they swam and clamored for *tosti*—ordinary melted cheese sandwiches made somehow glamorous by Italian vendors. Later, in the market we would buy basil so I could try my hand at pesto, about which I had only then learned, and when we came back to Portofino we sometimes strolled through the piazza, licking versions of that sublime sundae the *paciugo*.

Our terrace was lined with flowerpots and with tubs of rosemary, perhaps the first real (as opposed to dried) rosemary I'd ever seen. These were trimmed and watered by Elissa, our landlord's daughter, a young blonde woman who cleaned house for us several days a week. I could barely communicate with her in my broken Italian, so, since, like many Ligurians, she had some French, I usually spoke to her in my not quite so broken French. Often, in the late afternoon, she would appear on the terrace with garden shears, gesturing toward the tubs of rosemary and saying politely in our two languages, *"Rosmarino? Romarin?"* Watching her clip the fragrant branches and bear them away for some kitchen project, I too learned to clip branches of *rosmarino* and cook with the bittersweet dark green needles, chopped fine and so strongly perfumed that yes, Ophelia was right, they offer a medicine for memory. But it's sad that my memories of an Italy I never really knew are so partial, so incomplete, slanting and glinting from the stems of rosemary, the leaves of basil and oregano, then devolving into the tarragon that comforted my mother in her old age.

Before leaving for Europe, we had struggled to persuade my mother that she should join us on our trip, and, as always, she refused to stir from the apartment in which she had imprisoned herself, though she wrote us regularly, encouraging our travels. She forgot to tell us, however, that the internationally famous resort of Portofino was just across the wooded peninsula from Ruta, the Ligurian town from which her husband's family had emigrated to Nice in the nineteenth century. So the whole time we were in Portofino, eating *pasta al pesto* and inhaling the enlivening fragrance of *rosmarino*, we didn't know that the Via Mortola, with its herbs and bays, was just on the other side of the mountain.

Ubi Panis, Ibi Patris?

"Where bread is, there is home": so goes an old Latin saying. The Italian–American writer Anthony Di Renzo quotes it bitterly, noting that most of our Italian forebears were driven to the fruited plains of *L'America* by sheer destitution, "a raw, blind animal hunger born of centuries of poverty and disillusionment." Here, he goes on to argue, "those foolish enough to entertain political illusions quickly learned otherwise when they were "stacked in tenements like salami" as they learned to agitate for "grub first, then rights." Meanwhile, their culinary inheritance was lost: their sauces were diluted to suit American taste buds, and the once handcrafted artisanal sausages of their hometowns were ground out in filthy industrial kitchens. A cook named Boiardi became Chef Boy-Ar-Dee. *Pasta infornata* was replaced by frozen lasagna. Pizza became pizza pie (sort of like pie pie) and scampi became shrimp scampi (shrimp shrimp). Even when Italian dishes were made at home by nonnas with keen memories, they inevitably lost their Italianità and became Italian–American, sometimes even New Jersey Italian or Brooklyn Italian—because the ingredients were different, the terroir, as the French call it, wasn't the same.[3] To judge by the writings of many other foodoirists—I almost want to call them *foodoiristi,* so many are Italian–Americans—Di Renzo's anger at a simultaneously deprived and delicious past is matched by similar irritation at a culinarily diluted present. All of our parents and grandparents brought menus from the old countries, but what happened to the meats of memory in New World ovens? In my own family, certainly, oregano became dried oregano, and *basilico* virtually disappeared—at least from most mid-twentieth-century markets.

Nonetheless, speaking of markets, a few days ago my partner, Albert, and I lunched at a local spot called the Emeryville Public Market: a dimly lit, gymnasium-sized hall dotted with about a dozen gastronomically diverse stalls, vending food from a range of nations: Afghanistan to Italy, Jamaica to Japan and Korea, China and Vietnam to India and Persia. The fare on offer was cheaply priced international fast food, served on paper plates with plastic cutlery, prepared by cooks who really did seem to be from around the world. Chicken teriyaki, kung pao chicken, chicken kebabs, jerk chicken, chicken panini, chicken rice bowls, chicken tikka, chicken tacos, chicken with soy noodles—the poultry dishes, like most of the others, are pretty much staples of the contemporary American diet. The customers, largely working class, might as well have been at McDonald's, though the air was redolent with garlic, soy, curry and other spices that would perhaps have been unfamiliar to some in their childhoods.

There's nothing special about the Emeryville Public Market. Its cuisine is replicated at food halls around the country now, at the food trucks that circle many American cities, selling goodies from Asian fusion buns, Korean tacos and Niçoise sandwiches to homemade ice cream—and, needless to say, at far grander, *Zagat*-listed venues.[4] Diverse though New York was even in the pre–Julia Child forties and fifties, when I was a kid you could only get takeout versions of such exotic edibles at upscale urban groceries or fancy department stores. My aunt, for instance, purchased canned flageolets and white asparagus at Bloomingdale's, whence came also, I believe, our Crosse & Blackwell Christmas pudding. My grandmother found Russian delicacies (*paska* and *kulich*, say, for Orthodox Easter) on Madison Avenue in the Seventies. And my mother once bought a Mexican food "kit" somewhere (or maybe I bought it for her) featuring canned enchiladas in a sauce *picante* that struck us as intolerably hot.

At my Grandpa's Franklin Street restaurant in New York, he served customers straightforward "American" food: vegetable soup, Salisbury steaks, mashed potatoes with gravy, pot roast. If he had come to America from Nice now, would he have had a little "Mediterranean" spot somewhere, featuring the *caviar d'aubergines*, ratatouille, roast lamb, and ravioli of my childhood? A quick Google search along today's Franklin Street turns up a slew of surrounding restaurants, from the upscale Flor de Sol to the grittier Peace and Love Café. Might one of those have been Grandpa's? Or would he have sold pizza and ravioli out of a food truck or mall stall? And my mother: what would she have been able to cook, now, beyond chops and baked potatoes and canned vegetables?

The ubiquity of ethnic fast food seems, somehow, to parallel the proliferation not just of foodie culture but of ethnic foodoirs, though I'm not sure which came first, the foodie, the foodoir or the food stall. What all have in common, in any case, is a certain ambiguity of appetite, a sense of culinary loss accompanied by a sometimes obscure, sometimes very clear urge toward resolution. My mother's story is exemplary: her youthful anxiety to escape the Sicilian ghetto, its garlic and sausages and *pasta infornata*, was followed by a late-life yearning for the comforts of childhood, not just watery *scarola in brodo* but the real thing that she hoped she might find in Manhattan restaurants like Grotta Azzurra or Enrico & Paglieri. But I am exemplary too: my quite commonplace search for culinary (and other) ethnic roots ultimately issued in a sad recognition that those roots weren't mine. Growing up in New York, dining with my family at Grotta Azzurra or Larré's or the Russian Tea Room, I used to claim that I wasn't an American. But what was I, then? Sicilian, like my mother? French/Russian/Ligurian, like my father? Later, visiting Europe, I knew that I was none of those, yet not a representative American either. Or maybe, yes, a representative American precisely because of my blurred identity.

In *Crazy in the Kitchen,* her powerful memoir of "Food, Feuds, and Forgiveness in an Italian American Family," Louise DeSalvo describes a mother who evidently shared my mother's cultural confusion and anxiety. Although the household nonna skillfully produces a wonderfully "thick-crusted, coarse-crumbed Italian bread. A peasant bread," the narrator's mother "disdains" it "because it is everything that my grandmother is, and everything that my mother, in 1950s' suburban New Jersey, is trying very hard not to be." Unlike my mother, though, who did whatever she could to avoid cooking and disdained Jell-O, white bread and other culinary Americana, DeSalvo's parent buys "white bread, sliced bread, American bread . . . [She] thinks that eating this bread will change her, that eating this bread will erase this embarrassment of a stepmother. . . . Maybe my mother thinks that if she eats enough of this other bread, she will stop being Italian American and she will become American American."[5]

Laura Schenone, whose *Lost Ravioli Recipes of Hoboken* depicts the same kind of culinary dislocation, introduces us to another iteration of DeSalvo's mother—not a nonna-like mamma who stirs the pots of marinara and bolognese, but an American wanna-be whose cooking "spanned mid- to late-century American—that is to say, [it was] heavy on the home economics roasts, iceberg salads, and gelatin molds culled from women's magazines." And Schenone, whose book records the gustatory details of several pilgrimages to Liguria in search of the true, fine-skinned, herb-stuffed raviolis of that region, regretfully admits:

> I always knew the truth—I was not Italian. . . . I was born in the twilight of ethnicity, the barely tail end of it. As the years went on, Italians evolved into Italian–Americans, and a new generation emerged. With few connections left to the actual place of Italy, they carried out memories heavily faded by time and filtered through stereotypes from movies and television. Anthropologists might say that these Americanizations are creolized cultures in the United States—not inauthentic replicas but new cultures unto themselves. Yes, they deserve respect. But just the same, these latter-day New Jersey Italians trouble me and sometimes grated on my nerves.[6]

How well I know these feelings of cultural confusion and the culinary anxieties they inspire. It's one thing for an imperialist Anglo outsider like Elizabeth Barrett Browning to celebrate the Italian food that is glamorously *given* to her ("Dinner, 'unordered,' comes through the streets [of Florence] and spreads itself on our table") in a kind of nineteenth-century takeout, but quite another to be a person who ought to know exactly how to prepare that savory meal. Some summers ago David and I spent a week cruising the waters of the Mediterranean off southern Turkey with an Italian couple, a Turkish couple and a Turkish crew of three. We were (obviously) a lucky and elite little band: our boat, a traditional wooden *gulet* of the sort that has plied these seas for centuries, was fitted out with spacious cabins, a cosy galley and a shaded deck where we spent long, sybaritic mealtimes engaged in absorbing cross-cultural discussions of books, ideas, music, food, computers—the substance of contemporary lives. Our seminars, we began to call them.

I was wholly at ease until strange tensions began to develop between me and the rather elegant Italian couple. I'd told them, of course, that I'm an Italian–American and added even more specifics about my ethnicity—my mother's Sicilian origins, my Niçois grandfather's roots in Liguria. I meant these disclosures as a gesture of warmth, a sort of hands-across-the sea overture ("My people are your people") of a kind that one can only rarely make. But the Italians responded with curious indifference, even coolness.

The handsome, forty-something Milanese CEO, who liked to regale us with information about the opera CDs he often played while we sipped our aperitifs, seemed deaf when I not only waxed enthusiastic about some of the performances but ventured knowledgeable comments on them. His companion, a Roman woman who taught economics in Brussels and was also handsome, also forty-something, appeared, if anything, even more oblivious of my remarks, although she herself talked with considerable animation about her current efforts to educate herself in music, especially opera.

I finally realized that there was something peculiar happening when we had an odd exchange about, of all things, pasta. Although the Turkish crew unfailingly produced extraordinary meals, Pietro and Lucia (not their real names) had shopped assiduously for Italian delicacies in the port from which we'd embarked, and I thought there was something winsome in their determination to instruct our cook in the ways of an Italian kitchen. One night, after much discussion, they oversaw the assembly of a splendid pasta—a sort of spaghetti primavera, with lots of garlic and zucchini—that we had for a starter at dinner. Of course I complimented all concerned, congratulated the cook, praised the recipe, etc. But why was there a puzzling silence when I added that my Sicilian aunt made a very similar pasta primavera, as did, I am told, my grandmother before her? Mooning over garlic and zucchini as the *gulet* rocked in a glassy inlet, I confessed I was nostalgic for the lively Italian odors and flavors of home and celebrated the flavorful familiarity of this dish on which Pietro, Lucia and the Turkish cook had, I thought, so delightfully collaborated. But although Pietro and Lucia nodded and smiled politely, their smiles seemed forced and they contrived to nod a bit censoriously, as if I had been somehow impertinent.

Impertinent familiarity! That, I realized later, had been the social solecism I committed. I had professed familiarity with the ways of a culture that, from the perspective of "real" Italians, is not my own. My Italian is dreadful, practically nonexistent (my French-born father and my Sicilian-born mother could only speak English to each other, so that's the language we spoke at home when I was growing up), but I could grasp a few of the words I overheard Pietro and Lucia exchanging as we all lay on deck sunbathing the next morning. They spoke rapid, intimate Italian sentences that they assumed I'd never understand, and no, I can't reproduce their words accurately, but I caught their meaning. *She's just an American, what does* she *know about Italian cooking, about opera, about* being *Italian?*

And truly, after all, the answer is *almost nothing.* The easy cosmopolitanism of Pietro and Lucia was clearly grounded in an unproblematic ethnic sureness to which they had been born. The culture of which and for which they spoke was fully, seamlessly, theirs in a way in which it can never be mine—a way in which, as a matter of fact, it had probably ceased even to be my mother's within a year of her landing on Ellis Island. Thus, whether they saw my eagerness to show familiarity with things Italian as a competitive striving toward sophistication or as a sentimental gesture of recuperation, the (really) Roman woman and the (really) Milanese man must have at best ascribed a kind of pathos to me. To make matters worse, I was a *southern* Italian, a half-Sicilian, while my Ligurian grandfather was really Niçois. Thus, rather than supplying me with an engaging internationalism, my insistence that I was an Italian–American meant not that I was more than an American but that I was less than an Italian.

Less than an Italian: perhaps it is the sense of lessening or dilution that I associate with Italy, the lack that the Italian language especially signifies in my personal history, which gives particular poignancy to my experience of a cultural selfhood that is (yet is also somehow not) my own. I am an Italian–American who doesn't speak Italian just the way I'm a French–American whose French is pretty awful as well as a Russian–American who can barely read a word in the strange Russian alphabet. Because of all these complex combinations, moreover, I am an American–American who spent years denying *being* American. In other words, I inhabit a country (or perhaps countries) of hyphenation—maybe even a hyphen-nation. Indeed, in a confused and tentative fashion that Pietro and Lucia might never be able to understand, I don't just live on a hyphen in some abstract theoretical sense; I eat hyphenated food, sleep and dream among hyphens, and in a sense am a walking, talking hyphen. So are most of the foodoirists I study here.

When Louise DeSalvo returns with her husband to her family's native province of Puglia in search of the origins she has romanticized, she is horrified by the stony poverty she encounters. Does it explain the ferocity with which her Italian-born grandparents prepared food? She has unnerving memories of their kitchen in Hoboken, the one she preferred to her own mother's. As a frightened child, she explains, "I [was] curious about, horrified by how my grandparents wring birds' necks, pluck their feathers, kill eels with sharp blows to the head, kill fish by plunging a knife between their eyes. I watch them strip the skin off animals with pliers, remove entrails, drain animals' blood. I am beginning to wonder when life becomes nonlife, beginning to think about death, beginning to have nightmares in which I, too, am dressed for cooking."[7] Witnessing less traumatic but equally alienating culinary scenes in Liguria, on the other side of the Atlantic, Schenone confesses that "I was aware of myself as the outsider, the interloper who could not speak the language but had shown up here ignorant and unprepared." Inevitably, she decides, her cooking "is a translation project. I have no choice but to use the language of cookbooks, and I have read them all. . . . In this ridiculous manner, I figure out what my ancestors knew and passed down for hundreds of years." "Italian–American cooking [is] a bastardized cuisine," a restaurant reviewer for the *New York Times* remarked the other day. A chef at the place he was writing about chimed in to express his sense "that the food of Italy was legitimate food [and the food] I grew up eating was this weird thing we shouldn't talk about."[8]

Even while ethnic foodoirists report feelings of alienation from the *ur* food of the homeland, however, they often recall embarrassing confrontations with American food. I still remember my jealous confusion when I was first introduced to tuna casserole in the dorm at Cornell. Why didn't *my* mother use Campbell soups to make noodle dishes? To be sure, growing up in New York City, I wasn't embarrassed by the foods my family ate. So many of my friends were Jewish–American, Italian–American, Spanish–American, and African–American that it seemed quite logical for each person to have his or her own familial cuisine. But outside the city, things were certainly different. In her memoir *Were You Always an Italian?*, Maria Laurino reports being described as a "smelly Italian girl" in junior high school gym class (she was actually a third-generation American), and resolving to rid herself of the aromas of Italianità by renouncing the tastes of her youth: "the sweet scent of tomato sauce simmering on the stove [and the] oil-laden frying peppers." Even in college, though, she encounters what might be called food humiliation. After she has eaten some provolone cheese, her freshman roommate confuses its "odoriferous aroma" with vomit and inquires with concern about her weak stomach.[9]

Comparably unpleasant memories haunt Linda Furiya, a Japanese-American raised in Indiana, who derives the title of her foodoir, *Bento Box in the Heartland,* from an early elementary school trauma, when she discovered that her mother had packed her lunch box with glistening handmade stuffed rice balls instead of white-bread American sandwiches. "My *obento* lunches were a glaring reminder of the ethnic differences between my peers and me," she explains, although her mother comments (quite reasonably, it seems, from a current perspective), "Why go to trouble to make lunch for just plain old sandwich?" Ultimately, the little girl resolves the situation by symbolically dividing the time and place of her lunch in two. With her classmates, she eats the apple and cookies her mother provided; then she withdraws to one of the stalls in the girls' bathroom, where she wolfs down the rice balls. The cuisine of ethnicity, her decision implies, must be consumed furtively, and classified with excrement.[10]

Nor does a youthful pilgrimage to her homeland solve the vexed problem of her culinary identity. Furiya tells the tale of a trip to Tokyo that her mother brought her on when she was ten: alienated at first by strange furnishings—futons and sliding screens—the child soon fell in love with her Japanese relatives, spoke their language with ease, and adored the special foods they offered her. When the time came to return to Indiana, she found herself weeping with uncontrollable confusion. "I couldn't tell Mom I wanted to stay in Tokyo [and in any case] I missed Dad, and even my brothers. . . . My unhappiness was rooted in not knowing where I belonged. . . . I didn't know . . . that I had begun a lifelong journey in search of home." Arguably her recipe-studded memoir—like so many other ethnic foodoirs—is an attempt to create a sufficient gastronomic home: neither Tokyo nor Indiana, neither the lost original family table nor the uncomfortable New World lunchroom, the dematerialized but scrupulously described kitchen in the pages of the book becomes the only culinary place to which the writer feels she can belong.[11]

The Jordanian–American writer Diana Abu-Jaber recounts similar experiences of alienation and reconciliation. One of three daughters born to a calm, fair-skinned American mother and an exuberant, dark-haired Jordanian father (known throughout her book with cheery familiarity as Bud), she too remembers a childhood lived on the hyphen between the United States and Jordan, the snows of upstate New York and the winds of the desert outside Amman. Her parents fly back and forth between their two tentatively inhabited homes more frequently than Furiya's (and most of the memoirists I discuss here come from families where parents and grandparents never return to the homeland). But Abu-Jaber's cosmopolitanism fails to redeem her from the feelings of cultural dislocation and confusion that mark so many texts by her contemporaries. Both in her bestselling novel *Crescent* and her foodoir, aptly titled *The Language of Baklava*, she struggles, as others do, to create a space elsewhere through gastronomic memory and lyrical recipes. At one point, discovering a bustling Arabic restaurant inside what seems to be an American-style shopping mall eerily located in Bedouin country, she senses that she has entered a sort of time warp "that shows us another way that things could have gone. Our alternative lives emerge in bas-relief . . . I live contentedly in Jordan and understand exactly where in the world I belong." But more often Abu-Jaber struggles with the complexity of her identity.[12]

In her childhood, when her family is living in a suburb of Syracuse, she discovers that she dislikes the taste of American food and that "the neighbors don't barbecue in their front yards" as they would in Jordan; they use the backyard, which is "as private as other people's dreams." Deciding that the front yard "will allow us to share food . . . and gossip with the neighbors," the way they did in the old country, her parents bring out the grill—and scandalize some of the locals. A man "in belted beige slacks and tasseled loafers and [a] woman in a milky, synthetic blouse" wonder if "there might be some kind of . . . trouble going on" and admonish them that "this is a nice neighborhood." In response, the writer remembers a "feeling that starts somewhere at the center of my chest, as heavy as an iron ingot, a bit like fear or sadness or anger, but none of these exactly . . . I look up at the neighborhood and the mist has cleared. All the mean, cheaply framed windows are gaping at us, the sky empty as a gasp." Years later, returning to the States from a year spent in Jordan, she suffers again "from culture shock," a "sort of soul-sickness." Finally, she declares, "I am as surely a Bedouin as anyone who has traveled in a desert caravan." A reluctant Bedouin—"I miss and I long for every place, every country, I have ever lived"—she locates her dream kitchen in sentences and paragraphs, the "language of baklava."[13]

Ubi panis, ibi patris? Is the culinary homeland of immigrants, emigrants and refugees ultimately linguistic, as Abu-Jaber suggests? In *Mastering the Art of Soviet Cooking: A Memoir of Food and Longing*, the Russian immigrant Anya von Bremzen brilliantly implies this too. Remembering the frugal diet that marked her childhood in Soviet Moscow, she notes that in those years "dreaming about food . . . was just as rewarding as eating." Her book begins in contemporary Queens, New York, where she and her mother create a luscious version of the classic Russian salmon pie know as *kulebiaka*. It is to be the centerpiece of a dinner to which they have invited other Soviet refugees to help commemorate the last days of the tsars, and its inspiration comes, at least in part, from Chekhov's voluptuous description of the dish in his short story "The Siren":

> The kulebiaka must make your mouth water, it must lie before you, naked, shameless, a temptation. You wink at it, you cut off a sizeable slice, and you let your fingers just play over it. . . . You eat it, the butter drips from it like tears, and the filling is fat, juicy, rich with eggs, giblets, onions.

Yet the *kulebiaka* that originally inspired von Bremzen's fantasies was "a modest rectangle of yeast dough, true to Soviet form concealing a barely there layer of boiled ground meat or cabbage." Perhaps the bread, or the *kulebiaka*, that truly sustains the immigrant, the traveler among culinary worlds, is the bread of memory flavored by imagination, the bread that you can see in symbols on the page and consume in a hungry mind that creates its own ideal homeland.[14]

The Redeemed Kitchen

What, though, if the kitchen neither creates nor re-creates but transcends the homeland? For certain diasporic groups, flung from country to country by forces radically beyond control—slavery, persecution—the homeland and its culinary materiality basically disappear. If you were brought in chains from Africa, or fled a small Polish village obliterated by pogroms or the Holocaust, you almost certainly can't go home again. The only *there* that's there to long for is a kitchen of the mind.

African–Americans, whose ancestors were trafficked through the Middle Passage to the New World, often had little specific memory of origins. Their native cuisine, transmitted orally to those descendants who survived, was diluted by the poverty of the circumstances in which they struggled to live and feed their children. Frederick Douglass bemoaned the diet of "ash cake" on which he and his fellow slaves were obliged to live. "I have often been so pinched with hunger," he once recalled, "as to dispute with 'Nep,' the dog, for the crumbs which fell from the kitchen table." At the same time, some, at least, of the slaves were able to till little plots of land, so that the British writer Edmund Gosse, dispatching *Letters from Alabama*, noted that "The very negroes had their own melon 'patches,' as well as their peach orchards, and it is no small object of their ambition to raise earlier or finer specimens than their masters."[15]

What has come to be called soul food is a menu of necessity made various and voluptuous by improvisation. Worldwide, the cookbooks of aristocratic and bourgeois culture obviously didn't exist for the illiterate, though the recipes of European peasants were often perpetuated by scholarly gastronomes. Still, until quite recently few scribes recorded the basic maneuvers of slave kitchens in the New World. Yes, the black cooks who created an entire Southern cuisine for their masters built on instructions they were given by their owners, but as the food historian and cookbook writer Jessica B. Harris has incisively shown in *High on the Hog: A Culinary Journey from Africa to America*, her sweeping history of the African diaspora, enslaved captives also brought some of the riches of their own culture to New World kitchens, leaving a lasting mark on the cuisine of the Americas. Especially for their own families, they discovered roots and greens in the new land that were the equivalent of foods they had cooked in the old countries, and learned to manage in special delicious ways with the maize, rice and yams that grew in their regions, the parts of pigs (tails, feet, heads, offal) allotted to them, the black-eyed peas and beans and gravies they could prepare to go with local fish and shellfish, poultry, small game.[16]

Some of the earliest compilers of African–American cookbooks started out in slave kitchens, whose wisdom they brought to their own stoves. *What Mrs. Fisher Knows About Southern Cooking* (1881) and *Rufus Estes' Good Things to Eat* (1911) had such inceptions, as did *Cleora's Kitchens*, the more recent memoir of a free African–American cook who drew on family recipes handed down from harder times. In these works, the menu of ash cake described by Douglass becomes an affirmative feast of liberation and reinvention. Barbara Haber, the curator of Radcliffe College's famed (4,000-volume) cookbook library, picked *Cleora's Kitchens* as her favorite in the entire collection, explaining that "it expresses, through food, joy . . . you have the connection of food being celebratory in truly meaningful ways. Just wonderful stuff."[17]

More recent African-American foodoirs follow this same pattern, drawing on and delighting in the foods of the African diaspora, not only in the American South but in the West Indies and Brazil. Proclaimed Vertamae Smart-Grosvenor in her influential cookbook–memoir *Vibration Cooking, or, The Travel Notes of a Geechee Girl,* "If we couldn't have meat we had greens and rice and we ate plenty of that but my mother never cooked none of that weird 'tuna casserole.'" Maya Angelou's *Hallelujah! The Welcome Table* records "a lifetime of memories with recipes" that are mostly soul food ("Momma's Grandbabies Love Cracklin' Cracklin'," "Independence Forever," "Early Lessons from a Kitchen Stool," "Sweet Southern Memories"). Equally exuberant, Ntozake Shange produces in *If I can Cook/You KNow God can*, a compendium of foods from around the world all rooted in thoughts of

Africa and its New World offshoots: "Cousin Eddie's Shark with Breadfruit," "Mama's Rice," "Zaki's Feijoada," "Dominican Bread Pudding," and much more. "I . . . know we've done more than survive," she boasts. "We've found bounty in the foods the gods set before us, strength in the souls of black folks, delight in the *guele* (smell) of our sweating bodies . . . What and how we cook is the ultimate implication of who we are. That's why I know my God can cook—I'm not foolish enough to say I could do something the gods can't do. So if I can cook, you know God can."[18]

Arguably, in these books what was lost in the Middle Passage is found at a communal table defined by a recuperated cuisine that need not suffer by comparison with an original cookery that never really existed in the same way. Escaping the shadow of Douglass's ash cake, Smart-Grosvenor, Angelou and Shange recite the recipes of a home retrieved through food. Because Smart-Grosvenor had theatrical aspirations and became a radio personality, while Angelou and Shange are both poets—and novelists and playwrights—their recitations are lyrical performances, triumphant rather than elegiac. And even more lyrically and linguistically performative are the recipes offered in Austin Clarke's *Pig Tails 'n Breadfruit,* a culinary memoir of Barbados.

Born in the West Indies, Clarke is a poet, novelist and essayist who now lives and works in Canada but has taught on campuses around the United States as well. Though his foodoir is surely rooted in Barbados, that gastronomic home is neither lost nor distant: it lives and thrives in his pages, especially through his perfect command of, well, the *language* of pig tail 'n breadfruit, the "Wessindian" dialect in which he lists the procedures and "ingreasements" (ingredients) of the meals he describes in delicious detail. Each chapter of his book is in fact a performance of a particular recipe, as it might be described by a mother teaching her child the ways of the kitchen. Introducing his foodoir, he confesses that

> It is ironical to be suggesting a book about food cooked in Barbados, because in every self-respecting Barbadian household the woman [in charge of the kitchen] would not be caught dead with a cookbook. To read a book would suggest that she has not retained

> what her mother taught her. . . . There was never, and still is not, a cookbook in my mother's house.[19]

What Clarke performs on and off throughout his volume of food memories, then, are repeated and highly vivacious scenes of "Wessindian" instruction. His chapter titles includes such local specialties as "Bakes," "Meal-Corn Cou-Cou," "Breadfruit Cou-Cou with Braising Beef," "Souse," "Pepperpot," "Pelau" and the ironically named dish of rice, okra, pig tails and salt beef known as "Privilege." His devotion to culinary regionalism was clearly inspired by his mother's "characteristic dismissive prejudice against food cooked by Europeans, especially the French. 'What do French-people know about cooking food?' " But it is also energized by a fierce determination to dramatize the triumphs of the culinary imagination over slavery and poverty. Every recital of a recipe—and one can imagine these passages as staged events—is contextualized by the terrible reality of the colonial plantation that "was a pristine panorama of English pastoral beauty. . . . But you should fall on your two knees and thank God that you never had to be a labourer in [those] fields!" In "days of yore," he notes, "your belly was usually sticking to your back, through hunger. Slaves was always hungry. Food was always scarce. They had to learn how to 'cut and contrive,' to improvise." Thus, Barbadians "have always known that the food we eat is 'slave food,' based on leavings of left-overs, the remnants of the better cuts of meat eaten by the Plantation owners."[20]

Despite the bitterness of this context, however, Clarke's accounts of the cuisine that began as slave food are exuberant, even rollicking. Is your pantry almost empty on Sunday? You can make the pancakes known as bakes: for when "you are hungry and poor, it doesn't matter what kind o' food you eat on a particular day, so long as it is food and it taste sweet." And Clarke's performance of the recipe for bakes incorporates sociological analysis as well as culinary instruction:

> These bakes that I'm going to tell you how to make are bakes that middle- and upper-middle-class Barbadian people does make. With bakes, so too with everything. Food has always been

> tied up with social status and historical protocol. A middle-class person would add in certain other ingreasements with the flour, salt, sugar and water to reflect her status in society. The better the ingreasements you have in your bakes, the higher those ingreasements can lift you, even beyond the class to which you already belong; and they will make your bakes turn out lighter, too. Complexion of skin and social status, and the lightness of bakes, go hand in hand.[21]

The paradoxical elegance of bakes, a kind of transformation of ash cake risen out of tradition and improvisation, parallels the rich flavors of souse (head cheese) and black pudding (blood pudding), the "ultimate in slave food . . . made from the parts of the pig that nobody else wanted or had the heart to eat [but] the sweetest thing handed down by our ancestors, African slaves, to each and every one of us present-day Wessindians." Clarke describes with enthusiasm the weekly ritual of obtaining and devouring these nearly magical delicacies. "There is a special way, ordain in Barbadian culture and history, of eating pudding and souse. You eat it out in the open air, in the hot sun, with the sea breeze blowing in your face and the wind licking your body." And, he adds, "When you meet a woman who does make sweet pudding and souse, you will make sure that you keep her as a friend, as a wife or as a lover for the rest o' your life, the rest o' your born days."[22]

Perhaps even more enchanted than pudding and souse is the local specialty curiously known as Privilege. Clarke recounts his first experience with this dish when it is served to him by none other than the prime minister of Barbados. A melange of rice, okra, pig tail and salt beef, this too is a slave recipe redeemed through memory and performance. "Oh my God!" Clarke exclaims, once he has been introduced to it. "When you survey the contents of that pot . . . such a waft of historical and cultural goodness going blow in your face! . . . '*Why couldn't I have been a slave too?*' You are bound to ask yourself this question. 'Why did they have to abolish slavery before I learn how to cook Privilege?' " (emphasis added). Of course, his irony is palpable. But so is his gusto. For though the sufferings of history speak through him, Clarke speaks of his people's food *beyond* history, resurrecting the hard-won pleasures of the slavery table while transforming and transcending the pain of the colonial plantation.[23]

The resonant word "privilege" might also apply to the cuisine Elizabeth Ehrlich celebrates in *Miriam's Kitchen,* her memoir of learning to live with and through the difficulties and delights of kosher practice. Hers too is a diasporic table: her parents are Jewish–American immigrants, her mother-in-law (the Miriam of the book's title) and father-in-law are Polish-born Holocaust survivors. Like the concentration camp inmates whose scribbled fantasy recipes Cara De Silva introduced in *In Memory's Kitchen,* Miriam preserves the recipes of homes and villages that were blasted to the root by the Nazi occupation. But she also preserves, in her adhesion to traditional Jewish culinary rules, what she regards—and her daughter-in-law comes to consider—the sacred table that transcends the particularities of history.

Set forth in Leviticus 11 and Deuteronomy 14, then elaborated in countless rabbinical texts over the centuries, the laws of kosher are simple in the abstract but complex in implementation: you must not mix milk and meat ("do not seethe the kid in its mother's milk"), hence no dairy foods with meat meals, hence, no cheeseburgers or parmesan cheese on spaghetti bolognese. You must not eat animals that do not chew the cud or have cloven hooves. Hence no pork, no bacon, no rabbit. You must only eat fish with fins and scales. Hence no shrimp, no lobster, no clams or oysters, no seafood linguini or salad. You must not use the same dishes or cooking utensils for meat and dairy meals. Hence two sets of dishes. You must scour the house of risen bread before the ten days of Passover, when you are commanded to eat only matzoh, the unleavened bread that the Jews were able, so the story goes, to take with them into the desert when they fled Egypt. You must not use the same dishes for Passover that you use for the rest of the year. Hence *two* more sets of dishes for Passover—one for dairy meals, one for meat meals. To kosher your implements you must boil or scrub (or even iron) them in certain carefully defined ways. Similarly, you must prepare your stove for Passover with intricate cleansing rituals.[24]

And you must observe the Sabbath, the "queen" of weekly days, meaning that you must prepare not just a special meal, with lighted candles and chanted prayers, for Friday evening, but food—often a *cholent*, a kind of casserole—that will be waiting in the oven on Shabbat itself, the day when no observant Jew may light fires, handle money, drive cars or do any kind of labor—God's chosen day of rest which his chosen people must replicate.

Ehrlich compares the focused labor that all this entails to "Zen tea-making" with its concentrated abstraction of foodstuffs from quotidian cuisine. Yet she insists that there is "a heightened sense of reality in a kosher kitchen. You have to think about where your food comes from. . . . You need awareness. . . . You set limits on appetite. . . . It's discipline, a kosher kitchen. It is an encompassing way of life, in which discipline and meaning, the mundane and the spiritual, are inextricably tied." And indeed, although her foodoir is full of recipes, its emphasis is on the abstract concept of the sacred table, the one ordained by Torah, which transcends history. Sephardic Jews may do their eggplant one way; Ashkenazi Jews may do their chicken another way. And the Jews of old, all over the world, may have employed different manners and maneuvers through which they honored the Sabbath and its high holy cousins, Pesach and Rosh Hashanah. But the culinary rules transcend recipes, transporting cooks and diners out of ordinary history—the history of the Inquisition, the pogroms, the Shoah—into the sort of time-out-of-time or sacred time of which Mircea Eliade and others have written.[25]

Yet despite abstraction and devotion, the kitchen has its literality. It is the women, as Ehrlich points out over and over again, who "make" Shabbat and "make" Pesach, the Passover that centers on the seder meal. At one point in her foodoir, she meditates on the domestic labor that the sacred entails, as she decides to plan a seder:

> I should make the stove kosher for Passover, burn out the oven to clean it, take off the stove knobs and soak them, sear burners in their own flame. I should move out the stove and see what's underneath. Under the refrigerator, and under the sink. . . .
>
> I might as well invite a few more people to the Seder. I'll have to clean up a bit around the house. I'm in my living room, and

> there are hard, stale cookies under the cushions. The floors, the corners, crumbs everywhere! Hand me that mop, that bucket, that rag! I will make Pesach.[26]

To those of us who were born and brought up as Catholics—Italian–Americans like me and Louise DeSalvo and Laura Schenone and Maria Laurino—and perhaps to a range of other Christians from around the world, too, such a powerful meditation on the seder will recall Christ's Last Supper of holy bread and sacred wine, the West's paradigmatic sacred meal, which may originally have been a seder or at least a Shabat dinner. But Ehrlich's discussion of the preparations may force us to consider, too, that someone had to be in the kitchen cooking the Last Supper. Who mixed the flour and water for the bread—itself a kind of miracle bread not just like the Jewish matzoh but like the Barbadian bakes Clarke so lovingly describes? Who crushed the grapes for the wine? Who poured, who served? What did the cooks and diners remember of past meals like this one? Were they lonely for homes they had left somewhere else, as Abu-Jaber and Furiya were? Did they dislike the *kind* of bread they were eating? And the wine—even as they praised its holiness, did they wish for it to be more like the delicious drink of some faraway village?

The sacred table may transcend history, yet the history of each individual—as the recipes offered by every one of these foodoirs attest—is an inexorable part of the ongoing chronicle shaped by the culinary imagination. And after all, as most of these books also indicate, it is the cook who creates much of the history of both the sacred and the profane: the daily life shaped by kitchen practices around the world.

Chapter 8

Hail to the Chef! The Cook, the Camera, the Critic, and the Connoisseur

Every restaurant is a theater, and the truly great ones allow us to indulge in the fantasy that we are rich and powerful.

—RUTH REICHL, *GARLIC AND SAPPHIRES*

Who's cooking your food anyway? What strange beasts lurk behind the kitchen doors?

—ANTHONY BOURDAIN, *KITCHEN CONFIDENTIAL*

Many glorious battles have been fought in our beloved Kitchen Stadium. Battles were fought and gourmet dishes created, the memories of which are now forever etched in our minds.

—TAKESHI KAGA, *IRON CHEF: THE OFFICIAL BOOK*

The oven door opens and shuts so fast you hardly notice the deft thrust of a spoon as she dips into a casserole and up to her mouth for a taste-check like a perfectly timed double-beat on the drums. She stands there surrounded by a battery of instruments with an air of authority and confidence. Now & again a flash of the non-cooking Julie lights up the scene briefly, as it did the day before yesterday when with her bare fingers, she snatched a set of cannelloni out of the pot of boiling water with the cry, "Wow! These damn things are as hot as a stiff cock."

—PAUL CHILD, QUOTED BY NOËL RILEY FITCH

Soup Operas: Mysteries of the Kitchen Unveiled

Smoke rises out of strange vessels, and in the midst of the smoke secret ingredients appear, to the crashing of drums and banging of cymbals. It's the 1990s, and time for the Iron Chefs to work their wonders in Kitchen Stadium. But wait, they were hardly the first to light the fire of gastronomy on the screens of living rooms and dining rooms around the world. Look, here's a giant of a woman bouncing chickens around and wielding meat cleavers. It's just past the middle of the last century and Julia Child is working homelier wonders—no smoke and mirrors, but fabulous lessons and adorable mishaps. She spawns a throng of imitators, some comic, some competitively serious.

How many performing chefs there were and are! Forget Escoffier and Carême—let's just go back to the middle of the twentieth century, the era that gave birth to what we might consider the genre of the culinary spectacle. James Beard, on TV in 1946 (*I Love to Cook*, NBC); Dione Lucas, on TV in 1948 (*To the Queen's Taste,* CBS); Ernie Kovacs, on TV in 1950 (*Deadline for Dinner,* WPTZ) ; and of course, the incomparably exuberant, breathily electric and superbly articulate French Chef, Julia Child, whose culinary charisma (first seen on Boston's educational WGBH channel in 1961) transformed, if not the foodways of the nation, the styles of American video—and the tastes of the middle classes who were her devoted fans. In 1992 *Iron Chef* came along, first in Japan, then in the States. And then, beginning in 1993, there was the Food Network. And there were movies, too: including *Babette's Feast* (1987), *The Cook, the Thief, His Wife, and Her Lover* (1989), *Like Water for Chocolate* (1992), *Eat Drink Man Woman* (1994), *Big Night* (1996), *Dinner Rush* (2000), *Julie and Julia* (2009) and, perhaps most charming, the wonderfully animated *Ratatouille* (2007), whose brilliant cooking rodent, Remy, battles wicked imposter Chef Skinner and ice-hearted critic Anton Ego for control of the cuisine in a famous French restaurant.

Why and how did the kitchen invade the living room and the theater? As a character in *Dinner Rush* wonders, "When did eating dinner become a Broadway show?" The history of star chefs and their patrons, employers, fans and critics goes back to the Renaissance, when the young Catherine de' Medici supposedly journeyed across the Alps from Florence to Paris with a caravan of sophisticated cooks, bringing the glamour of haute cuisine Italian menus to the benighted Gauls. And kitchen wizards from the legendary Roman Apicius onward recorded elaborate recipes even before that. But the culinary names we still evoke with awe emerged from the private kitchens, manors and châteaus of the great in the course of the nineteenth century. Marie-Antoine Carême and, slightly later, Georges Auguste Escoffier, arguably the two major innovators, shed their gastronomic glow on menus throughout the period and on into the twentieth century (Escoffier died in 1935), and in particular they helped shape the relatively new institution of the public restaurant. So did such pioneering culinary theorists as Grimod de la Reynière and Jean Anthelme Brillat-Savarin.[1]

Nonetheless, these figures were by and large as distant from the average nineteenth-century and early-twentieth-century diner as the designers who dress First Ladies and Hollywood divas are from today's average shopper. Nor do twenty-first-century chefs as a rule inhabit spaces quite like the one Carême described when he wrote about his kitchen:

> Imagine yourself in a large kitchen before a great dinner. There one sees twenty chefs at their urgent occupations, coming and going, moving with speed in the cauldron of heat. Look at the great mass of burning charcoal, a whole cubic metre for the cooking of entrées and another mass on the ovens for the cooking of the soups, the sauces, the ragouts, the frying and the bains-maries. Add to that a heap of burning wood in front of which four spits are turning, one of which bears a sirloin weighing forty-five to sixty pounds, the other two for fowl and game. In this furnace everyone moved with tremendous speed, not a sound was heard; only I had the right to be heard and at the sound of my soft voice, everyone obeys. Finally, to put the lid on our sufferings, for about an hour the doors and windows are closed so that the air does not cool the food as it is being dished up.[2]

As the food writer Bill Buford has noted, the contemporary restaurant "grill station is hell," like "what Dante had in mind," and the same is true for other cooking stations.[3] But artists in our kitchens are no longer silent or invisible, like Carême's horde of muted, shut-in cooks. Along with their critics and followers, they've become a voluble lot, churning out memoirs, polemics and (yes) cookbooks while instructing the multitudes on countless TV shows. Their most astonishing dinners—those from Thomas Keller (The French Laundry, Per Se) and Ferran Adrià (El Bulli), for instance—are pictured in glossy albums on coffee tables in gourmet households or recorded in video homages. Needless to say, you have to have a certain income to patronize the restaurants ruled by such celebrities—venues where the stars may or may not actually cook, since most have long since trained platoons of followers, like Carême's dutiful workers, to imitate their moves. Posh dining rooms are populated by the fabled 1 percent, but also by eager 10 and 15 percenters who stretch their budgets for scintillating menus. My friends and colleagues sometimes wait weeks or months for reservations at The French Laundry, Gary Danko, Babbo, Momofuku, Per Se, Jean-Georges and on and on—and so do I. A schoolmate of my daughter Susanna's really won the culinary lottery: she was invited by a pal of hers who worked with the German art festival Documenta to dine at El Bulli, the pinnacle of postmodern gastronomy, just before it closed!

The media sends the messages, and dramatizes the menus of almost all these celebrated restaurants. Just this afternoon, I sat in an easy chair in my living room virtually dining at the French Laundry with Anthony Bourdain, Eric Ripert (of Le Bernardin) and several others: course after course floated gloriously by on the screen of my iPad, the fabled "ice cream cones" heaped with salmon tartare, the exquisite "oysters and pearls" (oysters and caviar), the extraordinary sorbets (mango, pear, even beet), the locally raised baby lamb, the parade of desserts and mignardises. More routinely, my friends and family peer at the Food Network and other culinary venues onscreen and online. When I'm riding my exercycle, I can watch Rachael Ray, Mario Batali, the Barefoot Contessa, even (if I want to have a culinary anxiety attack), Paula Deen. (A few days ago I checked out the video spectacle showcasing Deen's insultingly named Ghetto Breakfast Burger: two frosted doughnuts sandwiching a hamburger, a fried egg, and some bacon!) My twenty-seven-year-old grandson likes to watch *Top Chef*, a spinoff of *Iron Chef*, when he finds himself somewhere near a TV (he doesn't own one), or maybe he views it on his computer. Even my youngest grandchild, eight-year-old Sophia, can be riveted by *America's Test Kitchen*. And we don't just watch cooks cooking. As with Bourdain and co., or Mark Bittman, or Andrew Zimmern (of *Bizarre Foods* notoriety), we watch them eating. Bourdain elegantly nibbled that faux cone while eloquently singing its praises; before her recent fall from culinary grace, Deen gobbled up the grotesque burger, despite rumors of her diabetes. And, as the Travel Channel boasts, among other adventures "Andrew visits Cambodia to taste rotten fish, bats and tarantulas."

Which do we prefer, watching cooks cooking or watching them eating? In either case, we're dealing with, on the one hand, culinary exhibitionism, and on the other hand, culinary voyeurism. Whether chopping on camera, or chomping in the limelight, the celebrity chefs are performing. And we, the bedazzled audience, mouths watering and eyes glazed, are looking, listening, hungering. And as for reading—well, we love to read the chef's memoirs, and the memoirs of the critics who can make them or break them, and who have themselves, some of them, become spectacular figures. Perhaps most famously, Ruth Reichl, the *New York Times* critic, food memoirist and *Gourmet* editor earned esteem—and notoriety—for her impersonations of "ordinary" restaurant diners, many described in her charming *Garlic and Sapphires*. By pretending *not* to be a celebrated critic, she produced accurate appraisals of expensive establishments like Le Cirque and the Tavern on the Green from the perspective of just plain folks who couldn't easily afford their sky-high tabs. For, as Reichl herself claims to have told the *Times* when she accepted their job offer, "at a time when people are more interested in food and restaurants than they have ever been in the history of this country [you] shouldn't be writing reviews for the people who dine in fancy restaurants, but for all the ones who wish they could."[4]

Culinary performances online, onscreen and in print: food and cooking we can't stop looking at. Well, friends, that's twenty-first-century entertainment! And where did it all begin?

We Love Julia

The fifties drawing to an end. Eisenhower and his wife, Mamie, with her trademark curls and bangs, still in the White House. Here's a menu from one of their state dinners:

President and Mrs. Eisenhower's Dinner Menu
in Honor of King Paul and Queen Frederika of Greece,
October 28, 1955

Shrimp Cocktail
Cocktail Sauce Saltine Crackers

Sherry
Clear Consommé

Sliced Lemon
Celery Hearts Assorted Olives
Fairy Toast

White Fish in Cheese Sauce
Coleslaw
Boston Brown Bread Sandwiches

White Wine
Crown Roast of Lamb
Stuffed With Spanish Rice
Mint Jelly
French Peas Braised Celery
Bread Sticks

Orange and Roquefort Cheese Salad Bowl
French Dressing
Toasted Triscuits

Champagne
Caramel Cream Mold
Burnt Caramel Sauce
Lemon Iced Diamond Shaped Cookies
Nuts Candies Demitasse

Not bad for an era of Jell-O molds and tuna casseroles, although the saltines and toasted Triscuits do give a current diner pause. And what was that white fish, and what cheese was in the cheese sauce?[5]

Flouncy, full-skirted Dior-influenced dresses. Betty Crocker and Betty Furness in the TV kitchen. As noted earlier, a few efforts at onscreen cooking instruction by James Beard and Dione Lucas, both exceptionally accomplished chefs, for which neither gained mass audiences, since most viewers were still devoted to Ed Sullivan and Sid Caesar. But slowly the life of the little black box in the corner of the living room gains in variety and charisma. By the sixties, we're watching *I Love Lucy, Sesame Street*, the Beatles, *Dragnet, Mission Impossible* and (at the movies) Auntie Mame, James Bond, Mary Poppins.

And Julia Child. The "French Chef," who was neither French nor a chef (in the restaurant sense of the word) had coauthored what was to become one of the classic cookbooks of the century: *Mastering the Art of French Cooking.* Despite the obscurity of her debut on a small Boston channel she was an instant hit, and because her book was indeed masterful, she was instantly influential. Declares Paula Wolfert, herself a cookbook author and sophisticated gourmet, "Just as it's been said that all Russian literature has been taken from Gogol's overcoat, so all American food writing has been derived from Julia's apron." (Like Lucy, of *I Love Lucy,* Julia was always known by her first name, as if she were a beloved friend, aunt or neighbor.) But she didn't just help birth contemporary American food writing, a practice that owed much to such other innovators as M. F. K. Fisher, A. J. Liebling and Waverly Root. More important, it was Julia—gangly, breathless, always with (in her husband's words) "a slight atmosphere of hysteria" edging her inimitably swooping voice—it was Julia who "transformed cooking into entertainment."[6]

She herself was bemused by the swift response to her debut performance on WTVU. "There I was in black and white," she later recalled, "a large woman sloshing eggs too quickly here, too slowly there, gasping, looking at the wrong camera while talking too loudly, and so on." And she was indeed somewhat odd both in appearance and manner, especially when compared to the usual glamorous television star. Notes one observer, her hairdo was "unreconstructed Smith '34," and, adds another, she was "frumpy in a button-up blouse of stiff cotton, like a home-ec teacher." Yet there was something special—what was it?—about her eccentricity, her soprano voice, her intermittent gasps for breath, her height, her middle-aged hairdo (a bit Mamie Eisenhowerish) and her straightforward no-nonsense costume, that captivated. For even after her first show, letters came flying in from enchanted viewers, wanting to see—and learn—more.[7] What was so compelling—her performing (cooking as entertainment) or her teaching (cooking as a serious subject)? And how and why did she make the magic of the French Chef happen, along with the almost legendary lucidity and precision of *Mastering the Art of French Cooking* and its successor volumes?

An extra-tall Californian from a wealthy Pasadena family, six-foot-two-inch Julia Child came to womanhood literally looking down on most people, including her boyfriends, but graduated from Smith after the usual series of courses and crushes. After graduation she moved to New York, like so many ambitious young Americans, hoping to become a great novelist. Instead, she became an ad copywriter for W. & J. Sloane, a classy New York furniture company, then returned to California, where she dabbled in journalism and copywriting. When the Second World War broke out she quickly sought to enlist in the military, and since she was too tall for the WAVES or WACS, she became a diligent, patriotic employee of the OSS, the wartime precursor of the CIA. Posted to the Far East, she worked for General William J. ("Wild Bill") Donovan, sometimes known as the father of American intelligence, handling secret documents in Ceylon (Sri Lanka) and China. There she met and fell in love with her sexy gourmet colleague, the cosmopolitan Paul Child, four inches shorter than she and ten years older.[8]

Yes: Julia has been called a spy in the house of food, but in fact long before she infiltrated the Cordon Bleu cooking school in Paris she was a real-life spy, organizing extraordinarily confidential files for General Donovan and eventually assisting a team of other agents in the development of a special shark repellent to keep those predators away from American underwater missiles that targeted enemy submarines.[9] It all sounds like a 1940s' movie, doesn't it? Bogie and Bacall, analyzing crucial military information while dining and romancing in faraway places! And just think: Bogie was older and shorter, Bacall was younger and taller. Pictures of Paul in this period reveal a handsome, muscular, wide-awake guy—he was an artist and a poet as well as a spy—and Julia looks good in photos too, with her mile-long legs and slim torso, curly perm (not yet out of style) and frank, eager American face. Just this wartime love affair, conducted amid espionage and intrigue in the Far East, might have served as the basis for a Hollywood drama or even a television series like *M*A*S*H*. But if you read *My Life in France*, the memoir Julia coauthored with Paul's great-nephew Alex Prud'homme, you'll find there was a lot to come. Namely, as everybody knows, her life in France.

That life was not discontinuous with her wartime career. Paul was posted to Paris as a diplomatic attaché, and like most foreign service officers he very likely had connections with intelligence networks that his wife had to keep confidential. As for Julia herself, the organizational skills she had developed in overseeing blizzards of secret information for Donovan and others, together with the confidence and competence fostered by her years exploring parts of Asia, meant she was a very different person from the naive Smith graduate who had golfed and volunteered for Red Cross work in Pasadena. Coolly rational, she knew she could command, record and classify all kinds of documents. An experienced traveler, she wasn't subject to the kind of culture shock that might have shaken her had she gone straight to postwar Paris from Southern California. She disliked diplomatic ladies' teas—attended by people she called "frilly" or "fluffy"—but she could hold her own in sophisticated Parisian circles, among both expats and natives.

And Julia had, as everyone knows, fallen in love with France, its cuisine and its culture the moment she tasted her first bite of sole meunière. "It was heaven to eat," she proclaimed over and over again, and throughout her years in France she felt herself "opening like a flower." Muses Prud'homme,

> I think one of the reasons . . . she wanted to write all these recipes down and transmit them to Americans is it was a form of distilling experience, almost like a short story or a poem. She used the recipe as a way of talking about France and its values, which are so different from ours. You know, doing things correctly and taking the time to get it right, and to work hard and learn your technique, and also to have fun.[10]

A history major, Julia had graduated from Smith with (by her own account) a good command of spoken and written French, and she had minored in French literature. Now here she was in a land where (as in China) she loved to eat: "she's a wolf by nature," her husband once said.[11] And, equally important, the man she adored also loved to eat. She wanted to cook for him and for herself—and for everybody else too. She went to Berlitz to perfect her language skills. She went to the Cordon Bleu to perfect her culinary techniques. And when the famous cooking school relegated her to a class of utterly inexperienced women, she demanded a place in the professional program, to which female students usually weren't admitted. Thus she soon became not just a spy in the house of food but a spy at the Cordon Bleu, where slowly, steadily, with a will of iron and a knife of carbon steel, she began mastering the art of French cooking.

The life she lived in France—the core of her being, as her coauthored memoir reveals—was disciplined, delicious and sexy. She "would go to school in the morning," she told one interviewer, "then for lunch time, I would go home and make love to my husband," and then back she would go to the Cordon Bleu for the daily 3 p.m. cooking demonstration. My epigraph quoting Paul Child's narrative of her cannelloni making ("Wow! These damn things are hot as a stiff cock!") dates from this period, as her eagerly erotic self ("the non-cooking Julie") flashes through the authoritative culinary Julia, "surrounded by a battery of instruments." Describing her kitchen as an "alchemist's eyrie," her husband also exclaimed, "you ought to see that Old Girl skin a wild hare—you'd swear she'd just be comin' round the Mountain with her Bowie Knife in Hand." As she gained in gastronomic confidence—studying assiduously with the chef Max Bugnard and dining *à trois* with Simca Beck and Louisette Bertholle (fellow members of the association of "Gourmettes")—she remained a Francophile but had the chutzpah to critique some of the grandest names of the French culinary establishment. The famed critic known only as Curnonsky acted like "a dogmatic meatball who considers himself a gourmet but is just a big bag of wind," while the sainted Brillat-Savarin was "a kind of old brioche whose sole use is to furnish windbags [presumably like Curnonsky] with stupid quotations."[12]

Finally, as she came into her gastronomic own and grew closer to Beck and Bertholle, Julia understood that she didn't just want to cook, she wanted to teach cooking. She had discovered her vocation, as she always explained. She would be the emissary of French food to American kitchens—and in doing so she would also be a spy in the American supermarket, learning what passionate cooks in the servantless homes of the United States might find at Safeway and the A & P to substitute for unavailable French ingredients. Along with Simca and Louisette, she set about giving classes for visiting compatriots who wanted to understand the West's most famous cuisine. Her work on *Mastering* was almost an accidental by-product of her in-person pedagogy. Beck and Bertholle had signed a contract with an American publisher for a book about French cooking, and—after many ups and downs—it became clear that the project would need serious input from someone who knew more about Stateside food culture.

Julia was the one: she had studied at Cordon Bleu, she had spent night after night and day after day rehearsing recipes in her French kitchen at "Rue de Loo" (rue de l'Université) on the Left Bank, near the Sorbonne, and she had returned several times to the States to confirm her researches of American culinary practices in restaurants, homes and supermarkets. Who but she could rewrite French recipes—for boeuf bourguignon, crème caramel, *saumon soufflé*, potatoes Anna, tarte Tatin—so that they might be intelligible to American readers? "Housewives" around the country were a set with whom she herself didn't actually identify (she regarded herself, rightly, as a culinary professional) but she urgently wanted to convert them to the meticulous ways of French gastronomy, and she hoped to reach a range of other culinary practitioners, especially interested men.

As many of her viewers, admirers and readers know by now, Julia set to work immediately, testing recipes (at least three different versions of each), noting times, ingredients, techniques with the concentration of a chemistry professor, and finally writing each one up as if it were a magnificent theorem, complete with lemmas: the lemmas (assumptions and ingredients) carefully listed on the left, to match the carefully phrased instructions printed on the right. Her admonitions and explanations to the aspiring cook are notoriously detailed but such detail is, of course, the reason for her pedagogical success both on the page and on the screen. To give just one example: the recipe for boeuf bourguignon in the first volume of *Mastering* has been accused of excessive length and chastised for the multiple preparations it requires. The cook must simmer bacon for ten minutes (to rid it of salt) before browning it with the beef. When browning the beef she must sprinkle it with flour and toss to coat, then set the casserole in the oven for a few minutes before removing it and adding liquids. She must separately braise small white onions and sauté quartered mushrooms, then add them to the beef that has in the meanwhile stewed for three or four hours in stock, herbs and three cups of red wine. After the dish has cooked long enough, she must sieve the sauce (to remove the vegetables used for flavoring), skim it and test it for thickness. Et cetera.

How elaborate this is becomes quite clear when the *Mastering* recipe is juxtaposed with several other preparations for boeuf bourguignon from the same period. The well-known and widely publicized *Gourmet* cookbook (1950) offers instructions for braised beef in red wine but omits the small onions and quartered mushrooms, as well as the final sieving and seasoning. Dione Lucas's *Meat and Poultry Cook Book* (1955) does include the onions and mushrooms, separately browned, but then instructs the reader to cook them for hours along with the beef. And perhaps in a somewhat timid concession to American anxieties about alcohol, Lucas calls for only one cup of wine, the remainder of the cooking liquid to be stock or water.

Paul Child, *Julia Child on the Set of "The French Chef."*
Schlesinger Library, Radcliffe Institute, Harvard University, Boston, MA, USA.

Julia and her collaborators, by comparison, attend to and, given Julia's passion for pedagogy, analyze every step. The bacon should be simmered to give it the quality of French *lardons.* The beef must be dried in paper towels so it will not steam but rather brown properly. The onions and mushrooms should be cooked separately so they won't dissolve into the stew: they must maintain their integrity. The sauce must be skimmed and thickened so it won't be fatty or soupy. And these principles, as Julia repeatedly observes on the *French Chef* ("Boeuf Bourguignon" was one of her earliest programs on WTVU) can be applied to every comparable Gallic stew: coq au vin, *navarin d'agneau*, and on and on. The ingredients will vary but the foundational principles, like Euclidean rules of logic, will always hold true.

Julia herself knew that she was writing recipes for American audiences in an unprecedented way. Her step-by-step procedures, her application of new technologies like the Waring blender to classic French cuisine, her innovative directions for advance preparation, were designed for the servantless and perhaps nervous American cook. To be even more certain that her pioneering methods would work, Julia often sent her recipes to very close Stateside friends for them to test, after she had scrupulously tested and retested each recipe herself or with Simca. "What a book this will be, if we ever finish it!" she declared. Thus, as one of her biographers explains, "she was convinced that [her correspondents] must keep their work secret," so like the ex-OSS worker she was, she labeled each recipe she sent out "TOP SECRET" or "*YOUR EYES ONLY*" or "NEVER SEEN IN PRINT BEFORE."[13]

Her excitement was electric—and justified. Every self-respecting food historian knows the story. *Mastering* was greeted as a masterpiece, and Julia was quickly inducted into the innermost circle of American gastronomic luminaries. James Beard became one of her best friends, a kind of kissin' kitchen cousin. Dione Lucas gave a boozy party for her (where Julia prepared much of the food). Craig Claiborne praised her brilliance and precision. But what the American public immediately warmed to was not just—perhaps not even—her cooking skills but her extraordinary onscreen persona. For soon after *Mastering* appeared, Julia became the heroine of the TV kitchen, and more, a culinary wizard who fit right into the cultural setting of the mid-century like a key piece in a jigsaw puzzle. Though she's sometimes been seen as a matriarchal figure, sometimes compared to such female luminaries as Amy Vanderbilt and Eleanor Roosevelt, she was nothing like either of them, lacking Vanderbilt's society hauteur and Roosevelt's political gravitas. On YouTube or your PBS DVD, look at her looking at the camera. She talks straight *to* it, and hence to us, as if she were a friendly neighbor who has just dropped into the kitchen for a cup of coffee and to help with a recipe about which she's now imparting important information. Chuck is her favorite cut of beef for this stew, she confides. After you dry the chunks of meat so they won't steam, you put them into a sizzling hot pan. And look, here's how to space them in the pan—don't crowd them or that will make them steam. And look again, this amount of salt (in the palm of her hand) is, yes, a quarter of a teaspoonful, though it may seem like more.

But what a neighbor! Having Julia in your kitchen, even just an onscreen Julia, was like having some sort of fairy tale figure there—a great big tall Mary Poppins (or one of those giant sisters, Miss Fanny and Miss Annie, that

Mary Poppins and the children visit in the book). And this was an imposing sorceress who usually handled pots and pans and knives and spoons (including spoons full of sugar) with compelling deftness. But, too, having Julia in your kitchen or your living room was like having a sitcom heroine there, for instance that charming madcap Lucy, who almost always knew how to transcend her funniest errors. For Julia was not only deft, she was ebullient and improvisational. Has any true fan forgotten the famous story of the potato pancake that split in half when (by her own account) she "didn't have the courage" to flip it fiercely enough? Piecing it back together, "Remember," she confided winningly in a moment worthy of another mid-century show, *Candid Camera,* "if you're alone in the kitchen, who is going to see you?" And so she derived from what might have been a catastrophe a lesson that countless aspiring cooks have cherished to this day.[14]

Lessons—and not just in cooking! Having Julia onscreen in your house was also like having a prize-winning teacher on the premises, not the garden-variety home ec teacher with her tiresome cinnamon toast and Cream of Wheat, but a fabulous science teacher, probably a chemistry instructor, who knew how to command miraculous transformations. In fact, in one episode, called "Primordial Soup with Julia Child," she "cooks up a batch" of water, hydrogen, ammonia and methane to show how "these simple ingredients produce amino acids—the building blocks of life." Like Alec Guinness in *The Man in the White Suit* (1951), who hovers over bubbling retorts and test tubes, she stands in her own kitchen in a video that played for decades in the Smithsonian National Air and Space Museum's Life in the Universe gallery, and explains the molecular origins of the animate world. As she talks, in kid-friendly tones, she points to a list of the crucial elements—with her chef's knife! Why not? Life did begin in a kitchen crucible of sorts. Maybe some magician like Julia chopped up all the ingredients and devised the recipe.

When my children were little, they insisted on regularly watching three programs: *Sesame Street, Star Trek* and "Julia Child" (as they called *The French Chef*). I imagine they secretly believed that all three would teach them a lot about the universe: reading and counting, stars and galaxies, and the mysteries of cooking. Eventually, as television became more varied and sophisticated, cooking and cartoons and fantasy took different and more complex turns. As cartoons gathered momentum from postmodern irony (*The Simpsons, South Park*) and Leonard Nimoy was replaced by a new-generation Spock, Julia too moved on. Paul died after years in a nursing home. Julia vacated the little house in Provence where they had long wintered and took refuge in a Santa Barbara apartment complex. Onscreen, she watched other cooks cook, commented fondly and rarely stirred the pots herself. Nor did she seem regretful. As she wrote in *My Life in France,* when her niece asked her if she was going to miss the place, "I shrugged, and said: 'I've always felt that when I'm done with something I just walk away from it—*fin!*' "[15]

Viagra in the Kitchen

Of course, Julia couldn't and didn't simply walk away from her life in the kitchen. She went on cheerily cooking and coaching cooks on tapes and in videos, on YouTube and DVDs, and even, taking on the body of Meryl Streep, in the movie *Julie and Julia.* Hundreds of thousands of viewers still turn to the boeuf bourguignon show, the omelet show, and the infamous potato pancake episode. But many watch these scenes out of nostalgia for a kind of culinary instruction that no longer exists on television. For Julia's successors on the Food Network, the Cooking Channel, Bravo, and the Travel Channel are an entirely different kettle of cooks. Anthony Bourdain, one of the new century's most prominent culinary personalities, has paid his respects to her, even though his own career flourished through the development of an image almost directly the opposite of hers. The author of the best-selling memoir *Kitchen Confidential*—whose very title evokes *Dragnet* and *Mission Impossible*—Bourdain has also become a media celebrity. He appears on the Travel Channel eating exotic foods, he serves as a judge on *Top Chef* and *Iron Chef,* and he writes passionately about a range of restaurant practices, though (interestingly) he rarely produces recipes. Nonetheless, Bourdain scorns the Food Network and what he calls its "Ready-Made bobblehead personalities." Scathingly, he has compared the popular Rachael

Ray—labeled by Mario Batali the "cheerleader" among TV cooks—to her distinguished precursor, writing:

> Where the saintly Julia Child sought to raise expectations, to enlighten us, make us better—teach us—and in fact, did, Rachael uses her strange and terrible powers to narcotize her public with her hypnotic mantra of Yummo . . . "You're doing just fine. You don't even have to chop an onion—you can buy it already chopped. Aspire to nothing . . ."

"Aspire to nothing." The message of the Food Network, Bourdain implies, is Cooking for Dummies.[16]

His own authority, however, derives from the kind of macho fervor designed to take any kitchen stadium by storm. If Julia often seemed like a fairy tale cross between Lucy Ricardo and Mary Poppins, Bourdain is the tough guy hero of a hardboiled novel by Raymond Chandler, or he's Bogie at the stove, having seen to it that Mary Astor took the fall for the Maltese falcon. Julia introduced her memoir of life in France with a tender tribute to her husband ("This is a book about some of the things I have loved most in life: my husband, Paul Child; *la belle France;* and the many pleasures of cooking and eating"). But Bourdain's memoir, promising to be "about the dark restaurant underbelly," starts off with a bitter bang:

> So, it's not Super chef talking to you here. Sure, I graduated CIA, knocked around Europe, worked some famous two-star joints in the city—damn good ones, too. I'm not some embittered hash-slinger out to slag off my more successful peers (though I will when the opportunity presents itself). . . . This book is about street-level cooking and its practitioners. Line cooks are the heroes. I've been hustling a nicely paid living out of this life for a long time—most of it in the heart of Manhattan, the "bigs"—so I know a few things. I've still got a few moves left in me. Of course, there's every possibility this book could finish me in the

> business. There will be horror stories. Heavy drinking, drugs, screwing in the dry-goods area, unappetizing revelations about bad food-handling and unsavory industry-wide practices. Talking about why you probably shouldn't order fish on a Monday.[17]

Don't order fish on a Monday! That became one of the most notorious instructions in this book of unsavory restaurant revelations. It's leftover from before the weekend and it's probably close to rotten. But there's a kind of hilarity in the juxtaposition of this prudent admonition with the cigarette-dangling-out-of-the-corner-of-the-mouth "I've still got a few moves left in me" and the promise that "this book could finish me in the business." Food anxiety plus gastronomic gangsta rap! And the confidentiality of all this, akin to Julia's regular labeling of recipes as "TOP SECRET," suggests that the CIA from which the author graduated was what we ordinarily think of as the CIA—the network of spies—rather than the Culinary Institute of America that prepares its students for the Food Network.

To be fair, the personality that emerges now and then when the wise-cracking noir façade cracks can be endearing. "For me, the cooking life has been a long love," Bourdain admits before relating his own version of Julia's sole meunière episode: a tongue-tingling moment in his childhood when, as an eight-year-old traveling in France with his parents, he discovered the delights of eating an oyster. "It tasted of seawater . . . of brine and flesh . . . and somehow . . . of the future. Everything was different now. I'd not only survived—I'd enjoyed." Later still, he confesses that as a mere lad working the sweaty kitchens of Provincetown, he was in awe of his coworkers. "These guys were master criminals, sexual athletes, compared to my pitiful college hijinks. Highwaymen rogues, buccaneers, cut-throats, they were like young princes to me, still only a lowly dishwasher." But then the hard-boiled voice takes over, as he confides that he was more impressed still when during a raucous wedding party he caught a glimpse of his restaurant's head chef rear-ending a stoned "blushing bride" out by the trash cans. "I knew then, dear reader, for the first time: I wanted to be a chef."[18]

Sex in the kitchen: what with the hellish heat of the grill station, the close quarters, the bends and bumps and curses, and most of all the sheer fleshiness of the culinary arts—the chickens to be massaged, the bloody steaks, the oysters opening their salty mouths—it's not a surprising phenomenon. Even the fairy-tale Julia, always erotic and notoriously frank in her offscreen language ("Balls!" was a favorite dismissive remark) was roused to declare that her cannelloni were "hot as a stiff cock." Her comment was demure compared to British chef Gordon Ramsay's assertion that "Cooking is the most massive rush. It's like having the most amazing hard-on, with Viagra sprinkled on top of it, and it's still there twelve hours later." O those culinary men, "pillaging and rock-and-rolling through life with a carefree disregard for all conventional morality," as Bourdain puts it. And he notes, echoing Ramsay's testosterone-heated claim, "My vato locos are, like most line cooks, practitioners of that centuries-old oral tradition in which we—all of us—try to find new and amusing ways to talk about dick. . . . Does a locker-room environment like this make it tougher for women, for instance? Yep."[19]

Teaming up in various kitchen stadiums, the (mostly) male celebrity chefs might, yes, be football players or basketball stars. Michael Pollan points out that

> cooking in prime time is a form of athletic competition, drawing its visual and even aural vocabulary from *Monday Night Football.* On *Iron Chef America* . . . the cookingcaster Alton Brown delivers a breathless . . . play by play and color commentary, as the iron chefs and their team of iron sous-chefs race the clock to peel, chop, slice, dice, mince, Cuisinart, mandoline, boil, pan-sear, sauté, sous vide, deep-fry, pressure-cook, grill, deglaze, reduce and plate . . .[20]

Like warriors, too, the macho chefs even seem ready to devour each other, as if Homer's Laestrygonians had come again. Food critic and cooking acolyte Bill Buford describes the savage-tempered British chef Marco Pierre White throwing a risotto at his onetime apprentice Mario Batali, and beating up an "Irish kid who washed the dishes." Commented Batali, "I was frightened for my life, this guy was a mean motherfucker." As for White, he cannibalistically observed that Batali "Has big fucking calves, doesn't he? He should donate them to the kitchen when he dies. They'll make a great osso buco."[21]

Even literal butchery (not chef-on-chef carvery) is sexy, according to some accounts. After a session learning to cut up pigs and cows with famed Tuscan butcher Dario Cecchini, Buford bemusedly quotes his mentor: "A butcher never sleeps. A butcher works in meat during the day and plays in flesh at night. A true butcher is a disciple of carnality." Then the American glosses the statement, a "wordplay made possible in Italian": "Carne, flesh, carnality, sex, mean skin, dinner, sin [in] one continuous stream of association." The two, along with their women companions, have dined on blood-rare steak, and as a kind of digestif the master rather unnervingly admonishes his apprentice that "You must now make love like a butcher. For the rest of the night, you must enact the dark acts of carnality, a butcher's carnality. And then you will rise in the hours before dawn, smelling of carnality, and unload the meat from the truck, like a butcher."[22]

To be sure, the male cooking team is not all muscle, sweat and testosterone. In the last decade or so, many of their lightning-swift moves have been strategized by a sort of culinary science that is very different from the nutritional information imparted in old-fashioned home ec classes. For years the reigning master of avant-garde cookery has been Ferran Adrià, the Einsteinian innovator who long ran El Bulli, *the* gastronomic destination of the new century until it closed in 2011 so that the great man could devote more time to his culinary research. Coming in a close second have been Thomas Keller's similarly pioneering establishments, The French Laundry and Per Se. What distinguishes these scientizing chefs is their mastery not just of the ordinary transformations that are the bases of cookery (raw to cooked, thin to thick, pale to dark) but the laboratory investigations that empower them to produce foods that are wittily mimetic or surprising: "peanuts" with liquid interiors; "cones" that contain salmon tartare instead of sorbet or ice cream.

A Day at El Bulli, a Spanish-language documentary recording Adrià's command of his kitchen laboratory (and doesn't a chemistry lab look like a kitchen anyway?) focuses on the austere scientist surrounded by an almost entirely male platoon of attentive assistants, who might as well be working at (yes, Julia) a top secret facility somewhere in the bowels of a magic mountain. The food they produce, as devotees attest, is at least figuratively out of this world. "Someone asked me if the food at El Bulli was Spanish food," remarks one blogger, "and I said: 'No, it's Martian food.' Case in point, [a course] which tasted like biting into a marshmallowy mound of coconut-flavored snow. Light as air and intensely flavored. I have no idea how this was made or if NASA was involved." The same writer goes on to describe "Adrià's signature touch—that shocking moment when something that looks solid becomes liquid in your mouth."[23]

Where are women chefs in all this? A few, like the wonderful memoirist Gabrielle Hamilton, whose *Blood, Bones and Butter* is a kind of Kunstlerroman about her career at the stove, manage their own restaurants in the chef-eat-chef atmosphere of a primarily macho culinary battlefield. Hamilton has even beaten out Bobby Flay on *Iron Chef*, and maintains witty televised conversations with Anthony Bourdain and Charlie Rose. Other women, though, like "cheerleader" Rachael Ray and down-home Southern "butterball cook" Paula Deen, are treated with scorn. Bourdain wonders whether Ray "ever really cooks. She never said she was good at it." As for Paula Deen, he argues that she's "the worst, most dangerous person to America . . . She revels in unholy connections with evil corporations and she's proud of the fact that her food is f———ing bad for you."[24]

In fact, in recent years Deen has been castigated by many other commentators besides Bourdain. In 2012, she was widely denounced as hypocritical because she only announced that she herself was a diabetic—perhaps as a result of the sugary and fatty diet that included her doughnut Ghetto Burgers—when she became a spokesperson for a Danish producer of insulin, and in 2013 she was accused of racism for using the "n word" and exploiting African-American employees. The Food Network and Smithfield Foods both cancelled her contracts with them, as did a number of other corporations.[25]

Along with Hamilton, both the "saintly Julia" and (usually) the iconic and idealistic Alice Waters are exempted from the kind of contempt Bourdain expresses for both Ray and Deen, although the macho chef has scathingly claimed that Waters "annoys the living shit out of me" and that in her commitment to "expensive organic food" she is "very Khmer Rouge." Compared to the hard-driving men in Kitchen Stadium, comments Pollan, the women cooks (not really chefs) on the Food Network star in "dump-and-stir shows during the day" that "tend to be aimed at stay-at-home moms who are in a hurry and eager to please"—maybe those "fluffy" and "frilly" housewives that Julia too scorned. Yet even if Julia Child and Alice Waters don't dump-and-stir, they are frequently damned by faint praise: Julia is "saintly" as a beloved elementary school teacher though her recipes are "elaborate and time-consuming"; Waters is righteous—a "salad evangelist"—and, according to one former associate at Chez Panisse, "never had restaurant-cooking chops."[26]

Both, then, are in one way or another defined by their femininity: Julia as an outsized fantasy figure, Alice as lovely, innocent—and tough in her ruthless commitment not just to Chez Panisse but to her other culinary causes. Julia is also famous for the warmth of her marriage to Paul Child, whose immersion in her career, according to one biographer, made that career possible: at one point, Paul and Julia became "one person, and that person was Julia." Alice is noted for "her motley collection of ex-, current, and quasi-boyfriends," described by David Kamp in *The United States of Arugula* as "an amazing marshaling of disparate talents that she put to good use." Were both these female gastronomic stars rocketed to foodie heavens by male supporters? It's hard to believe that when you read the masterful recipes of *Mastering* or watch the brilliant presentations of *The French Chef,* when you sit down to dinner at Chez Panisse or stroll through one of Waters's "Edible Schoolyards." Paul Child himself declared in a birthday sonnet to his wife that her "unsurpassed quenelles and hot souffles / [her] English, Norse and German, and [her] French, / Are all beyond my piteous powers to praise," while even the colleague who considered that Waters "had no restaurant chops" admitted that she was "a bad motherfucker . . . Her determination and her strength, hidden behind that frailty, made that place continue and continue and continue. . . . She is the woman."[27]

Lights! Camera! Eat!

In an era of gastronomic obsession, it's inevitable that we encounter not just food memoirs and recipe poems but numerous food movies. Not surprisingly, most movies about women cooks present them as maternally and magically or even mysteriously nurturing. *Babette's Feast*, based on a wonderful tale of the same name by Isak Dinesen, dramatizes the sacrificial gesture of a brilliant woman chef who spends an unexpected financial windfall in creating an astonishing banquet for her (at least outwardly) unappreciative, puritanical Danish employers. *Like Water for Chocolate*, similarly based on a female-authored classic (by Laura Esquivel), depicts the thwarted desire and erotic passion of a gifted young cook whose enchanted foods are shaped by both her forced renunciation of love and her innate nurturing impulses. *Julie and Julia,* written by the novelist and screenwriter Nora Ephron, was derived from Julie Powell's blog about her enthralled determination to cook every one of Julia Child's *Mastering* recipes in a single year, and celebrates both Julia Child's influential career and the female kitchen bonding that opens doors of literary and culinary opportunity for Julie Powell, her young disciple.

By comparison, films about male chefs frequently have the same macho air as Bourdain's and Buford's memoirs. Both *Big Night* and *Dinner Rush,* for instance, bring the Mafia to the kitchen, building on the kinds of restaurant scenes featured in *Goodfellas* and *The Godfather.* On one hand, in each of these movies we witness the deliciousness of the pastas and sauces, the meats and wines that stream from stove to table, along with the swoons and sighs of the satisfied diners. On the other hand, we discover that the restaurants in which they're set are battlegrounds for rival thugs, bookmakers, gangsters. In these narratives, as in the famous Mafia dramas by Coppola and Scorsese, the kitchen itself, with its blood and garbage, its hellish burners and icy reach-ins—and its ever-lurking rats—becomes a metaphor for an underworld fight for survival. The most innocuous-seeming customers (spoiler alert: in *Dinner Rush* a bland Wall Street type hanging out at the bar) turn out to be murderers, while even when mafiosi are imprisoned (as in *Goodfellas*) they manage to slice garlic with a razor till it's almost invisible ("goodfella thin") and churn out fantastic sauces. Ratting on each other, owners and diners play out melodramas suggesting that behind the most exquisite gourmet spectacles lurk the diseased teeth, the poisonous tongues of rodents.

Rats! Anyone in the restaurant business, indeed anyone who walks the alleys of cities or harkens to the attics of the countryside, knows they're the worst. Bourdain at his grittiest describes his drug addiction and consequent fall into the lowest of Manhattan's low eateries:

> I worked at a Mexican restaurant on upper Second Avenue for a while, one of those places on the frat-boy strip with the obligatory margarita snocone machine grinding away all night and vomit running ankle-deep in the gutters outside. The place was owned by a very aggressive rat population, fattened up and emboldened by the easily obtained stacks of avocados left to ripen outside the walk-in each night. They ran over our feet in the kitchen, hopped out of the garbage when you approached and, worst of all, stashed their leavings in the walls and ceilings.[28]

Aggressive. Emboldened. Nothing more alarming. Our fear of rats is a fear of squirmy filth, bites, plagues, squealing hordes—conquest by a tiny, hairy, sickening other.

How, then, did so many moviegoers fall in love with Pixar's *Ratatouille* when it came out a few years ago? The rat gangs to whom we're introduced in this imaginatively animated film aren't Mickey Mouse or his pals, not even Remy, the hero. They really look like yucky rodents, as reviewers have pointed out over and over again. They eat garbage and are voracious, repulsive, reviled. They might even be allegorical figures standing in for scary immigrants—which only makes them worse, depending on how you feel about the alienness of immigrants. (If you're sympathetic, such symbolism horrifies you; if you're not, well. . . .) But although Remy's relatives gobble the most sickening objects out of the trash, our hero's journey toward chefdom begins when he first savors the epicurean combination of a crisp apple and a ripe cheese, then becomes a poignant narrative of the making of a culinary artist as he transforms himself and his human sidekick, the kitchen boy Linguini, into a single, collaborative chef.

No use recapitulating all the twists of the plot. If you don't know it already, rent the movie. Remy reaches Paris through the sewers, but his muse is the ghost of the great dead chef Gusteau, and—as in most male-centered culinary films—he has to fight a villainous gangster type, Chef Skinner, who has taken over the kitchen of the famous restaurant established by Gusteau (Linguini's real father, as it turns out). Worse still, "little chef" Remy has to appeal to the ice-hearted and tensile-tongued food critic Anton Ego, whose responses to food can make or break a restaurant. Every plot turn here recapitulates the schema of masculine culinary Kunstlerroman: the dedicated cooking hero who has to fight a wicked and corrupt system (Skinner, Ego) in order to achieve his vision of food; the kitchen whose technology is alarmingly fierce (especially for a tiny rat); the disturbing borders between the cooking space (dangerous and secret) and the dining space (leisurely and elegant). At the same time, the film dazzlingly turns our gastronomic belief systems upside down: the supposedly kindly food handlers abominate the heroic Remy; even the most disgusting rodents turn into kindly heroes.

The most famous scene in the movie, where the rats take over the Gusteau kitchen, underlines what Jacques Derrida would call the *renversement.* Here the creepy "villains" swarm over the burners and counters, stirring pots and finishing sauces in a dazzling culinary ballet that would ordinarily strike us as nightmarish. In the meantime, the human cooks, critics and customers side with the French health inspectors who seek to obliterate the rats. But the film, and Remy's career, reach a climax when the critic Anton Ego finally samples a dish of the "little chef's" devising—ratatouille, of course—and in a Proustian moment is transported back to boyhood innocence, praises the food and gives the restaurant a glowing review, declaring that "Not everyone can become a great artist, but a great artist can come from anywhere"—including the humble origin of a rathole. Though the health inspectors finally close the old Gusteau's down, it's ultimately reincarnated as the wildly popular bistro Ratatouille, one of whose principal investors is none other than Ego, and whose chef is, of course, that genius of a rodent, Remy. The expression of ecstasy on the critic's face when he tastes the elegantly presented vegetable dish that Remy has contrived for him is a wonder to behold, prepares us for this denouement, and reminds us, too, that it isn't easy, even for a cartoon figure, to eat on camera.

Yet, just as food movies and cooking shows continually increase in popularity, eating on camera has become a major business for (mostly) male cooks. Women cooks, of course, taste, sip and sniff. Julia Child brings to her lips a glass of Gravymaster-and-water masquerading as wine before she chirps her classic "Bon appetit!" Paula Deen swoons over her grotesque doughnut burger. But a number of celebrated culinary men make a living out of munching onscreen. Two of the most notorious are Guy Fieri, of *Diners, Drive-Ins and Dives*, who relishes down-home grungy stuff from around the country, and Andrew Zimmern, of *Bizarre Foods*, who devours weird stuff from around the world. "What can possibly be the appeal of watching Guy Fieri bite, masticate and swallow all this chow?" muses Michael Pollan, while even the most adventurous of diners might wonder why we should want to look on while Zimmern eagerly downs black chicken testicles in Taiwan, pig's windpipe in Osaka or raw camel in Ethiopia. One motive may be simply the gastronomic voyeurism that prompted crowds of courtiers and even a few lucky commoners to watch the king dine at the Grand Suppers of Versailles. Another is surely an anthropological curiosity about the varieties of quotidian experience around the world—a curiosity that *National Geographic* never really satisfied the way television can. Yet another may well be a certain *frisson* gained from the spectacle of someone politely eating something disgusting: Zimmern, Fieri and others of their ilk never flinch, gag or spit things out.[29]

And better still, besides taking us to unnerving culinary scenes around the world, the video camera gives us access to great restaurants where we might never be able to get reservations even if we could afford their prices. Bourdain—who does his share of strange eating on the Travel Channel—supplements spectacles of weirdness by taking us to such palaces of gastronomy as The French Laundry and El Bulli. As a TV host he's far more genial and considerably less hard-boiled than his writing persona would suggest. True, occasional bleeps punctuate his sentences, reminding us of his macho kitchen lingo. But even if, as he occasionally has, he teams up with Zimmern, he eats neatly and cheerfully onscreen, doesn't gobble, dribble or over-enthuse—just quietly and courteously marvels at miracles of cuisine. As a sometime chef, too, he occasionally goes backstage to the kitchen, where he knowledgeably comments on ingredients, stirs pots, peers in ovens. Food writer Mark Bittman and chef Mario Batali have done the same thing on gastronomic tours, most notably an idyllic pilgrimage through Spain with Gwyneth Paltrow and Spanish actress Claudia Bassols.

Interestingly, although most of the luminaries who guide us through eateries from dives and dumps to Michelin three-stars function as if they were food critics, none is really a critic in the way Anton Ego is: someone evaluating and rating restaurants on deadline for newspapers or other media. Indeed, if they really were critics, they wouldn't want to be caught on camera. As any chef's memoir will tell you, every cook worth his toque spends a lot of time trying to predict or detect visits from important critics. Gusteau's entire staff shivers with anxiety when Anton Ego sits at a table in the front of the house. And as Bill Buford discloses in *Heat,* Batali's signature restaurant Babbo is transfigured by the expectation of a visit from Ruth Reichl, then the food critic for the *New York Times* (defined as "the most important critic in the world"): "the strategies built around Reichl's visit call to mind a coach preparing for a big game . . . the whole restaurant. . . . was in a condition of constant dress rehearsal—waiting for Ruth. Joe [the co-owner] was in the front, overseeing the service. Mario was in the kitchen, whispering every order and inspecting it before it went out." But it was hard to know when and whether Reichl was there. She "was known to wear a wig" and was adept at disguising herself, even though a picture of her was posted in nearly every restaurant kitchen in New York.[30]

Molly, Miriam, Brenda, Chloe, Betty, Toni, Emily

I once went to dinner with a food critic—not as omnipotent a figure as the person who writes for the *New York Times*, but a well-known and quite important reviewer in the West Coast city where he lives and works. Several of us entered the restaurant ahead of him and gave the pseudonym under which he'd chosen to reserve our table. He came a bit later, with another friend, and seated himself unobtrusively among us. We ordered wine and a first course, then suddenly there was the server (or was it the chef?) hovering.

"I particularly wanted *you* to taste *this*," he said casually to my critic friend, who laughed and confided to the rest of us that "I've been *made.*" Identified. And from that moment on we ate the way people eat who dine with food critics: very well indeed. Nor was there any way, at that point, to know what our dinners would have been like had our host not been "made."

Throughout *Garlic and Sapphires,* as she catalogs her wonderful range of metropolitan impersonations, Ruth Reichl is ambivalent about the consequences of being "made." On the one hand, if she's recognized, she'll get the kind of extraordinary attention that only "the rich and the powerful"—and food critics—get, and as she claimed when she began her stint at the *Times,* she doesn't want to write "reviews for the people who dine in fancy restaurants, but for all the ones who wish they could." On the other hand, as she observes in a passage from which I've drawn one of my epigraphs, "Every restaurant is a theater, and the truly great ones allow us to indulge in the fantasy that we are rich and powerful"—and who wouldn't want that fantasy to become a temporary reality, as it does for the celebrity critic? Mostly, Reichl narrates her loyalty to the dilemmas of the ordinary diner, adopting a series of walk-on parts at New York's premier establishments. But every once in a while she tears off her wig of the moment and lets down her famously long and curly black hair to become her gastronomically expert self.

That self is an extraordinary one. Not just a critic and an actress, Reichl is a talented writer of both memoirs and cookbooks, an editor, a blogger and a major "food world" personage. As a memoirist, to be sure, she has quite a few counterparts among restaurant critics: from Craig Claiborne to Mimi Sheraton and Frank Bruni, the great powers of the *New York Times* have all shared their personal initiations into cuisine with thousands of fascinated readers. But Reichl is exceptionally productive. Her first autobiographical work, *Tender at the Bone*, begins as a Proustian recollection of her mother's terrible cooking ("The Queen of Mold") and how the taste of rottenness inspired her to take over the stove as quite a young child, then traces her evolution as a dedicated cook. The sequel, *Comfort Me with Apples*, interweaves food memories with tales of romance and the poignant story of a failed adoption, followed by the triumph of a late-life pregnancy. *Garlic and Sapphires*, the third volume in the trilogy, specifically recounts her years of daunting power at the *Times,* simultaneously celebrating the luxuries of the cosmopolitan table and deconstructing them from the ironic perspectives of gastronomic outsiders.

In a video interview, Reichl has confided that she had twelve different characters during her stint as New York's arbiter of tastiness, but *Garlic and Sapphires* profiles just six: Molly, Miriam, Chloe, Brenda, Betty, and Emily. (Oh yes, there's a weak seventh, Toni, whose performance is so halfhearted that the critic gets "made" almost immediately.) In the beginning of her period of performance, Reichl explains, her costume and makeup were constructed with the help of an old friend who was a drama coach, but after a while she learned how to shop for her own wigs, disguise her voice and manner, and even apply wrinkles with rubber cement. Her most striking successes, not surprisingly, are her impersonations of older middle- or lower-middle-class women. Molly, for instance, is a somewhat stout, middle-aged short-haired suburbanite in a good but well-worn Armani suit and sensible shoes. Dining at New York's top-tier glamour spot, Le Cirque, with an elderly friend (actually Reichl's drama coach), she's put at a bad table in the back of the room and rudely served: she practically has to beg for a wine list, isn't told of the specials and is even treated sullenly by the busboy. "Were we invisible because we were women?" Reichl/Molly wonders. "Or did we look too much like tourists to be worthy of recognition?" Internalizing Molly's pain, Reichl declares to her friend, Claudia, "I came here for glamour . . . and it has turned into a nightmare. I feel frumpy and powerless. I may be nobody, but I don't like paying to be humiliated."[31]

Needless to say, when the critic returns to Le Cirque as herself, all is changed, utterly changed. Sirio Maccioni, the owner, bows her and her escort to a large front table while declaring that he has kept the king of Spain waiting in the bar. "And then fireworks began shooting across the table: black truffles and white ones, foie gras, lobster, turbot, venison . . . as if we were the only people in the restaurant and fifty chefs were cooking just to please us." The well-known review that Reichl finally wrote was a consolidation (at the paper's behest) of two reviews, one by "Molly" ("despite the misery of the evening I let the restaurant keep one star") and one by the "real" Ruth

Reichl ("Of course I gave the restaurant four stars"). The negotiated evaluation? Three stars. The readership's reaction? Partly enraged ("You have destroyed the finest restaurateur in America") but mostly affirmative ("Keep up the good work. The silent majority needs you").[32] The very performance of the review was as deft as the critic's impersonation of an insecure, hopeful out-of-towner. As no longer a New Yorker but an out-of-towner myself, I can vaguely remember dining at Le Cirque on a trip to the city some years ago and finding the place glitzy but tasty; David and I had okay service (though we had to wait a while for our table) but the most memorable aspect of the evening was the big-top quality of the place—it too an impersonation—with its air of an old-time French circus. Far more memorable was Reichl's split-personality review.

The diners who help shape her other reviews are almost always as distinctive as Molly, and in each, as we learn in the course of her narrative, the author claims to have found a part of herself. After Molly, she becomes Miriam, a hoity-toity silver-haired old lady who's a reincarnation of her own mother and who commands excellent service at the Four Seasons. (But had she been "made"?) As a glamorous blonde, Chloe, Reichl picks up a wealthy guy at Palio and scores a meal (well, she splits the bill) at Lespinasse, where all goes well. Then she becomes Brenda, a happy-go-lucky redhead who somehow manages to have an excellent dinner at Daniel even though her guests include a couple of aging hippies.

Most poignant, however, is Betty, a down-at-heels spinster in her late sixties. Betty goes along with some friends to the Tavern on the Green, where, like Molly at Le Cirque, she's treated with indifference verging on contempt, even by a dining companion who doesn't realize she's the distinguished Ruth Reichl. Yes, ill-shod, badly dressed, limping elderly women are invisible in New York. Even Eric, the obsequious elevator man in Reichl's building (as she tells the tale) ignores Betty, though he had actually fallen for Brenda (he said he was a connoisseur of redheads). Betty's dilemma finally motivates the author to write a review that's really a manifesto: "Why I Disapprove of What I Do: It's indecent to glamorize a $100 meal. Or is it?" Beginning with a remark by one of her idols, M. F. K. Fisher—"You can't be a restaurant critic, unless you are one of those ambitious sorts, willing to walk on your grandmother's grave"—she worries that she's just telling rich people where to eat, then decides that the "more people pay attention to what and how they eat, the more attuned they become to their own senses and the world around them."[33]

Reichl's long and fascinating run as a culinary performer comes to a disturbing conclusion when she turns herself into Emily, a nasty lady modeled on the uptight, tweedy maitresse d' of the overpriced, slightly sleazy Box Tree restaurant, then supposedly the most romantic spot in New York. There, her old friend the cookbook author Marion Cunningham tells her off ("I don't like what you've become") with such severity that she rips off her wig mid-meal and resolves to change her life. The Box Tree gets a scandalous rating of "poor" and Reichl understands that if big-hearted Brenda was her best self, stony Emily is her worst. Too many masquerades have taken their toll; too many judgments have evidently been debilitating. By the end of the book, the narrator gets a serendipitous phone call from *Gourmet*, inviting her to apply for a job as its editor. At least one of her theatrical careers is over.[34]

But *Garlic and Sapphires* reminds us, as do the Food Network, the Cooking Channel, and all the other literary, cinematic and video representations of gastronomy that we've encountered in the last half century, that the food we tend to think of as the most material ingredient of our fleshly existence has become almost more virtual than real, almost more theatrical than quotidian. The twenty-first-century culinary imagination has transformed what we eat into what we read, watch, dream. Even the cookbooks of celebrity chefs are ghostwritten, said a story in the newspaper the other day: the chefs are too busy making themselves up for the camera to do their own recording of recipes. Nor are they (for the most part) cooking in the restaurants they own and maybe run. Do you think you'll really meet Mario Batali at Babbo? Jean-Georges Vongerichten at Jean-Georges?

The series of masquerades verges on infinite. The diner longs for the chef (who really isn't there). The chef yearns for the critic (who pretends to be someone else). The viewer salivates for the impalpable food. Garlic yearns for sapphires, as Reichl's title suggests, and sapphires need garlic. The dowdy diner wants rich food; the rich diner wants the luxury of power over the line cooks in the kitchen, who chop the garlic for pasta, sear the foie gras and grate the truffles. The Italian sommelier is far from home but impersonates Italy for New Yorkers. The French *patron* incarnates Paris but we are actually dining in Chicago or San Francisco, not in France.

Reichl's title comes from T. S. Eliot's *Four Quartets.* "Garlic and sapphires in the mud, / Clot the bedded axle tree, / The trilling wire in the blood / Sings below inveterate scars." [35] Eliot, who often wrote about food and its materiality with a mixture of revulsion and desire, implied that we are enthralled, rightly or wrongly, by the compelling (yet from his perspective vulgar) savor of garlic, even while we long for the (equally vulgar) wealth incarnated in deep blue radiant sapphires. Reichl herself may have been torn like that as she roamed from restaurant to restaurant, dining with the rich and powerful while longing to speak for the hungry vicissitudes of the middle and working classes, those who couldn't afford Le Cirque or Lespinasse or even, as it turns out, the shoddy Tavern on the Green. But what of the other chefs, critics, connoisseurs and masqueraders? As the smoke and mirrors perform their magic tricks in Kitchen Stadium, what can they do to feed the unfortunate Bettys of this world—or even Eric, the elevator operator in Reichl's building? What of the loiterers around Times Square, whom the food critic passes each day on her way to fancy restaurants? Are there greens and other goodies for their plates and palates? Would Julia and Tony Bourdain and Ruth's fancy blonde persona Chloe find something to offer them? Are the impoverished and lonely trapped among real rats, or can we hope that some might, sooner or later, have a chance to savor the amazing vegetable stew cooked up by Remy, the rodent hero?

Chapter 9

Cooking the Books: Cosiness, Disgust, Desire, Despair

> . . . this bottle was NOT marked "poison," so Alice ventured to taste it, and finding it very nice, (it had, in fact, a sort of mixed flavor of cherry-tart, custard, pine-apple, roast turkey, toffee, and hot buttered toast,) she very soon finished it off.
>
> —LEWIS CARROLL, *ALICE'S ADVENTURES IN WONDERLAND*

> When you're really down, focus on the food.
>
> —DIANE MOTT DAVIDSON, *STICKS AND SCONES*

> . . . back behind and to the left of the milk cans. Working dough. Working, working dough. Nothing better than that to start the day's serious work of beating back the past.
>
> —TONI MORRISON, *BELOVED*

In the First Kitchen

Lollipop trees and gingerbread houses. Bottles of cherry-tarts mingled with custard, roast turkey, toffee, and other goodies. Spoonfuls of sugar. Ice cream mountains. Landscapes of lusciousness like those from the medieval land of Cockayne. Tunnels in peaches. Rivers of chocolate. A world of cookies.

Children's books revel in the romance of food—and why not? When the baby is weaned from her first desire, the loss of the breast—with (if all goes well) its apparently ceaseless satisfactions—promotes further aspirations: the endless pleasures of Cockayne, the walls of sugar, the wells of delight, the spouts of syrup. Even before I read about such goodies in the Raggedy Ann and Andy stories—the Deep Deep Woods with its lollipop plants and Cookie Land with its sugar-frosted family and raisin-stuffed cake chickens—my father used to charm me with comparable tales. He was a man who loved the soda fountain at Schrafft's and often took me there to indulge in Broadway sodas (chocolate syrup, coffee ice cream, vanilla soda, a hint of mint) and big flat cookies that looked almost like the smiley heads of the Raggedies. "Imagine, Sandra," he'd say, "a land with ice cream mountains and chocolate rivers and candy bushes. . . ."

Does food in fiction begin with cosiness—which is to say, infantile pleasure—as it does in so many children's books, and, equally often, in parents' dreams of what such children's tales should be? Certainly the syrupy stories of Raggedy Ann and Andy tantalize sweet-toothed little ones with seemingly endless imaginings of what you can do with sugar. Despite their legendary clean white stuffing, the rag doll pals imbibe one ice cream soda after another and happily share them around with animals, fairies, elves and even cookie people. Raggedy Ann herself has a candy heart that flavors her dealings with just about everybody she meets, except a few nasty goblins (whom she ultimately converts to niceness). And though Andy is secondary to Ann, in a reversal of the old story of Eve-after-Adam, he too is stuffed with kindness. When, in their adventure in the Deep Deep Woods, she uses a "wishing pebble" to endow everybody with their just desserts, he joins her by wielding a "wishing stick." Wherever their shiny shoe-button eyes and perpetual smiles turn, the benevolent pair bestow the kind of sugary joy that psychoanalyst Melanie Klein associates with the abundance of the ever-giving "good breast."[1]

Yet even the cosiness of Cookie Land—one of Johnny Gruelle's most compelling culinary fantasies—is tainted by dread. In a realm founded on flour and sugar, appetite is a first principle of society; thus those who long to eat may themselves have to fear being eaten. The Raggedies are haunted by the threats of Hookie-the-Goblin, who insists he wants to make them into noodle soup, despite their very rational assertion that cloth dolls can't be boiled into noodles. Even more imperiled are the kindly cookie people. When Raggedy Ann first encounters the chocolate Cookie Man, he breaks in half, as any vulnerably brittle cookie might, and she is obliged to glue him together with molasses. Such shattering shadows all his family all the time: his Lemon Cookie son ends up with a vanilla leg after his original limb cracks apart; his daughter, little Strawberry, is stolen by the voracious Hookie, and indeed, the entire Cookie family, along with their cookie cows, chickens and ducks and their delicious cookie house, are always threatened by the mouth of the goblin—and by other hungry mouths that might come along.

Cookie Land is at the mercy of Cookie Monsters! "I can see that all of you are eating cookies right now, and it makes cold shivery crumbs run up and down my back," declares the Cookie Man to the Raggedies at their first meeting, and indeed, right after he falls down and splits in two, Ann's friend Little Weakie suggests that it would be "a good plan to break him into small pieces and put him in our pockets to nibble on when we leave here!" At the same time, even nasty Hookie, Cookie's opposite, is himself endangered by food. When the hungry goblin threatens her and her friends, Raggedy Ann points out that "you are sitting in the candy and can't get up!" Sugary syrupy stuff has literally glued him to the ground, immobilizing him. Sweet foods captivate and capture; sweet teeth threaten to nibble, rend, chew, and swallow.[2]

The perils of both food and appetite are emphasized in quite a few other ostensibly cosy children's books. Maurice Sendak's classic *In the Night Kitchen* begins when little Mickey overhears the pounding of bakers far below him in an indeterminately mythic kitchen and falls down and out of his clothes to land naked in the middle of their dough. Just before they can bake him in a "Mickey oven" he manages to reshape the sweet stuff surrounding him into an airplane and fly up into the Milky Way, with a cup for a jaunty cap. Yet the powerful bakers continue to chant their need: "Milk, milk, for the morning cake!" And as they do, the child falls back to earth and, divested of his getaway mechanism, plunges, naked again, into a giant milk bottle, singing "I'm in the milk and the milk's in me. God bless milk and God bless me!" Thus nurtured, he saves himself—as the Raggedies so often save themselves—through sharing. "Then he swam to the top, pouring milk from his cup into batter below," so that cooks can keep on making the morning cake—which by implication becomes the morning itself. And Mickey too becomes his materially embodied self, shouting "Cock a doodle doo" as he stands, now, on the outside of the milk bottle, with his gender-defining little penis as clearly outlined as the rest of his boy body. Whole and separate from the once engulfing milk, he returns to bed, clothes and civilization.[3]

Just as Melanie Klein's good, all-giving breast is always potentially a bad, denying or absent breast, so the good milk-giving mother might at any time turn into a devouring mother. By extension, even the most delicious food might become dangerous. Mickey didn't drown in the milk bottle (he could swim!), the Raggedies escaped the soup kettle, and the cookie people never did crumble. But: there's always a but. In such culinary tales as Tomie dePaola's *Strega Nona*, Judi Barrett's *Cloudy with a Chance of Meatballs* and perhaps most of all Roald Dahl's masterpiece *Charlie and the Chocolate Factory*, nurturing food turns nasty almost, as it were, of its own accord. A version of the old story of the sorcerer's apprentice, *Strega Nona* recounts the havoc wrought by greedy Big Anthony, who seeks to exploit the magic pasta pot from which Strega Nona, a good-hearted witch, feeds herself and him just enough every day. Nona knows the secret formula that stops the pot from overflowing; Big Anthony fails to blow the three kisses that seal the turn-off. When the pot floods the whole town with pasta, the citizens are ready to string Anthony up—until Nona comes home, halts the cooking and punishes her assistant by condemning him to eat all the pasta that has clogged the streets. What was marvelous becomes unsavory and sickening. Big Anthony, after all, had never signed up for a marathon eating contest. The book's concluding illustration shows him unhappily glutted and bloated, with the feminized stomach of late pregnancy.[4]

Cloudy with a Chance of Meatballs is, at least on the surface, morally neutral. In a bedtime story told by the speaker's grandpa, three hundred apparently lucky people live in the little town of Chewandswallow, where, as in the medieval land of Cockayne, the sky rains food upon them all day long. Breakfast, lunch and dinner are provided by incoming weather with clock-like regularity, although there is little choice of menu. Sometimes the meals are appropriate (one breakfast features orange juice, fried eggs, toast and milk), and sometimes not (one dinner consists merely of overcooked broccoli).

Slowly, however, the heavens grow fierce, sending down "a storm of pancakes and a downpour of maple syrup that nearly flooded the town," an "awful salt and pepper wind accompanied by an even worse tomato tornado," and "giant meatballs" that knock down houses and stores. Finally, the townsfolk determine to leave, and sail away on bread boats with swiss cheese sails, to live happily ever after in a world of supermarkets and refrigerators. Grandpa's lesson? Not so much that the modern industrialized world is preferable to the land of Cockayne, but that what at first appears to be celestial plenty can prove to be a purgatorial trial. And the implicit lesson of the plot? An elaboration of the disgust that so many children feel when they are helplessly subjected to menus over which they have no control and forced to eat unpleasant tornadoes of tomatoes and disgusting heaps of overcooked broccoli.[5]

Childhood disgust at unwanted food features more frankly and prominently in Henrik Drescher's over-the-top fantasy *The Boy Who Ate Around*. Served a yucky-looking dinner of "lizard guts and bullfrog heads" ("actually string beans and cheese soufflé"), little Mo is too polite to throw up his first bite of the meal but instead decides to "eat around it." As he metamorphoses into "a ferocious green warthog monster," he begins by gobbling up his mom and dad: "they were munchy" and, after all, they were responsible for the beans and the soufflé. Then, as his appetite intensifies, he becomes an ever huger monster, eating the table and chairs, the cars, the house, his best friend, his school, the president, the first lady, and finally the whole world in an infantile blast of hunger that leaves him, finally, bloated, flatulent, "tired and lonesome"—since he himself is all that's left. In the end, therefore, he disgorges the everything on which he has feasted and returns to the family table, from which, happily, the offending dinner has been removed. Instead, his resurrected parents and best friend join him in relishing banana splits, modest desserts considering the truly omnivorous feast that has preceded them.[6]

Superficially celestial plenty—the opposite of green beans and cheese souffle—is at the center of Roald Dahl's unnervingly riveting, yet often yummy *Charlie and the Chocolate Factory*, a work as classic as *In the Night Kitchen* and, almost, *Alice's Adventures in Wonderland*. Also at the center of this ambiguous book is the industrialized world of shops and factories that is so often at the periphery of popular children's stories. Where the Raggedies wander through forests and magic townships, as so many little heroines and heroes do, Charlie attains his dream of visiting Willie Wonka's chocolate factory only to enter what the grownup reader must recognize as a sort of sugary variation on Blake's dark satanic mills. Skinny and impoverished, the starving boy, his two sets of skeletal grandparents and his meek parents live on the meager rations of potatoes and cabbages that are all Charlie's father can provide with the wage he earns as a screwer-on of toothpaste caps in a factory that ludicrously shadows Wonka's luxurious establishment. When he loses even that job, the Bucket family are nearly reduced to the total emptiness their name signifies. Charlie's lucky find of a golden ticket to candy heaven is their only hope for survival.

I wish my father had lived long enough to read Dahl's book, but alas it was published just a year after he died, too early, in his late fifties. He would certainly have recognized some of its features as akin to those of the dreamy tales he related to me: the chocolate palace of the Indian prince, the fields of green sugar bisected by a great chocolate river and a roaring chocolate waterfall, the chambers of magic chewing gum, the Viking boat that is a colossal hollowed-out boiled pink sweet. What he might not have liked, or wanted to notice, was the parodic lottery in which, through a massive worldwide capitalistic distribution system, the five golden tickets to chocolate heaven are doled out to just a lucky few in a yearning population of hungry children. And what he might have chuckled at, but at bottom disliked, was the way chocolate heaven turns into chocolate purgatory, as four of the fortunate five meet punishments that fit their personal crimes. First, Augustus Gloop, a stereotypical greedy fat boy, drowns in the river of his desire; then Veruca Salt, the nuttily spoiled daughter of a peanut manufacturer, is nibbled nearly to death by squirrels and thrown, with her parents, into a garbage machine; next, Violet Beauregarde, an obsessive gum chewer, is herself turned into a stick of gum; and finally Mike Teavee, a compulsive televiewer, ends up as a tiny version of himself on a TV screen. Note the allegorical names: gloop, salt, beauregarde (self-regard), mike, and TV. Only Charlie Bucket, himself allegorically empty of any vile desire but filled only with natural hunger and the strength to "buck it," inherits the huffing, puffing, all-powerful factory of chocolate, with its huge pipes and chimneys, its floods of commercial sugar and dangerously sweet secret rooms, some with whips (cream, strawberry—and other, more pernicious whips) and some with beans (chocolate, coffee—and *has* beans).

As a left-leaning political liberal—a reader of *The Nation* and a supporter of Henry Wallace—my father would surely have been troubled by the enslavement of Willie Wonka's factory workers, the Oompa Loompas. A tiny people originally described as African pygmies and revised (after critical protests) into rosy-skinned little folks from an indeterminate "Loompaland" that continues to sound suspiciously African, the Oompa Loompas are the human property of Wonka, the factory owner, who has dismissed his original workers to replace them with the labor of these slaves. Cheerful yet censorious, the Oompa Loompas on the page and onscreen sing moralizing songs that justify the culinary trials intended for wrongdoing children. Perhaps their most exemplary chant (accompanied by the beating of "a number of very small drums") outlines the exemplary fate of greedy Augustus Gloop:

He'll be quite changed from what he's been,
When he goes through the fudge machine:
Slowly, the wheels go round and round,
The cogs begin to grind and pound;
A hundred knives to slice, slice, slice;
We add some sugar, cream, and spice;
We boil him for a minute more,
Until we're absolutely sure
That all the greed and all the gall
Is boiled away for once and all . . .
[Then] who could hate or bear a grudge
Against a luscious bit of fudge?[7]

My grandchildren, for whom *Charlie and the Chocolate Factory* has become a normative, indeed a much loved text, don't seem horrified by this, or if they are they are pleasantly scared at the prospect of the fat boy's transformation. But I think my father would have considered the punishment Dantesque (he knew his *Purgatorio*) and as a political thinker would have been distressed by the Oompa Loompas' subaltern part in working Willie Wonka's punitive will.

I'm not sure, though, whether my father would have given much thought to the physiological implications of the doings in the chocolate factory—its function, like that of many factories, as a gigantic set of intestines in which both raw materials (sugar, chocolate, cream) and people (children, Oompa Loompas) are digested and transformed. My father wasn't a Freudian and he would have been put off by discussions of what one commentator has called Dahl's "excremental vision" in this book. Yet the floods and waterfalls of rich brown chocolate gushing ever lower and lower into the bowels of the factory, along with the streams of filthy lucre into which they ultimately turn, supplement the orality of longings for sugar with the anality of play in shit. And demonic Wonka, on the surface the master of the moralizing Oompa Loompas, becomes also the embodiment of a Freudian id as he leads the children and their guardians down, down into the underworld that houses all "the most important rooms in my factory" while explaining the monstrosity of his ambition: "These rooms we are going to see are enormous! They're larger than football fields! . . . down here underneath the ground, I've got all the space I want. There's no limit—so long as I hollow it out."[8]

Hollowed out, himself, by hunger, Charlie Bucket is ultimately the mouth that Wonka chooses to fill with chocolate, along with the mind into which he will pour his magical trade secrets. At the end of the story, the little boy imports his starving family into the factory so he won't be alone, but in effect he alone, like Wonka alone and lonely, will be the master of all the sugars he surveys. Like his precursor, James in Dahl's earlier *James and the Giant Peach*, he may end as a celebrated hero—but consider the destiny of James! Once the giant peach has crushed this miserable orphan's wicked aunts, and once he and his friends have survived their travels in and on it by (among other strategies) devouring its luscious fruit, he ends up living alone in its desiccated pit, set up as a shrine in Central Park. Of course, he's visited by friends and admirers, as no doubt Charlie will be, but still, there he is, a retired traveler, all by himself in an inedible peach stone.

We imagine children's books as cosy, and so they often are, yet at the same time their cosiness compels because the strongest tales acknowledge the dread that always shadows comfort. To be sure, quite a few kids' classics are realistic in the usual sense of the word. From Louisa May Alcott's *Little Women* and Johanna Spyri's *Heidi* to Laura Ingalls Wilder's *Little House on the Prairie* and *Farmer Boy*, novelists represent children eating muffins, drinking goat's milk, gobbling apple turnovers in settings that are grounded in history and society—landscapes far less unlikely than the exotic places inhabited by Charlie, Mickey and the Raggedies. Yet these books too feature dream meals and dwell on the dangers of hunger, one's own hunger and the hungers of others. Lurking behind their quotidian scenes, as behind the gastronomic scenes in so many contemporary narratives, are both the satisfactions of primordial desires and the perils of the oven from which Hansel and Gretel escape but into which they shove the wicked witch, the deadly stickiness of candy, the grinding teeth of the machines that pulverize cacao beans—along with nasty little boy has-beens—into fudge, the glug-glug of the milk bottle out of which one might or might not rise into a milky way of one's own. In this fashion, the ambiguity of our first kitchens prepares us for the complex imaginings of the good, bad and weird flavors of kitchens to come in adulthood.

Mealtime Mayhem

If there was anyone who understood how childhood ambivalences could translate into adult terrors, it was Roald Dahl, who wrote many macabre stories for grownups, quite a few featuring interesting culinary strategies through which people get away with murder. In "Lamb to the Slaughter," for instance—one of his most famous pieces—a betrayed wife bops her erring policeman husband over the head with a frozen leg of lamb so deadly that "she might as well have hit him with a steel club." By the time his colleagues come to investigate, she has roasted the lamb and invited them all to participate in eating the evidence. In "Pig," a naive orphan slowly and tentatively turns carnivore after the death of his kindly vegetarian aunt, only to become, himself, meat for the slaughter when he goes to visit a packing house where pigs are butchered. In "Royal Jelly" an anxious father, whose baby has failed to thrive, supplements her feedings with royal jelly, which causes her to grow into what looks like "some gigantic grub that was approaching the end of its larval life and would soon emerge into the world complete with mandibles and wings." And perhaps most horrifyingly, in "Georgy Porgy," a finicky bachelor with a history of trauma imagines that he has been digested by an aggressive spinster who tried to kiss him. As she approaches him, he experiences her open mouth as a horrifying vagina dentata:

> I had never in all my life seen anything more terrifying than that mouth . . . [it] kept getting larger and larger, and then all at once it was right on top of me, huge and wet and cavernous, and the next second—I was inside it. . . . I could feel my legs being drawn down the throat by some kind of suction, and quickly I threw up my arms and grabbed hold of the lower front teeth and held on for dear life.

When his tale comes to an end, he is in a padded cell that he claims is part of the lady's intestinal tract: "Above me, I can see a pulpy sort of opening that I take to be the pylorus . . . and below me there is a funny little hole in the wall where the pancreatic duct enters the lower section of the duodenum." Killing with food, being killed as food, feeding dangerous food to a helpless infant, becoming food inside a system not unlike the chocolate factory's—all these fantasies haunted the imagination of a man who, paradoxically, was the author of a slew of beloved children's books.[9]

Even, or perhaps especially, in fiction it's hard to forget that, as I noted earlier in discussing the powers of the cook, the kitchen is murderous and so is life that lives on life. According to urban legend, carrots somehow scream when ripped from the ground, and other vegetables too may be sensitive. Imagine being boiled like a potato, gnawed like an ear of corn! And then, as we've seen in so many cannibal tales, imagine being devoured as oneself—a human being—in a stew! Such a stew features in Stanley Ellin's famous *The Specialty of the House*, where two friends, one an initiate, the other a regular, dine often at the mysterious Sbirro's restaurant, hungering for the nights when they will be served "lamb Amirstan," the diabolical specialty whose ingredients the reader slowly comes to understand, although it's clear the companions don't know what we know. All they're aware of, apparently, is the almost transcendent deliciousness of the food. No women can enter Sbirro's; no alcohol is served; no tobacco is smoked; not even salt and pepper are allowed. Only plates of mysterious meat and gravy, climaxing in the incomparable lamb Amirstan are offered to patrons. When the two finally consume the specialty, the "dripping chunks of meat" evoke a rapturous response from the newcomer: "It is as impossible . . . for the uninitiated to conceive the delights of lamb Amirstan as for the mortal man to look into his own soul." To which Sbirro, the patron, responds, "perhaps you have just had a glimpse into your soul, hurr? . . . but sit for a very little while in a dark room and think of this world—what it is and what it is going to be—then you must turn your thoughts a little to the significance of the Lamb in religion."[10]

Ah, the sacrificial Lamb! Imagine eating it in reality—or, indeed, becoming it! Even the Christ himself was never roasted, stewed, sautéed, baked and eaten in the very flesh! Remember those stout aunties who used to pinch rosy little cheeks exclaiming, "Oh you are so cute, I could just eat you up!"? As children, we shrank from their toothy smiles—at least I did. But Sbirro's manners are more insinuating, more subtly theological and revisionary. In a world of beast eat beast, man is his own lamb of God—a God who devours himself, in a sort of culinary black mass that twists the food chain into a spiral of Gothic horror. And Sbirro, with his face that reminds the narrator of Lewis Carroll's Cheshire cat, is the enforcer of this dire law of nature: his name is colloquial Italian for policeman or cop.

But perhaps such relatively short gobbets of dread are merely hors d'oeuvres to some of the full-length culinary fictions that have been produced in recent years. One of the eeriest of these is John Lanchester's *The Debt to Pleasure*, a bravura extended monologue spoken by the preening, psychotic Tarquin Winot, who has ostensibly decided to follow the example of Brillat-Savarin by producing a memoiristic set of gastronomic reflections. Often seen as Nabokovian in its construction of a narrator as crazed as the master's Humbert Humbert (*Lolita*) or Charles Kinbote (*Pale Fire*), Lanchester's novel is both brilliantly allusive and dazzlingly written. Indeed, the book's language—as intricately flavored and layered as a sauce by the great Carême—bathes us sometimes in tedium (at the speaker's pomposity), sometimes in desire (for the foods he conjures up) and, increasingly, in suspense, even fear (at the nature of the culinary plans that gradually emerge from his complex and evasive sentences). Structured like a menu, *The Debt to Pleasure* superficially focuses on the most delicious courses of the four seasons: winter offers blinis and caviar, Irish stew, queen of puddings and other goodies; spring tiptoes in with omelet, roast lamb with beans, peaches and red wine; summer more generally signifies "vegetables and saladings" along with "a selection of cold cuts"; and autumn brings an aioli along with meditations on breakfast, barbecues and more omelets, especially ones that feature mushrooms.[11]

As he muses, lectures, even hectors his readers on these foods, Winot—like the speaker of Browning's "My Last Duchess"—obliquely reveals not only his pernicious self-regard and his intense sibling rivalry but also his murderous history (spoiler alert). The brother of a world-famous sculptor, he repeatedly asserts that he is the great artist of his family, not the renowned Bartholomew. That his parents had some sense of his early oddness becomes clear when we learn that though his brother was sent away to regular schools, he himself was educated at home by tutors, until he went up to college for a short while, and saw to it that his lodgings, clothing and food were all a funereal black. As he outlines his culinary thoughts, which constitute a veritable encyclopedia of gastronomy larded with Brillat-Savarinesque moralizings, he rants against Bartholomew's bad taste—his fondness for HP sauce, bacon-egg-sausage breakfasts and other lowbrow pleasures. Gradually we become aware that, while he drives through France obsessively expatiating on its cuisine, he is also obsessively stalking a honeymoon couple. Wearing a range of disguises and using the Mossad manual of espionage, he follows them everywhere: he is fixated on the young wife, who is writing a biography of his brother but whom he self-delusively considers his own collaborator and biographer.

For the most part, Tarquin Winot practices a linguistic form of death by subordination—that is, his confessions of mayhem and murder come for the most part in asides, subordinate clauses, even parentheses. Indeed, as befits a disciple of Brillat-Savarin, he has folded them into stews, salads and especially omelets. Toward the end of the book, however, as his prey innocently drift into his Provençal kitchen, he becomes rather more open about his interest in poisonous mushrooms as well as about other inclinations. Eventually we learn that he has mysteriously managed to annihilate just about everyone who might have been an irritant to him—his nursemaid, the family cook, a nuisance of a neighbor, his parents, his brother, a family friend and ultimately the honeymooners. And finally Winot—or Whynot?—reveals that his given name was Rodney, but he himself changed it to Tarquin. "Tarquin Tarquinibus the Tarquin of Tarquins," he explains, "influenced by Shakespeare's charismatic villain. Ha ha. What a bore Lucrece is—all that virtue, all that wailing."[12]

But murder, not rape, is this Tarquin's forte, as it was that of Tarquin Superbus, the arrogant Roman emperor (and father of Lucrece's rapist) who removed anyone standing in his way. In fact, it becomes apparent that murder is the vocation to which Tarquin Winot has dedicated his life, just as art was his brother's. In their final conversation, he discloses, he and Bartholomew had discussed "the difference between the two most important cultural figures in the modern world, the artist and the murderer," with Tarquin noting that

> Destruction is as great a passion as creation, and it is as creative, too—as visionary and as assertive of the self. The artist is the oyster but the murderer is the pearl. . . . And then one must also face the sheer naturalness of murder, the unnaturalness of art. Paintings and music, books—they're so arbitrary, so overcomplicated, so full of invention and untruth, compared with the simple human act of taking a life because you don't want someone to carry on existing.[13]

Winot's killings aren't, of course, all culinary. He brings about deaths in all sorts of intriguing ways, only a few through the deployment of poisonous mushrooms. But his mad view of "the naturalness of killing," juxtaposed with the most lusciously elaborate menus, returns us to Alice B. Toklas's sardonic vision of murder in the kitchen. Every recipe, when prepared by a Tarquin, is a recipe for murder, every mealtime a chance for mayhem.

Just Desserts

Though Lanchester's Tarquin, along with a number of other gastronomic villains, gets away with murder, many of those who would wreak mealtime (and between-mealtime) mayhem regularly get their just desserts in the extraordinarily popular new genre of the culinary mystery. Rex Stout and Robert B. Parker were among relatively early writers who used kitchen talk to characterize their detective heroes. Stout's sedentary Nero Wolfe is famously dependent on his Swiss cook, Fritz Brenner, for the kind of elegant cuisine that recharges his brain cells. Between bouts of sleuthing, Archie Goodwin, Wolfe's amanuensis and the narrator of all the novels, often digresses to discuss the details of shad roe, broiled shad, duck in any form, chicken with tarragon and other dishes, along with the menus featured at the detective's favorite restaurant, Rusterman's. Indeed, *Too Many Cooks*, one of Stout's early *chef d'oeuvres,* turns on a meeting of master chefs at which the great gastronomes are tested in their knowledge of the recipe for *sauce printemps*, which will be served on roasted squabs; a subplot is devoted to Wolfe's personal search for the ingredients in *saucisse minuit*, a dish he adores.

Even before the conference, however, the famous detective spends part of a train ride celebrating the pleasures of American cuisine to a skeptical European cook, who declares that such dishes as "the New England boiled dinner and corn pone and clam chowder and milk gravy . . . are to la haute cuisine what sentimental love songs are to Beethoven and Wagner." To which Wolfe responds,

> Have you eaten terrapin stewed with butter and chicken broth and sherry? . . . Have you eaten a planked porterhouse steak, two inches thick, surrendering hot red juice under the knife, garnished with American parsley and slices of fresh limes, encompassed with

> mashed potatoes which melt on the tongue, and escorted by thick slices of fresh mushrooms faintly underdone? . . . Or the Creole Tripe of New Orleans? Or Missouri Boone County ham, baked with vinegar, molasses, Worcestershire, sweet cider and herbs? Or Chicken Marengo? Or chicken in curdled egg sauce, with raisins, onions, almonds, sherry and Mexican sausage? Or Tennessee Opossum? Or Lobster Newburgh? Or Philadelphia Snapper Soup? But I see you haven't. . . . The gastronome's heaven is France, granted. But he would do well, on his way there, to make a detour hereabouts.[14]

After one of the cooks is murdered during the *sauce printemps* contest, the detective of course plies his trade. His triumphant after-dinner speech at the end of the book features a further disquisition on the joys of American cooking, followed by a precise analysis of who done it, how and why, a clever denouement in which the satisfactions of the flesh seem almost to beget the satisfactions of the intellect. Not surprisingly, other culinary writers found the novel mouth-watering. "Best meal in English literature? The banquet in *Too Many Cooks* by Rex Stout," declared Nora Ephron, and M. F. K. Fisher noted that "I have a standing offer for second-hand copies of *Too Many Cooks*; it is more comfortable to give them to people than to know who has stolen mine, which happened three times before I learned that trick."[15]

Another cooking detective—not as obsessive a gourmet as Wolfe but nearly as influential—is Robert B. Parker's Spenser, who aptly defines himself thus: "Spenser's the name, cooking's the game." Unlike the sedentary Wolfe, however, Spenser is also a boxer—and a killer. His remarks about his culinary skills follow a masterful display of his fighting talents, in which he rescues Rachel Wallace, a kidnaped lesbian feminist, and offs two of her captors. He consoles himself, comforts her, and eases the mind of his girlfriend, Susan, with a meal of rice and beans, chopped tomatoes and grated cheddar, improvised on the spot to go with some corn bread he already has made. In another novel, he offers Susan (not herself a cooking type) an even more savory supper: "Grilled lemon and rosemary chicken, brown rice with pignolias, assorted fresh vegetables lightly steamed and dressed with Spenser's famous honey-mustard splash, blue corn bread, and a bottle of Iron Horse Chardonnay."[16]

Neither Wolfe nor Spenser uses cooking professionally, to be sure. So how do the culinary arts function in raveling or unraveling murderous plots? To begin with, where food in Dahl, Ellin and Lanchester is always fraught with danger, in Stout and Parker it at least superficially betokens comfort. When Wolfe isn't pushing his lips in and out as he ponders a crime, the (presumably) celibate detective erotically opens and closes his mouth around the consoling meals that Fritz provides. These, along with his extraordinary collection of exotic orchids, arguably represent life in the middle of death. Someone may have been stabbed, but Wolfe can still eat shad roe. More, a famous misogynist, he needn't be dependent on women for food. At the head of an all-male household—Archie, his quasi-son, and Fritz, a sort of spouse, along with Theodore, another consort in charge of his orchid collection—he exists to suggest that sustenance can be, must be, provided by males, not females. And consider the root of the word "orchid":

> from L. orchis, a kind of orchid, from Gk. orkhis (gen. orkheos) "orchid," lit. "testicle," from PIE *orghi-, the standard root for "testicle" (cf. Avestan erezi "testicles," Arm. orjik, M.Ir. uirgge, Ir. uirge "testicle," Lith. erzilas "stallion"). The plant so called because of the shape of its root.[17]

If his family of symbolic and literal testicles supports and sways him, Wolfe's kitchen nurtures his hungers as if with male breasts. And if he is horrifyingly obese (more than three hundred pounds, Archie tells us), his commitment to food as art rather than food as merely savage forage suggests that he aligns himself with the cooked (culture) rather than the raw (nature), no matter how fleshy he is.

As for Spenser, the very dissonance between his single poetic name (he is never given a first name) and his boxing prowess requires reconciliation. Parker, a onetime English professor, emphatically alludes to the sixteenth-century author of *The Faerie Queene*, and while his protagonist lacks lyricism he is curiously knightly and tough, though his weapons are fists and pistols instead of swords. But his confession that "cooking's my game" signals the redemptive measure that makes him into a more sympathetic Renaissance man. Punching, kicking, killing, Parker's hero needs to prove that he is also a gentle soul. The brooding eroticism of his relationship with the psychotherapist Susan Silverman helps establish his good taste. But "Spenser's my name, cooking's my game" also demonstrates his eroticism. An old-school hard-boiled detective, Spenser/Parker writes like Anthony Bourdain (or, rather, Anthony Bourdain writes like Spenser/Parker). But the difference between the two is the difference between the macho kitchen of a professional cook and the kindly kitchen of a professional killer. Food as goodness? Spenser, for all his toughness, needs to tenderize his meals and his mayhem. If killing is raw and bloody, cooking is cultured and well-seasoned—as is the sex life of the detective and his lover the psychotherapist, who clearly appreciates his saucy soul as much as she enjoys his toughened body. That in *Looking for Rachel Wallace* he even wins over the man-hating feminist—they weep together after he rescues her—adds the salt of tears to the literary broth.

If macho guys who beat suspects more often than eggs can be aligned with the venturesome masculinity portrayed by children's book authors like Dahl and Sendak, the so-called recipe novels by contemporary women writers who are the real queens of culinary mysteries might be said to descend from the sugary tales of the Raggedies. Joanne Fluke, the author of the Hannah Swensen books, actually focuses on the proprietor of a bakery/coffee shop called The Cookie Jar, and the titles of her works don't let us forget that sweetness is her theme, cosiness her aim. Just a few should give the general idea: *The Chocolate Chip Cookie Murder, The Strawberry Shortcake Murder, The Fudge Cupcake Murder, The Carrot Cake Murder, The Key Lime Pie Murder* and so on. For some readers, the books themselves are as addictive as cookies and ice cream; others find them saccharine and their plots crumbly. But is it a fluke that much of this writer's work parallels (or was influenced by) the equally addictive but more gastronomically diverse tales of Diane Mott Davidson?

Just as the Hannah Swensen stories revolve around a baker in the scenic small town of Lake Eden, Minnesota, Davidson's more wittily named protagonist Goldy Bear (later Goldy Bear Schulz) is home on the range in the super-scenic little community of Aspen Meadows, Colorado. Both places are cosy, with lots of people on a first-name basis—and at the same time each seems to have a higher homicide rate than New York or Chicago. Thus, when the culinary detectives aren't churning out the pies, cakes, pizzas and soups for which they give recipes to their readers, they're more often than not trying to decipher recipes for murder. But just as Davidson's titles are more punningly sophisticated than Fluke's (*Catering to Nobody, Dying for Chocolate, The Cereal Murders, The Last Suppers, Prime Cut, Tough Cookie, Sticks and Scones, Chopping Spree*), so her plots and plans, pots and pans are more upper-crust, and her storytelling style more suspenseful. Hannah's tales are told in the third person, giving the reader some distance from them; Goldy's, by contrast, are given in a fast-paced first person, suggesting that she is the narrator of her own life. As for their situations, Hannah has two boyfriends and a nudgy mother who only wants her to get married, but Goldy, at the center of a more complex circle, has a brilliantly characterized son, Arch, who plays Dungeons and Dragons in middle school but takes up fencing in high school; a vegetarian assistant, Julian Teller; a vile ex-husband who has been regularly abusive to her; a rich, overweight best friend who is also an ex-wife of the same ex-husband; an ambivalent relationship with the Episcopalian Church; grotesque ex-in-laws; problematic parents; and a range of other interesting connections. And where Hannah's gastronomic offerings are strictly sugary, the menus for the events Goldy caters are diversely elegant while they now and then turn out, though inadvertently, to be as dangerous as foods by Roald Dahl or Stanley Ellin.

Even if Davidson's mysteries are more sophisticated than Fluke's, the character of Goldy herself emphasizes Davidson's clear allusion to the kinds of fairy tales that underlie Fluke's works along with so many other culinary mysteries. Goldilocks Catering Where Everything Is Just Right has been founded by a short, slightly plump, curly-haired blonde named Goldy, née Gertrude Bear, who definitively didn't adopt the name of her abusive onetime mate John Richard Korman (a.k.a. the JERK, from his initials). But when the strong, tall, green-eyed detective Tom Schulz comes into her life, bringing a culinary passion akin to hers, she takes his name. He calls her "Miss G." but she is Goldilocks to his big bear hugs and happy to alternate her fabulous cuisine with the comfort food he regularly produces.

From the beginning of the series onward, however, Goldy doesn't just cook; she reflects, quite consciously, on the passions and pleasures of food. Kneading dough "as soft as flesh" for a friend's wake, she reflects that eating is "a way of denying death," and as for cooking, she affirms later that "Nothing equals mixing and baking to clear the mind." Elsewhere, she observes that "Cooking was the cure for loss" just as, in an epigraph I've used here, she decides that "When you're really down, focus on the food." "Cook," she tells herself over and over again; more than anything, cooking will "soothe the nerves." At the same time, cooking offers her tools for analysis. In *Double Shot*, for instance, she figures out a major clue to a murder while making a pie crust: "*Larding*. That's what I was doing with the pie crust. . . . But if you larded a crime scene with lots of items, responsibility for the crime could point in any number of directions." Yet even while cuisine is a creative way of mastering the universe, it is as vulnerable as all such strategies can be. At one of Goldy's parties, someone slips rat poison into the punch; before another, she discovers that her refrigeration system has been sabotaged and all the dishes she had made or planned to make are spoiled. Food can kill or be destroyed, and the richest delicacies can rot, the way the cookie man can snap in half and the greedy child can drown in chocolate. The meal you hunger for today may nauseate you tomorrow, as if it were the green beans and cheese soufflé that little Mo couldn't bring himself to eat.[18]

Nausea

As a famous concept in modern thought, nausea is more philosophical than culinary. It was wielded as a metaphor for existential angst in the 1930s by Jean-Paul Sartre, whose influential novel *La Nausée* is devoted to the metaphysical broodings of a reclusive bachelor living in a seaside town modeled on Le Havre. Roquentin, his protagonist, portrays himself as if he were an

Edgar Allan Poe speaker suffering from morning sickness. Nausea, we learn, is the poison gift of being, the dreadful consciousness of nothingness absurdly coiled at the heart of all. It settles on Sartre's unlucky hero when, understanding himself to be trapped in undesirable flesh and sexually frustrated, he succumbs to the illness of materiality: a waiter asks him what he would like to eat in a restaurant, and then "the Nausea seized me, I dropped to a seat, I no longer knew where I was; I saw the colors spin slowly around me, I wanted to vomit. And since that time, the Nausea has not left me, it holds me." Racist, anti-Semitic and misogynistic, Roquentin is most of all disgusted by the indifferent livingness of things—the black or almost-black bloated root of a chestnut tree that clots his vision "as a lump of food sticks in the windpipe," the slimy gelatinous cloud of being in which all that is human or nonhuman is sickeningly entwined. For him, sex is loveless and love (such as it is) is sexless. Desire turns against itself to issue in the nausea that is ubiquitous and absurd: although the word "nausea" implies food, the food that horrifies this proto-existentialist is the universe itself; he is trapped in an oxymoron, imagining life as an inedible feast.[19]

But if Sartre's nausea is ontological, the potent indigestion that overcomes the prize-winning college girl guest editors of a thinly disguised *Mademoiselle* in Sylvia Plath's *The Bell Jar* is triggered by the inedible feast of femininity. "Puking," as the narrator/protagonist Esther Greenwood puts it, is thematic throughout the book, and just about everything makes this nineteen-year-old want to puke, as if she were a teenage Roquentin. But, unlike Sartre's character, Esther is a hearty eater: "I love food more than just about anything else," she confides, noting that "No matter how much I eat, I never put on weight." So her puking is metaphorical—until, in two of the novel's bitterly funny scenes, it becomes literal. First, after a night on the town, the flirtatious Doreen, another editor, comes back from a drunken spree to vomit and then pass out in the corridor of the Amazon Hotel just next to Esther's room. Then, as if this little crisis were merely a token of more illness to come, all the lucky contest winners attend a banquet hosted (really, hostessed) by the food staff of another journal of femininity, *Ladies' Day,* at which they're poisoned by tainted crabmeat salad.[20]

Esther had enjoyed this meal with particular voluptuousness, spreading slices of chicken "thickly" with caviar and eating them, childishly, with her hands, before turning to avocado (her "favorite fruit") stuffed with the crabmeat salad. Sickness overtakes her while she's watching a bad romantic movie that reinforces all the nauseating stereotypes against which she frequently rages. On the way back to the Amazon, she and her friend Betsy begin vomiting in a cab, and then again in the elevator to their rooms, prompting Esther's sardonic observation that "There is nothing like puking with somebody to make you old friends." Later, after she too, like Doreen the night before, has passed out on the floor and been put to bed, she learns that all her associates had also been "keeling over like ninepins" because they were "poisoned, the whole lot of" them. The assessment of the allegorical *Ladies' Day* that ensues summarizes one of Plath's major themes as a poet and novelist:

> I had a vision of the celestially white kitchens of *Ladies' Day* stretching into infinity. I saw avocado pear after avocado pear being stuffed with crabmeat and mayonnaise and photographed under brilliant lights. I saw the delicate, pink-mottled crabmeat poking seductively through its blanket of mayonnaise and the bland yellow pear cup with its rim of alligator-green cradling the whole mess. Poison.[21]

Later in the novel, the poison of stereotypical femininity cooked up in the *Ladies' Day* kitchens resolves into an equally powerful vision of the seemingly natural world. Worried about what her choices for a future life might be, Esther imagines herself confronting a fig tree from whose branches alternative careers dangle—wife and mother, professor, editor, mistress, "Olympian crew champion." But as she sits "in the crotch of this fig tree, starving to death, just because I couldn't make up my mind which of the figs I would choose . . . the figs began to wrinkle and go black." Choosing one "meant losing all the rest," she explains, suggesting that the apparently natural tree (from which, needless to say, one could pluck many figs) is ultimately a cultural product embodying the old warning to women that "you can't have it all."[22]

If puking and starving are recurring motifs in *The Bell Jar*, the rather more sophisticated though equally allegorical ailment of heartburn permeates Nora Ephron's bestselling novel of that title. Just as Plath's Esther Greenwood suffers from a kind of proto-feminist nausea, Ephron's Rachel Samstat is felled by an emotional indigestion brought on by the betrayal of love. As such a tummy-twister, Ephron's confessional roman à clef *Heartburn* is the prototype of a number of other culinary novels that explore the flip side of the happy endings with which Davidson and Fluke conclude their tales. These stories of romantic nausea all explore situations in which women get their unjust desserts despite quite reasonable appetites. *The Bell Jar* is of course an anti-romantic roman à clef recounting Plath's own experience as a guest editor at *Mademoiselle* (she and her colleagues really were poisoned by crab salad!) followed by her notorious early attempt at suicide. Similarly, *Heartburn* reenacts the comically nasty drama of a real romance that issued in a real divorce—Ephron's breakup with her husband, Watergate journalist Carl Bernstein—and incorporates quite a few recipes reflecting the protagonist's vocation as a culinary writer. Yet where the rich dishes featured at the *Ladies' Day* banquet ultimately become literally or figuratively sickening as they elicit first Esther Greenwood's gluttony and then her nausea, the foods in *Heartburn* seem relatively neutral: cheesecake, lima beans and pears, sorrel soup, pot roast, pesto, oven-crisped potatoes, mashed potatoes, Key lime pie. What gives them their special flavor is neither the strangeness of the ingredients nor any flaws in the cookery, but the use to which Ephron puts them in a narrative that's part stream-of-consciousness confession, part stand-up comedy routine.

We learn, for instance, that the lima bean recipe was a special of Rachel's spoiled alcoholic Hollywood agent mother, Bebe Samstat, who (according to a series of filial one-liners) "loved to serve . . . something that looked like plain old baked beans and then turned out to have pears up its sleeve. She also made a bouillabaisse with Swiss chard in it. Later on, she got too serious about food—started making egg rolls from scratch, things like that." The pesto, in the words of another character, was "the quiche of the seventies." The mashed potatoes, as ultimate comfort food, turn up in a riff that begins "whenever I fall in love I begin with potatoes" but concludes with the more downbeat note that in "the end, I always want . . . mashed potatoes. Nothing like mashed potatoes when you're feeling blue." And the Key lime pie, of course, is the instrument of a slapstick pie-in-the-face denouement: when she realizes that her two-timing husband doesn't love her, Rachel flings the carefully baked pastry at him in a high-class Washington kitchen.[23]

In between offering recipes for these often comic dishes, Ephron's heroine rages that her husband's mistress serves "gluey puddings" while she nostalgically remembers the happily married days she spent as part of a dining-out foodie foursome that epitomized the gastronomic high life of the 1970s:

> . . . the four of us had a friendship that was a shrine to food. We had driven miles to find the world's creamiest cheesecake and the world's largest pistachio nut and the world's sweetest corn on the cob. We had spent hours in blind taste testings of kosher hot dogs and double chocolate chip ice cream. . . . Once, in New Orleans, we all went to Mosca's for dinner, and we ate marinated crab, baked oysters, barbecued shrimp, spaghetti bordelaise, chicken with garlic, sausage with potatoes, and on the way back to town, a dozen oysters each at the Acme and beignets and coffee with chicory on the wharf. Then Arthur said, "Let's go to Chez Helene for the bread pudding," and we did, and we each had two.[24]

Culinary yuppiedom ruled, so Rachel had evidently thought. Yet although she follows this account with a recipe for the famous bread pudding, food pilgrimages haven't saved her marriage. Cooking itself, she remarks, is comforting because it's "a sure thing" in an uncertain world: "if you melt butter and add flour and then hot stock, it will get thick!" But in a kind of meta-commentary on her narrative, she also remarks at one point that "It's hard to work in recipes when you're moving the plot forward"—just as it's hard to work in comfort in the midst of discomfort. In the end, Rachel literally throws away her pie in a moment of nauseated surrender—and then, in a further abandonment of consolation, she gives her traitorous husband the treasured vinaigrette formula for which his mistress has yearned. When your heart is burning with loss, recipes for romance might just make you sick. Let go of the oil. Let go of the spices. Let go of the vinegar.[25]

And of course you should also let go of the man, or so suggests the primary argument in some other female-authored novels of romantic nausea. Margaret Atwood's *The Edible Woman,* a work nearly contemporary with *The Bell Jar* and comparable in its bitter comedy, focuses on a young college graduate, Marian McAlpin, who works on customer surveys (laxatives, canned rice pudding, instant tomato juice, beer, sanitary napkins) and has drifted into a loveless engagement with a stodgily bourgeois and fiercely ambitious lawyer resonantly named Peter: behind his dark-suited demeanor, he's Mr. Macho, proud of a bedroom decorated with a "collection of weapons: two rifles, a pistol, and several wicked-looking knives." After Marian hears him laughingly telling friends about the pleasure he took in gutting a rabbit he had killed on a hunting expedition ("I whipped out my knife . . . and slit the belly and took her by the hind legs and gave her one hell of a crack, like a whip . . . and the next thing you know there was blood and guts all over the place"), she discovers—unsurprisingly—that she can no longer eat meat.[26]

Gradually, she becomes a vegetarian, but then, as Peter grows more domineeringly phallic, she is overcome by a wider-ranging anorexia, though she keeps herself going with (ironically) canned rice pudding. By the end of the novel, after a brief affair with another man, she gains perspective on her engagement and in a grandly perverse gesture of culinary rebellion bakes a large cake in the shape of a woman (the "edible woman") and offers it to her fiancé. "You've been trying to assimilate me," she charges. "But I've made you a substitute, something you'll like much better. This is what you really wanted all along, isn't it? I'll get you a fork." *Nothin' spells lovin' like somethin' from the oven!* Remember the old Pillsbury doughboy slogan? Well, Atwood reverses it, as she bakes a cake that's a culinary weapon against the man she never did love. Rachel Samstat's Key lime pie has a precursor here, though it isn't as complex as Marian McAlpin's cake, which the baker herself ends up devouring when her annoying fiancé is too shocked to pick up that fork. Turn and turn about. Romantic nausea has been inflicted on the *man*, sending him on his way![27]

What Atwood has herself described as a "proto feminist" novel (because when she wrote it the second-wave women's movement hadn't yet come into being) was a key text in an ongoing literary/culinary tradition. Perhaps its most curious parallel—and mirror image—is Fay Weldon's *The Fat Woman's Joke*. In this book, chubby protagonist Esther Sussman escapes from an unfaithful, diet-wielding husband to a dingy basement apartment in Earl's Court. Here, although she was once an accomplished cook, she defies the old rule that you can't be too thin or too rich, and eats and eats and eats endless junk foods: "frozen chips and peas and hamburgers, and sliced bread with bought jam and fishpaste, and baked beans and instant puddings and tinned porridge and tinned suet pudding, and cakes and biscuits from packets . . . sweet coffee, sweet tea, sweet cocoa and sweet sherry." Ballooning and rebellious, she tells a worried friend that her "real life" has begun: "Food. Drink. Sleep. Books. They are all drugs. None are as effective as sex, but they are calmer and safer."[28]

Did the diet, then, administered by a controlling, philandering husband, evoke such nausea that the only cure for the illness of marriage is food that would ordinarily disgust a gastronomically refined palate? Or did her marriage itself, with its threat of betrayal, nauseate Esther? Weldon juggles both possibilities, but both issue in culinary distress: "if I stop eating, I feel even sicker than I do if I don't stop eating. I will have to learn to live with nausea, I suppose," she decides. Nonetheless, by the end of the novel, after a round of romantic imbroglios among all the characters, the cynical "fat lady" reluctantly returns to the Victoriana-stuffed household from which she had fled. Weldon's view of her fate is jaded: the coercive coupledom from which both Rachel Samstat and Marian McAlpin manage to escape appears as inevitable as a virtuous, three-meals-a-day diet with no snacks in between. Tellingly, like *The Bell Jar, Heartburn* and *The Edible Woman*, *The Fat Woman's Joke* is a first novel, a kind of literary break-fast in which the writer anxiously scrutinizes the menu of femininity. Yet the problems these books dramatize endure. Not long ago, Fay Weldon gave an interview in which, responding to the question "What is your guiltiest pleasure?" she answered with one word, "Food," as if still reflecting the ambivalence that permeates all these tales.[29]

The critic Adam Gopnik has argued that in culinary novels like those I've been discussing recipes stand in, somehow, for sex scenes. If so, the sex in some of them is awful, except for what we encounter among jovial paperback detectives like Hannah Swensen and Goldy Bear. To be sure, certain fairly recent female- and indeed male-authored novels that investigate romantic nausea offer different recipes for revulsion. Abigail Stone's *Recipes from the Dump* and James Hamilton-Paterson's *Cooking with Fernet Branca* both function in various ways as meta-cookbooks, analyzing and even spoofing the strangeness of the recipe form itself from various perspectives. Stone's narrator, for instance, is a lonesome, impoverished single mom seeking both a man and a way out of destitution. Living near a literal dump and almost always figuratively in the dumps, loquacious Gabby Fulbriten composes scripts of misery using the recipe form—for instance, "Simple Clutter Consommé":

> 6 or 7 people a day calling you, offering fits and bonus points if you will give them cash
>
> Mailman arriving with 6 pieces of mail: 2 bills and 1 threatening letter from the Creditor's Marketplace in Honking, Ohio, and 3 letters confirming your name on the winners list of 3 different nationwide contests (never enter contests; they enter you on their own)
>
> A scary guy who keeps calling from somewhere in the world asking you to call him back on his 800 number
>
> Sift ingredients thoroughly, looking for any particles of truth. Add to water that has been mixed with beef jelly. Cover and simmer over low heat, making sure nothing jells or is connected. . . . Serve in bowls and garnish.[30]

But despite all her efforts to cook up protests and escapes, Gabby is still guarding her three children and her dilapidated house at the end of the novel. In conclusion, she offers hopeful recipes for "Polygamy Potluck" and "Life Juice," but the reader never finds out whether they're efficacious, or even tasty.

The recipes in Hamilton-Paterson's book masquerade as real, rather than meta, recipes, but they're neither tasty nor (one supposes) efficacious. A reclusive expat British novelist, Hamilton-Paterson sends up the whole recipe novel tradition with the grotesque menus his protagonist, Gerald Samper, proffers throughout *Cooking with Fernet Branca*. An aging queen sequestered in the hills of Tuscany, Samper feuds with his nearest neighbor, Marta, a "fizzy-haired frump" from the fictitious Eastern European country of Voynovia, who turns out to be a quite successful composer. But the two are united by their fondness for the bizarrely bitter liqueur Fernet Branca, usually taken in Italy as a medicinal digestif. Writes a commentator for the *Atlantic*, "Your first sip of Fernet Branca will be akin to waking up in a foreign country and finding a crowd of people arguing in agitated, thorny voices outside your hotel window. It's an event that's at once alarming and slightly thrilling."[31] But cooking with this stuff is weirder still. As narrator, Samper produces a number of odd recipes, ranging from "garlic and Fernet Branca ice cream" and "otter with lobster sauce" to his *chef d'oeuvre*, "Alien Pie," an extraordinarily parodic recipe whose ingredients must be read (not cooked!) to be believed:

1 kg. smoked cat, off the bone
500 gm baby beet
1tbs pureed prunes
50 gm kibbled peanuts
Nasturtium leaves
250 gm green bacon
250 gm lard
300 gm flour
Pepper
1 single drop household paraffin
500 gm old potatoes
500 gm rhubarb
4 pomegranates
1 baby hawksbill turtle

Fresh ginger
1 buzzard feather
Fernet Branca
White wine
Salt[32]

As for the strange procedure through which these ingredients (including the crucial drop of paraffin) are melded into a pie, that is too detailed to be quoted here, but suffice it to say that it's as odd as the substances it brings together. But finally, as a comment on recipe novels—or indeed on chatty cookbooks—which offer ideas for taking the just-completed masterpiece to table ("serve with a sturdy Cabernet and a crusty baguette," etc.), nothing can compare to Samper's instructions about the "realm of the sacramental" in which his dish belongs.

> All I can say is that Alien Pie, hot from the oven and with a jaunty buzzard feather stuck in the top, should be eaten on a terrace overlooking a distant ocean above which the remnants of sunset brood like old wounds seeping through a field dressing. It is one of those experiences poised exquisitely between sorrow and oblivion.[33]

Here nausea becomes comedy as the narrator's self-importance (comparable to the pomposity of Lanchester's Tarquin Winot) shows just what happens when a lifetime of misanthropy and misogyny reshapes the culinary arts. Of course, nausea is what only the reader experiences. Samper himself emphatically relishes his outrageous dishes, especially the "deep smoky, plummy, geological smell" of Alien Pie, which evidently, for him, evokes the plenitude of the cosmos.

Plenitude

It's unlikely that Gerald Samper's eccentric cookery would entice most diners, whose imaginings of plenitude might be Rabelaisian but are unlikely to be truly alien. Culinary pilgrims know of course about all the symbols of plenitude plated by foreign cultures: roast dog, monkey brains, camel stew, and—who knows?—maybe even smoked cat, off the bone. But even in other societies these foods tend to represent esoterica rather than plenitude. For what, after all, is plenitude? Isn't it the quotidian carried to some rainbow-reaching nth degree, the glitter of the culinary cosmos that mystically transforms us when we digest it? Plenitude is old-fashioned, innocent, erotic and so various in its kinds that it's almost impossible to define it. Plenitude is the Garden of Eden, the feast of the Eucharist, the Passover seder, a Kaiseki dinner in Kyoto, a *rijstaffel* in Amsterdam, the Cratchits' Christmas, Mrs. Ramsay's dinner party, Edna Pontellier's little feast of bread and wine and roasted chicken with her lover Robert Lebrun; it's even Leopold Bloom breakfasting on his emphatically *trafe* pork kidney. Plenitude is Raggedy Ann and Andy in the cookie house; it's the apple turnovers in *Farmer Boy*; it's the primordial breast in its first goodness, before the world turns over and the earlier pleasure is withdrawn. It's the land of Cockayne, the realm of milk and honey, the tasting menu of the gods. But it's always threatened, whenever and wherever someone devises a menu for it.

Films of plenitude abound, since beautifully cooked food is almost always delicious to look at. *Big Night, Ratatouille, Chocolat, Eat Drink Man Woman, Soul Food, Tortilla Soup, Babette's Feast* and *Like Water for Chocolate* all include scenes that gratify the hungry eye. But perhaps the last two of these are the most classic and influential; they're also based on superb texts. The great Danish writer Isak Dinesen composed "Babette's Feast" when a British friend advised her to "Write about food; Americans are obsessed with food."[34] In 1950 the tale appeared in the *Ladies' Home Journal*; later it was collected in a volume of Dinesen's short fictions, and later still it became a movie. Its representation of plenitude, however, is not just gastronomical but spiritual in its significance—like the symbolism of plenitude in so many theological rituals.

In a small Danish town the mysterious French refugee Babette has been taken in by a couple of austere Lutheran sisters who eschew all sensual pleasures in their lives as handmaids to their father, a beloved pastor with many disciples. But when Babette wins a lottery, she cooks a banquet to help the elderly spinsters and their fellow congregants celebrate the late clergyman's one-hundredth birthday. Ironically, all the devout guests—except for a cosmopolitan military man from the capital, who arrives unexpectedly—have vowed not to discuss food at the table, considering it unworthy, even satanic. Yet the menu Babette offers is so perfectly, even fabulously French that all are confounded, and their unforgiving silence begins to seem hateful. But while the villagers mistake champagne for lemonade, the visiting general recognizes it as Veuve Clicquot; and too, he understands that he's dining on delicacies his fellow guests would never have tasted: turtle soup, *blinis Demidoff, caille en sarcophage.* As course after course follows, along with rare wine after rare wine, all the congregants—despite their ignorance of what they're eating and drinking—are transformed by the meal, as if they had indeed participated in a rite of communion. Old quarrels are mended; former lovers remember their romance; friendships are renewed—and the general too is reminded of his youth, when he was in love with one of the aging sisters.

Babette, we ultimately learn, is a great culinary artist, a former cook at the grand Café Anglais in Paris, and she has spent her entire lottery prize on this feast for a group of people utterly ignorant of gastronomy. In her artistry and her generosity, she has created a plenitude that dispenses deliciousness even more spiritual than gustatory to the dour folk for whom she has cooked the meal. After they've dined, the ascetic guests "knew that the rooms had been filled with a heavenly light, as if a number of small halos had blended into one glorious radiance. Taciturn old people received the gift of tongues; ears that for years had been almost deaf were opened to it. Time itself had merged into eternity. Long after midnight the windows of the house shone like gold, and golden song flowed out into the winter air." And as they depart into the frozen streets of their town, the unknowingly inebriated elderly Lutherans romp in the new fallen snow "as if they had indeed had their sins washed white as wool, and in this regained innocent attire were gamboling like little lambs. It was, to each of them, blissful to have become as a small child; it was also a blessed joke to watch old Brothers and Sisters, who had been taking themselves so seriously, in this kind of celestial second childhood." The plenitude bestowed by Babette, though apparently secular, was effectively sacred too, and magical.[35]

An even more magical—because truly surreal—plenitude permeates Laura Esquivel's *Like Water for Chocolate*, another culinary text that was made into a very successful film. The subtitle of this work—"A Novel in Monthly Installments with Recipes, Romances, and Home Remedies"—suggests that the book is really the paradigmatic recipe novel, offering instructions for delicious dishes from Christmas rolls and Chabela wedding cake to walnuts in chili sauce. Through and with the spicy ingredients for these foods, Esquivel tells what she claims is the story of her great aunt Tita, a Cinderella who becomes a sorceress. Bound to what appears to be enslavement in the kitchen, this third daughter of nasty Mama Elena has been destined to spend her life serving her selfish mother hand and foot and forbidden to marry her lover, Pedro, who instead is married off to her older sister Rosaura. But for Tita, born on the kitchen table and nurtured by Nacha, the Hispanic family's native cook, "the joy of living [is] wrapped up in the delights of food," which become not only a sustenance for her but an impassioned language. Hence, even nausea is here part of the vocabulary of plenitude, for when her sister marries her lover, the bereft Tita joins Nacha in baking a magnificent wedding cake for 180 people—a confection that looks beautiful but sickens the entire company. After the first bite, "everyone was flooded with a great wave of longing. . . . But the weeping was just the first symptom of a strange intoxication . . . that seized the guests and scattered them across the patio and the grounds and in the bathrooms, all of them wailing over lost love" and engaged in a spasm of "collective vomiting."[36]

Unlike the nausea in Sartre or Plath, the illness elicited by Tita's cake is curiously purifying, arising from the intensity of the love that Mama Elena's viciousness has foiled. Nor can the censorious mother destroy her daughter's passion, which is expressed in further meals—for instance, when Tita prepares a dish of quails in rose petal sauce and, "as if a strange alchemical process had dissolved her entire being" in the food, enters "Pedro's body, hot, voluptuous, perfumed, totally sensuous," so with "that meal . . . it seemed they had discovered a new system of communication." Other members of the household, inevitably, are caught up in the powerful emotions that radiate from such cooking. Tita's opportunistic sister Rosaura grows fat and flatulent; her sister Gertrudis is seized by the fiery eroticism that flames from the thwarted lovers and runs away with a revolutionary; when Rosaura cannot nurse her own child, Tita magically supplies milk and becomes, in effect, a virgin mother; eventually, the strong-willed Mama Elena succumbs to gastric problems and dies, "wracked by horrible pains accompanied by spasms and violent convulsions." Both the savor of plenitude and the denial of plenitude haunt the culinary realm that Tita rules.[37]

For feminist readers, *Like Water for Chocolate* has been controversial. As Maite Zubiaurre has noted in a wide-ranging discussion, many have thought the book represents the kitchen as an "ideal site for establishing a female community from which to contest patriarchal power [and cooking as] a powerful language geared towards female liberation." From Zubiaurre's perspective, however, *Like Water for Chocolate* exemplifies "kitchen tales" that keep "women within the magic–domestic realm and at the margins of any real public influence." Indeed, she adds, "culinary art turns female power into magic transcendentalism. Tita . . . starts as a believable character, but rapidly converts into the misogynist stereotype of witch and sorceress." Yet surely the fantasy in Esquivel's novel is precisely the point of the work. Just as children's tales yearn for the abundance of love offered (and threatened) in Cookie Land, or in the nurturing Milky Way—the love that was once given by the lost breast—so Tita and Pedro and Gertrudis long for the love withheld by the witchy Mama Elena. But this Mama is cold steel, negative and knifelike: "when it came to dividing, dismantling, dismembering, desolating, detaching, dispossessing, destroying, or dominating, Mama Elena was a pro."[38]

Thus it is the lowly Tita, as in so many legendary tales, who controls the fire of a love as hot as "water for chocolate," a fire that can transform, transmute and purify. And thus, where Mama Elena failed to nurse Tita (her milk dried up when her husband died), the fire of Tita's love, as in the Christian story, metamorphoses a virginal breast into a sacred milk-giving vessel. "There really is not much difference between talking about food and talking about religion," Esquivel has written elsewhere, and she has also noted that from "its conception, *Like Water for Chocolate* was surrounded by love." More specifically, she has explained, the book was written to confront the "mother-witch" whose "binding [of] her children's jaws is one of spiritual malnutrition, the silencing of poetry, the chaining of the mind." If it's true, then, that in this book "culinary art turns female power into magic transcendentalism," that is because the feast of plenitude becomes a metonym for the lost breast, or even the lost satiety of the womb, from which, like the austere diners at Babette's banquet, satisfied communicants may be, if only briefly, reborn into a kind of "celestial second childhood."[39]

Ghost Milk

The thick cream of the breast and the magic of the body from which, if all goes well, it issues as if through some enchantment. The maternal body that must nurture its offspring. The womb in which the baby feasted without knowing what feasting was, and then the breast that offers plenitude, if all goes well. If all goes well. Inevitably (as in *Like Water for Chocolate*) culinary novels meditate on these subjects through various representations of the first meal, its presence, its absence.

Toward the end of the nineteenth century, George Moore introduced readers to the oppressed unwed mother Esther Waters, who has to become a wet nurse, feeding a rich woman's infant while her own child languishes in a "baby farm," until she can no longer bear her baby's suffering and seeks to support him through less well-paid jobs as a kitchen maid. Later, in the twentieth century, we encounter the image of Rose of Sharon, the eldest daughter of the Joads in John Steinbeck's *Grapes of Wrath*: after her own child is stillborn, she suckles a starving wayfarer in the book's final scene. And in the twenty-first century, there's Susann Cokal's *Mirabilis*, the tale of one Bonne La Mere, a young woman in medieval Poitou whose breast milk magically nurtures an entire village. But perhaps most important, in the late twentieth century there's Toni Morrison's *Beloved,* that extraordinary novel about slavery and its impact on the desire for mother's milk, the greed for milk, the theft of milk, the loss of milk and the ghost of milk.

Morrison's novels have always been obsessed with flesh and milk and food, in particular the ways in which black people, bereft of a mother country and taught to scorn their own dark bodies, turn against those bodies and the bodies of their children in self-loathing. In *The Bluest Eye* young Pecola despises her self, her skin, her hair, her eyes, and while her mother cooks delicacies for a spoiled white child she goes hungry, the way Esther Waters's baby does in George Moore's eponymous novel. In *Sula*, grandmother Eva incinerates her son, the dissipated (and resonantly named) Plum, while countless other deaths and dismemberments reflect the same loathing for African–American flesh and self. The hero of *Song of Solomon* is nicknamed Milkman because he has nursed so long, but his last name, ironically, is Dead. Milkman Dead. But *Beloved* perhaps most resolutely focuses on milk, breast, flesh, ghosts.

Based on the true story of Margaret Garner, an escaped slave who was captured by slave hunters and killed her two-year-old daughter rather than see her returned to bondage, Morrison's astonishing novel reformulates the historic event as a struggle not just for freedom but for mother's milk, the ultimate symbol of nurturance. The book's protagonist, Sethe, has escaped from the ironically named Sweet Home plantation in Kentucky, where she, her husband and five other good men have been enslaved for years, and en route to liberty has given birth to a baby girl, Denver. A little earlier, Sethe had managed to send her three children—two boys and a baby daughter—to their grandmother, Baby Suggs, in Ohio, but now she urgently needs to "bring her milk," as she puts it, to her older daughter, the "crawling already? baby girl" whom she is still nursing. Before she left Sweet Home, we learn, her milk was "stolen" in an episode of savage sexual assault by the two sons of Schoolteacher, the new manager of the plantation, a scene that was witnessed by her husband, who (in a deviation from the original history) went mad and smeared himself with the butter and clabber from the churn in the barn. When Schoolteacher and his posse arrive at what had seemed the safe haven of Baby Suggs's Ohio house, Sethe locks herself and her children in the woodshed and slits the "crawling already? baby girl's" throat with a saw, while trying to kill the other three as well.

Infanticide as a form of nurturance? Sethe wants her children liberated "on the other side"—in a heaven where slavery is unimaginable. The theft of milk as a form of rape? For Sethe, the "mossy teeth" of the white men clamped around her breast was the ultimate degradation—that and the scars of the whipping they gave her when they caught her after her first attempt at escape, a whipping that raised a numbed "tree" on her back, a tree of crucifixion. But is it the mother's right, or duty, to murder her child rather than return her to slavery? The original Margaret Garner claimed as much, as did her advocate, the abolitionist and feminist Lucy Stone. But through the voice and passion of the dead baby, known simply as "Beloved" because that word is the only one written on her gravestone, Morrison explores the complexity of the situation. Haunting what she experiences as her murderous mother's house, the ghost child tosses furniture around in rage, shakes the floors with the thunder of her thwarted desire for life and milk, and sometimes manifests herself as a column of bloody light at the front door. When her yearning for the face of the infanticidal mother whose nurturance she desperately needs becomes unendurable, she ferociously resurrects herself as a beautiful, unlined young woman who, like a newborn baby, can barely hold her head up. And like the neediness of a newborn baby, Beloved's need and greed for what only her mother can give—and what she feels her mother took away—is endless.[40]

Milk is at the center of *Beloved,* as it is, though very differently, at the center of so many children's tales. But food, more generally, is crucial throughout the book. After her release from prison, Sethe supports herself and her surviving children as a cook, working in a restaurant owned by a white man and taking home her rations as meals for the family. These rations are sparse but sufficient. We see Sethe kneading dough and baking biscuits for Paul D., another former Sweet Home slave who has become her lover and, in a way, her redeemer. For the black community, however, especially for Baby Suggs's household, plenitude has been dangerous. Exactly twenty-eight days after Sethe's arrival in Cincinnati, Baby Suggs, "holy"—the preacherly grandmother—hosted a lavish feast that aroused the envy of her neighbors, who failed to warn her, the next day, that the slave hunters were coming. Baby Suggs's house,

> rocking with laughter, goodwill and food for ninety, made them angry. Too much, they thought. Where does she get it all, Baby Suggs, holy? Why is she and hers always the center of things? How come she always knows exactly what to do and when? Giving advice; passing messages; healing the sick, hiding fugitives, loving, cooking, cooking, loving, preaching, singing, dancing and loving everybody like it was her job and hers alone. Now to take two buckets of blackberries and make ten, maybe twelve, pies; to have turkey enough for the whole town pretty near, new peas in September, fresh cream but no cow, ice and sugar, batter bread, bread pudding, raised bread, shortbread—it made them mad. Loaves and fishes were His powers—they did not belong to an ex-slave who had probably never carried one hundred pounds to the scale, or picked okra with a baby on her back.[41]

The community's rage at slavery metamorphoses into anger at one of their own, whose excess of material, maternal generosity reminds them of the nurturance they themselves have always lacked.

In the meantime, Beloved's need for nourishment of every kind has become gigantic, as Morrison depicts what it would mean for a "crawling already? baby girl" to be incarnated as a woman. To begin with, she has a voracious childlike desire for sweets, which could

> always be counted on to please her. It was as though sweet things were what she was born for. Honey as well as the wax it came in, sugar sandwiches, the sludgy molasses gone hard and brutal in the can, lemonade, taffy and any type of dessert Sethe brought home from the restaurant. She gnawed a cane stick to flax and kept the strings in her mouth long after the syrup had been sucked away.[42]

She might as well be one of the Raggedies in Cookie Land, and with her blank black eyes, frighteningly empty, and the suggestion of a smile under her chin—the scar where the saw slashed her open—she seems to have the look of a Gothic doll. But her hungers increase, and as her neediness balloons to inhabit the house she once haunted, she gradually destroys the family, seducing Paul D. and eventually driving him away to seek work in the slaughterhouse that is, tellingly, one of the major employers of African–Americans in the city. By the end of the novel, she is swollen to twice Sethe's size, pregnant (or so it seems) and devouring so much food that nothing is left for her sister, Denver, or Sethe, who has lost her job as a cook and is on the verge of starvation. The mother herself has become, thinks Denver, "like a rag doll."[43]

Eventually Denver seeks succor from the community that had ostracized her and her family for so many years, and as she reaches out to them they respond with gifts of food—a basket of eggs, a sack of white beans, a plate of cold rabbit meat. And then they come as a group in an effort to exorcize the ghostly incubus who has taken possession of the house where Baby Suggs, "holy," had once ruled. But after Beloved disappears and the house is silent, the ache of the dead child's sorrow still haunts Morrison's novel. The "crawling already? baby girl"—just on the brink of the upright stance that would make her into a free human being—has gone unfed because, arrested in the grave, she could never be fed enough. But would she have been nurtured at Sweet Home? Sethe herself was never properly nursed by her mother, and Denver has survived only through the mediation of a good runaway white girl, who defied the beastly laws that governed plantation life.

Did Beloved return as a symbol of Sethe's guilt? Or was it her own yearning that resurrected her, her search for the milk of human kindness that disappears when human enslaves human? Or did the dead girl rise from the grave in response to Sethe's own desperate yearning for the child to whom she had hoped to bring her milk? Certainly the mother recognizes her murdered child just when, after a strange evening during which she and Denver and the revenant had managed to brave a frozen pond on three ice skates, she is feeding them and herself a pan of warm milk into which she has stirred cane syrup and vanilla. There she is, the dark eyes with their bottomless longing, the "smile" of death under her baby chin. She is humming the song that her mother sang to her when she was nursing her. "Only my children know that song," Sethe thinks. The empty miracle of a resurrection that could never happen in slave society infuses the sweet warm milk—milk that can never really be returned to the mother from whom it was stolen. A ghost of milk. Milk meant for a child murdered here by inhuman bondage.

But is the ghost of milk always somewhere lapping at the edges of writings about food, whether they're intended for children or adults? The ghost of an unattainable satiety? And the ghost of a dread at the mother's power—does it even haunt the cosy tales of the Raggedies and the chocolate factory and the night kitchen?

PART III

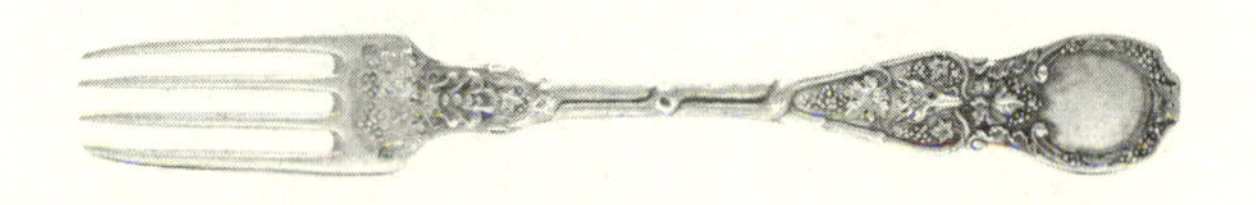

Food for Thought

Blessings and Curses

Chapter 10

The Poetics of Ice Cream: Eating Art at the Table, in the Gallery, and in a Grownups' Garden of Verses

Whip in kitchen cups concupiscent curds . . .
The only emperor is the emperor of ice-cream.

—WALLACE STEVENS, "THE EMPEROR OF ICE-CREAM"

From when I worked in restaurants, I can remember seeing rows of pies, or a tip of pie with one piece out of it, and one pie sitting beside it. Those little *vedute* in fragmented circumstances were always poetic to me.

—WAYNE THIEBAUD

. . . sometimes I just set the table
because meals are memorials
that teach us how to move,
history moves in us as we raise
our voice and then our glasses
to pour a little out for those
who poured out everything for us.

—JAKE ADAM YORK, "GRACE"

Eating the Body of Art

Birthday cakes, candy canes, chocolate bunnies, sugar eggs, real eggs all gussied up for rolling and trading—even when we were children, food wasn't just artful but art. Remember the gingerbread houses? They didn't only live in fairy tales; they appeared on our tables, with squiggles of icing around their make-believe windows; and our birthday cakes were and are studded with glorious pastel rosettes, as were the elegant larger-than-life sugar eggs through whose magic doorways we peered at pastoral scenes of ducks and bunnies. As for real-life Easter eggs, to this day, my daughter and granddaughter and I dip them in their ranges of colors, always arguing about how long to leave them in the magic solution that will transform them from plain old hard-boiled eggs to our annual spring treats. And all my grandchildren scribble little pictures on them, deck them out in stiff paper collars, affix decals. But before we do that, we polish them, as I learned in my own childhood from a beloved aunt, with just a smidgen of olive oil, so they glow almost as if lit from within by the new life they symbolize.

Food has been art at least since "Trimalchio's Feast," as described by Petronius, featured "a wild boar of the largest possible size . . . wearing a freedman's cap on its head" and a boiled calf decked out in a helmet. One Renaissance *trionfo da tavola,* a festive centerpiece for noble banquets, was designed by Andrea del Sarto to resemble the famous Florence Baptistery.

> The pavement was made of jelly and resembled a variously colored mosaic; the columns, which looked like porphyry, were large sausages; the bases and capitals parmesan cheese; the cornices were made of pastry and sugar, and the tribune of marzipan. In the center was a choir-stall made of cold veal, with a book made of pastry, the letters and notes formed by peppercorns. The singers were roast thrushes with open beaks, wearing surplices of pig's caul, and behind these were two large pigeons for basses, with six larks for the sopranos.[1]

But if the Baptistery *trionfo* was as much meat as sweet, the kinds of confectioneries many of us grew up with evolved as sugar became widely available in Europe after the colonization of the New World. By the eighteenth century, all over the continent skilled culinary artisans were carving delicate baskets, bowls and perhaps most important those nonutilitarian decorative works called *pièces montées.* Among the most extraordinary of these was a triumphal arch, with "gilded *pastillage* trophies," but there were plenty of others.[2] One writer on the subject described the sort of thing he had in mind:

> Let the table be well set, in the richest way possible. . . . At one end let there be a *trionfo* representing Pluto's palace. At the other end, Proserpina's palace. . . . In the center of the table a garden of sugar, its gates made of candied citrus, a fountain in the middle of good design with various figures, set off by two mountains of green gelatin, with wild beasts and hunters.[3]

The sugar from which these prized objects were molded—for the House of Savoie, British royalty, Marie Antoinette, and other rarefied clients—probably came from the backbreaking labor of Caribbean slaves: it was what Coleridge and others called "blood sugar" in impassioned diatribes against the sugar trade.[4] Yet its origins were of little account to the aristocrats whose households featured such items.

Indeed, by the early nineteenth century the great Marie-Antoine Carême, sometimes known as the first celebrity chef, ruled the continent. His view that the "main branch of architecture is confectionery" was undisputed in exclusive circles. His famed Patisserie de la rue de la Paix offered not only elaborate *pièces montées* but many of the latest pastries he had invented, including the Napoleon and the Charlotte russe. And despite the gradual disappearance of the *grande cuisine* Carême pioneered, such delicacies still flourish in France, as do *pièces montées.* I remember how impressed I was in the early 1990s when one of the waiters at Taillevent, then the reigning restaurant in Paris, wheeled out a cart containing a massive *Bon Anniversaire* plaque, like a great sugar sculpture, in honor of David's birthday. Birthday cakes and cupcakes with little candles—yes, I was used to those—but not this art nouveau creation. Yet even in the contemporary United States it's customary for important buildings to be dedicated at receptions featuring cakes in the shape of the new edifice, although, as one commentator has lamented, "the model cake endures destruction, slice after slice," prompting, for the architect, a nauseating "vision of the building's eventual demise."[5]

Cakes commemorating office buildings are merely commercial art, however, compared to most of the avant-garde culinary constructions assembled throughout the twentieth century by the Futurists and, after them, the Eat Art movement. The manifestos of Filippo Marinetti, the coauthor of *The Futurist Cookbook* and cofounder of its steely Holy Palate restaurant in Turin, were primarily political, often flirting with Fascism, but Daniel Spoerri, the (now) eminence grise of Eat Art, began his work as an impoverished poet of the table and dispassionate observer of contemporary culture. Like Marinetti, Spoerri was to become the *patron* of a restaurant—the eponymous Restaurant Spoerri in Dusseldorf, where he cooked often bizarre banquets (python schnitzels, ant omelets, lion steak) throughout the 1970s and above which he established the influential Eat Art gallery.[6] Before this, living with his wife in a tiny, cheap Paris hotel room in the early 1960s, he took to gluing dishes and cups, along with the leftovers they contained, onto blue tableaux (like his tabletop) and mounting them on the walls. They became his famous *Trap Pictures* (*Tableaux pièges*), curious collages inaugurating an aesthetic–culinary career based on an ironic interpretation of the old German saying that "When all the arts perish, the noble art of cooking will survive." In support of this point, Spoerri once argued that "humanity has two basic impulses, survival and reproduction, or, to put it more crudely . . . eating and fucking," and he chose "to focus his art on the former [since] the latter had been so much talked about already." Given the increasingly radical spirit of the sixties, his offbeat genre flourished. Eventually Spoerri produced *Trap Pictures* from remnants of meals by a range of celebrated artists, and one (a display of leftovers from a dinner consumed by Marcel Duchamp) sold at auction for more than a hundred thousand pounds.[7]

Of course, some of the foodstuffs trapped in Spoerri's collages were eaten by rats, and then the sadly diminished tableaux were recycled as rat-eaten *Trap Pictures*, an appropriate destiny given the paradoxical connection between the traditional glue trap used to catch rodents, often with bait analogous to the stuff the artist left on his table, and the helplessly trapped morsels of bread, cheese, meat that chance had arranged into graphic designs. But in addition, as poems of the present, Spoerri's early works—like, for instance, W. C. Williams's "This Is Just To Say"—literally capture the simultaneity of sensuality and disintegration, gastronomy and mortality. By "gluing together situations that have happened accidentally," he declared, he hoped to make the "observer uneasy," explaining:

> My trap pictures should create discomfort, because I hate stagnations. I hate fixations. I like the contrast provoked by fixating objects, to extract objects from the flow of constant changes and from their perennial possibilities of movement; and this despite my love for change and movement. Movement will lead to stagnation. Stagnation, fixation, death should provoke change and life, or so I like to believe.[8]

Ah, but the cruelty of the glue trap! I remember having to buy and set some real glue traps in Paris a decade ago, when David and I were suffering an invasion of mice let loose by renovation in the building. I didn't know Spoerri's work at the time, but the little arrangements of chocolate and cheese with which we made collages designed to tempt stray rodents onto a sticky board were in some sense comparable to his *Tableaux pièges.* We never did capture any mice—I think the *souris* haunting our apartment were as clever as Remy in *Ratatouille*—but my visions of abject creatures stuck in the darkest corners of the kitchen retrospectively illuminate the pathos of Spoerri's leftover *confitures,* crumbs of pastry or streaks of ice cream. Once, like Williams's plums, they may have been "so sweet and so cold"; now they are just so cold. Once, like Miss Havisham's wedding cake in *Great Expectations,* they might have been delicious with anticipation; now they are moldy with regret.

The aptly named still life or the even more aptly named *nature morte* is always at least as much an elegiac work as it is a celebration of life, a point that becomes especially clear when the art we contemplate is not figuratively but literally a dying fragment of nature. Cézanne's apples, joyous in their roundness and color, may seem to transcend time, but of course we know they have rotted by now. The materiality of their decay, concealed by the ripeness the artist has trapped in paint, suggests that theirs is a sort of "noble rot," to use a phrase that vintners employ to describe the overripe grapes from which the most exquisite wines are distilled. But after all, Cézanne, like most of his precursors in the genre, sought to represent nature, alive or dead, with a certain affirmative verve. Platters of oysters, baskets of bread, even dead birds waiting to be plucked and roasted may have been trapped in stillness, but their images were meant to tempt as well as taunt. The disillusioning works produced by Spoerri's contemporaries and disciples in the Eat Art movement, however, sardonically subvert the hubris of Roman centerpieces, Renaissance *trionfi*, Empire *pièces montées* and even currently popular architectural cakes while also questioning the semblance of eternity bestowed on fragile foodstuffs by painters, photographers and sculptors. If they are literalized, my alabaster peaches, my ceramic apples, my papier-mâché eggplants all become memento mori!

Spoerri's own musings on the food chain and its discontents were perhaps inevitably as scatological as they were morbid. In an early gastronomic diary, he proposed a film that would "start with a close-up of a fresh pile of shit returning through the intestines (X-ray image) back into the stomach where the chewed pieces of meat are collected that come out of the mouth in the form of a steak which is brought backwards to the butcher who attaches it back onto the ox which, at the end of the film, is awakened to new life, grazing in a sunny meadow full of flowers, and, naturally leaves behind a large pile of shit." Notes the art historian Renate Buschmann, this film was actually made in 1968 by two of Spoerri's colleagues, and premiered under the somewhat blasphemous title *Resurrection.*[9] In the early seventies, Spoerri hosted several banquets featuring similarly grotesque themes. At one, a *"diner cannibale,"* guests were offered foodstuffs carved in the shape of body parts belonging to the chefs, Claude and François-Xavier Lalanne, who used "baking moulds which reproduced the human body as a pâté." At another, a parodic *ultima cena,* diners were invited to consume culinary creations mirroring their own personalities; prints of the artworks were designed "in a style between a menu and a condolence card."[10]

Spoerri was hardly unique in his visions of dissolution and excrement.

His friend and countryman Dieter Roth produced a number of works "calculating [the] continuous decay and putrefaction" of "alimentary materials," putting in question "art's claim to eternity." One of his earlier projects was *Literaturwurst*—sausage casings stuffed with spices and literary texts—that he and a disciple crafted between 1961 and 1974; the series culminated in twenty pseudo sausages bulging with the complete writings of Hegel. Another, more scatological work was *Rabbit–Shit–Rabbit:* what appears to be a chocolate bunny (like those molded by the chocolatier Lindt) is actually made from rabbit shit. But perhaps Roth's most bizarre concoction was *Staple Cheese (A Race)* 1970—punning on "Steeple Chase"—a set of suitcases filled with cheese above which were mounted pictures composed of cheese. Inexorably both the cheeses on display and the boxed-in cheeses journeyed toward putrefaction, so that within a few days the stench of their dissolution, along with the maggots and flies they attracted, "made it impossible to enter the room."[11] More recently, similar excremental visions were converted into culinary (or, more accurately, anti-culinary) art by the Belgian artist Wim Delvoye and the Chinese filmmaker Fruit Chan. Delvoye's *Cloaca* (2001–) is a series of installations consisting of machines—some looking like washing machines, others like turbo engines—that efficiently turn food to shit before the bemused viewer's eyes.[12] Chan's film *Public Toilet* (2003) documents excremental spaces all over the world along with their users and their contents in graphic detail; the director, an important figure on the Hong Kong film scene, frankly called it "my shit movie."[13]

At least as shocking as these projects are the utilitarian items that the Canadian artist Jana Sterbak has fashioned over the years from flank steak. Her infamous *Vanitas: Flesh Dress for an Albino Anorectic* was an early version of the meat dress Lady Gaga wore to a 2010 music video awards ceremony. Now in the collection of the Pompidou Center in Paris, Sterbak's fifty pounds of heavily salted yet slowly rotting beef suggested to some the ways in which the female body has often been reduced to sheer, meaty materiality by carnivorous sexists. But that we are all, female or male, composed of gradually disintegrating flesh is also part of her point. And that point is made at least as dramatically in another of her creations, *Chair Apollinaire,* a superficially comfortable-looking easy chair covered not in leather but, again, in heavily salted flank steak. *Chair* puns grotesquely on the parallel between the La-Z-Boy we sit on and the flesh (*chair* in French) on which our spirit depends. And it also puns on *chère* (dear) in its affectionate evocation of the rhyme with "Apollinaire," the gourmand French poet who invented the term "surrealism." Thus the title of the work proposes a little menu of multiple meanings, including the notion that poetry itself is fleshly and transient as well as the idea that (as in surrealist poetry) even the commonest objects transcend themselves in a sort of dream life. Transience, though, rather than transcendence, is at the grisly heart of Sterbak's *Chair.* On her website right now—JanaSterbak.com—you can see two images of the work: one, the piece in its original form, red with bloody flesh and white with congealed fat; another, the piece some time later, blue-green with mold and decay.

From the temptations of the sugary *trionfo* to the morbid or scatological broodings of so many works produced by the Eat Art movement, the aesthetics of the literal *body* of art might seem to have disintegrated over the years, like Sterbak's dress and chair. It's worth noting, surely, that the grimmest presentations of food art date back to the second half of the twentieth century, when the nausea of Sartre and others rose in a postwar postmodernist era as citizens of the once-hopeful West were confronted with the wastes and wastings, the decimations and disillusionments of technology gone mad. Had the human body itself come to seem a mere tool for the sodderings of the soul? During the First World War parapets were built from the corpses of soldiers killed in combat, and during the Second the chimneys of Auschwitz and other camps literally devoured the remains of men, women and children. Had flesh itself come to seem excremental? The Nazis referred to the Jews they were transporting as pieces of "shit." Was aesthetic revulsion the only response?[14]

The Meat of the Matter

In Cassis, in the South of France, at a nurturing artist's colony called the Fondation Camargo, I spent some time discussing contemporary painting with my colleague Barbara Weissberger, an accomplished collagist, painter and photographer, because I shared a French teacher with her. We wrote little compositions for Josiane, our *professeur*, and Barbara riveted me with one in which she confessed that *"J'ai pensé que mes couleurs devaient s'inspirer de la viande crue: les rouges et les roses, les rouge-oranges, les jaunes"*—that is, she believed her characteristically vivid colors are inspired by raw meat. Indeed, she added, she often thinks of the reds, roses and blacks of Philip Guston, imagining him in his studio swallowed by a wave of red, simultaneously terrible and beautiful, and concludes that she often thinks, too, of the paintings of Chaim Soutine, *"les horribles rouges et jaunes de la viande"*: the horrible red and yellow of meat.

Not just in the art of the literal but in representational art, meat has been an aesthetic source, though it doesn't decay in paint as it does in reality. Still, the kitchen drowned in a tide of blood, and art the consequence of that brutal fact? We know, of course, that the cook must murder to create, but for those who aren't vegetarians, the conversion of the raw to the cooked inevitably confronts both chef and diner with unseemly butchery of some sort. True, lately there has been a movement of professional and amateur cooks to personally dismember the dead animals they plan to roast or stew. Influenced by such gastronomic celebrities as Gordon Ramsay, who butchered a lamb on television, Michael Pollan, who narrates his part in hunting, slaughtering, butchering and roasting a boar in one chapter of his bestselling *The Omnivore's Dilemma,* and Bill Buford, who apprenticed himself to a butcher in Tuscany, DIY (do it yourself) butchers learn "to slaughter and butcher" so that, according to the *New York Times*, "they can honor their pigs and eat them too." "I feel like if I'm going to eat meat," explains one magazine editor, "I don't want to eat stuff that I haven't had to work for."[15] Still, even that last remark encapsulates the notion of emotional as well as physical labor that's involved in butchery, with its connotations of murder and disgust.

At least since the Renaissance, however, painters have been way ahead of both Eat Art and DIY amateur butchers in their confrontation of meat as not just an aesthetic but also an existential subject. For centuries the genre of the still life—in French, *nature morte*; in Spanish, *bodegon*—has been obsessed

Pieter Aertsen, *Flight into Egypt* (1551).
Uppsala University Collection, Uppsala, Sweden.

with vegetables, flowers, fruit and fish as well as meat. And in exuberant variations on the still life, the Mannerist painter Arcimboldo created whimsical "people," some representing the seasons, out of fruits, vegetables, roots and fish, wittily reminding us that we are literally made out of what we eat. But some of the earliest and most powerful *natures mortes* quite literally laid out the assumptions of the form by zeroing in on the *facticity* of meat. Even still lifes featuring fruits and flowers frequently functioned as memento mori, sometimes with skulls depicted next to bowls of delicacies, sometimes with the dead bodies of game birds or empty oyster shells strewn across the canvas, sometimes even with worms crawling among apples. Pieter Aertsen's astonishing *Butcher's Stall with the Flight into Egypt* (1551) foregrounds sides of beef, sausages, chops, innards, limp poultry and the lugubrious head of a dead calf; behind these abject objects, there is a glimpse of a fresh exterior in which the Holy Family flee the reeking mortality (and materiality) of all this death as they journey toward redemption. A century later, Rembrandt's great

Rembrandt van Rijn, *The Slaughtered Ox* (1655).
Musée du Louvre, Paris, France.

Slaughtered Ox (1655) focuses on an enormous side of beef—an ox slit open and decapitated—hanging, in the pose of crucifixion, from a wooden beam.

As in Aertsen's work, there is an aperture at the back of the room where Rembrandt's butchered meat is displayed, here a doorway through which a young woman seems to be gravely peering. (In an earlier version of the work, pictured here, a servant girl bends below the cadaver, evidently scrubbing the floor, perhaps of blood.) Some critics see the painting as a reverent allusion to Christ's crucifixion, with the luminosity of blood and fat suggesting the holiness of sacrifice. But it might also be considered a blasphemous riff on a traditionally sacred event. Certainly, in either case, it is a powerful memento mori, like Aertsen's painting, glossing such sermonizings as that of the British theologian John Moore, who warned in 1617 that "in our meats (as in a looking glasse) we may learne our own mortalitie: for let us put our hand into the dish, and what doe we take but the foode of a dead thing . . . with which foode wee so long fill our bodies, until they themselves be meate for wormes?"[16]

Quite a few modern and contemporary paintings redeployed the images of butchery that Aertsen and Rembrandt so strikingly depicted. The Russian–Jewish–French painter Chaim Soutine based a famous series of canvases, *Le Boeuf Écorche* (circa 1924) directly on Rembrandt, but unlike Aertsen and Rembrandt he focuses with claustrophobic intensity on the splayed carcass, from which there is no escape: a blue background enfolds it, yet it appears to be still dripping what looks like a pool of blood onto the floor of the space in which it hangs. There's a story, perhaps apocryphal, that when Soutine was painting the work he kept the carcass in his studio for so long that neighbors complained of the stench and called the police—a foreshadowing of the problems caused by the stink of Dieter Roth's *Staple Cheese* installation. Clearly this early-twentieth-century artist was moving toward the materiality and immanence of his Eat Art successors. Where Aertsen's memento mori implies transcendence in its keyhole image of the Holy Family, and where Rembrandt (at least according to some critics) gives us a background glimpse of a whole, wondering, human being, Soutine offers—as do Roth, Spoerri, and Sterbak—pure abjection, though his is at least representational rather than literal.[17]

And that the Church itself is subject to the laws of the flesh rather than those of the Holy Ghost is suggested by Francis Bacon's *Figure with Meat* (1954), one of his notorious images of a screaming pope, in which he frames the figure of Pope Innocent X, derived from Velasquez's famous portrait (*Pope Innocent X,* c. 1650), with a raw and bloody *boeuf écorché* alluding to Rembrandt and Soutine. Notes one observer, "by linking the pope with these carcasses," Bacon implies that the Holy Father is either "a depraved butcher" or a "victim like the slaughtered animal hanging behind him."[18] Either way, the Trinity doesn't promise transcendence: like Sterbak's *Chair Apollinaire,* Christianity itself is doomed to decay. After all this, Philip Guston's *Painting Smoking Eating* (1973), whose raw reds drew the admiration of my friend Barbara, seems inevitable: here the artist lies prone in bed, felled like a rotting tree, with a cigarette in his mouth and cartoon eyes staring as if astonished at a tray of cigarette butts on his chest and a pile of bloody, perhaps inedible food at his side.

Blessing the Ice and the Cream

A felled body is also at the center of the poem from which I derive my title for this chapter: Wallace Stevens's enigmatic, often anthologized "The Emperor of Ice-Cream" (1922). Elegiac and incantatory, this work is a dirge for a mysterious female figure whose stony corpse is splayed out—not unlike a slaughtered ox—on what might be a kitchen table or perhaps an unmade bed. Here is the piece in its entirety:

> *Call the roller of big cigars,*
> *The muscular one, and bid him whip*
> *In kitchen cups concupiscent curds.*
> *Let the wenches dawdle in such dress*
> *As they are used to wear, and let the boys*
> *Bring flowers in last month's newspapers.*
> *Let be be finale of seem.*
> *The only emperor is the emperor of ice-cream.*
>
> *Take from the dresser of deal*
> *Lacking the three glass knobs, that sheet*
> *On which she embroidered fantails once*
> *And spread it so as to cover her face.*
> *If her horny feet protrude, they come*
> *To show how cold she is, and dumb.*
> *Let the lamp affix its beam.*
> *The only emperor is the emperor of ice-cream.*[19]

Employing the imperatives of a preacher, a funeral director or even a stage director, the speaker outlines the arrangements to be made with terse authority. First, "call" the muscular cigar maker and "bid him whip" ice cream in kitchen cups. "Let" girls wear their usual dresses, and "let" boys bring flowers in old newspapers, not fancy bouquets. "Let be"—what is—be the end result of what seems to be. Prepare for a folksy down-home ice cream social. Don't get dressed up. And as for the body of the dead woman, who has died in poverty (she had a cheap deal dresser, not mahogany, and one that lacks three knobs; her fanciest sheet was too small to cover her entirely), look at it in the scathing light of the daily: "let" the lamp of a disillusioned vision "affix its beam." Let there be light!

A bleak vision of quotidian death or a culinary fantasy? Stevens's great poem (it was one of his personal favorites) is both. Not a child of the Church, not a candidate for heaven, the dead woman has become merely lifeless meat: her "horny feet"—callused from years of trudging and drudging—"protrude" unattractively to tell how "cold she is, and dumb," how mute and wordless. Yet she is at the center of a worldly ceremony, her priest the secular "roller of big cigars" whose muscularity transforms nature (tobacco leaves, curds of milk) into the culture of daily pleasures: cigars and ice cream. And is he the emperor of ice cream, the ruler of the realm of hedonism? He may be or he may be that sovereign's acolyte. Either way, the poet argues, there is no "emperor"—no god—but the god of the living, ardent, concupiscent flesh, whose blessings we must celebrate while we can, before we too are cold and dumb. Against the inescapable reality of the corpse whose potential for decay drives the aesthetic of disillusionment that shapes artists from Soutine to Spoerri, Stevens sets his poetics of ice cream, a poetics of carpe diem that would bless the food we have while we are here, the delicious stuff that is, in Williams's words, "so sweet and so cold." In particular, Stevens celebrates the nurturing cream of the world, the treasure of mammalian milk, rather than the spilling blood of raw meat. Yet, just as Williams's plums were desirable not just for their sweetness but because they were coldly detached from the tree (and preserved in the icebox of culture), so the cream whipped by "the muscular one" is delightful because even while it is deathly cold it has been transformed into that specially sweet cultural product, ice cream.

Ice cream is at the center of one of the best-known food paintings of the mid-twentieth century, Wayne Thiebaud's *Girl with Ice Cream Cone* (1963), a picture that might almost seem to function as a companion piece to Stevens's much earlier poem, though it is in fact contemporary with Spoerri's more sardonic *Trap Pictures*. Brilliant and painterly in a traditional way, *Girl* depicts the artist's wife, Betty Jean, seated in a bathing suit on a pale blue ground and meditatively holding an ice cream cone. Her legs open before us in an inverted

V, foregrounding the blue-shadowed soles of her feet, but these are neither horny nor dumb. The woman with the cone (despite the title of the piece, she doesn't seem at all girlish) is very much alive, with a keen, dark gaze. Yet she isn't an erotic object either, though she is posed in a vaguely sexual position. Rather, she is clearly strong and well-muscled, with powerful-seeming shoulders and firm thighs—a desirous empress of ice cream, herself in command of her own appetite. Where Stevens's wenches and boys and even his roller of big cigars have to be told what to do about ice cream, Thiebaud's subject is displaying her cone with a kind of connoisseurship that would have pleased Stevens, who was himself a connoisseur of exotic fruits and rare wines. Plainly she admires its loopy whip, its suave pastels, its swirl of pleasure. In a minute, she will bite into it, but for now she is contemplative. As is the painter who represents her—her husband—who looks at her desirous looking with the same delight with which he looks at and depicts the lights and shades of her body.[20]

Thiebaud is famously a connoisseur of desserts—or, rather, of the look of

Wayne Thiebaud, *Girl with Ice Cream Cone* (1963).
Hirshhorn Museum and Sculpture Garden, Washington DC, USA.

desserts: not just ice cream but especially cakes and pies and candies, a range of sweetnesses that he portrays with a melancholy hedonism quite the opposite of the Eat Art aesthetic, even though he was focusing on food in exactly the same decades when Spoerri and Roth were working. The superb painting *Cakes* (1963), which now hangs in the National Gallery in Washington, is his signature piece in this genre and can be seen as yet another counterpart of "The Emperor of Ice Cream." Twelve full circles of color and a half circle, this baker's dozen of baked goods encompasses angel food cakes (two!), a Boston cream pie and a group of fancily decorated layer cakes, along with the half cake whose opened body reveals its sugary strata like a sort of culinary geology. In their shapeliness, however, Thiebaud's cakes are more geometrical than geological: indeed, the National Gallery uses their images in an interactive feature designed to teach school children, grades two to five, about fractions. At the same time, these contemporary *trionfi* (for that's what they seem to be) are as sensually tactile as they are abstractly geometric. Many critics have observed that Thiebaud laid on paint as if it were frosting: a *CBS News* special on his career opened with an image of someone icing a chocolate cake and then segued into an image of the artist brush-stroking paint as if it were butter cream. Is it the tension between Euclidean rounds of brilliance and heaps of concupiscent sweetness that gives *Cakes* its special charisma?

As he gained increasing renown for his representations of food on display, Thiebaud himself tended to emphasize the formal elements in his art. "It's not so much fun to be known as the pieman," he once confessed. Yet he had to admit that

> of course I do think a lot about the subject matter, which exercises some sort of mysterious pull. It's just very, very familiar. I spent time in food preparation, I sold papers on the streets, and I went into Kresges or Woolworths or Newberrys, to see the eccentric displays of peppermint candy. [My pictures are] mostly painted from memory—from memories of bakeries and restaurants—any kind of window display. It's the *exclusionary* aspect that gets me—there's a lot of yearning there.[21]

The exclusionary aspect! The phrase is a striking one and reminds us that we never see Thiebaud's tempting masses and morsels being consumed. Even his girl with an ice cream cone has her lips pursed as if in anticipation of a taste, but the cone appears untouched. As for the cakes—and the objects of such other well-known and delicious-looking paintings as *Pies, Pies, Pies* (1961) , *Sandwiches, Salads and Dessert* (1962) and *Five Hot Dogs* (1961)—they are all on view, often behind glass, but almost always intact. They seem meant to lure rather than to lunch on; they exhibit their geometry of desire while in their inaccessibility forbidding investigation of their geological layers of pleasure. They look finger-lickin' good, but no fingers are destined to clasp or crumble them, no teeth or tongue to munch and swallow. Hence the air of melancholy that haloes them, even at their most beautiful, the feeling they give, as Adam Gopnik eloquently puts it, of "a serene abundance that is always a window pane away."[22]

For a long time Thiebaud was often and wrongly classified as a Pop artist. One critic argued that he "preaches revulsion by isolating the American food

Wayne Thiebaud, *Cakes* (1963).
Cakes © Wayne Thiebaud / Licensed by VAGA, New York, NY

Claes Oldenburg and Coosje van Bruggen, *Dropped Cone* (2001).
Collection Neumarkt Galerie, Cologne, Germany.

habit."[23] It's true that his oeuvre, like the canon of Pop Art, began to emerge in the 1960s, along with the aesthetic of Eat Art. Yet if one briefly compares Thiebaud's seductive cakes with, say, Andy Warhol's famous soup cans and Coke bottles, a clear distinction emerges. Warhol's works are ironic, hard-edged critiques of industrial food, shiny images that replicate a world where artifice replaces appetite. Similarly, the Pop Artist Claes Oldenburg produced a series of influential soft sculptures and models of ordinary foods—hamburgers, pie à la mode—that deflate desire by making what might have been scrumptious appear inedible. And Oldenburg's monumental *Dropped Cone* (2001)—a giant sculpture on which he collaborated with his wife, Coosje Van Bruggen—implicitly comments on Thiebaud's *Girl with Ice Cream Cone* by depicting the comic collapse of a huge ice cream cone that seems to have fallen onto the roof of a mall in Cologne, Germany, like a missile from gastronomic outer space. "Coosje referred to the Dropped Cone as both a 'cornucopia of consumerism' and a 'sign of transience,'" explains a statement from the artists, noting that the "sculpture's tilt differentiated it from the surrounding church steeples"—as do, one might also add, its blasphemously secular lineaments.[24]

Comparable critiques of consumerism and of what's come to be called "commodity fetishism" were also mounted in two early Pop Art installations: Oldenburg's *Store* (1961) and the group project *The American Supermarket* (1964), in which Oldenburg also participated. Both of these were brief, successful shows in which a great deal of fake merchandise—much of it plaster, marble, cloth, bronze, wax or painted food—got sold to eager patrons whose aesthetic consumerism helped commodify the aesthetic of Pop Art while presumably joining in its attack on commodity culture. Oldenburg was earnest and passionate in his own manifesto, writing that:

> I am for art that is put on and taken off, like pants, which develops holes, like socks, which is eaten, like a piece of pie, or abandoned with great contempt, like a piece of shit.
>
> I am for art covered with bandages. I am for art that limps and rolls and runs and jumps. I am for art that comes in a can or washes up on the shore.[25]

His allegiance, then, like Thiebaud's and Warhol's, was to the quotidian. But his inclination, and more generally that of other Pop Artists, was not so much to bless as to curse its ubiquity or, at least, to construct a politics rather than a poetics of ice cream.

A more ambiguous figure in this group was Robert Indiana, who may be best known for his series of LOVE sculptures but also gained a measure of notoriety with his EAT and EAT DIE signs. One of the first of these, a huge piece consisting of five 300-pound discs, each six feet in diameter, and hundreds of lightbulbs, was built for the 1964 World's Fair in Flushing Meadows and proclaimed EAT so convincingly that it had to be turned off the day after it was installed because fairgoers thought it was advertising a real restaurant. Just a year earlier, Indiana had himself become the subject of a work of art—one of Andy Warhol's silent black and white films, this one a thirty-nine-minute creation appropriately titled *Eat.* In it, Indiana meditatively bites, chews and swallows what seems to be the same mushroom for the length of the movie, while Warhol films him from different angles. The work has a curious comic fascination, even beauty. Indiana's mouth is sensual, his eyes are dark and meditative, and he wears a vaguely clownish borsalino. His expression is bemused and Chaplinesque, as if he himself wonders what eating is all about and what it is for. Yet he is serene too, as if he were following the directions of a cinematic Wallace Stevens who had dictated that the artist eat a mushroom, and that he eat it with a certain absurd reverence.[26]

What I've called the poetics of ice cream, or more generally the poetics of appetite, as practiced by Stevens, Thiebaud and, here, Warhol is in its secular way an aesthetic of blessing, unlike the parodic aesthetic of most Pop Art. Much contemporary verse similarly blesses food as sacramental. If Indiana's motto EAT DIE, with its terse invocation of the food chain, summarizes the Eat Art philosophy, the meditative—perhaps mindful—act of eating filmed by Warhol reminds us of the sheer, odd pleasure we human animals take in simply tasting, chewing and swallowing. After all, if meat, fruit, cake and ice cream are the objects of contemplation in so much art, in real life—unless they are *pièces montées*—they are meant for consumption. And joyful consumption, one hopes.

The Imperatives of Pleasure

Stevens's poem teeters between celebration and instruction, as do so many prayers of blessing and thankfulness—or grace. "God is great. God is good. Let us thank him for our food. Amen." Grace, aligned with *gratias* and *gracias,* means thanks as well as blessing. Traditionally, many stand and hold hands, or bend their heads, in honor of the meal to come and in praise of its sources. Roman Catholics cross themselves and murmur, "Bless us, O Lord and these Thy gifts, which we are about to receive from Thy bounty. Through Christ, our Lord. Amen." Observant Jews speak in Hebrew, blessing the wine and the bread, which is broken and shared by all at the table, right after the *ha-motzi* prayer: "Blessed are you, God, King of the Universe, who brings forth bread from the earth." Hindus sometimes recite the fourteenth verse from the fifteenth chapter of the *Bhagavad-Gita,* which translates as "Becoming the life-fire in the bodies of living beings, mingling with the upward and downward breaths, I digest the four kinds of food."

Becoming the life-fire! Most blessings are ways of praising that fire and ensuring its continuance, through affirmations of our singular moment in the food chain, the moment when both we and what we eat are ripe and delicious. In the face of coldness and decay, Stevens's secular and decidedly anti-theological poem affirms that moment as did so many other poems of his and his contemporaries. We've seen that what I called the modernist fruit bowl was filled with fascinating edible objects by writers from Stein to Lawrence and Williams; Stevens of course was part of their cohort. All these artists were in one way or another descendants of that great American bard of the quotidian, Walt Whitman, but their works begot more and more elaborate spinoffs by writers from the Chilean Pablo Neruda (an acolyte of both Whitman's and Lawrence's) to Neruda's many disciples, most of whom would also have been devoted readers of Whitman, Williams, Stevens and Lawrence. And again, much of that work began in the sixties, the era of the beatniks and the diggers, the organic gardens at the People's Park, and the celebrations of a counterculture based on affirmations of life and LOVE, even while the Eat Art and Pop Art movements were sardonically subverting the industrialization of capitalist culture.

One might indeed argue that subversion, celebration and the imperatives of pleasure arrived together in a society whose young weren't quite sure what to do about industrialized food (hamburgers, hot dogs, ice cream) and its counter-cuisine counterparts (brown rice, organic tomatoes). In home kitchens and in restaurant kitchens, especially in California, both cooks and poets became locavores and organic: Alice Walker pioneered passions for baby lettuce and Meyer lemons, Allen Ginsberg and Denise Levertov preached the purity of "holy grains." Not always as political but often on the same wavelength, their colleagues and descendants began affirming and commending all the ways in which what we eat can be delicious. Many were indebted in particular to the writings of Neruda, whose *Odas Elementales* were brilliant variations on Lawrence's *Birds, Beasts and Flowers*: poems in which the poet celebrated the quotidian (the "elemental") by speaking with true seriousness to or about, say, his socks or his artichoke or his conger eel chowder, but also offered, as so many great poems do, recipes for pleasure.

What I've called the imperatives of pleasure are, in fact, at the center of much contemporary food poetry—meaning that such pieces are often recipe poems. Consider, after all, that a recipe is arguably a set of commands, just like Stevens's "The Emperor of Ice-Cream." *Take* three eggs, *add* a cup of flour, *stir* in melted butter . . . and on and on. "Let be be finale of seem." At the same time, a recipe is both an example of the quotidian and a set of directions for managing the quotidian. After you *beat* the eggs and the flour and sugar, and *bake* the batter, out of the oven come the layers of one of Thiebaud's cakes, and now the recipe writer often proposes further pleasure as a kind of blessing: delicious with whipped cream and strawberries. Or, as Julia Child sometimes does, she suggests the most appropriate wines and other accompaniments. "Garnish with parsley and serve over egg noodles. A hearty burgundy will complement this."

Neruda's "Ode to Conger Chowder" is very much in this recipe tradition, giving us the stipulations of a recipe in short lines of verse that are both terse and incantatory. Celebrating a special Chilean soup that features the conger eel, the poet lovingly describes the "rosy conger, / giant eel / of snowy flesh" and then instructs the reader, step by step, in the art of preparing this "thick and succulent" delicacy, "a boon to man." To begin with, Neruda notes, the cook must sauté garlic ("that precious / ivory"), along with onion and tomato, until they are golden. Then it's necessary to steam

our regal
ocean prawns,
and when
they are
tender,
when the savor is set in a sauce
combining the liquors
of the ocean
and the clear water
released from the light of the onion,
then
you add the eel

that it may be immersed in glory,
that it may steep in the oils
of the pot,
shrink and be saturated.
Now all that remains is to
drop a dollop of cream
into the concoction,
a heavy rose,
then slowly
deliver
the treasure to the flame,
until in the chowder
are warmed
the essences of Chile,
and to the table
come, newly wed
the savors
of land and sea,
that in this dish
you may know heaven.[27]

When is a recipe a blessing and when is a blessing a recipe? Why, when it's a poem, in which the "savors / of land and sea" marry in the kitchen, to produce "heaven" in a dish: the secular heaven that Stevens also praises. But besides being both celebratory and instructive, Neruda's poem is analytic and patriotic, as it investigates the gastronomic particularity of what he so famously called "residence on earth" (*Residencia en la Tierra*). "Our regal prawns"—steamed until tender—inhabit a sauce that combines "the liquors / of the ocean / and the clear water / released from the light of the onion," and after the eel steeps "in the oils / of the pot" it shrinks and is saturated with the "glory" of these flavors. The addition of a "dollop of cream . . . a heavy rose" finishes the chowder, giving it a local distinctiveness that captures "the essences of Chile," which become, too, the signatures of heaven on earth. And the poet–cook? He is in this case a sort of priest of the kitchen, reminding us of the magical metamorphoses that constitute the culinary art—not the hypothetical transformations of bread and wine into divine flesh and blood but the empirical changes, releases of liquors and shrinking of meat, flavoring of liquids and thickening of broth, that mark the magical turn from raw to cooked, from natural ingredients to a unique cultural product.

Another recipe poem very much in the mode of Neruda's ode to chowder, Gary Snyder's "How to Make Stew in the Pinacate Desert: Recipe for Locke & Drum" similarly sets forth a series of culinary commandments meant to issue in a blessed moment on "Turtle Island," Snyder's equivalent of the Chilean poet's "Residence on Earth." Less lyrical than Neruda, more radically quotidian, even humdrum, Snyder opens his poem with an urgent shopping list that calls for parsnips, onion, carrot, rutabaga and potato, green bell pepper, and "nine cuts of dark beef shank" because "They run there on their legs, that makes meat tasty." With equal urgency, the poet notes that by the time it's seven in Tucson, he and the other cooks have to get Bisquick for dumplings, along with bacon and herbs and spices. Next come the cooking instructions, as daily and straightforward as the shopping list though a bit more glamorous, since the stew is to be made in the desert, under the stars, where the chefs will "build a fire of Ocotillo, / broken twigs and bits of ironweed, in an open ring of lava," then set a Dutch oven across the embers. And finally, here's what to do:

Now put in the strips of bacon.
In another pan have all the vegetables cleaned up and peeled and sliced.
Cut the beef shank meat up small and set the bone aside.
Throw in the beef shank meat,
And stir it while it fries hot,
lots of ash and sizzle—singe your brow—

Like Locke says almost burn it—then add water from the jeep can—
add the little bag of herbs—cook it all five minutes more—and then
throw in the pan
of all the rest.
Cover it up with big hot lid all heavy, sit and wait, or drink budweiser
beer. . . .

And in the end, what do you do to celebrate your completion of this ordinary yet magical culinary project? "Dish it up and eat it with a spoon, sitting on a poncho in the dark." Matter-of-fact though they may be, the imperatives of pleasure will track you into the desert and nourish you even in the raw wilderness.[28]

If Snyder is urgent and colloquial, Nancy Willard offers a more fantastic yet sardonic set of instructions in her frequently anthologized "How to Stuff a Pepper," a recipe poem that is spoken by a philosophically digressive cook who intends to teach the poet "how to stuff a pepper with rice." Beginning with the observation that you must "Take your pepper green, and gently, / for peppers are shy," the cook eroticizes the vegetable, remarking that in its "silk tights" it dreams "of somersaults and parsley," and "of the days when the sexes were one." Yet after observing that the acolyte should enter this culinary object as if it were "a moon, spilled like a melon" or "a temple built to the worship / of morning light," this speaker withdraws from the didactic mode, admitting a kind of defeat.

> *I have sat under the great globe*
> *of seeds on the roof of that chamber,*
> *too dazzled to gather the taste I came for.*
> *I have taken the pepper in hand,*
> *smooth and blind, a runt in the rich*
> *evolution of roses and ferns.*
> *You say I have not yet taught you*
>
> *to stuff a pepper?*
> *Cooking takes time.*[29]

For as this professorial cook muses on the properties of the raw material at hand, she is distracted by reverence for the veritable *ding an sich*—the pepper itself, in all its blooming materiality. Confessing that she regards this vegetable as itself "a temple," the speaker imaginatively inhabits it, confiding that "I have sat under the great globe / of seeds on the roof of that chamber, / too dazzled to gather the taste I came for." Rather than stuffing the pepper with rice, the cook has comically enough stuffed the pepper with herself, and emerging from her dream of green interiority, admits that she has failed to convey any recipe at all! But then, "cooking takes time," and perhaps some of the time it ought to take is time spent on reflection. A successful children's book writer, Willard uses the (ostensible) recipe form to bless rather than to instruct, while also producing a luminous fantasy in which the main ingredient of the dish baffles the intentions of the would-be culinary instructor, turning her instead into a dazed worshipper.

While a recipe may in itself be an act of instruction and at least implicit celebration, the telling of a recipe may of course have different overtones. There are recipes for poisons, recipes for witches' brews, recipes for revenge and recipes shot through with grief. Carol Ann Duffy's startling "Circe"—spoken by Homer's legendary enchantress—is an instance of vengefulness posing as culinary instruction, although, in the course of the poem, the sorceress who turned Odysseus's sailors into pigs also reveals her own wistful vulnerability. "Circe" begins authoritatively, as the speaker addresses her attendants, noting that "I'm fond, nereids and nymphs, unlike some, of the pig, / of the tusker, the snout, the boar and the swine. / One way or another, all pigs have been mine— / under my thumb." We know from Homer how and why the pigs became hers, but her subsequent summary of what she does with them is as hilarious as it is furious. Commenting that "I want to begin with a recipe from abroad," Duffy's Circe, a broad wronged by Odysseus, punningly explains that her preparation of pork "uses the cheek—and the tongue in cheek / at that." Then she proceeds with her enraged commands, outlining her grievances as she goes along, and only toward the end reveals the wound that inspires what we might consider her gastronomic reflux.

Well-cleaned pig's ears should be blanched, singed, tossed
in a pot, boiled, kept hot, scraped, served, garnished
with thyme. Look at that simmering lug, at that ear,
did it listen, ever, to you, to your prayers and rhymes,
to the chimes of your voice, singing and clear? Mash
the potatoes, nymph, open the beer. Now to the brains,

to the trotters, shoulders, chops, to the sweetmeats slipped
from the slit, bulging, vulnerable bag of the balls.
When the heart of a pig has hardened, dice it small.

Dice it small. I, too, once knelt on this shining shore
watching the tall ships sail from the burning sun
like myths; slipped off my dress to wade,
breast-deep, in the sea, waving and calling;
then plunged, then swam on my back, looking up
as three black ships sighed in the shallow waves.
Of course, I was younger then. And hoping for men. Now,
let us baste that sizzling pig on the spit once again.[30]

How this Circe hates Odysseus and his crewmen, with their "piggy eyes" and their hardened hearts, the hearts she longs to dice so small—hates them because, after all, they humiliated her as she swam from her shining shore, "waving and calling" and "hoping for men." Now all she wants is to "baste that sizzling pig on the spit once again."

Compared to "Circe," Patricia Smith's "When the Burning Begins" is nostalgic, sorrowful and only obliquely angry. Ostensibly a recipe for "hot water cornbread," the poem eulogizes and elegizes the poet's father, Otis Douglas Smith, who taught her to make the delicious bread and while doing so became her muse, telling her that she will be "*a wonderful writer / and you will be famous someday and when / you get famous . . . would you write about me?*" Only gradually, and in a few asides, does the poet reveal that he was murdered by a gunman in his own part of Chicago, but eventually it becomes clear that the poem's title refers not just to a step in the cooking of cornbread but to a phase of grief.

The recipe for hot water cornbread is simple:
Cornmeal, hot water. Mix till sluggish,
then dollop in a sizzling skillet.
When you smell the burning begin, flip it.
When you smell the burning begin again,

dump it onto a plate. You've got to wait
for the burning and get it just right.

Before the bread cools down,
smear it with sweet salted butter
and smash it with your fingers,
crumple it up in a bowl
of collard greens or buttermilk,
forget that I'm telling you it's the first thing
I ever cooked, that my daddy was laughing
and breathing and no bullet in his head
when he taught me.

Mix it till it looks like quicksand, *he'd say.*
Till it moves like a slow song sounds.[31]

In its sorrowful reiteration of the way the burning will begin and will smell, followed by its celebration of the momentary pleasure of eating, Smith's poem, too, "moves like a slow song sounds," reminding us in a Proustian way of how much the savor of humanity can infuse even the simplest recipe, one that has only a few ingredients—cornmeal, hot water, a father, a daughter, a sizzling skillet, and a bullet—and how, as her conclusion declares, "sometimes the burning / takes such a long time, / and in that time, / sometimes // poems are born."

The Flesh Made Word

Inevitably, just as painters fixated on the often fascinating material spectacle of food, poets begin thinking of poems as food and food as poems. We poets, after all, are inclined to taste and chew, mouth and tongue our words, though we don't always want to eat them, swallow them or bite them back. But poems are born from the mouth, and the profusion of culinary metaphors associated with language itself emphasizes the connection that has probably inspired a number of recipe poems along with other verses destined for what the poet and anthologist Kevin Young has called "the hungry ear." What is special to contemporary writing and painting is the turn away from festal food to quotidian food, a move that goes back to the modernists—Lawrence, Williams and others—as I've shown, but becomes especially notable at the mid-century, as Allen Ginsberg lyrically strolls through a supermarket in California and Wayne Thiebaud frosts bakery layer cakes with paint.[32] Arguably, such art owes much to the shift in aesthetic values described by the distinguished philosopher Arthur C. Danto in his influential *Transfiguration of the Commonplace*, a work analyzing the institutional changes in the art world that facilitated the widespread acceptance of Pop Art works (*Brillo Box*, Campbell's soup cans) but whose thesis also illuminates the general ascendence of seemingly ordinary, "low" subject matter in a range of genres.[33]

As a poet myself, I remember vividly the era in my own life when, after a childhood and girlhood of "poetic" versifying in what now look to me like lyrical abstractions, I too suddenly swerved toward the quotidian. I was an acolyte of Yeats and Stevens (and, yes, Edna St. Vincent Millay) but then, in the early seventies, I was reading Lawrence, Whitman, Williams, Ginsberg, and I began to speak in a voice that felt somehow more "real"—more like daily life. My first poem in that vein—I called it "Mafioso"—was political, and as angry in its way as Smith's or Duffy's, but I'm struck, today, by its general foodiness. I had wanted to protest the stereotyping of Italian–Americans that I felt permeated even such masterworks as Francis Ford Coppola's *The Godfather*—which I've never been able to watch without distress. As I began to write, I found in some surprise that I was juxtaposing the foods of my Sicilian mother's family with the ludicrous images of gangsters whose criminality seemed to me to pollute my inheritance.

Frank Costello eating spaghetti in a cell at San Quentin,
Lucky Luciano mixing up a mess of bullets and
calling for parmesan cheese,
Al Capone baking a sawed-off shotgun into a
huge lasagna—
are you my uncles,
my only uncles?

O Mafiosi,
bad uncles of the barren
cliffs of Sicily—was it only you
that they transported in barrels
like pure olive oil
across the Atlantic?[34]

After this unexpected culinary breakthrough, my ancestral cuisines (and there were several—Sicilian, Ligurian, Niçois, Russian) offered countless wonderful "objective correlatives," as T. S. Eliot would say, for my explorations of personal and public history. In one series of verses, I meditated on my mother's baffling habit of kissing the bread before she threw it away; in another poem, I set my Italian–American family's meals of artichokes and pasta against my Jewish mother-in-law's "brisket, and good rye bread"; in another, I memorialized my mother's last days in a nursing home, when she would eat "chocolate, nothing but chocolate," so sick was she of this world; and in yet another I remembered the happiness, even the holiness, of dining with my beloved on oysters Rockefeller "in the icy / gut of winter." "Love calls us to the things of this world," wrote Richard Wilbur in a wonderful poem about laundry, and I think in many of these writings I was inspired by a variation of that statement: "The food of this world calls us to love."[35]

Like the late Jake Adam York, who has provided me with one of my epigraphs here, I was coming to an aesthetic as well as personal understanding that "meals are memorials," for "history moves in us as we raise / our voice and then our glasses / to pour a little out for those who poured out everything for us." Such an understanding, I'm sure, informs almost all the recipe poems I've considered here, along with a host of other poems of blessing and memory and, yes, politics and cursing. About cursing I'll write further in the next chapter, but here I want to note how vast and varied what we might consider the anthology of poetic gratitude has become in the years since Williams celebrated the sweetness and coldness of the plums his wife had sequestered in the icebox.[36]

Needless to say, writers have continued to praise the fruits of the earth, and many, like Williams, have recorded the pleasures of such gifts on the kitchen table. Both the late Craig Arnold and Gerald Stern focus on grapefruit, with Arnold recording bemusement at the strangeness of our morning ceremonials and Stern ceremonially testifying to the joys of grapefruit at breakfast time or indeed around the clock. What grips Arnold is the oddity of the experience of waking "when all is possible / before the agitations of the day / have gripped you" and going to the kitchen to "peel a little basketball / for breakfast"—a "sweet" and "devout" discipline that is "precisely pointless."[37] Stern, however, is extravagant in his ritual celebration, though he locates himself ironically in the midst of an absurd dailiness:

> *I'm eating breakfast even if it means standing*
> *in front of the sink and tearing at the grapefruit,*
> *even if I'm leaning over to keep the juices*
> *away from my chest and stomach and even if a spider*
> *is hanging from my ear and a wild flea*
> *is crawling down my leg. My window is wavy*
> *and dirty. There is a wavy tree outside*
> *with pitiful leaves in front of the rusty fence*
> *and there is a patch of useless rhubarb, the leaves bent over, the*
> *stalks too large and bitter for eating,*
> *and there is some lettuce and spinach too old for picking beside the*
> *rhubarb. This is the way the saints*
> *ate, only they dug for thistles . . .*

The saints, whom he has invoked so ironically, ultimately offer Stern a clue that leads him through the body of the poem, and the body of the world, to benediction:

> *. . . Ah sky,*
> *my breakfast is over, my lunch is over, the wind*
> *has stopped, it is the hour of deepest thought.*
> *Now I brood, I grimace, how quickly the day goes,*

how full it is of sunshine, and wind, how many
smells there are, how gorgeous is the distant
sound of dogs, and engines—Blessed art Thou,
Lord of the falling leaf, Lord of the rhubarb,
Lord of the roving cat, Lord of the cloud.
Blessed art Thou oh grapefruit King of the universe,
Blessed art Thou my sink, oh Blessed art Thou
Thou milkweed Queen of the sky, burster of seeds,
Who bringeth forth juice from the earth.[38]

In this eloquent comedy of the ordinary, the secular has become sacred as it does in so many contemporary poems of gastronomic communion.

Li-Young Lee is even more reverent in linking food to origins, as he celebrates the metamorphoses of blossoms to a "brown bag of peaches / we bought from the boy / at the bend in the road." Gradually, as he considers the pleasure brought from "laden boughs" and the hands of pickers and "sweet fellowship in the bins," he achieves a state of beatitude not unlike Neruda's or Stevens's, as he concludes that there are "days we live / as if death were nowhere / in the background" while we journey "from blossom to blossom to / impossible blossom, to sweet impossible blossom." But of course, it is the paradox of blossoming—its transience, its impossible impersonation of unending delight in the "round jubilance of peach"—that causes us to treasure it. The blossom, as Stevens wrote in "Sunday Morning," his classic secular ode to joy, is the opposite of what we imagine eternity to be, for "Death is the mother of beauty," and the mother, too, of our rapidly passing moments of gastronomic pleasure. What is good to eat must be good to think, so Lévi-Strauss declared, because the actual process of eating is so quickly over.[39]

Toward the end of the century, verses that think about eating became increasingly radical in their imaginings. In one piece, Chana Bloch fantasizes eating babies as if they were ice cream cones; in another, Mark Strand affirms that he has been eating poetry itself; and in another, Seamus Heaney prophesies the gastronomic transformation of a foodstuff—oysters—into language, which is after all, the mission of the culinary poem. "Eating Babies," as Bloch scandalously titles her poem, might seem cannibalistic, and there is indeed an edge of gloating witchiness in the text. At the same time, however, there is a lovingly (if perversely) maternal urge to reassimilate the creamy flesh she has nurtured with the milk of her own breasts. And besides, she is riffing on that old line, so scary to so many kids, "You're so cute I could just eat you up."

> *I bend down, taste the fluted*
> *nipples, the elbows, the pads*
> *of the feet. Nibble earlobes, dip*
> *my tongue in the salt fold*
> *of shoulder and throat.*
> *Even now he is changing,*
> *as if I were*
> *licking him thin.*

The adoration of the infant: who is not susceptible to it? What, after all, is the secret message of so many images of the sacred baby, Jesus, plumply throned on the Madonna's lap, triumphantly incarnate in cherubic chubbiness. "Fat / is the soul of this flesh," Bloch affirms, "Safety-fat, / angel-fat," as she proceeds to steal it into a poem, for safekeeping.[40]

But perhaps every poem itself is a form of "angel-fat," a metaphorically edible mutation of transcendent spirit. So Mark Strand implies in "Eating Poetry," as he confesses that "Ink runs from the corners of my mouth. / There is no happiness like mine. / I have been eating poetry." By the time he has finished his meal, he has terrified the librarian in charge of the verses he consumes, and is turning into a different creature, maybe half dog. Is eating poetry an animal action or an aesthetic performance? Perhaps both. Strand's poem suggests that poetry is as nourishing and delicious as flesh, yet it is also transformative, like an alchemical concoction. But where Circe's sorcery turned Odysseus's sailors into grunting swine, the delights of verse release new animal energies, as the diner barks and "romp[s] with joy in the bookish dark."[41]

Beyond animal joy, however, there is language itself, the primordial substance of poetry. Duffy's pigs grunt, Strand's speaker barks, but the speaker of Seamus Heaney's "Oysters" envisions the gift of active language as he recounts a meal with friends.

Our shells clacked on the plates.
My tongue was a filling estuary,
My palate hung with starlight:
As I tasted the salty Pleiades
Orion dipped his foot into the water.

We had driven to that coast
Through flowers and limestone
And there we were, toasting friendship,
Laying down a perfect memory
In the cool of thatch and crockery. . . .

. . . I ate the day
Deliberately, that its tang
Might quicken me all into verb, pure verb.

Though elsewhere in the poem Heaney admits that the oysters are not only "alive and violated" but also the "glut of privilege," he redeems what might be the venial sin of devouring them with a prayer that the "tang" of this day of communion with the fruits of the "philandering ocean" might transform him into poetry—"Might quicken me all into verb, pure verb"—or might at least issue in a poetry of action not just on the page but in the world.[42]

As we turn from the existential poetics of ice cream to a politics of prose and poetry that calls even more specifically for action in the world, we'll explore the range of ways in which writers—journalists, novelists, essayists and poets too—have begun to critique the disasters of the industrial food chain. To mount such assaults, however, all have to have had a sense of the ontological pleasures and perils of eating. Thiebaud's visions of culinary delight and Spoerri's decaying leftovers are equal reminders of what have come to be called "real foods" as compared to the "foodish" or "foodlike" products of the great manufacturers who fill the shelves of our supermarkets. And even unlikely poems about eating babies as if they were ice cream cones, poems about eating poems as if they were pastries, and poems about eating oysters that turn into poems constitute a ground of exuberance out of which, as we'll see, rise diatribes of protest.

Chapter 11

Food Chained: Food Fights, Fears, Frauds—and Fantasies

How can a nation be great if its bread tastes like Kleenex?

—JULIA CHILD

C'mon Pigs of Western Civilization Eat More Grease.
Eat Eat more marbled Sirloin more Pork 'n gravy!
Lard up the dressing, fry chicken in boiling oil

—ALLEN GINSBERG, "C'MON PIGS OF WESTERN CIVILIZATION EAT MORE GREASE"

The ideal industrial food consumer would be strapped to a table with a tube running from the factory directly into his or her stomach. Think of the savings, the efficiency, and the effortlessness of such an arrangement. Perhaps I exaggerate but not much. The industrial eater, is, in fact, one who does not know that eating is an industrial act, who no longer knows or imagines the connections between eating and the land, and who is therefore necessarily passive and uncritical—in short, a victim.

—WENDELL BERRY, "WHAT ARE PEOPLE FOR?"

Diets and Diatribes

I just took a quiz on the *New York Times* website that showed I'm eating a "strong Mediterranean diet": I got thirteen out of fourteen points by disclosing that olive oil is my primary cooking fat, that I eat fish three times a week, consume three portions of vegetables daily, drink wine every night, eat a lot of legumes and tomato sauce, and rarely consume "commercial pastries." I would have had a perfect score if I had declared that I ate fruit three times a day instead of two, and maybe I do eat fruit three times a day on some days, but I was being conservative. Perhaps I should go back and retake the test?

Yesterday the *Times* announced that the Mediterranean diet has been "shown to ward off heart attack and stroke."[1] I guess I should be especially pleased to learn this not only because, as half Sicilian and a quarter Niçoise by descent, I've always based my culinary life on olive oil, wine, and tomatoes, but also because I'm writing right now at the Bogliasco Foundation villa, a gorgeous study center actually on the shore of the Mediterranean where, needless to say, we eat an almost Platonic version of the Mediterranean diet. Fish maybe four times a week, modest amounts of wine at lunch *and* dinner, salads, vegetables, healthful pastas and risottos, and lots of *frutta*! The administrators of the place are three fit young women who heap their plates with such foods at meals and are clearly thriving. And yet already there are critiques of this latest "diet fad" popping up online. The *Times* article, for instance, quotes dissents from two proponents of low-fat diets, Dr. Caldwell Blakeman Esselstyn Jr., the vegan author of *Prevent and Reverse Heart Disease: The Revolutionary, Scientifically Proven, Nutrition-Based Cure*, and Dr. Dean Ornish, a gastronomic guru of Bill Clinton's, both of whom dismissed the study. Opined Dr. Esselstyn, all this project revealed was that "the Mediterranean diet and the horrible control diet [a more or less typical Western diet] were able to create disease in people who otherwise did not have it," this because although heart attacks and strokes were reduced by 30 percent they were not eliminated. His own regime, presumably, promotes eternal life.

Of course not. I realize I'm being unfair to Esselstyn and others because I am so personally bemused by what any halfway literate eater confronts: the frantic advocacy of an extraordinary range of diets through which people in America and Europe have tried to regulate their food intake in the last thirty years or so. At a minimum, these range from high-fat/low-carb (Atkins), to high-protein/low-carb (Dukan, South Beach) to low-fat/vegan or vegetarian

(Ornish, Esselstyn), to "real food, mostly plants" (Pollan) to plain old calorie counting (Weight Watchers, Jenny Craig) to radical fasting (CRON diet, Okinawa diet) and on and on. Nor is this proliferation of culinary advice a recent phenomenon. In the mid–century, there were Carlton Fredericks (low or no-sugar), and Gayelord Hauser (yogurt, skim milk, wheat germ, blackstrap molasses). A popular radio personality, Fredericks regularly inveighed against refined sugars and flours, as did Hauser, who was Greta Garbo's nutrition guru—and my husband's grandmother's. In their time, both were considered charlatans; you can still find them discussed online at quackwatch.org. Yet their diatribes against refined sugar, Wonder bread and other industrially processed foods were certainly prophetic. And Grandma Levitt thrived on Hauser's carrot, parsley, spinach and beet juice drinks.[2]

Just within the last century there have been quite a few other strange diets. How many readers remember the grapefruit diet, the hard-boiled egg diet, or the Metrecal pseudo-liquid diet? What am I leaving out? The first of these combined severe calorie restriction with a half grapefruit at every meal, on the assumption that grapefruit reduces insulin levels, facilitating fat loss. The second often segued into a more traditional low-fat diet or into an Atkins diet. The third, which I once undertook and remember with revulsion, involved drinking protein-enriched, unpleasant-tasting chocolate or vanilla shakes whose calories were carefully measured. (More recently, these diet drinks have been replaced by Slim Fast shakes, which are also supplemented by various 100-calorie salty snacks, on the assumption that the contemporary diner's appetite is almost entirely focused on sugar and salt—forget sour, bitter and, certainly, umami!)

Despite their fervor, these latest dining prescriptions aren't historically unprecedented. As Louise Foxcroft points out in her history of dieting, the ancient Greek physician Hippocrates advocated a regimen of "light and emollient foods, slow running, hard work, wrestling, sea-water enemas, walking about naked and vomiting at lunchtimes." But following the invention of printing, books about weight control and food health more generally became increasingly popular. The great Brillat-Savarin was himself a dieter, following a high-protein/low-carb diet (à la Atkins or Dukan): "a more or less strict abstinence from all farinaceous food will tend to diminish corpulence," he asserted, adding that without exercise a gourmand will "finally die in [his] own melted grease." At the same time, in the United States such vegetarian advocates of "farinaceous food" as Sylvester Graham and John Harvey Kellogg preached the virtues of whole-grain diets. Graham denounced the evils of white bread (shrewdly criticizing its chemical additives) and invented the graham cracker, which was consumed in great quantities by his disciples. He was also a crusader for temperance and against masturbation; like Kellogg, he believed that meat, milk, alcohol and other dietary indulgences promoted the evils of masturbation—which, the two agreed, could lead to insanity. ("Neither the plague, nor war, nor small-pox, nor similar diseases, have produced results so disastrous to humanity as the pernicious habit of onanism," declared one contemporary commentator on this subject.) Kellogg, a Seventh-day Adventist and one of the pioneers of industrial breakfast food who contributed cornflakes to our culture, also founded the influential Battle Creek Sanitorium, where patients were treated with daily enemas of water and yogurt; just as celebrities currently flock to "fat farms," major figures of the day were his patients—Sarah Bernhardt, William Howard Taft, Thomas Edison—with some journeying to Battle Creek for colon-cleansing and sunbaths.[3]

The most popular diet of the nineteenth century, though, was devised by William Banting, a London undertaker, whose *Letter on Corpulence, Addressed to the Public* (1863) influenced both Robert Atkins and the recent food journalist Gary Taubes. Himself suffering from obesity, Banting claimed that he undertook his diet at the suggestion of the physician William Harvey, and discovered that he could keep fit on four meals a day, consisting of "meat, greens, fruits, and dry wine." Like Atkins and Dukan—and, earlier, Fredericks and Hauser—he preached against sugar and starch, and also advocated eschewing beer, milk and butter. His regimen became so popular that his name turned into a verb: "Are you banting?" one citizen might ask another, or "I think I'm going to bant"—meaning to diet. Some decades later, Fletcherizing—a procedure also named for its proponent—was for a long time a practice of choice in the United States. Horace Fletcher, who became known as the Great Masticator, insisted that each mouthful should be chewed at least one hundred times in order for "a pitiable glutton" to become "an intelligent epicurean." Among those who experimented with his diet were John D. Rockefeller and Upton Sinclair. So charismatic was this dietary strategy that it became the subject of a popular ditty:

> *Eat somewhat less but eat it more*
> *Would you be hearty beyond fourscore.*
> *Eat not at all in worried mood*
> *Or suffer harm from best of food.*
> *Don't gobble your food but "Fletcherize"*
> *Each morsel you eat, if you'd be wise.*
> *Don't cause your blood pressure e'er to rise*
> *By prizing your menu by its size.*

A further motto—"Nature will castigate those who don't masticate"—may once again become popular. Not too long ago the *Scientific American* online blog reported the results of a Chinese study showing that "both healthy-weight and obese men consumed fewer calories (about 12 percent less) at an unlimited half-hour meal when they chewed their food more."[4]

By the early twentieth century, weight control had become an urgent cultural imperative. The food historian Katharina Vester, noting that nineteenth-century banting had mostly appealed to men, who associated virility with lean muscularity and femininity with voluptuous roundness, shows how dieting became a sign of health and modernity. The newly emerging genre of diet advice books, which now often addressed both men and women, fought over which sex had it worse.

> In *The Fun of Getting Thin* (1912), Samuel Blythe claimed: "A fat man is a joke; and a fat woman is two jokes—one on herself and the other on her husband." In contrast, Amelia Summerville argued in *Why Be Fat?* four years later: "It is hard to tolerate an overfat woman; it is absolutely impossible to look at an obese man without a feeling of disgust, because if he were living the life of a

> normal, healthy man, he would not be fat. Hence the lack of love and, I may add, respect, for the fat man."

The stout body that had once been a signifier of strength and prosperity had become an object of scorn, indeed contempt.[5]

The passions aroused by dieting—not just for weight loss but for good health—should remind us that the etymological roots of the word "diet" are more far-reaching than what we might understand as a simple set of menus. The noun derives from Old French *diete* (thirteenth century) signifying "diet, pittance, fare," and before that from medieval Latin *dieta*, "parliamentary assembly," also "a day's work, diet, daily food allowance," from Latin *diaeta*, "prescribed way of life," from Greek *diaita,* originally "way of life, regimen, dwelling," related to *diaitasthai*, "lead one's life," and from *diaitan*, originally "separate, select" (food and drink). Thus our diet—as our set of rules not just for eating but for acquiring food and preparing it—has significant moral overtones, some of which surely explain the heatedness of our debates. Gluttony has always been one of the seven deadly sins, and such practices as the consumption of spicy or fatty foods, the drinking of alcohol and coffee, and the indulgence in chocolate and other luxurious desserts have long been the subject of sermonizing. Vegetarianism, along with its more radical cousin, veganism also has a history that goes back to Plutarch, Horace and earlier. But following the industrialization of food production and the rise of ecological sensitivity, the contemporary Western diet—and its relationship to a problematic food supply and a perhaps contaminated water supply—has become the object of anxious, even obsessive attention. Once upon a time (or so we believe) we knew something about where our vegetables and fruits came from, maybe even the farms where they grew, and we watched closely as the local butcher sliced, chopped or ground the meat we were going to dine on. Once upon a time (or so we believe) we drank pure water from our own springs and wells. But now, with anonymously packaged, distantly manufactured foods chained to supermarkets—and indeed to nationwide chains of supermarkets—we know little or nothing about the origins of what we put in our mouths. No wonder millions feel suspicion, aversion and rage.

Suspicion: who hasn't feared E. coli (in popular foods from hamburger to bagged spinach), salmonella (available in your soft-boiled eggs or at your local diner), mad cow disease (beef, veal, where, what, when, remember?), the evocatively named "pink slime" (yucky odds and ends of beef treated with ammonia), trichinosis (now no longer a worry with domesticated pigs in the West but an anxiety that haunted my mother in my childhood, meaning that pork chops seemed to have been made of cardboard), hormones and antibiotics in meat and milk, various kinds of worms in fish (cod worms, spaghetti worms, round worms) and just recently horsemeat (little bits of it, even in our beloved Ikea meatballs, and sometimes it comes *tout ensemble* with a scary equine painkiller called phenylbutazone)? And think, too, how as children we feared tapeworms and ringworms and all those other parasites! Consider what might enter your stomach. If you can possibly help it, do NOT open your mouth to admit any poisons!

Aversion: no wonder, considering what food might contain, that we are so often repelled by its moisture, even indeed its sliminess, its sourness, its bitterness, its ersatz sweetness, its odd saltiness. What poisons do these tastes mask? And consider the taboo foods we might unwittingly consume—not just horsemeat but, from a Western perspective, cat, rat, dog, snake, and—shudder—bugs! Of course, one can try to make the best of it. Remember the old limerick:

> *There was a young man from Peru*
> *Who found a small mouse in his stew—*
> *Said the waiter,* Don't shout
> And wave it about,
> Or the rest might be wanting one too!

As for the industrial ingredients that flavor, thicken, preserve and otherwise quite literally constitute so many of the processed foods we consume, "barely a day goes by," writes columnist Mark Bittman, " that someone doesn't say to me, 'There's nothing I can safely eat.' Many of us are afraid of our food and of the way it's produced, and to some extent that fear is justified."[6] Our anxiety about such dangers has led to the founding of whole food movements (indeed, of the Whole Foods chain of supermarkets) and to countless exposés in various genres. Just a short list of the most noted of these would include Frances Moore Lappé's *Diet for a Small Planet* (1971), Peter Singer's *Animal Liberation* (1975), Ruth Ozeki's *My Year of Meats* (1998), J. M. Coetzee's *The Lives of Animals* (1999), Eric Schlosser's *Fast Food Nation: The Dark Side of the All-American Meal* (2001), Marion Nestle's *Food Politics: How the Food Industry Influences Nutrition and Health* (2002) and *What to Eat: An Aisle by Aisle Guide to Savvy Food Choices and Good Eating* (2006), Michael Pollan's *The Omnivore's Dilemma: A Natural History of Four Meals* (2006) followed by his *In Defense of Food: An Eater's Manifesto* (2008), Jonathan Safran Foer's *Eating Animals* (2009), Michael Moss's *Salt Sugar Fat: How the Food Giants Hooked Us* (2013) and Melanie Warner's *Pandora's Lunchbox: How Processed Food Took Over the American Meal* (2013)—not to mention such widely distributed films as Morgan Spurlock's *Super Size Me* (2004) and Robert Kenner's *Food, Inc.* (2009).

Rage: in one way or another, all these works articulate or elicit rage as they reveal the dangerous particulars of the American industrial food chain: the corn-fed antibiotic-dosed cattle who once roamed free but are now imprisoned in filthy feedlots, surrounded by "lagoons" of manure; the corn that has "colonized" vast portions of the Midwest and infiltrated much of our food supply in unlikely forms, especially that of the high-fructose corn syrup that sweetens all our soft drinks; the heavy doses of salt, sugar and fat that huge corporations deploy in luring Americans to buy more processed foods (breakfast cereals, chips, Lunchables, fraudulent yogurts and cheeses, and of course Twinkie-like goodies with all they stand for); and the bizarre range of chemicals out of which "nutrition scientists" devise ever more elaborately faked dishes. About these last, Melanie Warner makes a sweeping statement that may well summarize one major set of anxieties that torment thoughtful diners:

> The avalanche of prefabbed, precooked, often portable food into every corner of American society represents the most dramatic

> nutritional shift in human history. If we really are what we eat, then Americans are a different dietary species from what we were at the turn of the twentieth century. As a population, we ingest double the amount of added fats, half the fiber, 60 percent more added sugars, three and a half times more sodium, and infinitely greater quantities of corn and soybean ingredients than we did in 1909.[7]

Nor can we necessarily escape the chemical chains in which American food has been imprisoned by making alternative choices at the local market. As Pollan shows in *The Omnivore's Dilemma,* what was once high-minded back-to-the-land organic has become "industrial organic," with pesticide-free fields bordering on pesticide-laden fields, and once independent organic farms are now subsidiaries of huge agribusiness corporations.

Even the foods at the fabled Whole Foods chain aren't always whole or pure of "scientific" meddling. Warner notes that "Whole Foods co-founder John Mackey once acknowledged that some of what his stores sell is a 'bunch of junk.'" And as for the usual fast food sources, she offers a breakdown of a purportedly fresh Subway sweet onion chicken teriyaki sandwich, observing that of the "105 ingredients, 55 are dry, dusty substances that were added to the sandwich for a whole variety of reasons." Cumulatively her list sounds like something from mid-century science fiction:

> The chicken contains thirteen: potassium chloride, maltodextrin, autolyzed yeast extract, gum Arabic, salt, disodium inosinate, disodium guanylate, fructose, dextrose, thiamine, hydrochloride, soy protein concentrate, modified potato starch. The teriyaki glaze has twelve: sodium benzoate, modified food starch, salt, sugar, acetic acid, maltodextrin, corn starch, spice, wheat, natural flavoring, garlic powder, yeast extract. In the fat-free sweet onion sauce, you get another eight: sugar, corn starch, modified food starch, spices, salt, sodium benzoate, potassium sorbate and calcium disodium EDTA. And finally the Italian white bread has twenty-two:

> wheat flour, niacin, iron, thiamine mononitrate, riboflavin, folic acid, sugar, yeast, wheat gluten, calcium carbonate, vitamin D2, salt, ammonium sulfate, calcium sulfate, ascorbic acid, azodicarbonamide, potassium iodate, amylase, wheat protein isolate, sodium stearoyl lactylate, yeast extract and natural flavor.[8]

Is such a concoction, too, a product of the culinary imagination? It doesn't sound any more unlikely than one of Daniel Spoerri's or Dieter Roth's Eat Art projects. And consider: almost anyone could make the same thing at home with a slice of roast chicken, a slice of onion, fresh baked bread and a dash of traditional soy sauce.

But the anxiety and anger that the industrial food chain elicits in so many commentators doesn't just focus on chemical fakery and its discontents—its consequences for our health, its annihilation of the historical pleasures of dining. Starting in the 1970s, with Lappé's *Diet for a Small Planet* (which went through several editions and was followed by a number of sequels) and gaining in urgency with the entry of such nutritionists and journalists as Nestle, Schlosser and Pollan into the fray, political critiques of our food system turned to the horrors of industrial meat production. Vegetarians and animal rights advocates had long decried the cruelty of killing animals for dinner-table pleasures. Wrote Plutarch in the second century, "You ask me why I refuse to eat flesh. I, for my part, am astonished that you can put in your mouth the corpse of a dead animal, astonished that you do not find it nasty to chew hacked flesh and swallow the juices of death-wounds." And in 1999, the vegetarian novelist J. M. Coetzee created the character of Elizabeth Costello, herself a novelist, who quotes Plutarch in a lecture at "Appleton University" and scandalously declares to a mostly meat-eating audience that living as we do by and among industrial abattoirs, "we are surrounded by an enterprise of degradation, cruelty, and killing which rivals anything that the Third Reich was capable of, indeed dwarfs it, in that ours is an enterprise without end, self-regenerating, bringing rabbits, rats, poultry, livestock ceaselessly into the world for the purpose of killing them."[9]

Coetzee, who first delivered his quasi-fictional *The Lives of Animals* at

Princeton, where the noted animal liberationist Peter Singer had just been appointed to an honorific chair, may have been outlining an extraordinarily radical notion in comparing modern industrial slaughtering to the Holocaust. But when he published this book, a number of contemporary writers had also begun to investigate the dystopias of the slaughterhouse, the meat-packing plant, and the feedlot. A mounting sense of dread at the thought of the perilous substances we might be ingesting was accompanied by an increasing dismay at what we might be doing to our fellow creatures and to the earth itself. "The consequences of a grain-fed meat diet may be as severe as those of a nation of Cadillac drivers," proclaimed Lappé, picking up on American worries about gas-guzzling automobiles. She cited a "detailed 1978 study sponsored by the Departments of Interior and Commerce showing that *the value of raw materials consumed to produce food from livestock is greater than the value of all oil, gas and coal consumed in this country*," and wondered, "How can this be?"[10] And from Schlosser to Pollan and Foer, the polemicists who followed her shared her view that terrestrial resources were being exhausted by the food-factory system, but went further in their diatribes against the death-dealings of what had become a meat machine.

Dystopias

If today's dietary sermons have their origins in the polemics of such nineteenth-century gurus as Banting and Kellogg, our assaults against the application of factory techniques to the preparation of meat—beef, veal, pork, chicken—for the family table can be traced back to Upton Sinclair's ferocious novel *The Jungle* (1906). A classic of "muck-raking," this work also brilliantly characterizes the culture of a huge Chicago meat-packing plant as virtually a culinary dystopia, providing a paradigm of the grisly details and infernal settings that will appear in every succeeding work of this sort. Argues Elizabeth Costello in Coetzee's *The Lives of Animals*, "We need factories of death; we need factory animals. *Chicago showed us the way; it was from the Chicago stockyards that the Nazis learned how to process bodies*" (emphasis added).[11] Here, early in *The Jungle,* the narrative follows a group of astounded observers as they tour a Chicago meat-packing plant:

> Then the party went across the street to [where] every hour they turned four or five hundred cattle into meat. Unlike the place they had left [a hog-slaughtering plant], all this work was done on one floor; and instead of there being one line of carcasses which moved to the workmen, there were fifteen or twenty lines, and the men moved from one to another of these. . . . Along one side of the room ran a narrow gallery, a few feet from the floor [into which] the cattle were driven by men with goads which gave them electric shocks. Once crowded in here, the creatures were prisoned, each in a separate pen, by gates that shut, [and] over the top of the pen there leaned one of the "knockers," armed with a sledge hammer, and watching for a chance to deal a blow. The room echoed with the thuds in quick succession, and the stamping and kicking of the steers. The instant the animal had fallen, the "knocker" passed on to another; while a second man raised a lever, and the side of the pen was raised, and the animal, still kicking and struggling, slid out to the "killing bed." Here a man put shackles about one leg, and pressed another lever, and the body was jerked up into the air. There were fifteen or twenty such pens, and it was a matter of only a couple of minutes to knock fifteen or twenty cattle and roll them out. Then once more the gates were opened, and another lot rushed in and so out of each pen there rolled a steady stream of carcasses, which the men upon the killing beds had to get out of the way. The manner in which they did this was something to be seen and never forgotten. They worked with furious intensity, literally upon the run—at a pace with which there is nothing to be compared except a football game.[12]

The dispassionate tone of the narrative here is impressive in its ostensible acceptance of the necessities of the business being described, and notable too for a kind of naive wonder at a scene that "was something to be seen and never forgotten," marked by the "furious intensity" of a football game. And Sinclair continues in the same understatedly bloody vein, noting coolly that "it was all highly specialized labor," with first, the " 'butcher,' to bleed" the carcass with "the flash of [a] knife," leaving the floor "half an inch deep with blood, in spite of the best efforts of men who kept shoveling it through holes," and then "the 'headsman,' whose task it was to sever the head with two or three swift strokes," then other workers to cut and rip the skin, to gut the carcass, to scald it with "jets of boiling water," to remove the feet and transport "the finished beef" to the "chilling room." At last, in a finale to the little drama,

> the visitors were taken to the other parts of the building, to see what became of each particle of the waste material that had vanished through the floor; and to the pickling rooms, and the salting rooms, the canning rooms, and the packing rooms, where choice meat was prepared for shipping in refrigerator cars, destined to be eaten in all the four corners of civilization.[13]

Sinclair's understatement here, magnified by the nonjudgmental perspective of the innocent immigrant "visitors" (who are mostly longing for jobs in the meat-packing plant), achieves a masterful irony that almost evokes the enduring irony of Jonathan Swift's "Modest Proposal"—although (with the possible exception of a few animal rights activists) we would almost all agree that eating babies is a lot worse than killing and butchering plunging, bellowing cattle. But the dismal fate of cows, calves and steers, as well as hogs and chickens, becomes increasingly central in the work of writers following in the path Sinclair pioneered, as does the dreadful destiny of those who do the killing and those who clean up after the killers.

"Cattle Metropolis" is Michael Pollan's sardonic label for the nightmarish feedlot he visits, a "city" of 36,000 cattle being fattened for slaughter: so grim a dystopia that it might indeed seem to support Elizabeth Costello's comparison to a Nazi concentration camp. Known euphemistically as a CAFO (concentrated animal feeding operation), this particular patch of urban blight seems to be located, ironically enough, near Garden City, Kansas—and it is anything but blooming. Testifies Pollan:

> You'll be speeding down one of Finney County's ramrod roads when the empty, dun-colored January prairie suddenly turns black and geometric, an urban grid of steel-fenced rectangles as far as the eye can see—which in Kansas is really far . . . And then it's upon you: Poky Feeders, population, thirty-seven thousand. A sloping subdivision of cattle pens stretches to the horizon, each one home to a hundred or so animals standing dully or lying around in a grayish mud that, it eventually dawns on you, isn't mud at all. The pens line a network of unpaved roads that loop around vast waste lagoons on their way to the feedyard's thunderously beating heart and dominating landmark: a rhythmically chugging feed mill that rises, soaring and silvery in the early morning light, like an industrial cathedral in the midst of a teeming metropolis of meat.[14]

As the journalist goes on to note, the specialized stomachs, or rumens, of these cattle have evolved to digest a diet of grass, so the feed they're given—a mixture of flaked corn, dried fibers, animal fat (sometimes from their own species) and a sort of goopy protein substance—has to be treated with antibiotics to keep the hapless diners from getting ill on what they weren't meant to eat. They stand, feed and sleep on heaps of their own manure, and gaze out at great manure "lagoons" into which the shit is eventually siphoned off. Slowly, insidiously, the chemical runoff from the cornfields and the CAFO filters down to the Gulf of Mexico, where it creates a further natural disaster, an ever-growing mass of algae that swallows all other viable life in the water. "A feedlot is very much a premodern city," comments Pollan, "teeming and filthy and stinking, with open sewers, unpaved roads, and choking air rendered visible by dust." Because the "urbanization of the world's livestock" is a recent development, he adds, "it makes a certain sense that cow towns like Poky Feeders would recall human cities centuries ago, in the days before modern sanitation." At the same time, however, he observes that "if the modern CAFO is a city built upon commodity corn, it is a city afloat on an invisible sea of petroleum"—all the fuel necessary, as Frances Moore Lappé pointed out in the seventies, to process and transport the corn, the cows, the meat.

But though Pollan discusses the CAFO in compelling detail, he says little or nothing about how slaughterhouse procedures have evolved one hundred years after Sinclair wrote *The Jungle.* This is partly because while there were actual "visitors' galleries" in the old Chicago plants, at least according to Sinclair, it's now almost impossible to tour a slaughterhouse except through a kind of espionage, as an "undercover" worker. From the testimony of such witnesses, we get reports that issue in strikingly different views. On the one hand, the *New York Times* nature writer Verlyn Klinkenborg writes approvingly of the innovations put in place by the famed animal scientist Temple Grandin, cheerfully explaining that

> if you eat at fast-food restaurants—McDonald's, Wendy's, Kentucky Fried Chicken—you're eating meat that's been slaughtered in plants audited to Grandin's standards, meat from cattle and pigs that walked calmly to their fate through handling systems she designed. In the human scheme of things, those animals are economic units whose death is inevitable. By designing chutes and alleys that respect a cow's sensibilities—reducing its fear and uncertainty—Grandin has done more to improve animal welfare than almost any human alive. Increasing a cow's comfort as it nears death may seem like a futile subtlety to many humans. But fear is one of the critical differences between humane and inhumane slaughter. It also happens to be one of the differences between good meat and bad.[15]

On the other hand, in *Eating Animals* the vegetarian novelist Jonathan Safran Foer offers an account of "inhumane slaughter" that ratchets Sinclair's horrific particulars up a notch. For, declares Foer, "knocking" the cattle destined for butchery doesn't always succeed in rendering them unconscious, and then, he writes bitterly, "No jokes here, and no turning away. Let's say what we mean: animals are bled, skinned, and dismembered while conscious."[16]

As for the slaughterhouse workers themselves, Sinclair's portrayal of their situation in *The Jungle* is still apt, but many more recent writers have chimed in with new tales of misery. Eric Schlosser exposes the nightmares faced by those who clean the killing floor once the day's butchery is finished:

> When a sanitation crew arrives at a meatpacking plant, usually around midnight, it faces a mess of monumental proportions. Three to four thousand cattle, each weighing about a thousand pounds, have been slaughtered there that day. The place has to be clean by sunrise. Some of the workers wear water-resistant clothing; most don't. Their principal cleaning tool is a high-pressure hose that shoots a mixture of water and chlorine heated to about 180 degrees. As the water is sprayed, the plant fills with a thick, heavy fog. Visibility drops to as little as five feet. The conveyor belts and machinery are running. Workers stand on the belts, spraying them, riding them like moving sidewalks, as high as fifteen feet off the ground. Workers climb ladders with hoses and spray the catwalks. They get under tables and conveyor belts, climbing right into the bloody muck, cleaning out grease, fat, manure, leftover scraps of meat. Glasses and safety goggles fog up. The inside of the plant heats up; temperatures soon exceed 100 degrees. "It's hot, and it's foggy, and you can't see anything," a former sanitation worker said. The crew members can't see or hear each other when the machinery's running. They routinely spray each other with burning hot, chemical-laden water. They are sickened by the fumes [and] the stench . . . is so powerful that it won't wash off.[17]

And the meat itself, the object of all this furious effort in the feedlot and the slaughterhouse—is it worth the trouble and expense?

I've focused on writing about cattle rather than hogs or poultry, but most investigators of the food industry wouldn't give high marks to any of the industrial producers of these meats. The corn-fed beef that issues from today's feedlots, comments Pollan, "is demonstrably less healthy for us [than traditional grass-fed beef], since it contains more saturated fat and less omega-3 fatty acids. . . . A growing body of research suggests that many of the health problems associated with eating beef are really problems with corn-fed beef." Thus, if the metropolis of the feedlot is one dystopia and the slaughterhouse another, the supermarket meat counter (or do I mean the American kitchen) would seem to be yet a third. And still another dystopia, certainly, is the empire of fast-food eateries that has colonized the whole world. Morgan Spurlock dramatizes its dangers in *Super Size Me*, where he makes himself into a kind of lab rat, eating nothing but food from McDonald's for thirty days: his blood pressure and cholesterol shoot up, his liver gets fatty, he gains twenty-five pounds, doesn't have a sex life with his girlfriend, and is exhausted, moody, headachy. "You are sick," one of his doctors tells him.[18]

While journalists and documentarians have churned out dystopian visions of industrial eating at an ever-increasing rate, poets and novelists have hardly been silent. "C'mon Pigs of Western Civilization Eat More Grease" (1993), the rant by Allen Ginsberg from which I draw one of my epigraphs, savagely threatens "Agh! Watch out heart attack, pop more angina pills" while continuing with sardonic fury to urge crazed diners on: "Turkeys die only once, / look nice, next to tall white glasses / sugarmilk & icecream vanilla balls" so "Pass out in the vomitorium come back cough up strands of sandwich still chewing pastrami at Katz's delicatessen." "Diabetes & stroke," along with a host of other ills, he concludes (as does Spurlock's doctor), are "monuments to carnivorous civilizations." Nearly twenty years earlier, Ginsberg's old friend Gary Snyder had also, though rather more gently, chastised carnivores for their industrial practices in "Steak" (1972). Like Pollan and a number of other polemicists, Snyder is neither a vegan nor a vegetarian; his concerns are ethical and ecological. Thus in his poem he describes steak houses with stereotypical names (The Embers, Fireside) "up on the bluff," where a range of diners enjoy themselves: the chamber of commerce, "the visiting lecturer, / stockmen in Denver suits, / Japanese–American animal nutrition experts / from Kansas, / with Buddhist beads." In front of the restaurants, cheery representations lure more diners in, a "smiling disney cow" or a "huge / full-color photo of standing Hereford stud / above the very booth / his bloody sliced muscle is / served in:/rare"—but there is worse to come, for "down by the tracks / in frozen mud, in the feed lots, fed surplus grain/(the ripped-off land)/the beeves are standing round— / bred heavy." And they are "long-lashed, slowly thinking / with the rhythm of their / breathing," not unlike the doomed sufferers who would be described a few decades later by Coetzee's Elizabeth Costello.[19]

Of course, not all disturbing poems and stories about food focus on meat, although historically it has been the most controversial part of the food chain, for moral, political and medical reasons. Processed breakfast cereal, for instance, is a problematic, even bizarre innovation that goes back just to the late nineteenth century, and as early as 1906 the British writer Saki (H. H. Munro) penned the hilarious "Filboid Studge," a short story about an attempt to market a singularly unappetizing breakfast cereal originally called Pipenta. When its manufacturer complains that no one will "buy that beastly muck," an ambitious young marketer, who hopes to marry the man's daughter, gives the product the "resounding name of 'Filboid Studge'" and advertises it in a Dantesque poster that depicts "the Damned in Hell suffering a new torment from their inability to get at the Filboid Studge which elegant young fiends held in transparent bowls just beyond their reach. [A] single grim statement ran in bold letters along its base: 'They cannot buy it now.'" Instantly, the "beastly muck" appeals to a sense of duty that causes consumers to turn it into a best-selling health food. Indeed, notes the author, once women "discovered that it was thoroughly unpalatable, their zeal in forcing it on their households knew no bounds. 'You haven't eaten your Filboid Studge!' would be screamed at the appetiteless clerk [whose] evening meal would be prefaced by a warmed-up mess which would be explained as 'your Filboid Studge that you didn't eat this morning.'"[20]

More understated but equally sardonic and perhaps more political in its implications, Ruth Stone's short poem "American Milk" takes on the dairy industry. Here is the whole piece:

Then the butter we put on our white bread
was colored with butter yellow, a cancerous dye,
and all the fourth grades were taken by streetcar
to the Dunky Company to see milk processed; milk bottles
riding on narrow metal cogs through little doors that flapped.
The sour damp smell of milky-wet cement floors:
we looked through great glass windows at the milk.
Before we were herded back to the streetcar line,
we were each given a half pint of milk in tiny
milk bottles with straws to suck it up. In this way
we gradually learned about our country.[21]

Consider that not a cow is to be seen in this poem, where children, not cattle, are "herded" around, bread is white by default, butter is dangerously dyed yellow, bottles ride on conveyor belts and children are given straws "to suck it up"—not just milk but the nature of "our country." With sly wit, Stone condenses into just eleven lines what many journalists later used thousands of words to elaborate.

A broader irony suffuses Campbell McGrath's "Capitalist Poem #5" a little monologue spoken by an habitue of 7–Eleven, an impoverished dishwasher who describes in flat, straightforward tones the daily meals he is able to afford at that venue.

I was at the 7–11.
I ate a burrito.
I drank a Slurpee.
I was tired . . .
I did it every day for a week.
I did it every day for a month . . .
On the way out I bought a quart of beer for $1.39.

All that mars the hard-won understatement of this brief snapshot of culinary life at one of the "7–11's all across the nation" where countless citizens dine on similar microwaved burritos is the unnecessarily editorial conclusion: "I was aware of social injustice // in only the vaguest possible way." The poem, after all, makes the point quite clearly, and the dishwasher might just be too exhausted to muse on "social injustice": he embodies it.[22]

A thousand particulars of social injustice, and a good deal of editorializing about them, are central to Ruth Ozeki's lively, incisive and often hilarious novel *My Year of Meats*, a chronicle of a year in which Japanese–American documentary filmmaker Jane Takagi-Little takes a job making what are supposed to be promotional TV episodes for the massive conglomerate Beef-Ex. Destined for viewing by Japanese housewives in an effort to encourage them to cook more meat, each segment of *My American Wife!* features a different proud homemaker along with her recipes for (ideally) beef. And the series does start off with a bang, as a woman from the Midwest prepares a wonderfully parodic dish of "Coca-Cola beef": 2 kilograms rump roast, 1 can cream of mushroom soup, 1 package onion soup mix, and 1 liter of Coca-Cola (*not* Pepsi). Needless to say, things go wrong as the episode deteriorates into slapstick. The hostess runs out of Coke and is forced to substitute Pepsi (which must be carefully decanted into a Coke bottle); in a scripted Valentine's Day episode, her husband kisses her too fast so that he bangs his teeth against her upper lip; and in an unscripted scene at the end of the program, he laughingly reveals that he's been unfaithful to her, eliciting a *boinnggg* of horror.[23]

Still, despite all this absurdity, "Meat is the Message" of the show, as commanded by the TV production company and the advertising agency. "Each weekly half-hour episode of *My American Wife!* must culminate in the celebration of a featured meat, climaxing in its glorious consumption." But "of course, the 'Wife of the Week' is important too . . . She is the Meat Made Manifest: ample, robust, yet never tough or hard to digest. Through her, Japanese housewives will feel the . . . traditional family values symbolized by red meat in rural America." One such housewife is Akiko Ueno, the downtrodden, bulimic spouse of Joichi Ueno, the Japanese advertising executive in charge of the Beef-Ex account. Joichi, who demands to be called "John" (John Wayne-o?) because that sounds more modern, is an alcoholic bully who lectures, hectors, and beats his wife; her bulimia, alternating with anorexia, has made her temporarily infertile, as well as skeletal; and she is covered with bruises. But she dutifully cooks the meat dishes featured on *My American Wife!*, some of which are quite as amazing as Coca-Cola beef: beef fudge, for instance.[24]

Gradually, the spirited comedy of the novel dissolves into an ever more dystopian portrait of the meat industry and its various spokesmen. Jane, following her instincts for a good story, introduces some American wives who don't fit the cookie-cutter image Beef-Ex has called for. "John" Ueno is enraged when she features a lesbian couple who serve a meatless pasta primavera to their family. And he is equally infuriated when another show focuses on "Hallelujah lamb chops"—the favorite dish with which a pair of devoted parents celebrate the return to consciousness of their crippled little girl, who was devastatingly injured when a Walmart truck ran into her as she was bicycling home from school. "Australian lamb!" exclaims Ueno apoplectically, as he tries, yet again, to fire Jane. As the plot thickens and darkens, Akiko and Jane are drawn ever closer, doubling each other's pain. Jane, who's been involved in an intense romance, has gotten pregnant, though she thought she was infertile because her mother may have been given DES (diethylstilbestrol, an anti-abortifacient) when she—Jane—was in utero. Akiko, whose eating disorder mysteriously improved when she ate the Hallelujah lamb chops of which her husband disapproved, has begun to menstruate, but "John" Ueno doesn't know it. Discovering that she's been in touch with Jane by fax, he drunkenly beats and rapes her vaginally and rectally. Meanwhile, Jane determines to do a shoot at a feedlot in Colorado, a take on the destructive world of Beef-Ex that initiates a further drama of dread and disease.

In Colorado, Jane encounters an ag major who scrupulously initiates her into the bad news about meat production and its effect on global warming that journalists from Eric Schlosser to Michael Pollan would later popularize: "do you know that the average American family of four eats more than two hundred sixty pounds of meat in a year? That's two hundred sixty gallons of fuel [and] every McDonald's Quarter Pounder represents fifty-five square feet of South American rain forest destroyed forever, which of course affects global warming as well." As for the feedlot itself, it looks to her not quite like a city but like "an enormous patchwork comprising neatly squared and concentrated beef-to-be. . . . The only aspect of [the cattle's] animal nature that could not be contained by the gridwork was the stench [which] rose and spread like anarchy on the autumn wind. The closer we came the stronger it got."[25]

But the secret of *this* feedlot is not just the horror of killing animals and not just the devastated and stinking space in which they are imprisoned: it is the secret of their preparation. In a horrifying riff on the reports that have long circulated about feedlots, these cattle are fed grotesquely recycled foods: "byproducts from potato chips, breweries, liquor distilleries, sawdust, wood chips," Gale, the owner's son, tells Jane. "We even got byproducts from the slaughterhouse—recycling cattle right back into cattle. Instant protein"—and then, worse and worse, plastic, cement dust. And even their own manure. ("You gotta understand the way feedlots work. The formulated feed we use is real expensive, and the cattle shit out about two-thirds before they even digest it. Now, there's no reason this manure can't be recycled into perfectly good feed.") When Jane weakly protests about mad cow disease, Gale brushes her off with, "It's all done local." But further revelations are to come, for it turns out that the animals are being, quite illegally, treated with DES, which has had dire effects on Rosie, the owner's five-year-old daughter: she has developed breasts and pubic hair and has had a premature menarche. As for the managerial son, who injects his cattle with this growth hormone, he himself has developed breasts and a higher voice.[26]

The crisis of the book originates in food-borne diseases, several of them. In what is just barely a parody of real-life practices, Beef-Ex taints its products, its employees and of course its animals.[27] As the tale crashes to a close, Jane suffers a miscarriage in a dramatic confrontation in the slaughterhouse the family also runs, and Akiko flees Japan to seek a new home in the States. Ironically, her husband's rape has impregnated her, though it also caused a rectal hemorrhage that put her in the hospital for some time. Perhaps predictably, Akiko takes shelter with the vegetarian lesbian couple, while Jane's tapes of the feedlot, the slaughterhouse, and especially the prematurely voluptuous Rosie go viral. If meat is the message and the good wife is meat made manifest, both dinner and sexuality might be deadly, or at least diseased.

Disorders and Diseases

Diseased dinner, diseased sexuality? The bulimarexic Akiko Ueno is a particularly striking and prophetic figure in *My Year of Meats,* for she literally incarnates—and the pun is intended—what are not only central issues in the novel but also persisting, even exploding, problems for contemporary thinkers about food and its chains of significance. To begin with, of course, both the bulimic and the anorexic—90 percent of them young women—are representative "hunger artists" in modern developed societies, whose vexed eating practices (bingeing, purging, starving) have often been seen as either protests against cultural norms of feminine submissiveness, slenderness and fragility or excessive internalizations of such norms. Whether these problems originate in rebellion or in perfectionist acceptance of contemporary ideals, both are in a way celebrity disorders, a fact that gives them a certain glamour. Anorexia notoriously caused the 1983 death of the pop star Karen Carpenter, in whom extravagant crash dieting led to the cardiac disasters that kill so many sufferers from the illness. That Carpenter also purged using laxatives may, according to some sources, have prompted later revelations that bulimia, once called "the Princess Di disease," was the unhappy Diana's "shameful friend," assuaging (she said) the feelings of emptiness she suffered in her marriage to Charles, but clearly also associated with the enormous pressures on her to be the beauty queen she became. Countless other public figures (mostly women performers)—from Katie Couric and Jane Fonda to Sally Field, Diane Keaton and Lady Gaga—have confessed to comparable eating problems.[28] Their disclosures, indeed, have intensified the charisma of such disorders, prompting some dieters to comment, with or without irony, that "I wish *I* could have just a little bit of anorexia!" Surely, too, that charisma influences participants in so-called "Pro-Ana" (pro anorexia) and "Pro-Mia" (pro bulimia) websites like "Tumblr.Proana," where impassioned adolescents claim that "Pretty girls don't eat," wonder "Why the fuck do I eat at all," trade tips about diet or purging tricks, and post proud pictures of their own emaciation—or, indeed, of themselves vomiting into toilets.

For some years, much contemporary poetry and fiction about bulimarexia has focused on the engendering of the confused desires and dreads expressed online by these fasting girls. Works like Frank Bidart's superb dramatic monologue "Ellen West" (1975) almost uncannily predicted both the obsession with hunger and the conflicting obsession with thinness-as-perfection that postmodern sufferers from eating disorders regularly reiterate on their websites and blogs. Based on the psychoanalyst Ludwig Binswanger's 1944 history of a severely ill young woman who regularly purged with laxatives (sometimes sixty or seventy packages a night), Bidart's poem captures the cadences not just of Ellen West (a pseudonym employed by Binswanger) but also the cultural imperatives she simultaneously questions and introjects. Claims Ellen,

> *My true self*
> *is thin, all profile*
> *and effortless gestures, the sort of blond*
> *elegant girl whose*
>
> *body is the image of her soul.*

Yet at the same time she admits that "I love sweets,—heaven / would be dying on a bed of vanilla ice cream." Ambitious and literary, the historical woman who became the subject of so many analyses was torn between what she considered the spiritual and aesthetic beauty of the "thin, all profile" self and the fleshliness of the body that longed for sweets. When her physicians counseled that she "must give up / this ideal"—so Bidart has her say—she eventually poisoned herself, after remarking that her husband "married / meat, and thought it was a wife."[29]

The theme of woman as meat was later, as we've seen, elaborated in Ozeki's novel, with its injunction that the American wife must be meat made manifest. But Ellen West's story reflects the long history of the entanglement of feminine sexuality with food, appetite, eating and materiality or meatiness. Must a woman take in food so that she can *be* food for others—husband, children, lovers, even parents? If she renounces food, can she escape the voracious appetites of others, as well as her own desires? In an early essay, I argued that the enigma of anorexia may be precisely its parodic use of femininity to deny or subvert femaleness, and in a larger sense its strategic use of self-denial as an ironic form of self-assertion. In support of my claim, I tried to trace literary representations of anorexia to roots in the writings of nineteenth-century women from the Brontës to Christina Rossetti and Emily Dickinson. The connections between women and food are both deep and mythic, I noted, for besides being cooks—converters of nature into culture, of the raw into the cooked—women are themselves both foodlike and producers of food: milk, blood, womb-fruit. Presiding at the feast of life, everywoman both provides the goodies and is herself a delicacy on the great table: at her sweetest, a honey, a cookie, a muffin, a peach, but at her fleshiest a piece of meat. Is it possible, then, I wondered, that anorexia is metaphorically a mad form of cooking, a kind of lunatic *cuisine minceur* in which the patient/chef converts herself with special fervor from raw (flesh) to cooked (spirit)? If so, how can she eat the feast?[30]

Looking at the writings of women who were dramatizing or analyzing the gender dynamics of bourgeois Victorian society, I defined *Wuthering Heights,* where Heathcliff and the first Cathy both starve themselves to death, as a kind of bible of anorexia; studied the strangely eroticized representations of appetite in Christina Rossetti's "Goblin Market"; and mused on Emily Dickinson's "I had been hungry, all the Years," with its ultimate repudiation of culinary desire:

> *. . . I found*
> *That Hunger—was a way*
> *Of persons outside Windows—*
> *The Entering—takes away*[31]

Bidart's "Ellen West" is clearly rooted in this tradition of feminine, perhaps proto feminist, ambivalence about food, with its concomitant hunger pains. So, too, are more recent poems about this problem. Louise Glück's "Dedication to Hunger" analyzes the origins of what she calls "The Deviation" (from conventional eating):

It begins quietly
in certain female children:
the fear of death, taking as its form
dedication to hunger,
because a woman's body
is a grave; it will accept
anything.[32]

And Eavan Boland's "Anorexic" captures the disturbing self-definitions that underlie the practice of culinary renunciation, with her speaker proclaiming that "Flesh is heretic," and because "My body is a witch. I am burning it" by eschewing food in an effort to return to woman's origins, where she will be "thin as a rib."[33]

These poems, however, like my own early writing on the subject of eating disorders, basically investigate the issues raised by ideals of the feminine, with little or no exploration of the relationship between the gender imperatives that shape women's bodily fantasies and the consumer culture that increasingly informs those imperatives. But as many scholars of the subject have rightly noted, anorexia and bulimia are diseases afflicting advanced industrialized societies; how many sufferers from these illnesses could be found, after all, in impoverished African or South Asian communities?[34] Akiko's problems, therefore, are crucial in representing not only the gender strictures that govern her life as a supposedly dutiful Japanese wife but also because they reveal her place in a globalized community where Western—really, American—ways of preparing meat (Coca-Cola beef! beef fudge!) are being peddled to populations for whom such foods are so new as to be either repellent anomalies or ambiguous curiosities. As Ozeki represents her story, it isn't *any* food that prompts Akiko's purging; it is specifically American-style meat, and even more specifically beef. "After dinner, when the washing up was done, she would go to the bathroom, stand in front of the mirror, and stare at her reflection. Then . . . she'd start to feel the meat. It began in her stomach, like an animal alive, and would climb its way back up her gullet, until it burst from the back of her throat. She could not contain it." After vomiting it up, she regularly feels "a small flutter in her stomach, which she identified as success." Given what we eventually learn about the meat peddled by Beef-Ex, it's hard not to sympathize with Akiko. If cattle eat shit, then eating cattle is eating shit, and like e. e. cummings' famous "Olaf glad and big," the Japanese wife seems to be saying, "there is some shit I will not eat." Tellingly, she recovers from her illness after defying her beefy bully of a husband by preparing the Hallelujah lamb chops favored by the little American girl who was crippled by a Walmart truck. "Australian lamb!" he rages, but Akiko keeps the food down. And after her recovery, she begins preparing a cornucopia of traditional Japanese fish and vegetable dishes.[35]

"There is some shit I will not eat": this fierce assertion by cummings's Olaf, a dedicated conscientious objector, should remind us that the refusal of food has long been an important political strategy. As such a maneuver, the so-called hunger strike has roots in ancient Celtic and Indian practices. In both cultures, it was customary to fast as a way to protest injustice; the faster frequently placed himself outside the door of his adversary while undertaking a period of self-starvation. In more draconian circumstances, African captives would sometimes refuse food in the course of the infamous journey of the Middle Passage that carried them toward slavery. According to Jessica Harris's history of African-American food and foodways, this practice "occurred in numbers great enough to necessitate the invention by slavers of the speculum oris, a diabolical three-pronged screw device designed to force open the mouths of the stubborn so they could be force-fed with a funnel."[36] Much more recently, the hunger strike was deployed by early twentieth-century women battling for suffrage, by Mahatma Gandhi in his struggle for Indian independence, by Irish Republican revolutionaries, and—quite lately—by inmates of the US internment camp at Guantánamo Bay.[37]

In these cases authorities countered (and still counter) with tactics as brutal as the slavers' use of the speculum oris. When they deemed it necessary, they force-fed the protester, usually pouring a gruel-like substance through a nasal tube into the striker's stomach—a horrific and often dangerous procedure that regularly inspires further fasting. Arguably Akiko Ueno's bulimarexia is a kind of hunger strike analgous to desperate moves made by political prisoners and protesters: although her despotic husband doesn't actually force-feed her, he has metaphorically done so by commanding her to cram what she regards as oppressive American beef into her gullet. Her anorexia and her vomiting are thus ways of defying both the gender imperatives imposed on her (the American *wife* is "meat made manifest") and the culinary imperialism implicit in the very concept of *American* beef.

That both bulimia and anorexia are very much about control of the materiality of consumption in an increasingly materialistic culture of consumables becomes quite clear in one of the most popular recent eating disorder memoirs—a literary genre that has proliferated along with the diseases it records. Marya Hornbacher's *Wasted* envisions "Thinness" as a mode of transcendence. As the author admits, "It is more than Thinness, per se, that you crave. It is the implication of Thin. The tacit threat of Thin. The Houdini-esque-ness of Thin, walking on hot coals without a flinch, sleeping on a bed of nails. You wish to carry Thinness on your arm, with her cool smile. " Recalling a crucial summer when she worked at "McD's," she outlines the extremity of a behavior to which she was driven by her desire for Thinness and her fear of being considered "cute":

> That summer, I had decided that "cute" was the last thing I wanted to be. At my lunch break, I would eat a quarter-pounder with cheese, large fries, and a cherry pie. Then I would throw up in the antiseptic-scented bathroom, wash my face, and go back on the floor, glassy-eyed and hyper. After work, I would buy a quarter-pounder with cheese, large fries, and a cherry pie, eat it on the way home from work, throw up at home with the bathtub running, eat dinner, throw up, go out with friends, eat, throw up, go home, pass out. My parents watched me transform that summer, the constant purging thinning me quickly.[38]

That this almost orgiastic frenzy of bulimia—later to be followed by what Hornbacher considers the "purer" disorder of anorexia—is set like a little psychodrama on the now nearly universal stage of McDonald's is hardly irrelevant. Remember *Super Size Me*? Perhaps the inevitable counterpart of that imperative is *Undersize Me!* Over and over again, "Pro-Ana" sites carry conflicted messages from teenage girls about junk food. They are drawn to the Golden Arches, toward ubiquitous mounds of fries and almost meltingly erotic double cheeseburgers, neatly decorated with pickle slices and festively wrapped in golden paper. How to resist? Yet even while they're beckoned toward the fantasy of endlessly available and strangely inexpensive pleasure, they are taught to resist, to be thin, to be—at their most "successful"—fashion-model skeletal size zeros.

Even the acclaimed gender theorist Susan Bordo, whose *Unbearable Weight* has become a touchstone work for those interested in studies of eating disorders and "body sculpting," seems curiously oblivious to the connection between a globalized food chain and bulimarexia. In her preface to the second edition of her book, she reports taking her four-year-old daughter to a McDonald's for a Happy Meal, where she was disappointed that the little girl received a miniature Barbie instead of a tiny truck as the prize that comes with the burger, fries and shake. That there might be some weirdly dissonant relationship between the Barbie, the Happy Meal and the very subject she studies doesn't seem to occur to her. But it is precisely the Barbie *in* the Happy Meal that triggers so many troubles. For the Happy Meal itself turns out to be almost as gravely disordered as the fasting girls who gorge themselves on it and then so passionately purge. Is the tale of the year-old McDonald's Happy Meal an urban legend? In 2010, newspapers on both sides of the Atlantic carried a story whose headline in the UK *Daily Mail* read:

> Fast food, frighteningly slow decay: Mother keeps McDonald's Happy Meal for a whole year . . . and it STILL hasn't gone off

and then went on to relate an anecdote about a Colorado housewife nutritionist who decided to keep a Happy Meal (burger, bun, pickle, fries, shake) on a counter in her kitchen for twelve months. Online photos show that nothing disintegrated. "Flies won't go near it," said Mrs. Bruso. The patty curled up a bit at the edges and the bun cracked, but that was that. McDonald's denied the story, of course, but commentators attributed the miracle of the meal to chemical preservatives.[39]

Postmodern Pastorals

Are there happier alternatives to these unhappy industrial meals? Dreams of what Charles Reich long ago called "the greening of America" abound (although Reich's "green" was more likely marijuana than kale). For instance, in one of the *New York Times Magazine*'s food and wine issues, Mark Bittman explored a range of "McVegan" franchises in and around Los Angeles as he sought healthful but speedy culinary possibilities for fastidious travelers. One of the first places he tested was a chain called the Veggie Grill, where he tried a number of meatless substitutes for such all-American favorites as burgers, chicken nuggets, carne asada and crab cakes. But his description of these dishes was disheartening, as a number of readers commented:

> The "chickin" in the "Santa Fe Crispy Chickin" sandwich is Gardein, a soy-based product that has become the default for fast-food operators looking for meat substitutes. Although there are better products in the pipeline, Gardein, especially when fried, tastes more or less like a McNugget (which isn't entirely "real" chicken itself). The "cheese" is Daiya, which is tapioca-based and similar in taste to a pasteurized processed American cheese. The "steak," "carne asada," "crab cake" (my favorite) and "burger" are also soy, in combination with wheat and pea protein.[40]

Not very appetizing, right? In fact, these sad recipes make me nostalgic for the bad old days of the 1950s, when a vegetarian boyfriend used to take me out for nutburgers that were probably a whole lot tastier and more healthful than these dishes, especially given the problematic consequences of eating too much soy, which can dangerously mimic estrogen. To be sure, as Bittman notes, "In terms of animal welfare, environmental damage and resource usage, these products are huge steps in the right direction. They save animals, water, energy and land." But equally ersatz "gardenburgers"—long available in your local supermarket's freezer case—do the same for animal welfare. Inevitably, therefore, Bittman himself laments the absence of real whole foods in such products and includes in a sidebar his own "McBitty's" recipes for black bean burgers, sweet potato fries and Mexican chocolate shakes.[41]

"Whole foods!" What would that phrase have meant to my parents or my grandparents? And what about "slow food"? (Would they, in fact, have recognized the phrase "fast foods"?) That in the industrialized world we have come to inhabit a culinary landscape marked by the dichotomy between "whole" ("slow," "real") food and technologically produced "fast" food has given rise to a literary genre—half polemic, half memoir—that might be called postmodern pastoral. "Victory gardens," of course, date back to the Second World War, while community gardens became popular with the rise of the counterculture analyzed by Reich and Theodore Roszak. But more prominent proponents of postmodern pastoral, with its utopian visions of healthy farms and bucolic landscapes, include writers from Wendell Berry, Alice Waters, Carlo Petrini and Michael Pollan to Barbara Kingsolver, Novella Carpenter and a host of other culinary gurus. Berry, a poet, novelist and farmer, has had a deep influence on most of these other thinkers through such volumes as *The Unsettling of America* and *The Unforeseen Wilderness.* Alice Waters followed the establishment of Chez Panisse, the restaurant that virtually pioneered locally sourced foods, with a series of best-selling cookbooks, autobiographical essays, and most recently the Edible Schoolyard Project, which seeks to provide garden-grown foods to children around the country while introducing them to a cuisine that might wean them away from McDonald's. Carlo Petrini founded the Slow Food movement, which now has chapters all over the world. Michael Pollan has clearly lived his research for such volumes as *The Omnivore's Dilemma, Food Rules*, and most recently *Cooked.* Barbara Kingsolver wrote *Animal, Vegetable, Miracle* to record a year she and her family spent subsisting almost entirely on the foods they grew or raised on their farm in the North Carolina hills. Novella Carpenter's *Farm City* tells the more paradoxical story of her experience raising vegetables, chickens and pigs in the heart of downtown Oakland, California.

As practitioners of postmodern pastoral, all these figures counsel back-to-the-land (even city land) projects and back-to-the-kitchen practices that might help save us from our overfed, hyper-sugared, excessively fatted selves and the dystopic ingredients that turned us into such creatures. In his popular *In Defense of Food*, Michael Pollan tersely defines the central axioms that animate the writings of all these thinkers: "Eat food. Not too much. Mostly plants," and then (importantly) elaborates: "Don't eat anything your great-grandmother wouldn't recognize as food." For after all, as Wendell Berry has proclaimed, eating isn't just an "industrial act" (as he notes in one of my epigraphs for this chapter) but also an "agricultural act." Thus a return to the farm, the farmer's market and the roadside fruit stand is a key dream of postmodern writers who resist the dystopia shaped by the scientists who gave us processed foods and their worldwide distribution by McDonald's and its cohorts.[42]

Pollan's declaration is, to be sure, shaped for and by the middle class. What would *my* great-grandmothers have "recognize[d] as food"? At least one lived on a farm outside Nice, where I think both Pollan and Alice Waters would have found her Mediterranean/Provençal menus compelling. Yet even her family ate frugally, as I know from the foods my grandparents served on *non*-festive occasions. And so did my other forebears, I'm sure—the Russians, the Sicilians, the Eastern European ancestors on my husband's side. As Rachel Laudan points out in her magisterial *Cuisine and Empire: Cooking in World History*, for millennia—indeed, well into the nineteenth century—most of the world's people subsisted on what she calls "humble" cuisine, a monotonous and often dangerous diet of grains, maize or potatoes rarely, if ever, supplemented by the nourishing meats, nuts, greens and fruits that (if they were peasants) they may have supplied to the tables of the wealthy. She notes that modern "Western cuisine [is] thought to be unhealthy and unsafe, processed and marketed" by greedy corporations. But the "agrarian-romantic story about culinary history [that extolls] the fresh, natural, and healthful bounty of the earth, lovingly prepared by peasant women" is "of course, a myth, just like older stories of cooking being taught by the gods, or forced on humans on leaving the Garden of Eden." Thus though the multinational corporations we have come to call "Big Food," in parallel with "Big Pharma," are hardly heroic, she argues that if "our vision of the way to have better food is to have less processing, more natural food, more home cooking, and more local food, we will cut ourselves off from the most likely hope for better food in the future."[43]

Her view is surely controversial, and I quail even to repeat it here, given the power of the postmodern pastorals outlined by so many activists in the whole foods and slow food movements, nor do I wish to repudiate the extraordinarily important transformations that these movements have wrought in the ways we eat and, equally important, think and write about eating. But yes, I would have to respond to Michael Pollan's stricture about the foods available to my great-grandmothers and grandmothers, that I can't sentimentalize the food of poverty or near poverty. My Russian grandmother, whom I knew well, grew up on *kasha* and I don't know what else. She was glad to recognize frozen *petits pois* as food when they appeared in supermarkets. She was prudent with leftovers, once even (according to my mother) adding a bit of last night's salad to the soup! As for the soup, I'm sure it must often have been what I came to call, when spending ten days or so with a broken-down icebox in Paris, "refrigerator soup"—everything one can salvage that won't go bad, tossed into a pot and seasoned *however.* Not bad at all, in my opinion—perhaps the ancestor of pot au feu—but nothing much like the recipes you'll find in today's pastoral utopias. And my Sicilian grandmother? She once camped out in the ruined *sala* of a palazzo in the little town of Sambuca–Zabut where she lived with her seven children. Although I've been told that chickens wandered in and out of the formerly golden space (it had originally been a gilded ballroom!) it's hard to believe that I would want to replicate the scanty diet Nonna Petronella was able to offer her five little sons and two daughters, although recipes for "regional food" from the impoverished culture she fled have also taken their place in the foodoirs and cookbooks that memorialize her hardscrabble native Sicily, metamorphosing it too into one among a number of pastoral utopias.

For utopias they are. Consider Michael Pollan's memoir of hunting and foraging (the last section of *The Omnivore's Dilemma*), or Barbara Kingsolver's wonderful tale of sustainable living on an Appalachian farm. Let's say you dwell in an urban ghetto: where are you going to get the down payment on the farm? Or, for that matter, access to the woods where you can hunt, fish and forage? Strong, young and hip, Novella Carpenter found a way to raise a pig in the concrete heart of the city, but how many of her neighbors could have followed suit? I remember that when I used to ask my Sicilian-born mother, a New York City schoolteacher, what she dreamed of most in the world, she said—jokingly—"a farm!" Growing up in Queens, I hadn't a clue what a row of corn would look like, nor a field of wheat, nor (even) a lettuce patch. But as I was later to learn, my mother was being deeply ironic. When she returned to her native village in Sicily, not far from Agrigento, she was shocked to find herself living in a cousin's house where the ground floor was even in the 1960s occupied by pigs, chickens and goats; the family slept upstairs, inhaling their aromas. My mother never really meant that she wanted a farm, and now she was repelled by agricultural odors! No wonder she preferred to live in a shadowy apartment in Jackson Heights, Queens, where we rarely ate the food of her homeland, dining instead on pseudo-American delicacies like lamb chops and instant mashed potatoes.

Nonetheless, the fantasy of self-sufficiency dates back almost to forever, as does the celebratory pastoral mode. The seventeenth-century poet Andrew Marvell praised the delicious quiet of "The Garden," where "Ripe apples drop about my head / The luscious clusters of the vine / Upon my mouth do crush their wine" and fruitful peace annihilates "all that's made / To a green thought in a green shade." And after those curiously sham meals of my childhood, I'd often snuggle up in my little white bed and read "desert island" books, the paradigms of which were probably *Robinson Crusoe* and (my personal favorite) *The Swiss Family Robinson.* What luck, I must have secretly thought, to be stranded on a desert island where, like the Swiss family, you can end up with several plantations, a first home *and* a second home. Or, like Crusoe, with a willing manservant! And now memoirs of such dream settlements abound, influenced perhaps not just by various desert island tales but also by, say, Laura Ingalls Wilder's *Farmer Boy* and other works in the *Little House on the Prairie* series, where children confront the pleasures and pains of a difficult countryside and are rewarded with plump steaming apple turnovers.[44]

O pioneers! Take a look at *Slow Food Nation's Come to the Table: The Slow*

Food Way of Eating, which profiles a slew of beautiful California organic farms. On every fifth or sixth page, we see a photo of a family feasting in the fields, raising glasses, dining on home-grown delicacies. I want to visit them all, to eat their peaches, strawberries, potatoes, asparagus. But how many urban Americans will be able to purchase that produce, even with the burgeoning of the organic food movement? Now Safeway offers "O Organic," factory-farmed, presumably pesticide-free fruits and vegetables. Most of these veggies don't come from Full Belly Farm and the other sacrosanct acres from which Waters sources the menus for Chez Panisse. And what if, on another continent, you do grow your own stuff in a Third World garden?

The fantasy of self-sufficiency! My oldest grandchild is living that out right now as a Peace Corps agro-forestry volunteer in a West African village. He gardens, keeps bees, bicycles eight kilometers to a nearby town for staples. He tells me he has a friend in that town who has electricity, running water and an oven; he himself has none of these amenities. "Don't you want to take a shower when you visit him?" I asked. "No," he said, "I'd just have to bicycle home again—and I'm used to bucket showers." But he did bake cookies with his friend, and though he's used to all kinds of local foods, he welcomes boxes of junk food that we send from the States. But, he says, his "standards have changed." He used to fantasize about what he might get here in California. Now his dreams are what he might find to eat in Conakry, the capital of Guinea, the country where he lives. The self-sufficient village food is scanty—mostly rice with peanut sauce and "mashed-up bits of fish" as well as lots of mangoes when they're in season—so maybe that's why he has those dreams—dreams very different from the ones Barbara Kingsolver and Alice Waters outline. If we gave his village more money, better seeds, would things be different?

Not long ago, my three other grandchildren and I strolled through the Edible Schoolyard—the original one!—that Alice Waters and her associates planned and planted at a nearby Berkeley junior high school as part of their ambitious nationwide project. The leaves of the olive trees rustled in the breeze. Birds sang among the burgeoning broccoli. Two large globe artichokes, as shiny with newness as if someone had polished them, dangled from hairy stalks. It was almost May. Everything was thrusting upward, alive with vegetable ambition. "A green thought in a green shade," said Andrew Marvell so long ago. The culinary imagination goes back that far, and farther still, to Virgil's *Georgics* and to the Garden of Eden, with its eternal fruits. It isn't clear that either Slow Food Nation or the Edible Schoolyard project can realize those dreams. But at least here and there, in the vast concrete expanses of our century's shopping malls, where the only local vegetables used to be decorative cabbages in ornamental planters, some farmers' markets set up shop among the industrial chains—McDonald's, Burger King, Safeway, Walmart—helping us to reimagine and sustain our culinary hopes. Here's to the green thought, *salute* to the green shade!

Notes

Epigraphs: Ernest Hemingway, "Gastronomic Adventures," *Toronto Star Weekly* (November 24, 1923); Virginia Woolf, *Diary* (Mar 8, 1941); William Dickey, "Killing to Eat," *Rainbow Grocery*.

Chapter 1: ADD FOOD AND STIR: LIFE IN THE VIRTUAL KITCHEN

Epigraphs: Filippo Marinetti, *The Futurist Cookbook*, 36; Joe-Anne McLaughlin, "Existentially Speaking," *The Banshee Diaries*; Anthony Bourdain, *The Nasty Bits*, 277.

1. Lobel, "The Joy of Cookbooks." Lobel adds that "cookbook sales increased by 5 to 10 percent each year," notes that there "are thousands of websites devoted to cooking," and that a "good search for 'recipes' yields over 29 million hits."
2. Gopnik, "Cooked Books." For more of Gopnik's views, see *The Table Comes First: Family, France, and the Meaning of Food*.
3. For competitive eating, see Fagone; for Food Network vs. cable news, see Pollan, "Out of the Kitchen, Onto the Couch": "The Food Network can now be seen in nearly 100 million American homes and on most nights commands more viewers than any of the news channels" (28).
4. In his recent *Cooked*, Pollan formulates what he calls "the Food Paradox": "Why is it that at the precise historical moment when Americans were abandoning the kitchen, handing over the preparation of most of our meals to the food industry, we began spending so much of our time thinking about food and watching other people cook it on television? The less cooking we were doing in our own lives, it seemed, the more that food and its vicarious preparation transfixed us" (3).
5. Brillat-Savarin, 15; Miller, 36; Buford, 73.
6. Capon, xxvi.
7. Fisher, *Alphabet for Gourmets*, 79; http://www.deandeluca.com/butcher-shop/beef/foie-gras-burger.aspx; http://www.foodnetwork.com/recipes/robert-irvine/cheddar-onion-bangers-and-mash-with-guinness-essence-recipe/index.html; http://eater.com/archives/2012/11/30/french-chain-quick-to-unleash-its-foie-gras-burgers-again.php
8. *Food, Inc.*
9. For more on the legendary McRib, see Hendel; see also Jargon and Kesmodel.
10. For more about Terrace, see Harper.
11. Jones, 26.
12. Ibid., 3, 5, 16.
13. Ibid., 129.
14. Ibid.

15. Batterberry, 221.
16. Gabaccia, 5.
17. King, 93. For a lively analysis of the California–Paris trajectories that shaped not only Child but also Fisher and Toklas, see Schmidt.
18. Dione Lucas was a precursor to Julia Child in many ways; like Child a Cordon Bleu graduate, she proselytized for French cooking, and had a cooking school and several restaurants in New York, along with her own television show at a time when, lamented a writer for *Time*, "Gone are the old days when TV cooking simmered along on full-length programs over most stations around the country and the meringue melted under hot lights" ("Radio: Cooking for the Camera"). For other cookbooks, see Boni, *The Talisman Italian Cookbook*, and Heth, *The Wonderful World of Cooking*.
19. Lowell 187. Shapiro, passim. For the Pillsbury Bake-Off, see 34–40, especially the advice of one contestant: "When your recipes do not win, then *dare* to go beyond the conventional. . . . Dream–experiment–measure" (38).
20. For a scrupulous history of the counterculture's gastronomic effect in this period, see Belasco. On the history of the restaurant, see Spang.
21. Pollan, "Out of the Kitchen, Onto the Couch," quoting Simone de Beauvoir. He elaborates, noting: "Curiously, the year Julia Child went on the air—1963—was the same year Betty Friedan published *The Feminine Mystique*, the book that taught millions of American women to regard housework, cooking included, as drudgery, indeed as a form of oppression. You may think of these two figures as antagonists, but that wouldn't be quite right. They actually had a great deal in common, as Child's biographer, Laura Shapiro, points out, and addressed the aspirations of many of the same women. Julia never referred to her viewers as 'housewives'—a word she detested—and never condescended to them. She tried to show the sort of women who read *The Feminine Mystique* that, far from oppressing them, the work of cooking approached in the proper spirit offered a kind of fulfillment and deserved an intelligent woman's attention. (A man's too.) Second-wave feminists were often ambivalent on the gender politics of cooking. Simone de Beauvoir wrote in *The Second Sex* that though cooking could be oppressive, it could also be a form of 'revelation and creation; and a woman can find special satisfaction in a successful cake or a flaky pastry, for not everyone can do it: one must have the gift.' This can be read either as a special Frenchie exemption for the culinary arts (*féminisme, c'est bon*, but we must not jeopardize those flaky pastries!) or as a bit of wisdom that some American feminists thoughtlessly trampled in their rush to get women out of the kitchen."
22. For a thread discussing these issues in response to Pollan's "The Food Movement, Rising," see Clark, "The Foodie Indictment of Feminism" available at http://www.food-culture.org. On this subject, see also Shapiro, who discusses the intricate parallels between Friedan and Child not only in her biography of Child but in the penultimate chapter of *Something from the Oven*.
23. Plath, *The Bell Jar*, 53; Bundtzen; Kumin 42; Jong.
24. de Silva, 52.

Chapter 2: BLACK CAKE: LIFE (AND DEATH) ON THE FOOD CHAIN

Epigraphs: Plato, *Timaeus*, 492; Hegel, *Lectures on Fine Art*, 138; Whitehead, *Dialogues*, 246; Dickinson, 1311.

1. Bierce, 28.
2. Chaucer, "Pardoner's Tale," line 68.
3. Goldhaber, unpublished translation.
4. Kafka, 65.
5. Giono, quoted in Storace.
6. Bierce, 30.
7. Song of Songs, 2:5.
8. Brillat-Savarin, 182.
9. Ibid., 182, 181.
10. See Gilbert, "Suckled by Manly Bosoms: Culinary Transvestism."
11. Quoted from *Slate,* in Sullivan.
12. Allen, 74. For more about Mitterrand's last meal, see also Paterniti.
13. *Hamlet,* Act 1 Sc. 2; Gaskell, 130; Carver, 402–26.
14. Wrangham; Bauman; for more on food sharing, see, for instance, Kaplan and Gurven.
15. Homer, 247, 252; Rogak, 30, 38; Lawrence, *Etruscan Places*, 64.
16. Rogak, 20, 80, 68, 150.
17. Allen, 47.
18. Narayan, 89.
19. For quotes relating to Día de los Muertos, see F. Gonzalez-Crussi, 68–70, passim; Rogak, 94–5, and (for a more extended discussion) Gilbert, *Death's Door,* 4–5.
20. Artusi, 302.
21. Webb, 30–1.
22. See Rogak, 58, 130, 84, 74, 8, 62, 108. Bakhtin, 283.
23. Rando, 46; Vanderbilt, 339; Post, "Funerals," 407–9.
24. Bauer.
25. On designer funerals, see, for instance, Davis, "a little AC/DC": "Designer Funerals: The Final Getaway."
26. Boswell, *Life of Samuel Johnson*, 273; Halpern, 180.
27. Indeed, as the critic Susan Leonardi has pointed out, this root "implies an exchange, a giver and a receiver. Like a story, a recipe needs a recommendation, a context, a point, a reason to be." Thus, she argues, a recipe is "an embedded discourse" (340).
28. Fisher, *Serve It Forth,* 12, 16. The tome known as *Apicius* was not in fact authored by the luxury-loving gourmet named Marcus Gavius Apicius but is rather of unknown origin.
29. Dalby and Grainger, 68.
30. *The good huswifes Iewell* (1596).
31. Dalby, 176.
32. Dickinson, *Letters*, 783–4.

Chapter 3: ALL THAT IS TOOTHSOME? SACRED FOOD, DEADLY DINING

Epigraphs: Brillat-Savarin, *The Physiology of Taste*, 53; Genesis 2–3.

1. Child and Beck, 2:26.
2. Toklas, 39–40. Toklas goes on to recount how she was taught to "smother" pigeons, prefatory to the preparation of Braised Pigeons On Croutons, and later she describes the orange sauce that was the culinary fate of Blanchette, a pet duck who was "frightened . . . to death" by a barking dog (42–5).

3. Stone, 69; Capon, 45; Dickey, 25–6; Brillat-Savarin, 54.
4. Ruskin, 145.
5. Milton, *Paradise Lost*, V:344–7, 434–7.
6. Genesis, 4:1–8.
7. Byron, 790.
8. Exodus 16:31; on lichens, see Allen, 62–3; on the Jewish dietary laws, see, for example, Jean Soler, "The Semiotics of Food in the Bible" and Marvin Harris, "The Abominable Pig," both in Counihan and Van Esterik.
9. A number of commentators on Jesus's role as a Jewish rabbi have pointed out similarities between his doctrines and those of his famed precursor Rabbi Hillel; others have suggeted that many theological doctrines about the Last Supper were provided later, by disciples and other acolytes in the early Christian movement. In addition, various historians have cast doubt on the notion that the Last Supper was actually a seder. See, e.g., Theissen and Merz, 423–7; see also Funk, 139.
10. Bynum, 51. For a contemporary Catholic take on transubstantiation, see http://www.just forcatholics. org/a34.htm: "When Jesus said, 'This is my body,' He was physically present with the disciples. They could see, hear and touch him. John was actually leaning on His bosom. So when Jesus took bread and said, 'This is my body,' it was only natural for the apostles to understand that the bread was the symbol rather than His actual body. The tangible proof that the bread did not become Jesus' body, is the bodily, physical, substantial and material presence of the man Jesus Christ standing with the apostles. Similarly, when He said, 'This is my blood,' Jesus added, '. . . which is shed for you.' Which blood shed for us? The wine in the cup or the blood in Jesus' veins? Since the wine was never shed, it must represent the blood that was actually shed on the cross." "Cannibal feast": Milton, *Complete Prose Works,* 553–4.
11. Bynum, 2.
12. Ibid at 46.
13. Ibid at 66, 60.
14. Visser, *Much Depends on Dinner*, 138.
15. As Felipe Fernandez-Armesto notes in his fine *Near a Thousand Tables*, "In most cultures, the origins of cooking are traced to a divine gift, Promethean fire, or to the luck of a culture hero. Fire is a secret betrayed by a defector from Olympus. In ancient Persia it was elicited from the heart of rock by a hunter's misdirected missile. For the Dakota Indians it was struck from the earth by the claws of a jaguar-god. For the Aztecs, the first fire was the sun, kindled by the gods in the primeval darkness. To the Cook Islands, it was brought by Maui after his descent into the bowels of the earth. An Australian aboriginal found it secreted in the penis of a totemic animal, while for another tribe it was an invention of women, who cooked with it during the men's absence on the hunt and hid it inside their vulvas" (7–8).
16. See Foley, line 372.
17. Pseudo-Apollodorus, I.v.2.
18. Foley, lines 208–9.
19. See Luck. The word "entheogen"was coined in 1979 by a group of ethnobotanists and scholars of mythology; see Ruck, et al. The translation "creating the divine within" is sometimes given, but it should be noted that "entheogen" implies neither that something is created (as opposed to just perceiving something that is already there) nor that that which is experienced is within the user (as opposed to having independent existence).

20. Ovid, 134–42.
21. *Titus Andronicus,* Act 5, Sc. 3. Titus's daughter Lavinia has been raped by Tamora's sons, who then cut out her tongue and chop off her hands so she can't tell the story; but in a scene where Titus's grandson, Marcus, is reading to her, she points to his book indicating the tale of Philomela, inspiring him to give her a stick to hold with her mouth and stumps; she writes the names of her attackers in the dirt and Titus begins to plan a revenge that parallels those of Procne and Thyestes.
22. Korsmeyer, passim, esp. 190–200. In 2011 a fascinating exhibition on artistic representations of cannibalism was mounted in Paris: http://www.lamaisonrouge.org/spip.php?article726.
23. Visser, *Rituals of Dinner*, 53.
24. Ibid., 5.
25. Montaigne, 105–18.
26. The anthropologist Marvin Harris has speculated that the meat of sacrificial victims provided those who ate it with animal protein that was otherwise largely absent from the ancient Mexican diet.
27. Montaigne, "On Vehicles," 264–84; but, the essayist adds bitterly, "I am very much afraid that we have greatly precipitated its declension and ruin [of this new world] by our contagion; and that we have sold it our opinions and our arts at a very dear rate. It was an infant world, and yet we have not whipped and subjected it to our discipline, by the advantage of our natural worth and force, neither have we won it by our justice and goodness, nor subdued it by our magnanimity. Most of their answers, and the negotiations we have had with them, witness that they were nothing behind us in pertinency and clearness of natural understanding." On the Aztecs, see Visser, 3–4, 8–12. For recent views of Aztec society which regard the contemporary Spanish accounts on which Visser relies as ethnocentrically biased, see, e.g., Hart and Arens; Arens, in particular, argues that the "myth" of cannibalism is a form of "cultural libel," based on secondhand or hearsay evidence. For a discussion of the views of Arens and others, see also Osborne.
28. Leigh Fermor, 30. See also Fernandez-Armesto, 21.
29. Visser, *The Rituals of Dinner*, 11.
30. Homer, 220, 234, 274–5, 279. For a lively discussion of cannibalistic practices (and myths of cannibalism) around the world, along with some of their more dismaying medical consequences, see Allen, 154–72.
31. Swift, 492–9.
32. *Don Juan*, 2.LXXVI, in Byron, 452.
33. Poe, 81.
34. For an interesting discussion of the origins of Twain's "Cannibalism in the Cars" in newspaper stories, see Branch. For a particularly gripping tale of what's called "survival cannibalism," see Hanson, and for a fine commentary on this and similar works, see Rawson. As Rawson notes, the unfortunate seaman who is cannibalized in the real-life 1885 episode central to *The Custom of the Sea* was actually called Richard Parker, the name Poe gave to his fictional victim fifty years earlier! For the Donner party, see Houghton and, among many other histories, Johnson. For the Andes air disaster, see Read.
35. Rawson, 13; on Dahmer, see Morton, 31; Rivera. Rivera explained that he and his fellow students "purchased cadavers from the city morgue choosing the bodies of persons who had died of violence—who had been freshly killed and were not diseased or senile. We lived on this cannibal diet for two months, and everyone's health improved" (20).

36. See Jenkins.
37. *Inferno*, Canto 34, lines 61–7, in Dante, 365–7.
38. See Caporael, 25.
39. Bynum, 44.
40. Alan Davidson, 678; the author adds that the problem of ergot, posed by the "exceptionally poisonous" fungus *Claviceps purpurea* growing on rye, "remains in less wealthy countries where food supplies are so meager that to sieve the grain and so diminish the harvest seems more perilous than to trust to luck."
41. Freeman; for a different interpretation of this legend of the Buddha's death, see Wasson and O'Flaherty.
42. On Medea and Theseus, see Graves, 332–5; on the "charm of Prometheus," see Rhodius, 282 (11.828–90).
43. On Dionysus, see Kerényi; on Carrie Nation and her hatchet, see Batterberry, 152–3; on the history of the WCTU, see Rosenberg, especially 242–5. On the history of viticulture in general, see Unwin.
44. Some believe the Pope's death was brought about by mistakes and confusion at a dinner party. According to one account, he was killed by wine that he himself had caused to be poisoned in order to murder Cardinal de Corneto. In another account, he ate a box of sweetmeats that had been poisoned by the cardinal: see Mack, 802–12.
45. Zimmern has said that the "one thing he won't eat" is "human beings"; see Hutton.
46. In her semi-autobiographical trilogy *Lark Rise to Candleford* (1945), the English novelist Flora Thompson has someone calling them both "love-apples" and "nasty horrid things": see Thompson, 111. For more on the tomato, see Allen, 18–20, and Thompson, cited in Alan Davidson, 803.
47. On the eggplant, see Safire.
48. Allen, 267.
49. Dickens, 100.
50. Fernandez-Armesto, 181. "The Women's Petition," often considered a satirical work, was also a protest against emerging coffeehouse culture. On coffee's behalf, Francis Bacon noted in 1627 that "they have in Turkey a Drinke called Coffa, made of a Berry of the same Name . . . Which they take, beaten into powder, in water, as Hot as they can drinke it. And [the] Drinke comforteth the Braine and Heart and helpeth digestion" (*Natural History,* quoted in Colquhoun, 145).
51. Homer, 214; "The Lotos-Eaters," line 98, in Tennyson, 79; "lotus" as jujube: see Alan Davidson, 425.
52. Carroll, 33.
53. Ibid., 10–1, 41; see also Bimberg.
54. For an extended discussion of food in "The Eve of St. Agnes," see Morton, 153ff., who sees stanza 30 as "a profound meditation on food as emblem."
55. Rossetti, 5–19.
56. "Kubla Khan," lines 53–4, in Coleridge, 183.
57. Baudelaire, 16. Despite warning of the dangers of hashish, Baudelaire also observed, in much the same vein as many other writers on drugs, that under its influence "Sounds cloak themselves with colour; colours blossom into music. . . . Musical notes become numbers; and if your mind is gifted with some mathematical aptitude, the harmony to which you listen, while keeping its voluptuous and sensual character, transforms itself into a vast rhythmical operation, where numbers beget numbers, and whose phases and

generation follow with an inexplicable ease and an agility which equals that of the person playing."

58. Gautier, 89.
59. Benjamin, *On Hashish*. On drugs and Romanticism, see Pollan, *The Botany of Desire*, 145–9; also see Lenson, Hayter, and Boon.
60. Toklas misspells his name, which was Brion Gysin.
61. Toklas, 273–4: "*évanouissement*": a sort of waking swoon.
62. Dickinson, 1715.
63. "Adam lay ybounden," lines 9–12, in Wright, 32–3; ("If the apple hadn't been taken, our lady would never have been heaven's queen; blessed be the time the apple was taken, therefore we must sing Thanks to God").

Chapter 4: MASTER BELLY AND OUR DAILY BREAD: A BRIEF HISTORY OF THE LITERARY KITCHEN

Epigraphs: Homer, *Odyssey*, 363; Rabelais, *Gargantua and Patagruel*, 408.

1. Proust, 32–3.
2. On Benjamin's "profane illumination," see this volume, chapter 2.
3. Quoted in Suzuki, 275–6.
4. Current neuroscience supports Proust's assertion that "When from a long distant past nothing subsists . . . taste and smell alone . . . bear unflinchingly . . . the vast structure of recollection." See Max.
5. Bakhtin, 281.
6. Lévi-Strauss, 89. The origin and intention of the concept "good to eat, good to think" is vexed. According to one scholar, "Lévi-Strauss first used the phrases 'bon à manger' and 'bon à penser' . . . in his book *Le Totémisme aujourd'hui* (1962)," to explain "why certain animals are chosen" as totems and "Food choice was not directly implicated": see Santich, 4.
7. Brillat-Savarin, 3.
8. Again, see the arguments of the anthropologist Richard Wrangham on the connection between cooking fires and the evolution of human physiology, in *Catching Fire*.
9. Barthes, 21, 23; Douglas, 53.
10. Alcott, *Little Women,* 16.
11. Dickinson, "207," 96. For "celestial bread," see Bynum, 40; Gregory of Nyssa, see Bynam, 38.
12. Thoreau, 56–7.
13. Alcott, *Transcendental Wild Oats*.
14. Ibid., 37.
15. Alcott, *Little Women*, 38.
16. *Hobomok* (1824) and *Hope Leslie* (1827) are both quoted in McWilliams, "Distant Tables," 377, 379; "republican simplicity": 370; "monstrous and hellish": 371.
17. Barlow, II:1–15.
18. Plato, *The Republic*, 81 (dialogue between Socrates and Adeimantus); Telfer, 37; on the Pythagorean diet see Riedweg, passim, especially 31, 75, 100; Porphyry, 52.
19. "Disquisition on gastronomy": Horace, Satire 4, 56–8; "a hungry stomach" and "a deep-rooted inclination": Satire 2, 43; "vegetarian food": Epistle 5, 84; to be sure, in his dinner invitation he did extol "the wonders uncorked by wine!" but presumably he referred to the pleasures of civilized imbibing.

20. Seneca, 201; Petronius, 60, 75, 90; Horace, Satire 8, 72–3.
21. On Gregory of Nyssa, see Dudley, 138; "Essay on Man," lines 172–4, in Pope, 294; Hawthorne, 117; Thoreau, "Watermelons," 107.
22. *Inferno*, VI:16–19, in Dante, 45.
23. Stuart; Cheyne, 78; Richardson, vol. 1, 1; Rousseau, 373.
24. P. Shelley, 18; M. Shelley, 120.
25. Douglass, 114.
26. Flaubert, 59, 45, 185, 281, 286, 295.
27. Dickens, *Oliver Twist*, 15.
28. C. Brontë, 57, 74–5, 38, 86.
29. Dickens, *A Christmas Carol*, 83.
30. See Kim.
31. Bakhtin, 7, 9; *Twelfth Night*, Act 2 Sc. 2.
32. "Land of Cockayne," lines 53–60, in Glaser, 151–2.
33. Franklin, 2; Dahl, *James and the Giant Peach*, *Charlie and the Chocolate Factory*; Gruelle, *Raggedy Ann in the Deep Deep Woods*.
34. Rabelais, 224–6; in Tutuola's *The Palm-Wine Drinkard,* an enormous, voracious baby is born from his mother's thumb, suggesting, as Rabelais does, that just as there is an infantile fear of what Melanie Klein calls the "bad breast," there is a parental fear of the devouring offspring.
35. Dickens, 12; Bakhtin, 276.
36. Chopin, 42, 96; see also Cather, *Essay on Chopin.*
37. For a more comprehensive study of *The Awakening*, see Gilbert, "The Second Coming of Aphrodite."
38. Joyce, "The Dead," 141.
39. Woolf, *To the Lighthouse,* 52.
40. Mauss, 115.
41. See http://www.fruitlandsevents.com/files/FMC=lunch=4=13=asia.pdf. Accessed May 13, 2013.

Chapter 5: THE KITCHEN MUSE: THE MODERNIST COOKBOOK AND ITS SEQUELS

Epigraphs: Whitman, 226; Stein, *Writings*, vol. 1, 329.

1. See Fontaine.
2. Elias, 479.
3. Dickens, *American Notes for General Circulation*, 164.
4. Chopin, 43 ; Joyce, *Ulysses,* 55; Woolf, *Mrs. Dalloway,* 161.
5. Steedman; "Crumble-Hall," lines 115–20, in Leapor, 209.
6. Woolf, *Diary*, 358.
7. De Certeau, et al., 152, 154.
8. Hemingway, "Big Two-Hearted River," 184–5; Hemingway, "The Wild Gastronomic Adventures of a Gourmet," 376, 371.
9. "To Be Hungry Is To Be Great," in Williams, *Collected Poems*, 400.
10. "This Is Just To Say," ibid., 372; for the interview with Williams conducted by John Gerber in 1950, see Wallace.

11. For an interesting theoretical analysis of Williams's ambiguities and rhetorical strategies in this poem, see Altieri.
12. Williams, *Collected Poems*, 536ff.
13. For more information about Keats's influence on Williams, see Mariani (passim, esp. 11–2). I'm grateful to my son, Roger Gilbert, for illuminating the connections between "This Is Just To Say" and "Ode on a Grecian Urn."
14. On taste and Romanticism, see Kolb, esp. 11–24; also see Gigante, Morton, Abrams (esp. 392–401).
15. "Song of the Exposition," in Whitman, 225–35; "Against the Weather: A Study of the Artist," in Williams, *Selected Essays*, 216; "A Pact," in Pound, 89.
16. "The Love Song of J. Alfred Prufrock," in Eliot, *Collected Poems*, 3–7.
17. "Peach," in Lawrence, *Complete Poems*, 279.
18. Lawrence, "Walt Whitman," *Studies in Classic American Literature*, 148–61; "An Elegy for D. H. Lawrence," in Williams, *Collected Poems*, 392–5; Eliot, *After Strange Gods*.
19. See "The Visual Appetite: Representing Taste and Food" in Korsmeyer, 146–84.
20. "The Relations Between Poetry and Painting," in Stevens, 740–54; "The Dwarf," 189–90; "A Dish of Peaches in Russia," 206.
21. "Someone Puts a Pineapple Together," in Stevens, 693–8; "Floral Decorations for Bananas," pp. 43–4; "The Motive for Metaphor," 257; "The Comedian as the Letter C," 22–36.
22. Jong, 43; "appleyness": Lawrence, *The Paintings of D.H. Lawrence,* 34.
23. Perloff, 66–7.
24. Korsmeyer, 141; Stein, *Writings*, vol. 1, 327.
25. Stein, *Writings*, vol. 1, 336, 331, 341.
26. Ibid., 491; Garland, 41–2.
27. On Bilignin see Stein, *Writings*, vol. 1, 679; Brillat-Savarin, 215.
28. Unfortunately we could not obtain permission to reproduce "Five Apples," the painting Leo owned, but the work we offer here represents the "appleyness" of apples with the same verve.
29. Stein, *Writings*, vol. 1, 181; for Cézanne on apples, see Trachtma; for the quote from Leo Stein, see Wineapple, 374.
30. Stein, *Writings*, vol. 1, 181, 329; Toklas, 139.
31. Marinetti, 32; David, 65.
32. Marinetti, 37, 47.
33. Ibid., 8, 36–7.
34. See Hathaway.
35. Marinetti, 66, 39.
36. Petronius, 27–30; Delville, 10.
37. Stein, "American Food and American Houses," 187.
38. Ginsberg, *Howl*, 29.
39. Stein, "American Food and American Houses," 191.

Chapter 6: TASTES OF CLAY: THE MANY COURSES OF THE CULINARY MEMOIR

Epigraphs: Liebling, 3; Buford quoted in Garner, 22; Fisher, *Gastronomical Me*, vi.

1. Fisher, "Savoring Winter," 8.
2. For a use of the noun "foodoir," see, e.g., Muhlke: " Done well, memoirs about love and food go together like steak and martinis. Meals are a perfect application for the 'show,

don't tell' directive, from proposal soufflé to break-up pastina. These foodoirs have become a successful subset, one part chick lit mixed with one part chicken lit."

3. Fisher, *Gastronomical Me*, 51; Fisher, "Savoring Winter," 8.
4. Scarry, 13
5. On food and sex, see Eberstadt; see also Gopnik, "Cooked Books."
6. For the quote from Updike, see Reardon, 492; Fisher, "The Most Important Meal I Ever Ate"; Fussell, 107; Child and Prud'homme, 18.
7. Fisher, *The Gastronomical Me,* ix.
8. Ibid., 11.
9. Woolf, "Mr. Bennett and Mrs. Brown," 36; Joyce, *Ulysses,* 741: if Bloom's choice of kidneys is vaguely scatological, his purchase of pork kidneys is transgressive considering his Jewishness.
10. Woolf, "Mr. Bennett and Mrs. Brown," 36; Woolf, *To the Lighthouse*, 132.
11. Garner, 22.
12. Fisher, *Serve it Forth,* 20, 50.
13. Ibid., 4–5.
14. Ibid., 6–7, 19.
15. Ibid., 51–2; see *The Gastronomical Me,* 183, for another passage on dining alone, in which the author declares that it saves her from officers and "predatory passengers" who might bother her "just because I was under ninety and predominantly female."
16. Fisher, *The Gastronomical Me*, 190–1.
17. Lukanuski, 115.
18. Fisher, *The Gastronomical Me*, 190.
19. Fisher, *Consider the Oyster*, 181.
20. Fisher, *The Gastronomical Me,* 190.
21. Fisher, *Serve It Forth*, 119.
22. Fisher, *The Art of Eating*, 63.
23. Fisher, *The Gastronomical Me*, 3.
24. Ibid., 11–3.
25. Ibid., 13–5.
26. Ibid., 28–30.
27. Ibid., 34–5.
28. Ibid., 75.
29. Ibid., 76.
30. Ibid., 148.
31. Ibid., 101.
32. Ibid., 151, 155–6.
33. Ibid., 165.
34. Ibid., 209.
35. Fisher, *An Alphabet for Gourmets*, 744. For more on "the category of Two," see Pennell.
36. J. Moore, *Never Eat Your Heart Out*, 140–1, 149.
37. Ibid., 182, 203.
38. J. Moore, *Fat Girl*, 5.
39. Levi, 116; Orwell, 65.
40. J. Moore, *The Left Coast of Paradise*, 192.
41. J. Moore, *Never Eat Your Heart Out*, 51.

42. J. Moore, *Fat Girl*, 12–4.
43. "Poem for a Birthday" in Plath, *Collected Poems,* 131–7.
44. See Ellwanger, 139.

Chapter 7: BITTER HERBS OR THE SPICES OF LIFE? THE AMBIGUITIES OF THE TRANSNATIONAL FOODOIR

Epigraphs: Browning, 341; DeSalvo, 5; Schenone, 194.

1. "The Love Song of J. Alfred Prufrock," in Eliot, 3.
2. Downie, 99.
3. Di Renzo, 31.
4. For food trucks, see, e.g., Gallagher and Gold.
5. DeSalvo, 9, 12–3.
6. Schenone, 14, 33.
7. DeSalvo, 66.
8. Schenone, 45, 5; Wells. To be sure, many other presumably authentic ethnic cuisines have also been effectively "bastardized" in the United States—and in other countries. For a discussion of the ways in which Chinese–American cooking isn't really Chinese, see Lee.
9. Laurino, 17, 24–5.
10. Furiya, 5.
11. Ibid., 173.
12. Abu-Jaber, *The Language of Baklava,* 282
13. Ibid., 81, 317.
14. Von Bremzen, 18, 12; Chekhov, "The Siren," 357.
15. Douglass, 91–2; Gosse, 246.
16. Harris, 21–40.
17. See Koch.
18. Smart-Grosvenor, 145: a well-known NPR personality, Smart-Grosvenor declares that "Poor as we was, we never ate no bad meat. My mother would take it back or throw it away before she cooked it for us. Black folks spend more money for food than white folks. White folks can take a can of tuna fish and feed multitudes." Angelou, 31–40, 65–70, 71–8, 161–70; Shange, 29–30.
19. Clarke, 3.
20. Ibid., 42.
21. Ibid., 49–50.
22. Ibid., 162.
23. Ibid., 65.
24. Leviticus 11:1–4; Deuteronomy 4:1–29.
25. Ehrlich, 16. On "Sacred time" see Eliade, 68–115.
26. Ehrlich, 195.

Chapter 8: HAIL TO THE CHEF! THE COOK, THE CAMERA, THE CRITIC, AND THE CONNOISSEUR

Epigraphs: Reichl, *Garlic and Sapphires*, 82; Bourdain, *Kitchen Confidential*, 61; Kaga, iii; Paul Child, quoted in Fitch, 178.

1. For the history of the restaurant in the West, see Spang.
2. Quoted in Kelly, 26.
3. Buford, 81.
4. Reichl, *Garlic and Sapphires*, 18.
5. For this and other White House dinner menus, see M. Barrett.
6. Wolfert quoted in Fitch, 275; Paul Child quoted in Conant, 114.
7. "Black and white": Child and Prud'homme, 242; "unreconstructed" and "frumpy": "Our Lady of the Ladle."
8. Fitch, 85, 65.
9. Ibid., 180.
10. "It was heaven": Shapiro, *Julia Child*, 27–8; "opening like a flower" and Prud'homme: Jacobs.
11. Fitch, 23.
12. "Would go to school in the morning": Child quoted in Jacobs; "alchemists' eyrie": Child and Prud'homme, 178; "wild hare": ibid., 112; "dogmatic meatball": Fitch, 200; "old brioche": Fitch, 209.
13. Fitch, 207.
14. Ibid., 285–6.
15. Child and Prud'homme, 301.
16. "Bobblehead personalities": Bourdain, *Kitchen Confidential*, 358; Bourdain on Rachael Ray, see "Nobody Asked Me, But. . . ." There are in fact quite a few cookbooks in the "Dummies" series, including *Gourmet Cooking for Dummies, Jewish Cooking for Dummies,* and *Cooking Basics for Dummies.*
17. Child and Prud'homme, 3; Bourdain, *Kitchen Confidential*, 2.
18. Bourdain, *Kitchen Confidential,* 4.
19. Ibid., 6, 18, 24, 26.
20. Pollan, "Out of the Kitchen, Onto the Couch."
21. Buford, 79.
22. Ibid., 9.
23. See Roberts.
24. Bourdain, "Nobody Asked Me, But . . ."
25. See Moskin and Severson.
26. For Bourdain on Waters, see Pelecanos; Pollan, "Out of the Kitchen, Onto the Couch"; "elaborate and time-consuming": Kamp, 91; "never had restaurant-cooking chops": Kamp, 146.
27. On Julia and Paul Child, see Shapiro, 133; Paul Child's sonnet: Fitch, 269.
28. Bourdain, *Kitchen Confidential,* 170.
29. Pollan, "Out of the Kitchen, Onto the Couch."
30. Buford, 306.
31. Reichl , *Garlic and Sapphires,* 33.
32. 2bid., 82, 18.
33. Ibid ., 227.
34. Ibid., 226-8.
35. Eliot, "Burnt Norton," *Four Quartets,* 3.

Chapter 9: COOKING THE BOOKS: COSINESS, DISGUST, DESIRE, DESPAIR

Epigraphs: Carroll, 6; D. M. Davidson, 297; Morrison, *Beloved*, 84.

1. Klein, 53.
2. Gruelle, *Raggedy Ann in Cookie Land*, 26–7.
3. Sendak, 12, 31, 13, 10.
4. dePaola, 12.
5. J. Barrett, 21.
6. Drescher, 8.
7. Dahl, *Charlie and the Chocolate Factory*, 79–80.
8. On Dahl's "excremental vision," see Bosmajian; Dahl, *Charlie and the Chocolate Factory*, 62.
9. Dahl, *Collected Stories*, 108, 126–8.
10. Ellin, 374.
11. Lanchester, 8, 127.
12. Ibid., 207.
13. Ibid., 245.
14. Stout, 7.
15. Ephron, "Just a Minute"; Fisher, quoted in McAleer, 432.
16. Parker, *Looking for Rachel Wallace,* 208; Parker, *Crimson Joy*, 19.
17. *American Heritage Dictionary*.
18. D. M. Davidson, *Catering to Nobody*, 1; D. M. Davidson, *Double Shot*, p. 440.
19. Sartre, 19, 131. For a charming take on *Nausea*, see Roz Chast's cartoon "Recipes from the Jean-Paul Sartre Cookbook," which includes parodic directions for "Free Will Soup," "Angsty Tuna Salad," and "Any Cake At All": *New Yorker*, September 23, 2013: 85.
20. Plath, *The Bell Jar*, 47, 49, 26.
21. Ibid., 29–30, 49, 52–4.
22. Ibid., 86.
23. Ephron, *Heartburn*, 21, 98, 124.
24. Ibid., 4, 102.
25. Ibid., 131, 97.
26. Atwood, 53, 60.
27. Ibid., 193.
28. Weldon, 8.
29. Ibid., 135; Greenstreet.
30. Stone, 132.
31. Hamilton-Paterson, 166. For Fernet Branca, see Curtis.
32. Ibid., 170.
33. Ibid., 199.
34. Brantley, 186.
35. Dinesen, 41, 43.
36. Esquivel, *Like Water For Chocolate,* 5, 29.
37. Ibid., 38, 97.
38. Zubiaurre, 30–1; Esquivel, *Like Water For Chocolate,* 69.
39. Esquivel, *Between Two Fires*, 96–7, 149.
40. Morrison, *Beloved*, 81; on Margaret Garner and Lucy Stone, see Reinhardt.

41. Morrison, *Beloved*, 159–60.
42. Ibid., 64.
43. Ibid., 259.

Chapter 10: THE POETICS OF ICE CREAM: EATING ART AT THE TABLE, IN THE GALLERY, AND IN A GROWNUPS' GARDEN OF VERSES

Epigraphs: Stevens, 50; Thiebaud quoted in Nash, 18; York poem: see Shahin.

1. Petronius, 60; Varriano, 183.
2. For more on *pièces montées*, see Day.
3. Varriano, 194.
4. Morton, 175.
5. See Morris.
6. Buschmann, 238.
7. For more on Spoerri, see Hatch.
8. Piene and Mack, 217.
9. Buschmann, 238.
10. Ibid., 241.
11. Ibid., 239; also see Danto, 280–2.
12. For sketches and photographs of these, see http://www.wimdelvoye.be/#.
13. On Fruit Chan's "excremental vision," see Morrison.
14. For a further discussion of Nazi attitudes toward Jews as "shit" see Gilbert, *Death's Door*, 155–6; parapets: see 150.
15. A. Williams, ST1.
16. Fudge, 74; see also Deam.
17. For more on Soutine and *Le Boeuf Écorché*, see Wheeler.
18. For more information, see "Francis Bacon's 'Figure with Meat.'"
19. Stevens, 50.
20. For a color image of *Girl with Ice Cream Cone*, see Nash, 103.
21. Quoted in Gopnik, "An American Painter," 54–5.
22. Ibid., 41.
23. "The Slice of Cake School."
24. See the statement by the artists on Claes Oldenburg: website: http://www.oldenburgvanbruggen.com/largescaleprojects/droppedcone.htm.
25. Oldenburg, 39.
26. On Indiana, see Ryan.
27. Neruda, 47–9.
28. Snyder, *The Back Country,* 28–9.
29. Willard, 8–9.
30. Duffy, 47–8.
31. Smith, 89.
32. "The hungry ear": Young; "A Supermarket in California," in Ginsberg, *Howl*, 29–30.
33. Danto, 208, 142.
34. "Mafioso," in Gilbert, *In the Fourth World*, 22.
35. "Kissing the Bread," in Gilbert, *Kissing the Bread*, 171–5; "No thank you, I don't care for artichokes" and "Chocolate," in Gilbert, *Belongings*, 37–9, 40–1; "Oysters Rockefeller" in

Gilbert, *Aftermath*, 98–9; "Love Calls Us to the Things of This World," in Wilbur, *Collected Poems*, 307–8.

36. York, "Grace": see Shahin.
37. Arnold, "Meditation on a Grapefruit."
38. "Grapefruit," in Stern, 397.
39. "From Blossoms," in Lee, 21; Stevens, 53–5.
40. "Eating Babies," in Bloch, 34–6.
41. "Eating Poetry," in Strand, 3.
42. "Oysters," in Heaney, 3.

Chapter 11: FOOD CHAINED: FOOD FIGHTS, FEARS, FRAUDS—AND FANTASIES

Epigraphs: Child, quoted in Fitch, 308; Ginsberg, "C'mon Pigs of Western Civilization Eat More Grease"; Berry, "What Are People For," 146.

1. See Kolata.
2. Hauser, 73. Hauser believed in the healthful effects of "whole foods" and urged people to avoid starch, gluten, sugar and excessive consumption of meat. When enriched white breads were introduced in the 1950s, Hauser denounced them as "devitalized." See the bibliography for other diets from Fredericks, Atkins, Dukan, Agatston, Ornish, Esselstyn, Pollan (*Food Rules*), etc.
3. For Hippocrates, see Markowitz; Brillat-Savarin, 254; for more by Graham, see his *A Treatise on Bread*; for more by Kellogg, see his *The Natural Diet of Man*. A *New York Times* columnist recently plugged a similar weight-loss program, featuring a wider range of ersatz soups, snacks, puddings and shakes: see Adam Davidson.
4. Banting, 7–11; Fletcher; for the poem on Fletcher, see "Medicine: Fletcherizing"; mastication study, see Harmon.
5. On Banting and "virility," see Vester; "A fat man is a joke": Blythe, 9; "overfat woman": Summerville, 38. All quoted in Vester.
6. Bittman, "Bad Enough." For an ambitious and sweeping analysis of food anxieties in the context of contemporary American politics, see Lavin.
7. Warner, xiv.
8. Ibid., xv, 11.
9. Plutarch as quoted in Coetzee, 38; "we are surrounded": ibid., 21.
10. Lappé, 65–6.
11. Coetzee, 53.
12. Sinclair, 32.
13. Sinclair specifies further: " No tiniest particle of organic matter was wasted in Durham's. Out of the horns of the cattle they made combs, buttons, hairpins, and imitation ivory; out of the shinbones and other big bones they cut knife and toothbrush handles, and mouthpieces for pipes; out of the hoofs they cut hairpins and buttons, before they made the rest into glue. From such things as feet, knuckles, hide clippings, and sinews came such strange and unlikely products as gelatin, isinglass, and phosphorus, bone black, shoe blacking, and bone oil. They had curled-hair works for the cattle tails, and a 'wool pullery' for the sheepskins; they made pepsin from the stomachs of the pigs, and albumen from the blood, and violin strings from the evil-smelling entrails. When there was nothing else to be done with a thing, they first put it into a tank and got out of it all the tallow

and grease, and then they made it into fertilizer. All these industries were gathered into buildings near by, connected by galleries and railroads with the main establishment; and it was estimated that they had handled nearly a quarter of a billion of animals since the founding of the plant by the elder Durham a generation and more ago. If you counted with it the other big plants—and they were now really all one—it was . . . the greatest aggregation of labor and capital ever gathered in one place. It employed thirty thousand men; it supported directly two hundred and fifty thousand people in its neighborhood, and indirectly it supported half a million. It sent its products to every country in the civilized world, and it furnished the food for no less than thirty million people!" Sinclair, 32–4.

14. Pollan, "Power Steer"; see also Singer, who inveighs against "speciesism" and argues that all beings capable of suffering deserve equal treatment, for giving lesser importance to beings based on their species is no more justified than discrimination based on skin color. Declaring that animals should have rights based on their ability to suffer rather than their intelligence, he observes that while animals show lower intelligence than the average human, many severely intellectually challenged humans show equally diminished, if not lower, mental capacity. See Pollan, *The Omnivore's Dilemma*: "One-fifth of America's petroleum consumption goes to producing and transporting our food" (183).
15. Klinkenborg, quoted in Sacks, 273. See also Grandin and Johnson.
16. Foer, 230.
17. Schlosser, 165; for more recent investigations of slaughterhouses, see Pachirat and also Conover.
18. Pollan, "Power Steer"; *Super Size Me*.
19. Ginsberg, "C'mon Pigs of Western Civilization Eat More Grease"; Snyder, *Turtle Island*, 10.
20. Munro, 104–5.
21. R. Stone, *American Milk*, 1.
22. "Capitalist Poem #5," in McGrath, 23.
23. Ozeki, passim.
24. Ibid., 8.
25. Ibid., 250, 255.
26. Ibid., 258, 260.
27. On cattle feed, see Pollan, "Cattle Futures?": "despite the FDA's 1997 ban on feeding cattle cattle meat and bone meal, feedlots continue to rear these herbivores as cannibals. When young, they routinely receive 'milk replacer' made from bovine blood; later, their daily ration is apt to contain rendered cattle fat as well as feed made from ground-up pigs and chickens—pigs and chickens that may themselves have grown up on a diet of ground-up cows. But the grossest feedlot dish we read about in our newspapers over breakfast has to be 'chicken litter,' the nasty stuff shoveled out of chicken houses—bedding, feathers and overlooked chicken feed. Since this chicken feed may contain the same bovine meat and bone meal that FDA rules prohibit in cattle feed, those rules are, in effect, all but guaranteed to break themselves. Oh, yes, I forgot to mention one of the ingredients in chicken litter: chicken feces, which the US cattle industry regards as a source of protein."
28. See Diana, Princess of Wales: "I had bulimia for a number of years. And that's like a secret disease. You inflict it upon yourself because your self-esteem is at a low ebb, and you don't think you're worthy or valuable. You fill your stomach up four or five times a

day—some do it more—and it gives you a feeling of comfort. It's like having a pair of arms around you, but it's temporary, temporary. Then you're disgusted at the bloatedness of your stomach, and then you bring it all up again. And it's a repetitive pattern, which is very destructive to yourself."

29. "Ellen West," in Bidart, 109.
30. See also Gilbert, "Hunger/Pains."
31. Dickinson, "439," 203.
32. Glück, 1284.
33. Boland, 52–3.
34. On bulimia and anorexia, see Brumberg; Bordo; Chernin; Levenstein.
35. Ozeki, 37–8, 137; "I sing of Olaf glad and big," in cummings, 37–8.
36. Harris, 35.
37. For a comprehensive look at the history of hunger strikes, see Beresford.
38. Hornbacher, 69, 91.
39. Bordo, 30ff.; "Fast food, frighteningly slow decay."
40. For a reasoned and moderate discussion of the possible problems of soy, see http://www.mayoclinic.com/health/soy/NS_patient-soy/DSECTION=safety.
41. Pollan, *In Defense of Food*, 148 and passim.
42. Laudan, *Cuisine and Empire*, 352.
43. Bittman, "Yes, Healthful Fast Food Is Possible. But Edible?," MM26.
44. Marvell, "The Garden," in Rumrich and Chaplin, 553–5; see also Laudan, "A Plea for Culinary Modernism.

Bibliography

Abrams, M. H. *Natural Supernaturalism*. New York: W. W. Norton, 1973.

Abu-Jaber, Diana. *Crescent*. New York: Norton, 2004.

———. *The Language of Baklava*. New York: Anchor, 2006.

Agatston, Arthur. *The South Beach Diet*. New York: St. Martin's Press, 2003.

Alcott, Louisa May. *Little Women*. New York: Bantam Classics, 1983.

———. *Transcendental Wild Oats*. Carlisle, MA: Applewood, 1873.

Allen, Stewart Lee. *In the Devil's Garden: A Sinful History of Forbidden Food*. New York: Ballantine, 2002.

Altieri, Charles. "Presence and Reference in a Literary Text: The Example of Williams' 'This Is Just to Say'." *Critical Inquiry*, Spring 1979: 489–510.

The American Heritage Dictionary. 2011.

Angelou, Maya. *Hallelujah! The Welcome Table: A Lifetime of Memories with Recipe*. New York: Random House, 2007.

"Apicius: Cookery and Dining in Imperial Rome." August 19, 2009. Project Gutenberg. http://www.gutenberg.org/files/29728/29728-h/29728-h.htm. Accessed December 6, 2013.

Arens, William. *The Man-Eating Myth: Anthropology and Anthropophagy*. Oxford: Oxford University Press, 1979.

Arnold, Craig. "Meditation on a Grapefruit." *Poetry*, October 2009.

Artusi, Pellegrino. *The Art of Eating Well: An Italian Cookbook*. Trans. Kyle Phillips. New York: Random House, 1996.

Atkins, Robert C. *Doctor Atkins' Diet Revolution*. New York: Bantam, 1981.

Atwood, Margaret. *The Edible Woman*. New York: Anchor, 1998.

Babette's Feast. DVD. Directed by Gabriel Axel. 1987. Denmark: Orion Classics, 2001.

Bakhtin, Mikhail. *Rabelais and His World*. Trans. Helene Iswolsky. Bloomington: Indiana University Press, 1984.

Banting, William. *Letter on Corpulence: Addressed to the Public*. London: Harrison, 1864.

Barlow, Joel. *The Collected Works of Joel Barlow*. New York: Scholars' Facsimiles and Reprints, 1970, 85–93.

Barr, Luke. *Provence, 1970*. New York: Clarkson Potter, 2013.

Barrett, Judi. *Cloudy with a Chance of Meatballs*. New York: Aladdin, 1982.

Barrett, Mary Brigid. "A Taste of the Past: White House Kitchens, Menus, and Recipes." 2008. *Our White House*. http://www.ourwhitehouse.org/tasteofpast.html. Accessed May 16, 2013.

Bart, Lionel. *Lionel Bart's Oliver!* New York: TRO, 2000.

Barthes, Roland. "Toward a Psychosociology of Contemporary Food Consumption." Trans. Counihan and Van Esterik. In Counihan and Van Esterik.

Batterberry, Michael, and Ariane Batterberry. *On the Town in New York: The Landmark History of Eating, Drinking, and Entertainments from the American Revolution to the Food Revolution*. New York: Routledge, 1998.

Baudelaire, Charles. *Artificial Paradises*. Trans. Stacy Diamond. New York: Citadel, 1998.

Bauer, Anne. "Mourning Meal." http://citypages.com/databank/ 27/1311/article14043.asp. January 18, 2006. Accessed May 11, 2013.

Bauman, Zygmunt. *Mortality, Immortality, and Other Life Strategies*. Palo Alto: Stanford University Press, 1992.

Beauvoir, Simone de. *The Second Sex*. Trans. H. M. Parshley. New York: Vintage, 1989.

Belasco, Warren. *Appetite for Change: How the Counter Culture Took on the Food Industry*. Ithaca: Cornell University Press, 2006.

Benjamin, Walter. *On Hashish*. Trans. Scott J. Thompson. Cambridge: Harvard University Press, 2006.

Beresford, David. *Ten Dead Men*. New York: Atlantic Monthly, 1997.

Berry, Wendell. "The Pleasure of Eating." *What Are People For?* Berkeley: Counterpoint, 2010, 145–52.

———. *The Unforeseen Wilderness: Kentucky's Red River Gorge*. Emeryville, CA.: Counterpoint, 2006.

———. *The Unsettling of America: Culture and Agriculture*. San Francisco: Sierra Club Books, 1996.

Bidart, Frank. *In the Western Night: Collected Poems 1965–1990*. New York: HarperCollins, 1990.

Bierce, Ambrose. *The Devil's Dictionary*. New York: Dover, 1993.

Big Night. DVD. Directed by Campbell Scott. 1996. Los Angeles: Samuel Goldwyn Company, 2002.

Bimberg, Christiane. "The Importance of Eating and Drinking in British Children's Classics." *Inklings: Jahrbuch für Literatur und Ästhetik* (1999): 10–34.

Bittman, Mark. "Bad Enough." *New York Times*, May 14, 2013.

———. "Yes, Healthful Fast Food Is Possible. But Edible?" *New York Times Magazine*, April 3, 2013: MM26.

Bloch, Chana. *The Past Keeps Changing*. Rhinebeck, NY: Sheep Meadow Press, 1992.

Blythe, Samuel G. *The Fun of Getting Thin: How to be Happy and Reduce the Waist Line*. Chicago: Forbes, 1912.

Boland, Eavan. *New Collected Poems*. New York: Norton, 2009.

Boni, Ada. *The Talisman Italian Cookbook*. New York: Clarkson Potter, 1950.

Boon, Marcus. *The Road of Excess: A History of Writers on Drugs*. Cambridge, MA: Harvard University Press, 2005.

Bordo, Susan. *Unbearable Weight: Feminism, Western Culture, and the Body*. Berkeley: University of California Press, 2004.

Bosmajian, Hamida. "Charlie and the Chocolate Factory and Other Excremental Visions." *The Lion and the Unicorn* (1985): 36–49.

Boswell, James. *Journal of A Tour to the Hebrides*. New York: Literary Guild, 1935, 12.

———. *The Life of Samuel Johnson*. New York: Everyman's Library, 1993.

Bourdain, Anthony. *Kitchen Confidential, Insider's Edition: Adventures in the Culinary Underbelly*. New York: Ecco, 2012.

———. *The Nasty Bits: Collected Varietal Cuts, Usable Trim, Scraps, and Bones*. New York: Bloomsbury, 2006.

———. "Nobody Asked Me, But . . ." n.d. *Wild Style Chef.* http://www.wildstylechef.com/AnthonyBourdainNews.htm. Accessed May 16, 2013.

Branch, Edgar M. "Mark Twain: Newspaper Reading and the Writer's Creativity." *Nineteenth-Century Fiction*, March 1983: 576–603.

Brantley, Susan. *Understanding Isak Dinesen*. Columbia: University of South Carolina, 2002.

Brillat-Savarin, Jean-Anthelme. *The Physiology of Taste: Or Meditations on Trascendental Gastronomy*. Trans. M. F. K. Fisher, New York: Norton, 2009.

Brontë, Charlotte. *Jane Eyre.* New York: Norton, 2000.

Brontë, Emily. *Wuthering Heights.* New York: Norton, 1990.

Browning, Elizabeth Barrett. *The Letters of Elizabeth Barrett Browning*. New York: Macmillan, 1899.

Brumberg, Joan Jacobs. *Fasting Girls: The History of Anorexia Nervosa*. New York: Vintage, 2000.

Buford, Bill. *Heat: An Amateur's Adventures as Kitchen Slave, Line Cook, Pasta-Maker, and Apprentice to a Dante-Quoting Butcher in Tuscany*. New York: Vintage, 2007.

Bundtzen, Lynda. "Lucent Figs and Suave Veal Chops: Sylvia Plath and Food." *Gastronomica* 10.1 (2010): 79–90.

Buschmann, Renate. "Evocations of Pleasure and Disgust. Daniel Spoerri and the Establishment of Eat Art." In Elodie Evers, et al., eds., *Eating the Universe: Vom Essen in der Kunst*. Dusseldorf: Kunsthalle Düsseldorf, 2009.

Butler, Cleora. *Cleora's Kitchens: The Memoir of a Cook and Eight Decades of Great American Food*. Tulsa: Council Oak, 2003.

Bynum, Caroline Walker. *Holy Feast and Holy Fast: The Religious Significance of Food to Medieval Women*. Berkeley: University of California Press, 1987.

Byron, George Gordon, Lord. *The Major Works*. Oxford: Oxford University Press, 2008.

Capon, Robert Farrar. *The Supper of the Lamb*. New York: Modern Library, 2002.

Caporael, Linda R. "Ergotism: The Satan Loosed in Salem?" *Science*, April 2, 1976: 21–6.

Carpenter, Novella. *Farm City: The Education of an Urban Farmer*. New York: Penguin, 2010.

Carroll, Lewis. *Alice's Adventures in Wonderland and Through the Looking-Glass*. Oxford: Oxford University Press, 2009.

Carver, Raymond. "A Small, Good Thing." *Collected Stories*. New York: Library of America, 2009, 402–26.

Cather, Willa. "Kate Chopin." *Pittsburg Leader*, July 8, 1899.

Chaucer, Geoffrey. *The Canterbury Tales*. New York: Norton, 2005.

Chekhov, Anton. "The Siren." Trans. Avrahm Yarmolinsky. *American Mercury* (March 1947), 354–8.

Chernin, Kim. *The Obsession: Reflections on the Tyranny of Slenderness.* New York: Harper and Row, 1981.

Cheyne, George. *The Natural Method of Curing the Diseases of the Body, and the Disorders of the Mind Depending on the Body*. Farmington Hills: Gale ECCO, MI: 2010.

Child, Julia, and Simone Beck. *Mastering the Art of French Cooking*. 2 vols. New York: Knopf, 1961, 1970.

Child, Julia, and Alex Prud'homme. *My Life in France*. New York: Anchor, 2009.

Chopin, Kate. *The Awakening.* New York: Norton, 1993.

Clark, Anna. "The Foodie Indictment of Feminism." *Salon*, May 26, 2010. http://www.salon.com/2010/05/26/foodies_and_feminism/. Accessed May 11, 2013.

Clarke, Austin. *Pig Tails 'n Breadfruit: A Culinary Memoir*. New York: New Press, 1999.

Coetzee, J. M. *The Lives of Animals*. Princeton: Princeton University Press, 1999.

Cokal, Susann. *Mirabilis*. New York: Putnam, 2001.

Coleridge, Samuel Taylor. *Coleridge's Poetry and Prose*. New York: Norton, 2004.

Colquhoun, Kate. *Taste: The Story of Britain Through Its Cooking*. New York: Bloomsbury, 2007.

Conant, Jennet. *A Covert Affair*. New York: Simon and Schuster, 2011.

Conover, Ted. "The Way of All Flesh: Undercover in an Industrial Slaughterhouse." *Harper's*, May 2013.

The Cook, The Thief, His Wife, and Her Lover. DVD. Directed by Peter Greenaway. 1989. Los Angeles: Allarts Cook, 2001.

Counihan, Carole, and Penny Van Esterik, eds. *Food and Culture: A Reader*. New York: Routledge, 1997.

Craig, Diana. *Arcimboldo, The Life and Works*. London: Smithmark, 1996.

cummings, e. e. *100 Selected Poems*. New York: Grove Press, 1954, 37–8.

Curtis, Wayne. "The Bitter Beginning." *Atlantic,* November 2008.

Dahl, Roald. *Charlie and the Chocolate Factory*. New York: Penguin, 2011.

———. *Collected Stories*. New York: Everyman's Library, 2006.

———. *James and the Giant Peach*. New York: Puffin, 1996.

Dalby, Andrew. *Flavours of Byzantium*. Devon, UK: Prospect, 2003.

Dalby, Andrew, and Sally Grainger. *The Classical Cookbook: Revised Edition*. Los Angeles: J. Paul Getty Museum, 2012.

Dante Alighieri. *The Inferno*. Trans. Robert Pinsky. New York: Farrar, Straus, and Giroux, 1997.

Danto, Arthur C. *The Transfiguration of the Commonplace*. Cambridge, MA: Harvard University Press, 1983.

———. *Unnatural Wonders: Essays from the Gap Between Art and Life*. New York: Columbia University Press, 2007.

David, Elizabeth. *Italian Food*. New York: Penguin, 1999.

———. *An Omelette and a Glass of Wine*. Guilford, CT: Lyons, 1997.

Davidson, Adam. "How Economics Can Help You Lose Weight." *New York Times Magazine*, March 10, 2013: MM17.

Davidson, Alan. *The Oxford Companion to Food*. Ed. Tom Jaine and Jane Davidson. Oxford: Oxford University Press, 2006.

Davidson, Diane Mott. *Catering to Nobody*. New York: Random House, 2002.

———. *Double Shot*. New York: HarperTorch, 2005.

———. *Sticks and Scones*. New York: Bantam, 2002.

Davis, Jeanie Lerche. "Designer Funerals: The Final Getaway." http://www.webmd.com/balance/features/designer-funerals-final-getaway. Accessed December 13, 2013.

———. *MedicineNet.com*, October 29, 2003. http://www.medicinenet.com/script/main/art.asp?articlekey=52294. Accessed May 11, 2013.

Day, Ian. *Royal Sugar Sculpture*. Durham, UK: Bowes Museum, 2002.

de Certeau, Michael, Luce Giard, and Pierre Mayol. *The Practice of Everyday Life*. Trans. Timothy J. Tomasik. Vol. 2. Minneapolis: University of Minnesota Press, 1998.

de la Pradelle, Michelle. *Market Day in Provence.* Trans. Amy Jacobs. Chicago: University of Chicago Press. 2006.

de Quincey, Thomas. *Confessions of an English Opium-Eater*. New York: Penguin, 2003.

de Silva, Cara, ed. *In Memory's Kitchen: A Legacy from the Women of Terezin*. Lanham, MD: Jason Aronson, 1996.

Deam, Lisa. "Bloom: Rembrandt, Red Meat, and Remembering the Flesh." *The Cresset* LXX.5 (2007): 6–13.

Defoe, Daniel. *Robinson Crusoe*. New York: Barnes and Noble Classics, 2003.

Delville, Michel. *Food, Poetry, and the Aesthetics of Consumption: Eating the Avant-Garde*. New York: Routledge, 2008.

dePaola, Tomie. *Strega Nona*. New York: Aladdin, 1979.

DeSalvo, Louise. *Crazy in the Kitchen: Foods, Feuds, and Forgiveness in an Italian American Family*. New York: Bloomsbury, 2004.

di Renzo, Anthony. *Bitter Greens: Essays on Food, Politics, and Ethnicity from the Imperial Kitchen*. New York: State University of New York Press, 2010.

Diana, Princess of Wales. Interview with Martin Bashir, BBC, November 1995.

Dickens, Charles. *American Notes for General Circulation*. New York: Penguin, 2001.

———. *Oliver Twist*. New York: Penguin, 2010.

———. *A Tale of Two Cities*. New York: Barnes and Noble Classics, 2004.

———. *A Christmas Carol and Other Christmas Books*. Oxford: Oxford University Press, 2008, 5–84.

Dickey, William. *The Rainbow Grocery*. Boston: University of Massachusetts Press, 1978, 25–6.

Dickinson, Emily. *The Letters of Emily Dickinson*. Cambridge, MA: Harvard University Press, 1998.

———. *The Poems of Emily Dickinson*. Ed. R. W. Franklin. Cambridge, MA: Harvard University Press, 1999.

Dinesen, Isak. *Seven Gothic Tales*. New York: Vintage, 1991.

Dinner Rush. DVD. Directed by Bob Giraldo. 2002. Los Angeles: Access Motion Picture Group, 2003.

Douglass, Frederick. *The Complete Autobiographies of Frederick Douglass*. Radford, VA: Wilder, 2008, 73–270.

Downie, David. *Enchanted Liguria: A Celebration of the Culture, Lifestyle and Food of the Italian Riviera*, with photographs by Alison Harris. New York: Rizzoli, 1997.

Drescher, Henrik. *The Boy Who Ate Around*. New York: Hyperion, 1996.

Dudley, Sandra H. *Museum Objects: Experiencing the Properties of Things*. New York: Routledge, 2012.

Duffy, Carol Ann. *The World's Wife*. New York: Faber and Faber, 2001.

Dukan, Pierre. *The Dukan Diet Life Plan*. New York: Random House, 2013.

Eat Drink Man Woman. DVD. Directed by Ang Lee. 1994. Taipei: Ang Lee Productions, 2002.

Eberstadt, Mary. "Is Food the New Sex?" *Policy Review*, January 27, 2009.

Ehrlich, Elizabeth. *Miriam's Kitchen*. New York: Penguin, 1998.

Eliade, Mircea. *The Sacred and the Profane: The Nature of Religion*. Trans. Willard Trask. New York: Harcourt Brace, 1987.

Elias, Norbert. *The Civilizing Process: Sociogenetic and Psychogenetic Investigations*. London: Blackwell, 2000.

Eliot, T. S. *After Strange Gods*. London: Faber and Faber, 1934.

———. *Collected Poems 1909–1962*. New York: Harcourt Brace, 1963.

———. *Four Quartets*. New York: Mariner, 1943.

Ellin, Stanley. *The Specialty of the House and Other Stories*. New York: Random House, 1990.

Ellwanger, George Herman. *The Pleasures of the Table*. New York: Doubleday, 1902.

Ephron, Nora. *Heartburn*. New York: Vintage, 1996.

———. "Just a Minute: Ten Questions for Nora Ephron." *The Observer*, February 25, 2007.

Esquivel, Laura. *Between Two Fires: Intimate Writings on Life, Love, Food, and Flavor*. Trans. Stephen Lytle. New York: Crown, 2000.

———. *Like Water for Chocolate: A Novel in Monthly Installments with Recipes, Romances, and Home Remedies*. Trans. Carol and Thomas Christensen. New York: Anchor, 1995.

Esselstyn, Caldwell B. *Prevent and Reduce Heart Disease*. New York: Avery, 2008.

Estes, Rufus. *Rufus Estes' Good Things to Eat: The First Cookbook by an African–American Chef*. New York: Dover, 2004.

Fagone, Jason. *Horsemen of the Esophagus*. New York: Crown, 2006.

"Fast food, frighteningly slow decay: Mother keeps McDonald's Happy Meal for a whole year . . . and it STILL hasn't gone off." *Daily Mail*, March 23, 2010.

Fernandez-Armesto, Felipe. *Near a Thousand Tables: A History of Food*. New York: Free Press, 2003.

Fisher, Abby. *What Mrs. Fisher Knows About Southern Cooking*. Bedford, MA: Applewood, 1995.

Fisher, M. F. K. *An Alphabet for Gourmets*. New York: North Point Press, 1989.

———. *The Art of Eating*. Boston: Houghton Mifflin Harcourt, 2004.

———. *Consider the Oyster*. New York: North Point Press, 1988.

———. *The Gastronomical Me*. New York: North Point Press, 1989.

———. *How to Cook a Wolf*. New York: North Point Press, 1988.

———. "The Most Important Meal I Ever Ate." *Napa Valley Tables*, Spring/Summer 1990.

———. "Savoring Winter." *New York Times*, October 27, 1985: 8.

———. *Serve It Forth*. New York: North Point Press, 2002.

———. *Two Towns in Provence: Map of Another Town and a Considerable Town*. New York: Vintage, 1983.

Fitch, Noël Riley. *Appetite for Life: The Biography of Julia Child*. New York: Anchor, 2012.

Flaubert, Gustave. *Madame Bovary*. Trans. Margaret Mauldon. Oxford: Oxford University Press, 2008.

Fletcher, Horace. *The New Glutton, or Epicure*. New York: Frederick A. Stokes, 1903.

Foer, Jonathan Safran. *Eating Animals*. New York: Little, Brown, 2009.

Foley, Helene P., ed. *The Homeric Hymn to Demeter: Translation, Commentary, and Interpretative Essays*. Princeton: Princeton University Press, 1993.

Fontaine, Stanislas. "The Civilizing Process Revisited: Interview with Norbert Elias." *Theory and Society*, March 1978: 243–53.

Food, Inc. DVD. Directed by Robert Kenner. 2008. Los Angeles: Magnolia Pictures, 2009.

Foxcroft, Louise. *Calories and Corsets: A History of Dieting Over 2000 Years*. London: Profile, 2012.

"Francis Bacon's 'Figure with Meat' (1954)." *Food Culture Index*, July 12, 2010. http://www.foodcultureindex.com/2010/07/francis-bacons-figure-with-meat-1954.html. Accessed May 17, 2013.

Franklin, Benjamin. "Information to Those Who Would Remove to America." 1782. http://nationalhumanitiescenter.org/pds/makingrev/independence/text8/franklininfoamerica.pdf. Accessed May 13, 2013.

Fredericks, Carlton. *Carlton Fredericks' Program for Living Longer*. New York: Simon and Schuster, 1983.

Freeman, Mary E. *The Revolt of "Mother" and Other Stories*. New York: Dover, 1998, 81–97.

Friedan, Betty. *The Feminine Mystique*. New York: Norton, 2001.

Fudge, Erica. "Saying Nothing Concerning the Same: On Dominion, Purity, and Meat in Early Modern England." *Renaissance Beasts: Of Animals, Humans, and Other Wonderful Creatures*. Chicago: University of Illinois Press, 2004, 70–86.

Funk, Robert W. *The Acts of Jesus: The Search for the Authentic Deeds of Jesus*. New York: HarperCollins, 1998.

Furiya, Linda. *Bento Box in the Heartland: My Japanese Girlhood in Whitebread America*. Emeryville, CA: Seal Press, 2006.

Fussell, Betty. *My Kitchen Wars*. New York: North Point Press, 2009.

Gabaccia, Donna R. *We Are What We Eat: Ethnic Food and the Making of Americans*. Cambridge, MA: Harvard University Press, 2000.

Gallagher, Aileen. "Trucks on a Roll." *New York Restaurants*, July 11, 2010. http://nymag.com/restaurants/cheapeats/2010/67139/. Accessed May 15, 2013.

Garland, Sarah. "'A cook book to be read. What about it?': Alice Toklas, Gertrude Stein and the Language of the Kitchen." *Comparative American Studies*, March 2009: 34–56.

Garner, Dwight. "The Charisma of Food." *New York Times Book Review*, July 9, 2006.

Gaskell, Elizabeth. *Cranford*. New York: Dover, 2003.

Gautier, Théophile. "The Hashish-Eaters' Club." Trans. Peter Haining. *The Hashish Club: An Anthology of Drug Literature*. London: Owen, 1975, 84–100.

Gigante, Denise. "Romanticism and Taste." *Literature Compass*, March 2007: 407–19.

———. *Taste: A Literary History*. New Haven: Yale University Press, 2005.

Gilbert, Sandra M. *Aftermath*. New York: Norton, 2011.

———. *Belongings*. New York: Norton, 2005.

———. *Death's Door: Modern Dying and the Ways We Grieve*. New York: Norton, 2006.

———. "Hunger/Pains." *University Publishing*, Fall 1979.

———. *In the Fourth World*. Tuscaloosa: University of Alabama Press, 1979.

———. *Kissing the Bread*. New York: Norton, 2000.

———. "The Second Coming of Aphrodite." *The Kenyon Review* 5.3 (Summer 1983): 42–66.

———. "Suckled by Manly Bosoms: Culinary Transvestism." *Michigan Quarterly Review*, Fall 1996: 676–89.

Ginsberg, Allen. "C'mon Pigs of Western Civilization Eat More Grease." *Literal Latte*, November 1994.

———. *Howl and Other Poems*. San Francisco: City Lights, 1959.

Glaser, Joseph, ed. *Middle English Poetry in Modern Verse*. Indianapolis: Hackett, 2007, 149–52.

Glück, Louise. *Descending Figure*. New York: Ecco, 1981.

"The Good Huswifes Jewell." December 20, 2008. *Medieval Cookery*. http://medievalcookery.com/notes/ghj1596.txt. Accessed December 6, 2013.

Gold, Jonathan. *Counter Intelligence: Where to Eat in the Real Los Angeles*. Los Angeles: L.A. Weekly Books, 2000.

Goldhaber, Judith. "Translation of Aesop's Fables." Unpublished ms.

Goldstein, Joyce. *Inside the California Food Revolution*. Berkeley: University of California Press, 2013.

Gonzalez-Crussi, F. *The Day of the Dead and Other Mortal Reflections*. New York: Harcourt Brace, 1993.

Gopnik, Adam. "An American Painter." *Wayne Thiebaud: A Paintings Retrospective*. San Francisco: Fine Arts Museum of San Francisco, 2000, 39–70.

———. "Cooked Books: Real food from fictional recipes." *New Yorker*, April 9, 2007.

———. *The Table Comes First: Family, France, and the Meaning of Food*. New York: Vintage, 2011.

Gosse, Philip Henry. *Letters from Alabama: Chiefly Relating to Natural History*. Tuscaloosa: University of Alabama Press, 1993.

Gourmet Cookbook. 2 vols. New York: Gourmet Distributing Corp., 1952.

Graham, Sylvester. *A Treatise on Bread*. Boston: Light and Stearns, 1837.

Grandin, Temple, and Catherine Johnson. *Animals in Translation: Using the Mysteries of Autism to Decode Animal Behavior*. New York: Scribner, 2005.

Graves, Robert. *Greek Myths*. London: Penguin, 1955.

Greenstreet, Rosanna. "Q & A: Fay Weldon." *Guardian*, February 15, 2008.

Gruelle, Johnny. *Raggedy Ann in the Deep Deep Woods*. New York: Simon and Schuster, 2002.

———. *Raggedy Ann in Cookie Land*. New York: Simon and Schuster, 2002.

Hamilton, Gabrielle. *Blood, Bones and Butter: The Inadvertent Education of a Reluctant Chef*. New York: Random House, 2012.

Hamilton-Paterson, James. *Cooking with Fernet Branca*. New York: Europa, 2005.

Hanson, Neil. *The Custom of the Sea*. New York: John Wiley and Sons, 2000.

Harmon, Katherine. "Chew on This: More Mastication Cuts Calorie Intake by 12 Percent." *Scientific American*, August 3, 2011.

Harper, Lisa. "Eating Ivy." *Gastronomica* 6, no. 2 (2006).

Harris, Jessica B. *High on the Hog: A Culinary Journey from Africa to America*. New York: Bloomsbury, 2011.

Harris, Marvin. *Cannibals and Kings: The Origins of Culture*. New York: Random House, 1977.

Hart, Jonathan. "Public/Private Subjectivity in the Early Modern Period: The Self Colonizing and Colonizing the Self." *Early Modern Literary Studies*, January 2002: 1–23.

Hatch, John G. "On the Various Trappings of Daniel Spoerri." *ARTMargins*, March 28, 2003.

Hathaway, Susan. "Molecular Gastronomy Spreads to Home Kitchens." *Mercury News*, January 5, 2011.

Hauser, Gayelord. *House & Garden* (1972): 73.

———. *Look Younger, Live Longer.* New York: Fawcett, 1976.

Hawthorne, Nathaniel. *The American Notebooks*. In *The Centenary Edition of the Works of Nathaniel Hawthorne*. Vol. 8. 23 vols. Columbus: Ohio University Press, 1962.

Hayter, Alethea. *Opium and the Romantic Imagination*. Berkeley: University of California Press, 1968.

Heaney, Seamus. *Field Work*. New York: Farrar, Straus, and Giroux, 2009.

Hegel, G. W. F. *Hegel's Aesthetics: Lectures on Fine Art, Vol. I*. Trans. T. M. Knox. Oxford: Oxford University Press, 1998.

Heider, Frederick, and Barbara Loots, eds. *The Romance of Food*. Kansas City, MO: Hallmark, 1976.

Hemingway, Ernest. "Big Two-Hearted River." *The Nick Adams Stories*. New York: Scribner, 1981, 177–99.

———. *A Moveable Feast*. New York: Scribner, 1996.

———. "The Wild Gastronomic Adventures of a Gourmet." *Dateline Toronto: The Com-*

plete Toronto Star Dispatches, 1920–1924. Ed. William White. New York: Scribner, 1985. 371–6.

Hendel, John. "The Cult of the Elusive McDonald's McRib." *Atlantic*, October 13, 2010.

Heron, Katrina, and Alice L. Waters. *Slow Food Nation's Come to the Table: The Slow Food Way of Living*. New York: Modern Times, 2008.

Hesser, Amanda. *Cooking for Mr. Latte, A Food Lover's Courtship with Recipes*. New York: Norton, 2004.

Heth, Edward Harris. *The Wonderful World of Cooking*. New York: Simon and Schuster, 1956.

Homer. *The Odyssey*. Trans. Robert Fagles. New York: Penguin, 2006.

Horace. *Satires and Epistles*. Trans. Niall Rudd. London: Penguin, 2005.

Hornbacher, Marya. *Wasted: A Memoir of Anorexia and Bulimia*. New York: Harper Perennial, 2006.

Houghton, Eliza Donner. *The Expedition of the Donner Party and Its Tragic Fate*. Lincoln: University of Nebraska Press, 1997.

Hughart, Barry. *Eight Skilled Gentlemen*. New York: Doubleday, 1991.

Hugo, Victor. *Les Miserables*. Trans. Norman Denny. New York: Penguin, 1982.

Hutton, Rachel. "Andrew Zimmern talks eating penises and stealing to buy drugs on Nightline." July 29, 2010. *The Hot Dish*, http://blogs.citypages.com/food/2010/07/andrew_zimmern.php. Accessed May 12, 2013.

Jacobs, Laura. "Our Lady of the Kitchen." *Vanity Fair*, August 2009.

Jargon, Julie, and David Kesmodel. "Bona Fide Fans Chase Rib-Free Rib Sandwich." *Wall Street Journal*, October 11, 2010.

Jenkins, Russell. "Girl's body 'put in mincing machine.'" *The Times* (London), June 22, 2007.

Johnson, Kristin, ed. *"Unfortunate Emigrants": Narratives of the Donner Party*. Logan: Utah State University Press, 1996.

Jones, Judith. *The Tenth Muse: My Life in Food*. New York: Knopf, 2007.

Jong, Erica. *Fruits and Vegetables*. New York: Ecco, 1997.

Joyce, James. *Dubliners*. New York: Penguin, 1993.

———. *Ulysses*. New York: Vintage, 1990.

Julie and Julia. DVD. Directed by Nora Ephron. 2009. Los Angeles: Columbia Pictures, 2009.

Kafka, Franz. *A Hunger Artist and Other Stories*. Trans. Joyce Crick. Oxford: Oxford University Press, 2012.

Kaga, Takeshi. *Iron Chef: The Official Book*. Tokyo: Fuji Television, 2001.

Kamp, David. *The United States of Arugula: How We Became a Gourmet Nation*. New York: Clarkson Potter, 2006.

Kaplan, Hillard, and Michael Gurven. "The Natural History of Human Food Sharing and Cooperation: A Review and a New Multi-Individual Approach." *Moral Sentiments and Material Interests*. Cambridge, MA: MIT Press, 2005, 75–113.

Keats, John. *Complete Poems and Selected Letters*. New York: Modern Library, 2001.

Kellogg, John Harvey. *The Natural Diet of Man*. Battle Creek, MI: Modern Medicine, 1923.

Kelly, Ian. *Cooking for Kings: The Life of Antonin Carême, the First Celebrity Chef*. London: Short Books, 2003.

Kerényi, Carl. *Dionysos: Archetypal Image of Indestructible Life*. Trans. Ralph Manheim. Princeton: Princeton University Press, 1996.

Kim, Suk-Young. "The Shade of Saturnalia in *The Satyricon* of Petronius." *Carnival: A History of Subversive Representations, Actes du huitième colloque étudiant annuel de littérature française, francophone, et comparée*. Ed. Joanna Augustyn and Eric Matheis. New York: Columbia University Press, 1999.

The King James Bible. Oxford: Oxford University Press, 2008.

King, William. *The Poetical Works of William King V1: Containing His Art of Cookery, Imitation of Horace's Art of Poetry*. Edinburgh: Kessinger, 2009.

Kingsolver, Barbara. *Animal, Vegetable, Miracle: A Year of Food Life*. New York: Harper Perennial, 2008.

Klein, Melanie. *Selected Melanie Klein*. New York: Free Press, 1986,

Koch, John. "Barbara Haber." *Boston Globe*, November 22, 1998: 10.

Kolata, Gina. "Mediterranean Diet Shown to Ward Off Heart Attack and Stroke." *New York Times*, February 26, 2013: A1.

Kolb, Jocelyn. *The Ambiguity of Taste: Freedom and Food in European Romanticism*. Ann Arbor: University of Michigan Press, 1995.

Korsmeyer, Carolyn. *Making Sense of Taste: Food and Philosophy*. Ithaca: Cornell University Press, 2002.

Kumin, Maxine. *The Nightmare Factory*. New York: Harper and Row, 1970.

Lamb, Charles. *A Dissertation Upon Roast Pig and Other Essays*. New York: Penguin, 2011.

Lanchester, John. *The Debt to Pleasure*. New York: Picador, 1996.

Lappé, Frances Moore. *Diet for a Small Planet*. New York: Ballantine, 1991.

Laudan, Rachel. *Cuisine and Empire*. Berkeley: University of California Press, 2013.

———. "A Plea for Culinary Modernism: Why We Should Love New, Fast, Processed Food." *Gastronomica* I:1 (Winter 2001).

Laurino, Maria. *Were You Always an Italian?: Ancestors and Other Icons of Italian America*. New York: Norton, 2001.

Lavin, Chad. *Eating Anxiety: The Perils of Food Politics*. Minneapolis: University of Minnesota Press, 2013.

Lawrence, D. H. *Birds, Beasts and Flowers!: Poems*. Boston: Black Sparrow Press, 2007.

———. *Complete Poems*. New York: Penguin, 1964.

———. *Etruscan Places*. Cambridge: Cambridge University Press, 1992.

———. *The Paintings of D.H. Lawrence*. London: Mandrake Press, 1929.

———. *Studies in Classic American Literature*. New York, Penguin, 1990.

Leapor, Mary. *The Works of Mary Leapor*. Oxford: Oxford University Press, 2004.

Lee, Jennifer 8. *The Fortune Cookie Chronicles*. New York: Twelve Books, 2008.

Lee, Li-young. *Rose: Poems*. Rochester, NY: BOA, 1986.

Lehrer, Jonah. *Proust Was a Neuroscientist*. Boston: Houghton Mifflin, 2007.

Leigh Fermor, Patrick. *The Traveler's Tree: A Journey Through the Caribbean Islands*. New York: NYRB Classics, 2011.

Lenson, David. *On Drugs*. Minneapolis: University of Minnesota Press, 1995.

Leonardi, Susan. "Recipes for Reading: Summer Pasta, Lobster à la Riseholme, and Key Lime Pie." *PMLA* 104.3 (1989).

Levenstein, Harvey. *Fear of Food: A History of Why We Worry about What We Eat*. Chicago: University of Chicago Press, 2012.

Levi, Primo. *The Periodic Table*. Trans. Raymond Rosenthal. New York: Schocken, 1995.

Lévi-Strauss, Claude. *The Raw and the Cooked*. Trans. Doreen Weightman and John Weightman. Chicago: University of Chicago Press, 1983.

———. *Totemism*. Trans. Rodney Needham. Boston: Beacon, 1963.

Liebling, A. J. *Between Meals: An Appetite for Paris*. New York: Modern Library, 1995.

Like Water for Chocolate. DVD. Directed by Alfonso Arau. 1992. Mexico City: Arau Films Internacional, 2000.

Lobel, Cindy R. "The Joy of Cookbooks." *Reviews in American History* (2005): 263–71.

Lowell, Robert. *Collected Poems*. New York: Farrar, Straus and Giroux, 2003.

Lucas, Dione. *The Dione Lucas Meat and Poultry Cook Book*. New York: Gramercy, 1955.

Luck, George. "Review of R. Gordon Wasson, Albert Hofmann, Carl A. P. Ruck, et al. *The Road to Eleusis*, new edition with preface by Huston Smith." *American Journal of Philology* (2001): 135–8.

Lukanuski, Mary. "A Place at the Counter: The Onus of Oneness." *Eating Culture*. New York: State University of New York Press, 1998.

MacDonald, Betty. *The Egg and I*. New York: Harper Perennial, 2008.

Mack, Maynard. *Alexander Pope: A Life*. New York: Norton, 1986.

Mariani, Paul J. *William Carlos Williams: A New World Naked*. New York: Norton, 1990.

Marinetti, Filippo. *The Futurist Cookbook*. Trans. Suzanne Brill. San Francisco: Chronicle, 1991.

Markowitz, Terry. "All About Food: How Would Jesus Diet—or William the Conqueror?" *Daily Pilot*, May 7, 2013.

Marvell, Andrew. *The Complete Poems*. New York: Penguin, 2005.

Mauss, Marcel. *The Gift: The Form and Reason for Exchange in Archaic Societies*. Trans. W. D. Halls. New York: Norton, 2000.

Max, D. T. "When artists pave the way for scientists." *International Herald Tribune*, November 3–4, 2007: 9.

McAleer, John. *Rex Stout: A Biography*. Boston: Little, Brown, 1977.

McGrath, Campbell. *Capitalism*. Middletown, CT: Wesleyan University Press, 1990.

McLaughlin, Joe-Anne. *Banshee Diaries*. Toronto: McArthur, 1998, 19.

McLean, Alice L. *Aesthetic Pleasure in Twentieth-Century Women's Food Writing: The Innovative Appetites of M. F. K. Fisher, Alice B. Toklas, and Elizabeth David*. New York: Routledge, 2012.

McWilliams, Mark. "Distant Tables: Food and the Novel in Early America." *Early American Literature* 38.3 (2003): 365–93.

"Medicine: Fletcherizing." *Time*, September 17, 1928.

Miller, Henry. "The Staff of Life." *Remember to Remember*. New York: New Directions, 1947, 35–53.

Milton, John. *Complete Prose Works*. Ed. Don M. Wolfe. Vol. 6. New Haven: Yale University Press, 1953–82, 8 vols.

———. *Paradise Lost*. New York: Norton, 2004.

Montaigne, Michel de. *Essays*. Trans. John M. Cohen. New York: Penguin, 1993.

Moore, George. *Esther Waters*. New York: Oxford University Press, 2012.

Moore, Judith. *Fat Girl: A True Story*. New York: Penguin, 2006.

———. *The Left Coast of Paradise*. New York: Soho Press, 1987.

———. *Never Eat Your Heart Out*. New York: North Point Press, 1998.

Morris, Mark. "Ingestion/Why Architects Look Sick at Building Dedication Ceremonies." *Cabinet*, Fall 2005.

Morrison, Susan. "Fruit Chan's 'excremental vision': Public Toilet." *CineAction*, March 22,

2003. http://www.thefreelibrary.com/Fruit+Chan's+'excremental+vision'%3A+Public+Toilet.-a0106941461. Accessed May 17, 2013.

Morrison, Toni. *Beloved.* New York: Vintage, 1987.

———. *The Bluest Eye*. New York: Vintage, 1970.

———. *Song of Solomon*. New York: Vintage, 1977.

———. *Sula.* New York: Penguin, 1973.

Morton, Timothy. *The Poetics of Spice*. Cambridge, UK: Cambridge University Press, 2000.

Moses, Kate. *Cakewalk*. New York: Dial, 2010.

Moskin, Julia. "Chef Has Diabetes." *New York Times*, January 17, 2012, C4.

Moss, Michael. *Salt Sugar Fat: How the Food Giants Hooked Us*. New York: Random House, 2013.

Muhlke, Christine. "Kiss the Cook." *New York Times*, December 3, 2009, B6.

Munro, H. H. "Filboid Studge." *The Complete Short Stories of Saki*. New York: Digireads.com, 2010, 104–5. http://books.google.com/books?id=za_EkodPlQgC&printsec=frontcover#v=onepage&q&f=false.

Narayan, Shoba. *Monsoon Diary: A Memoir with Recipes*. New York: Random House, 2004.

Nash, Steven A. "Unbalancing Acts: Wayne Thiebaud Reconsidered." *Wayne Thiebaud: A Paintings Retrospective*. San Francisco: Fine Arts Museum of San Francisco, 2000, 11–38.

Neruda, Pablo. *Selected Odes of Pablo Neruda*. Trans. Margaret Sayers Peden. Berkeley: University of California Press, 1990.

Nestle, Marion. *Food Politics: How the Food Industry Influences Nutrition and Health, Revised and Expanded Edition*. Berkeley: University of California Press, 2007.

———. *What to Eat: An Aisle by Aisle Guide to Savvy Food Choices and Good Eating*. New York: North Point Press, 2006.

Neuhaus, Jessamy. *Manly Meals and Mom's Home Cooking: Cookbooks and Gender in Modern America*. Baltimore: Johns Hopkins University Press, 2003.

Newton, Judith. *Tasting Home: Coming of Age in the Kitchen*. Berkeley, CA: She Writes Press, 2013.

Oldenburg, Claes. "I am for an art." *Store days: documents from The Store, 1961, and Ray Gun Theater, 1962*. Ed. Emmett William. New York: Something Else Press, 1967, 39–42.

———. "Statement by the Artists." 2001. http://oldenburgvanbruggen.com/largescaleprojects/droppedcone.htm. Accessed December 6, 2013.

O'Neill, Molly, ed. *American Food Writing*. New York: Library of America, 2007.

Ornish, Dean. *Eat More, Weigh Less*. New York: HarperCollins, 2013.

Orwell, George. *Down and Out in Paris and London*. New York: Houghton Mifflin, 1972.

Osborne, Lawrence. "Does Man Eat Man?" *Lingua Franca* (1997): 28–38.

"Our Lady of the Ladle." *The Errant Aesthete*, August 6, 2009. http://theerrantaesthete.com/2009/08/06/our-lady-of-the-ladle/. Accessed May 16, 2013.

Ovid. *Metamorphoses*. Trans. A. D. Melville. Oxford: Oxford University Press, 1986.

Ozeki, Ruth L. *My Year of Meats*. New York: Penguin, 1998.

Pachirat, Timothy. *Every Twelve Seconds: Industrialized Slaughter and the Politics of Sight*. New Haven: Yale University Press, 2011.

Parker, Robert B. *Crimson Joy*. New York: Dell, 1989.

———. *Looking for Rachel Wallace*. New York: Dell, 1980.

Paterniti, Michael. "The Last Meal." *Esquire*, May 2, 1998. http://www.esquire.com/features/The-Last-Meal-0598. Accessed May 11, 2013.

Pelecanos, George. "Chewing the Fat: No Reservations' Anthony Bourdain." *dcist*, January 19, 2009.

Pennell, Elizabeth Robins. *The Feasts of Autolycus: The Diary of a Greedy Woman*. Berkeley: University of California Libraries, 1900.

Perloff, Marjorie. *21st-Century Modernism: The "New" Poetics*. New York: Wiley–Blackwell, 2002.

Petrini, Carlo. *Slow Food: The Case for Taste*. Trans. William McCuaig. New York: Columbia University Press, 2004.

Petronius. *The Satyricon and The Apocolocyntosis of the Divine Claudius*. Trans. J. P. Sullivan. New York: Penguin, 1986.

Piene, Otto, and Heinz Mack. *Zero: 1–3, 1958–1961*. Cambridge, MA: MIT Press, 1973.

Plath, Sylvia. *The Bell Jar*. New York: Harper Perennial, 2005.

———. *Collected Poems*. New York: Harper Perennial, 2008.

Plato. *The Republic*. Trans. G. M. A. Grube and C. D. C. Reeve. New York: Hackett, 1992.

———. *Timaeus*. Trans. Benjamin Jowett. London: Macmillan, 1892.

Plutarch. *Moralia*. Trans. Edward N. O'Neil. Cambridge, MA: Harvard University Press, 1936.

Poe, Edgar Allan. *The Narrative of Arthur Gordon Pym of Nantucket*. New York: Dover, 2005.

Pollan, Michael. *The Botany of Desire: A Plant's Eye View of the World*. New York: Random House, 2001.

———. "Cattle Futures?" *New York Times*, January 11, 2004.

———. *Cooked: A Natural History of Transformation*. New York: Penguin, 2013.

———. *The Omnivore's Dilemma: A Natural History of Four Meals*. New York: Penguin, 2007.

———. *Food Rules: An Eater's Manual*. New York: Penguin, 2009.

———. *In Defense of Food: An Eater's Manifesto*. New York: Penguin, 2008.

———. "The Food Movement, Rising." *New York Review of Books*, June 10, 2010.

———. "Out of the Kitchen, Onto the Couch: How American Cooking Became a Spectator Sport, and What We Lost Along The Way." *New York Times Magazine*, August 2, 2009.

———. "Power Steer." *New York Times Magazine*, March 31, 2002, T3.

Pope, Alexander. "An Essay on Man." *The Major Works*. Oxford: Oxford University Press, 2009, 270–308.

Porphyry. *On Abstinence from Animal Food*. Trans. Gillian Clark. Whitefish, MT: Kessinger, 2006.

Post, Emily. *Etiquette*. New York: HarperCollins, 2009.

Pound, Ezra. *Personae*. New York: New Directions, 1990.

Proust, Marcel. *Swann's Way*. Trans. C. K. Scott Moncrieff. New York: Modem Library, 1998.

Pseudo-Apollodorus. *Bibliotheca*. Trans. Sir James George Frazer. Cambridge, MA: Harvard University Press, 1921.

Rabelais, François. *Gargantua and Pantagruel*. Trans. Burton Raffel. New York: Norton, 1991.

"Radio: Cooking for the Camera." *Time Magazine*, May 30, 1955.

Rando, Therese. *How to Go On Living When Someone You Love Dies*. New York: Bantam, 1991.

Ratatouille. DVD. Directed by Brad Bird and Jan Pinkava. 2007. Emeryville, CA: Pixar, 2007.

Rawlings, Marjorie Kinnan. *Cross Creek Cookery*. New York: Fireside, 1996.

Rawson, Claude. "The Ultimate Taboo." *New York Times Book Review*, April 16, 2000.

Read, Piers Paul. *Alive: The Story of the Andes Survivors*. New York: Avon, 1974.

Reardon, Joan. *Poet of the Appetites: The Lives and Loves of M. F. K. Fisher*. New York: North Point Press, 2005.

Reichl, Ruth. *Comfort Me with Apples: More Adventures at the Table*. New York: Random House, 2001.

———. *Garlic and Sapphires: The Secret Life of a Critic in Disguise*. New York: Penguin, 2005.

———. *Tender at the Bone*. New York: Random House, 1998.

Reinhardt, Mark. *Who Speaks for Margaret Garner?* Minneapolis: University of Minnesota Press, 2010.

Richardson, Samuel. *The Correspondence of Samuel Richardson*. 4 vols. Cambridge: Cambridge University Press, 2014.

Rhodius, Apollonius. *The Argonautica*. Trans. E. P. Coleridge. New York: Book Jungle, 2009.

Riedweg, Christoph. *Pythagoras: His Life, Teaching, and Influence*. Ithaca: Cornell University Press, 2008.

Rivera, Diego. *My Art, My Life: An Autobiography*. Trans. Gladys March. New York: Dover, 1992.

Roberts, Adam. "Dinner at El Bulli: The Greatest Restaurant in the World." *The Amateur Gourmet*, August 11, 2009.

Rogak, Lisa. *Death Warmed Over: Funeral Food, Rituals, and Customs from Around the World*. Berkeley, CA: Ten Speed Press, 2004.

Root, Waverly. *The Food of France*. New York: Vintage, 1992.

Rosenberg, Emily S. "Missions to the World: Philanthropy Abroad." *Charity, Philanthropy, and Civility in American History*. Ed. Mark D. McGarvie. Cambridge, UK: Cambridge University Press, 2004, 241–58.

Rossetti, Christina. *Complete Poems*. New York: Penguin, 2001.

Rousseau, Jean-Jacques. *Julie, or the New Heloise: Letters of Two Lovers Who Live in a Small Town at the Foot of the Alps*. Trans. Jean Vadié. Hanover, NH: Dartmouth, 1997.

Ruck, C. A., et al. "Entheogens." *Journal of Psychedelic Drugs* (1979): 145–6.

Ruskin, John. *The Ethics of Dust*. In *The Works of John Ruskin*. Vol. 18. 39 vols. Cambridge: Cambridge University Press, 2010.

Ryan, Susan Elizabeth. *Robert Indiana: Figures of Speech*. New Haven: Yale University Press, 2000.

Sacks, Oliver. *An Anthropologist on Mars*. New York: Knopf, 1995.

Safire, William. "The Multifarious Aubergine." January 16, 2006. *Language Hat*, http://www.languagehat.com/the-multifarious-aubergine/. Accessed May 12, 2013.

Santich, Barbara. "Reflections on References in Lévi-Strauss." *Newsletter for the Research Centre for the History of Food and Drink*, 2001: 4.

Sartre, Jean-Paul. *Nausea*. Trans. Lloyd Alexander. New York: New Directions, 2007.

Scarry, Elaine. *The Body in Pain: The Making and Unmaking of the World*. New York: Oxford University Press, 1987.

Schenone, Laura. *The Lost Ravioli Recipes of Hoboken: A Search for Food and Family*. New York: Norton, 2008.

Schlosser, Eric. *Fast Food Nation: The Dark Side of the All-American Meal*. New York: Mariner, 2012.

Schmidt, Paul. " 'As if a cookbook had anything to do with it,'—Alice B. Toklas." *Prose* (1974): 179–203.

Sendak, Maurice. *In the Night Kitchen*. New York: HarperCollins, 1996.

Seneca, Lucius Annaeus. *Morals of a Happy Life*. Trans. Roger L'Estrange. Chicago: Belford, Clark, 1882.

Severson, Kim. "Paula Deen's Cook Tells of Sights, Steeped in History." *New York Times*, July 24, 2013, A7.

Shahin, Jim. "Jake Adam York's barbecue poetry: a state of 'Grace.'" *Washington Post*, November 20, 2012.

Shakespeare, William. *Hamlet*. London: Arden, 1982.

———. *Henry IV, Part 1*. London: Arden, 2002.

———. *Macbeth*. London: Arden, 1985.

———. *Titus Andronicus*. London: Arden, 1995.

———. *Twelfth Night*. London: Arden, 2009.

Shange, Ntozake. *If I can Cook/You KNow God can*. Boston: Beacon, 1998.

Shapiro, Laura. *Julia Child: A Life*. New York: Penguin, 2009.

———. *Something from the Oven: Reinventing Dinner in 1950s America*. New York: Penguin, 2005.

Shelley, Mary. *Frankenstein: or, The Modern Prometheus: The 1818 Text*. Oxford: Oxford University Press, 2009.

Shelley, Percy. *A Vindication of Natural Diet*. London: F. Pitman, 1994.

Sheraton, Mimi. *Eating My Words: An Appetite for Life*. New York: Harper Perennial, 2006.

Silva, Nikki, and Davia Nelson. *Hidden Kitchens*. New York: Holtzbrinck, 2005.

Sinclair, Upton. *The Jungle*. New York: Dover, 2001.

Singer, Peter. *Animal Liberation*. New York: HarperCollins, 2009.

"The Slice-of-Cake School." *Time*, May 11, 1962.

Smart-Grosvenor, Vertamae. *Vibration Cooking: or, The Travel Notes of a Geechee Girl*. Athens: University of Georgia Press, 2011.

Smith, Patricia. *Teahouse of the Almighty*. Minneapolis: Coffee House Press, 2006.

"Snow White and the Seven Dwarfs." *The Golden Bird and Other Fairy Tales of the Brothers Grimm*. Trans. Randall Jarrell. New York: Macmillan, 1962.

Snyder, Gary. *The Back Country*. New York: New Directions, 1968.

———. *Turtle Island*. New York: New Directions, 1974.

Spang, Rebecca L. *The Invention of the Restaurant: Paris and Modern Gastronomic Culture*. Cambridge, MA: Harvard University Press, 2000.

Steedman, Carolyn. "Poetical Maids and Cooks who Wrote." *Eighteenth-Century Studies*, Fall 2005: 1–27.

Stein, Gertrude. "American Food and American Houses." In Molly O'Neill, ed. *American Food Writing*. New York: Penguin, 2007, 187–91.

———. *Writings, 1903–1946*. 2 vols. New York: Library of America, 1998.

Steinbeck, John. *The Grapes of Wrath*. New York: Penguin, 2006.

Stern, Gerald. *Early Collected Poems: 1965–1992*. New York: Norton, 2010.

Stevens, Wallace. *Collected Poetry and Prose*. New York: Library of America, 1997.

Stone, Abigail. *Recipes from the Dump*. New York: Norton, 1980.

Stone, Ruth. *American Milk*. Fanwood, NJ: From Here Press, 1986.

———. *Second-Hand Coat: Poems New and Selected*. Boston: Godine, 1987.

Storace, Patricia. "A Country Made for Living." *Condé Nast Traveler*, September 2006.

Stout, Rex. *Too Many Cooks*. New York: Bantam, 1995.

Strand, Mark. *Reasons for Moving*. New York: Atheneum, 1968.

Stuart, Tristram. *The Bloodless Revolution: A Cultural History of Vegetarianism: From 1600 to Modern Times*. New York: Norton, 2008.

Sullivan, Andrew. "The Daily Dish—Last Meals." *Atlantic,* November 15, 2009.

Summerville, Amelia. *Why Be Fat?: Rules for Weight-Reduction and the Preservation of Youth and Health*. New York: Frederick A. Stokes, 1916.

Super Size Me. DVD. Directed by Morgan Spurlock. 2004. Los Angeles: Kathbur Pictures, 2004.

Suzuki, D. T. *Zen and Japanese Culture*. Princeton: Princeton University Press, 1970.

Swift, Jonathan. "A Modest Proposal." *Major Works*. Oxford: Oxford University Press, 2008, 492–99.

Telfer, Elizabeth. *Food for Thought: Philosophy and Food*. New York: Routledge, 1996.

Theissen, Gerd, and Annette Merz. *The Historical Jesus: A Comprehensive Guide*. Minneapolis: Fortress, 1996.

Thompson, Flora. *Lark Rise to Candleford*. Boston: Godine, 2009.

Thoreau, Henry David. *Walden*. New Haven: Yale University Press, 2004.

———. *Wild Fruits*. Ed. Bradley P. Dean. New York: Norton, 2001, 107–10.

Toklas, Alice B. *The Alice B. Toklas Cook Book*. New York: Harper Perennial, 2010.

Trachtma, Paul, "Cézanne: The man who changed the landscape of art." *Smithsonian Magazine*, January 2006, 37–43.

Tutuola, Amos. *The Palm-Wine Drinkard*. New York: Grove/Atlantic, 1953.

Twain, Mark. "Cannibalism in the Cars." *The Best Short Stories of Mark Twain*. New York: Modern Library, 2004, 14–21.

Unwin, Tim. *Wine and the Vine: An Historical Geography of Viticulture and the Wine Trade*. New York: Routledge, 1996.

Vanderbilt, Amy. *The Amy Vanderbilt Complete Book of Etiquette: 50th Anniversay Edition*. New York: Doubleday, 1995.

Varriano, John. *Tastes and Temptations: Food and Art in Renaissance Italy*. Berkeley: University of California Press, 2009.

Vester, Katharina. "Regime Change: Gender, Class, and the Invention of Dieting in Post-Bellum America." *Journal of Social History* 44, no. 1 (2010): 39–70.

Virgil. *Georgics.* Trans. David Ferry. New York: Farrar, Straus, and Giroux, 2006.

Visser, Margaret. *Much Depends on Dinner: The Extraordinary History and Mythology, Allure and Obsessions, Perils and Taboos of an Ordinary Meal*. New York: Grove Press, 2010.

———. *The Rituals of Dinner: The Origins, Evolution, Eccentricities, and Meaning of Table Manners*. New York: Penguin, 1992.

Von Bremzen, Anya. *Mastering the Art of Soviet Cooking*. New York: Crown, 2013.

Wallace, Emily M. "An Interview with William Carlos Williams." *Massachusetts Review*, Winter 1973: 130–48.

Warner, Melanie. *Pandora's Lunchbox: How Processed Food Took Over the American Meal*. New York: Scribner, 2013.

Wasson, Gordon R., and Wendy Doniger O'Flaherty. "The Last Meal of the Buddha." *Journal of the American Oriental Society*, October–December 1982: 591–603.

Waters, Alice. *The Art of Simple Food: Notes, Lessons and Recipes from a Delicious Revolution.* New York: Clarkson Potter, 2007.

Webb, Mary. *Precious Bane.* New York: Penguin, 1982.

Weldon, Fay. *The Fat Woman's Joke*. Chicago: Academy Chicago, 2005.

Wells, Pete. "No Disrespect for the Meatball Hero." *New York Times*, January 25, 2012: D6.

Wheeler, Monroe. *Soutine*. New York: Arno Press, 1966.

Whitehead, Alfred North. *Dialogues of Alfred North Whitehead*. Boston: Godine, 1954.

Whitman, Walt. *The Complete Poems*. New York: Penguin, 2004.

Wilbur, Richard. *Collected Poems*. New York: Harvest, 2004.

Willard, Nancy. *A Nancy Willard Reader*. Middlebury, VT: Middlebury College Press, 1991.

Williams, Alex. "Slaughterhouse Live." *New York Times*, October 23, 2009: ST1.

Williams, William Carlos. *The Collected Poems of William Carlos Williams*. Vol. 1. New York: New Directions, 1986, 2 vols.

———. *Paterson*. New York: New Directions, 1958.

———. *Selected Essays*. New York: New Directions, 1969.

Wineapple, Brenda. *Sister Brother: Gertrude and Leo Stein*. New York: Putnam, 1996.

"The Women's Petition Against Coffee Representing to Publick Consideration the Grand Inconveniences Accruing to their Sex from the Excessive Use of that Drying, Enfeebling Liquor." *University of Giessen*, December 7, 2003. http://www.uni-giessen.de/gloning/tx/won-pet.htm. Accessed May 5, 2013.

Woolf, Virginia. *The Diary of Virginia Woolf*. Vol. 5. New York: Harcourt/Harvest, 1985.

———. "Mr. Bennett and Mrs. Brown." *Selected Essays*. Oxford: Oxford University Press, 2008, 32–6.

———. *Mrs. Dalloway*. New York: Harvest, 1990.

———. *To the Lighthouse*. New York: Harcourt, 2010.

Wrangham, Richard. *Catching Fire: How Cooking Made Us Human*. New York: Basic Books, 2010.

Wright, Thomas. *Songs and Carols from a Manuscript in the British Museum of the Fifteenth Century*. London: T. Richards, 1856. http://books.google.com/books?id=BDFOAAAAcAAJ&q=ybounden#v=onepage&q&f.

Wyss, Johann. *The Swiss Family Robinson*. New York: Signet Classics, 2004.

Young, Kevin, ed. *The Hungry Ear: Poems of Food and Drink*. New York: Bloomsbury, 2012.

Zola, Émile. *In the Belly of Paris*. Trans. Ernest Alfred Vizetelly. Copenhagen and Los Angeles: Green Integer, 2006.

Zubiaurre, Maite. "Culinary Eros in Contemporary Hispanic Female Fiction: From Kitchen Tales to Table Narratives." *College Literature*, Summer 2006: 29–51.

Acknowledgments

Portions of this book have appeared in slightly different form in:

"Feeding the Foodoir: Hunger Artistry." *Gastronomica* (Fall 2014).

"Female Spoons and Male Forks." *Women's Review of Books* (May/June 2008): 3–4.

"The Casserole Inquisition." *The American Scholar* (Winter 2008): 236–41.

"Bitter Herbs?' *In Our Root Are Deep with Passion*. Eds. Lee Gutkind and Joanna Clapps Herman, 159–77. Ann Arbor: The University of Michigan Press, 2006.

"Mysteries of the Hyphen: Poetry, Pasta, and Identity Politics." In *Beyond the Godfather: Italian American Writers on the Real Italian American Experience.* Eds. Marianne Hirsch, A. Kenneth Ciongoli, and Jay Parini, 49–61. Hanover, NH: University Press of New England, 1997.

"Suckled by Manly Bosoms: Culinary Transvestitism." *Michigan Quarterly Review* (Fall 1996): 676–89.

"Hunger/Pains." *University Publishing* (Fall 1979): 1–12.

Credits

Images

Paul Child, *Julia Child on the Set of "The French Chef,"* courtesy of Schlesinger Library, Radcliffe Institute, Harvard University.

Wayne Thiebaud, *Girl with Ice Cream Cone,* © Wayne Thiebaud/Licensed by VAGA, New York, NY.

Wayne Thiebaud, *Cakes,* © Wayne Thiebaud/Licensed by VAGA, New York, NY.

Claes Oldenburg and Coosje van Bruggen, *Dropped Cone*, Collection Neumarkt Galerie, Cologne, Germany. Copyright © 2001 Claes Oldenburg and Coosje van Bruggen.

Text

Judith Goldhaber, "A popular revolt against the belly . . ." Copyright © 2012 Judith Goldhaber. Reprinted by permission of the author.

Ruth Stone, "American Milk." Copyright ©1986 Ruth Stone. Reprinted by permission of the Ruth Stone Foundation.

William Carlos Williams, "This Is Just To Say." From *The Collected Poems: Volume I, 1909–1939*, copyright ©1938 by New Directions Publishing Corp. Reprinted by permission of New Directions Publishing Corp and Carcanet Press Ltd.

Index

Page numbers in *italics* refer to illustrations.